Y0-BQI-006

Jarring witnesses

POSTMODERN THEORY

Series editor:

THOMAS DOCHERTY
School of English, Trinity College Dublin

A series which openly and rigorously confronts the question of the postmodern in contemporary debates, and which boldly proposes a refiguration of what is understood as 'the modern' in all its forms: aesthetic and political, cultural and social, material and popular.

Other titles in the series include:

Justice miscarried: Ethics and aesthetics in law
COSTAS DOUZINAS and RONNIE WARRINGTON

Modern wasteland to postmodern wilderness
RODNEY GIBLETT

POSTMODERN THEORY

Jarring witnesses
Modern fiction and the
representation of history

ROBERT HOLTON

HARVESTER WHEATSHEAF

New York   London   Toronto   Sydney   Tokyo   Singapore

LIBRARY
COLBY-SAWYER COLLEGE
NEW LONDON, NH 03257

PN
3503
.H57
1994
c.1

33819683

First published 1994 by
Harvester Wheatsheaf
Campus 400, Maylands Avenue
Hemel Hempstead
Hertfordshire, HP2 7EZ
A division of
Simon & Schuster International Group

© Robert Holton 1994

Earlier versions of Chapters 6 and 7 have appeared in *Textual Practice* and *English Studies in Canada*.

All rights reserved. No part of this publication may be reproduced, stored in a retrieval system, or transmitted, in any form, or by any means electronic mechanical, photocopying, recording or otherwise, without prior permission, in writing, from the publisher.

Typeset in 9½/12 pt Melior
by Photoprint, Torquay, Devon

Printed and bound in Great Britain by
Biddles Ltd, Guildford and King's Lynn

British Library Cataloguing in Publication Data

A catalogue record for this book is available
from the British Library

ISBN 0–7450–1283–3

1 2 3 4 5   98 97 96 95 94

LIBRARY
COLBY-SAWYER COLLEGE
NEW LONDON, NH 03257

For my family

Contents

Foreword   ix

Part I History and narrative   1

1 Historical narrative and the politics of point of view   3

2 Common sense and historical narrative   36

Part II Modernism and orthodoxy   55

3 *Nostromo* and the 'torrent of rubbish'   57

4 *Parade's End*: 'Has the British this or that
come to *this*!'   93

5 *Absalom, Absalom!*: The 'nigger in the woodpile'   128

Part III Postmodernism and heterodoxy   161

6 Bearing witness: African–American women's fiction   163

7 *V.*: In the rathouse of history with
Thomas Pynchon   217

Conclusion   246

Notes   258
References   280
Index   297

Foreword

As we all know there are at least two sides to every story. This caveat is traditionally expressed, however, when one of those sides is displacing the others in a particular narrative representation. A seeming contradiction inherent, perhaps, in narrative itself, this is the basic problem to be discussed in the chapters that follow: how does point of view, with its inevitable limitations of perspective, function as a necessary locus for the organisation of narrative representation? While the problem of point of view has been a central one in Anglo-American modernist fiction and criticism, at least since Henry James (the work of Percy Lubbock or Wayne Booth being notable instances[1]), my own appropriation of the term is less formalist, less purely literary perhaps, and owes much to the discussion of the function of narrative representation of history. The narratives I examine are all in the twentieth-century novels concerned with historical or pseudo-historical events. For this reason the problem of point of view in narrative historiography, as well as in narrative fiction, is important, and I begin by discussing how this problem is handled in modern Anglo-American philosophy of history. Part I follows a line starting with F. H. Bradley and running through to Hayden White; it analyses how each theorises the process of making a coherent narrative out of the admittedly diverse materials that comprise the totality of the historical field. Some of the ideas that emerge out of the discussion are then addressed in relation to concepts of the heterodoxic and the heteroglossic in the work of Pierre Bourdieu and Mikhail Bakhtin respectively.

Part II examines three modern novels, Conrad's *Nostromo*, Ford's *Parade's End* and Faulkner's *Absalom, Absalom!* In particular, problems concerning the construction of coherent narrative in each of the novels are explored in relation to the historical and cultural point of view grounding this act of representation. While many interesting novels are relevant to such an enquiry, these three have been chosen both for their similarities and their differences. Most obviously, they share a common language (in a non-Bakhtinian sense[2]) and historical period. Further, all claim a certain stature in the modern (and modernist) canon. A final quality linking them, as I will argue, is an orthodoxy in Bourdieu's sense of the word.[3] On the other hand, in each of these novels the cultural division, in terms of which this orthodoxy is registered, presents a different aspect of the problem. In *Nostromo*, Conrad explores the problems of (post)colonial expansion, as a European-based community confronts a cultural 'other' on the terrain of that 'other' – South America. In Ford's *Parade's End* and Faulkner's *Absalom, Absalom!*, however, the 'other' is within: in the former, class and, to a lesser degree, race and gender are the loci for the orchestration of heteroglossia; in the latter, the problem of slavery and its legacy has created a unique heterodox situation combining a powerful sense of racial alterity with an internal and national struggle for coherence.[4]

In Part III, two alternative approaches to historiographic narrative are considered. The penultimate chapter focuses on how members of a marginalised group, African–American women, retell history, positioning themselves very differently in relation to orthodox (dominant) historical discourse. Once again, while many works might have been selected for discussion here, the fiction of African–American women has seemed most appropriate for a number of reasons. Marginalised primarily on the basis of race and gender perhaps, they have tended as a result to become victims of socio-economic class barriers as well. Nevertheless, these writers have struggled against the cultural aphasia that is a part of this condition and produced not only a remarkable body of fiction, but a body of fiction whose exploration of history is as extensive as it is intense.

Finally, Pynchon's *V*. provides the basis for the discussion of another response – postmodernist – to the problems of hetero-doxy and point of view in historical narrative. As one of the most important American postmodernists, and as an author whose questioning of history and of historiography is profound,

Pynchon's work investigates some of the political and philosophic
– as well as the novelistic – ramifications of postmodernism. One
problem crucial to postmodern discourse to be considered
involves the charge that the abandonment of traditional concepts
of Truth and Objectivity inevitably leads to a relativist paralysis
that is injurious to political dissent and resistance.

In the conclusion, I will turn to a more general examination of
modernism and postmodernism as literary and social phenomena
in relation to what might loosely be termed the historical sense of
the cultural communities from which these phenomena have
arisen. Issues related to heterodoxy, heteroglossia and common
sense will be considered in the light of the preceding discussions
of the novels and the historical worlds they represent.

I

History and narrative

Historical narrative and the politics of point of view

Since the eighteenth century, history has come to be most commonly thought of as an orderly narrative.[1] More recently though, the academic and scientific respectability of historians has at times been impugned on the basis of the dubious truth-claims that can be made for the works of scholars whose main task may appear to be 'mere' story-telling, in however erudite a form. In 1979, Lawrence Stone, noting a revival of narrative form in the writing of history, pointed out that 'in the last fifty years . . . this story-telling function has fallen into ill repute among those who have regarded themselves in the vanguard of the profession' (1979: 3). Similarly, Hayden White has observed that in the opinion of some historians and philosophers of history, the use of narrative in historiographic discourse appears as

an index of a failure at once methodological and theoretical. A discipline that produces narrative accounts of its subject matter as an end in itself seems methodologically unsound; one that investigates its data in the interest of telling a story about them appears methodologically deficient.   (1987: 26)

This implies a need for a more rigorous positivist methodology, but historians have also run into problems when applying scientific models to history. One important attempt of this kind in Anglo-American philosophy of history has been the Covering Law Model which held 'that general laws have quite analogous functions in history and in the natural sciences [and] that they form an indispensable instrument of historical research' (Hempel, 1942: 35). In recent years, however, as the laws of history have remained stubbornly elusive, the influence of this scientific model has waned – as F. R. Ankersmit puts it, the 'CLM failed because historical *reality* proved too complex' (1986: 13).[2]

More influential yet, perhaps, has been the example of the *Annales* school in France. While its roots go back to the work of Lucien Febvre and Marc Bloch in the early decades of this century, the *Annales* school has continued to extend its range and depth in the post-war years through the contributions of Fernand Braudel, Emmanuel Le Roy Ladurie and others. Indeed, as Georg Iggers notes, 'the *Annales* have become a model of scientific history to historians throughout the world today' (1975: 79). The *Annales* school arose in part as a reaction against the traditional approach to history which concentrated on the narration of great events and the lives of great men who make history. Despite the claim of narrative historians to be the simple communicators of 'what happened', Braudel objects that

in its own covert way, narrative history consists in an interpretation, an authentic philosophy of history. To the narrative historians, the life of men is dominated by dramatic accidents, by the actions of those exceptional beings who occasionally emerge, and who often are the masters of their own fate and even more of ours. And when they speak of 'general history,' what they are really thinking of is the intercrossing of such exceptional destinies, for obviously each hero must be matched against another. A delusive fallacy, as we all know.   (1980: 11)

While the benefits in terms of plot and narrative tension are evident, Braudel argues that what is lost in any 'great man' theory is the degree to which 'anonymous history, working in the depths and most often in silence' in fact shapes the lives of people (1980: 10). This anonymous history, then, becomes the object of a discipline that focuses not on individuals and events but on

the major forms of collective life, economies, institutions, social structures, in short and above all, civilizations – all the aspects of reality which earlier historians have not exactly overlooked, but . . . have all too often regarded as a backdrop, there only to explain the behavior of the exceptional individuals on whom the historian so complacently dwells.   (Braudel, 1980: 11–12)

While the positive effect of the *Annales* example is not in doubt, it could be argued that narrative has not been banished from the scene of history by the work of historians such as Braudel, so much as it has been reformulated or renegotiated. In concentrating on the *longue durée* at the expense of *histoire événementielle*, the anonymous population rather than the exceptional individual, their work is not necessarily in essence anti-narrative and, as Paul Ricoeur notes in his discussion of Braudel's work, it even retains important aspects of that genre (1984: v.1, 209–17).[3] In discussing his work on the history of climate – hardly a typical narrative subject – Le Roy Ladurie (who once declared that soon 'the historian will be a [computer] programmer or he will be nothing' (Stone, 1979: 13)) tellingly speaks of the 'story of fluctuations over whole centuries ... that the great glaciers have to tell' (1979b: 289). I do not mean to argue that Ladurie has simply replaced narratives of great men with narratives of great glaciers in his pursuit of a 'history without people', but merely to suggest that narrative is too fundamental to be summarily swept from what Stone has termed the 'mansions' of history (1979: 4). Indeed, despite Ladurie's claim that 'in the last decade [historiography] has virtually condemned to death the narrative history of events and individual biography' (1979b: 111), these genres continue to flourish. In fact, two of Ladurie's own most acclaimed works, *Montaillou* and *Carnival at Romans* might be compared with modernist novels.[4]

Georg Iggers argues further that while the shift in focus accomplished by the *Annales* school has been a positive one, political events have necessarily been downplayed and as a result the '*Annales* have made little contribution to bringing greater conceptual rigor into the analysis of the elements of purposive human action which enter into specific historical change' (1975: 78). A similar comment might be made in relation to the work of Michel Foucault whose important archaeological or genealogical studies of discursive formations (or *epistemes*) similarly tend to minimise conscious human agency. Yet, as Ian Hacking points out, Foucault's approach is in another sense the opposite of the *Annales* school: rather than an emphasis on continuity and the *longue durée*, Foucault focuses on the discontinuities and ruptures that many forms of historiography have tended to elide in order to construct the past as coherent. Foucault recommends that the study of history abandon 'the certainty of absolutes' that guarantees as truth its unifying perspective: 'The traditional devices for constructing a comprehensive view of history and for retracing the past as a patient and continuous process must be systematically dismantled' (1977: 153). One aspect of this dismantling process that has enormous implications for historiography and for narrative generally can be found in the opening pages of *The Order of Things* where he defines a history of the Other, 'of that which, for a given culture, is at once interior and foreign, therefore to be excluded (so as to exorcise the interior danger)' (1973: xxiv). The degree to which this reconception of history and historiography, by means of the introduction of irreducible discontinuity and difference, will affect the writing of practicing historians is not as yet clear, but its potential for disturbing the orderly narrative structure posited in the eighteenth century is obvious:

We want historians to confirm our belief that the present rests on profound intentions and immutable necessities. But the true historical sense confirms our existence among countless lost events, without a landmark or a point of reference.   (Foucault, 1977: 155)

Clearly, the very possibility of coherent historical narrative in any traditional sense founders with the acceptance of this description of the temporal situation.

Whatever its problems, narrative history will not easily be displaced as one (if not *the*) essential historiographic genre. The attempt to make the knowledge of history wholly scientific seems finally unlikely to succeed. No matter how sophisticated the techniques of social science become, no matter how 'scientific', historical data will always remain incomplete. Furthermore, the results produced by the analysis of historical data – even the legitimate definition of what constitutes historical data – are always limited by the questions posed by its analysts, whose own historical and cultural contexts inevitably impose limits on their range of enquiry. While the value of the research accomplished by the many historians who use the various scientific methodologies now incorporated into the study of history, can hardly be overstated, the problems of historical knowledge and historiographic representation cannot really be said to have been solved. This is not, in any case, the place to reopen the long-standing debate over the distinction between nomothetic (general law) and idiographic (individual description) sciences and over the position of history in this scheme.[5] The importance of narrative form in historiography is not really in question: whether or not the narrative element can be proven to be problematic or even inferior, it persists, both in academic and in more popular works of history. Also (as Gramsci almost says) all people *are* historians to the degree that each person carries a sense of the past in his or her mind, and there is a strong narrative element in the discourse that we all conduct about that past.[6]

Aristotle states in the *Poetics* that a plot 'must be an imitation of an action that is one and whole'. He acknowledges that there are, however, 'many actions in the life of a single person from which no overall unity of action emerges' and which are therefore not appropriate to poetry, but only to history. In poetry 'the parts of the action' must be arranged so that 'if any one part is transposed or removed, the whole will be disordered and disunified. For that whose presence or absence has no evident effect is no part of the whole.' Aristotle is not concerned here with the problems that might arise from the fact that judgements involving evident effects and definitions of the whole may be neither absolute nor universal, but instead may be intricately connected to point of view. The task of the historian, he continues, is to narrate what has actually happened rather than, like the poet, to write about what might have occurred or might occur; and for this reason poetry is more significant than history (1968: 16–17). When poetry comes closest to history, presenting the disorder of actuality rather than the unity of art, it is most inferior: 'Of the simple plots and actions the episodic are the worst; and I mean by episodic a plot in which the episodes follow each other without regard for the laws of probability or necessity' (1968: 18).[7] In the late twentieth century, however, the historical laws of narrative probability or necessity are far from self-evident.

Sidney, in a restatement of the Aristotelian position in *An Apology for Poetry*, characterises the historian as 'tied, not to what should be but to what is, to the particular truth of things and not to the general reason of things'. As a result, 'his example draweth no necessary consequence, and therefore a less fruitful doctrine' (1966: 107). Unlike the poet, 'the historian, bound to tell things as they were, cannot be liberal (without he will be poetical) of a perfect pattern' (1966: 110). Still, without the poet's pattern of artistic unity as a guide, how, he wonders, 'will you discern what to follow, but by your own discretion'. The imposition of order on historical events, or the extraction of meaning from them is not the function of the historian according to this theory, and history is to that extent an inferior discipline.

One of the founders of modern historiography, Leopold von
Ranke, accepted some of these strictures with evident satisfaction.
In a classic statement on the nature of the historical project, he
writes:

To history has been assigned the office of judging the past, of instructing the
present for the benefit of future ages. To such high offices this work does not
aspire: It wants only to show what actually happened.   (Stern, 1956: 57)[8]

Yet, whether it is by the discretion of the historian or the
discretion of the reader (or some combination of the two),
historical narratives generally do manifest a sense of order in their
representation of the episodic chaos of temporality. This sense of
order is based, at least in part, on the discretion (Sidney) or point
of view of the historian, whose task it is – either implicitly or
explicitly – to arbitrate between the various accounts of the past
and to decide which episodes have an evident effect (Aristotle)
and what that effect may be. In general, historians have not
contented themselves with the mere chronicling of more or less
discrete events: von Ranke and his successors often recount
history in narrative form, thus bestowing both significant order
and causal logic on the historical field. As von Ranke himself
acknowledges, an historian's intentions depend on his viewpoint
and 'writers differ in the positions from which they view the
history' (1973: 135, 148). He alters the previous assessment of
history as excessively episodic by balancing the claims of fact and
form: accurate 'presentation of facts, no matter how conditional
and unattractive they might be is the supreme law. The development of the unity and progress of the events [comes] next in order
of importance' (1973: 137). In the end, he is convinced that the
internal logic of a historical work is derived from the intentions of
the author in combination with the available information (1973:
150). Authorial intentionality, narrative point of view: these then
are mediating terms between episodic chaos and coherent narrative in the representation of history.

   Hegel is well aware of the difficulties involved in the writing of
history: while insisting that we must 'apprehend the historical
faithfully', he adds that even in the use of such terms 'as
"faithfully" and "apprehend" [there] lies an ambiguity' since the
historian always 'brings his categories with him and sees the data
through them' (1953: 13). Nevertheless, despite this awareness,

Hegel's own categories seem evident in his assertion that the 'cultured human mind' (1953: 21) cannot help distinguishing among the various manifestations of the world spirit 'as they appear in the struggle of world-wide historical interests'. Some of the interests Hegel cites as examples, however, seem quite specific to nineteenth-century European concerns with nationalism and colonialism. When we read about the ancient Greeks, or about Alexander's conquests, he argues, 'we know very well what interests us. We want to see the Greeks saved from barbarism, we want the Athenian state preserved, and we are interested in the ruler under whose leadership the Greeks subjugated Asia.' 'We have here', he concludes, 'a substantial, an objective interest.' The degree to which this historiographic discretion may truly be termed objective, or the interests be conceived as world-wide or having a universal aim is no longer as clear as it may have appeared from the European perspective of the last century.[9] Hegel, however, bases his claim on an idea of a universal human nature, a concept whose universality appears ultimately to be undermined to some degree by its ascription of normative and deviant status:

The concept of human nature must fit all men and all ages, past and present. This universal concept may suffer infinite modifications; but ... [t]hinking reflection disregards the variations and adheres to the universal, which under all circumstances is active in the same manner and shows itself in the same interest. The universal type appears even in what seems to deviate from it most strongly; in the most distorted figure we can still discern the human.

(1953: 21)

What begins as descriptive tends toward the prescriptive as the ill-defined norms of human nature are characterised as suffering modification, subject to deviance and distortion. Yet there exists a necessary connection between this positing of a normative human nature and the tacit adoption of a very definite viewpoint on history as a vantage point from which to order events into coherent narrative. In the developing discussion of historiographic point of view since Hegel (a discussion I will explore in the next section), problematic terms such as 'human nature' occupy a central place.

It might seem to be belabouring the obvious to argue that acts of narrative representation necessarily exclude as well as include information; only by virtue of exclusion can the included be organised into any comprehensible order. The filtering out of the noise from the information, the relevant from the irrelevant, the background from the foreground, occurs only as a result of a complex series of judgements, the criteria of which bear close examination. Further, as Robert Young writes, 'History, with a capital H . . . cannot tolerate otherness or leave it outside its economy of inclusion' (1990: 4). The trace of the excluded, then, may remain within the borders of the narrative although in a transformed or misrecognised form which enables the narration itself to proceed. A comparison might be made with psychoanalytic models of repression, in which material that cannot easily be dealt with is repressed but continues to exert pressure on the psyche, thereby deforming it and threatening to disrupt its sense of coherence. Narrative accounts of the past, however successful their establishment of a smooth surface coherence and continuity, can be interrogated like palimpsests for traces of the competing (but excluded) narratives which remain at some level embedded. It is in this sense, remarks Hans Kellner, that 'the *text* of history [is] a text that can only be seen by "getting the story crooked" ' (1989: x).

To get the story crooked is to understand that the straightness of any story is a rhetorical invention and that the invention of stories is the most important part of human self-understanding and self-creation.   (1989: xi)[10]

In recent years the question of the coexistence of different, even incommensurable or competing historical narratives, each with its own claims to objective status, each with its own (sometimes mutually exclusive) claims to legitimacy, has become a vitally important issue. On the one hand, philosophical challenges such as Kuhn's theory of paradigm shifts, for example, put our grasp on truth in doubt; on the other, the global politics of the postcolonial world increasingly demonstrate that the models of historical reality long taken for granted by the world's dominant groups may not tell 'the whole story', may, in fact, be part of an attempt (conscious or otherwise) to repress much of the story that they have not wished to contemplate. Indeed, as a number of recent philosophers of history have argued, the very conceptual possibility of a 'whole story' has been thrown into doubt. Furthermore, as Foucault has indicated,

The more History attempts to transcend its own rootedness in historicity, and the greater the efforts it makes to attain, beyond the historical relativity of its origin and its choices, the sphere of universality, the more clearly it bears the marks of its historical birth, and the more evidently there appears through it the history of which it is itself a part.   (1973: 371)

The impact of these developments on a discipline that simply aspired to 'show what actually happened' (von Ranke) has been enormous. While fiction and history ought by no means be conflated, the similarity of the mediating roles played by concepts such as intentionality and point of view in the discussion of the writing both of history as narrative and of narrative fiction tends to work against the absolute separation of these two genres. Generic differences certainly exist, yet inasmuch as both seek to construct coherent narrative representations of events the similarity is worth examining. As a result, the following survey of the discussion in Anglo-American philosophy of history of narrative and point of view in the writing of history can (and will) be extended to elucidate some analogous problems in fiction as well.

BRADLEY AND CRITICAL PRESUPPOSITIONS

In his early work, The Presuppositions of Critical History (1874), F. H. Bradley was responding to the controversy that followed the sceptical attitude taken by positivist historians of his time, towards traditional claims for the literal historical truth of the Bible.[11] His discussion of the construction of historical narrative moves far beyond this specific debate, however. With brevity and clarity, he poses a problem that has continued to be a major source of difficulty in historiography:

We ask for history, and that means that we ask for the simple record of unadulterated facts; we look, and nowhere do we find the object of our search, but in its stead we see the divergent accounts of a host of jarring witnesses, a chaos of disjoined and discrepant narrations, and yet, while all of these can by no possibility be received as true, at the same time not one of them can be rejected as false.   (1968: 85)

From their differing points of view, these jarring witnesses may, of course, have very different ideas of what constitutes representational unity (Aristotle), a perfect pattern (Sidney), an objective interest (Hegel), even concerning what actually happened (von Ranke). It is evident that for Bradley the possibility of accepting without intervention 'the divergent accounts of a host of jarring witnesses, a chaos of disjoined and discrepant narrations', is not to be considered.

Early in the essay, Bradley presents a suggestive metaphorical discussion of history. His target is the uncritical historical method that would passively accept testimony and authority at face value, and the metaphor employed is sexual. Throughout the essay Bradley uses, not surprisingly, the masculine pronoun 'he' to refer to historians; in this passage he characterises history as 'she', and pursues the metaphor at some length. History can, it seems, be a difficult Victorian mistress: her unresponsive body is presented as a 'tranquil expanse no breath of thought can ruffle' (1968: 85). History has many would-be lovers and, in effect, leaves a trail of historiographical broken hearts behind:

> Writer after writer in rapid succession takes up the never-exhausted theme . . . the passion of the mind to be at home in its object, the longing to think the thing as it is in itself, and as all men have failed to think it before.   (1968: 86)

Such ardor is not easily discouraged, and the urge returns 'with every rise of the spirit'. Due to the incommensurable claims made on history by her many suitors, each of whom seems to represent her differently and none of whom can claim to possess her fully, the uncritical historian faces a dilemma: how can the beloved body truly be possessed? This dilemma then leads to an erotic impasse: 'Impotent to deny the existence of these facts, and powerless to explain them, the uncritical consciousness refuses to advance, or advancing loses hold on all reality.' The result, then, is a kind of historiographic detumescence, perhaps premature narration or even an act of narration that violates the available facts.

Without consummation, of course, there can be no reproduction, and in the end the disillusioned historian/lover

> is forced to see in the place of its reproduction an origination, in the place of its witness a writer of fiction, in the place of its fact a theory; and its consistent issue is the barren skepticism which sees in history but a weary labyrinth of truth and tangled falsehood, whose clue is buried and lost in the centuries that lie behind.   (1968: 86)

Although some kind of reproductive relationship is clearly called for by Bradley, he finds it necessary to limit and control the creative relationship within strict bounds. History may no longer remain chaste, but promiscuity cannot be allowed.

While expressing reservations concerning the practical consequences, Bradley accepts it as 'the task of the historian', even 'his
mission', to bring order to this promiscuous chaos. As he himself
recognises though, this mission runs immediately into a serious
obstacle. Admitting the historian's responsibility to exercise a
corrective influence implies, he observes, a preconception, even a
'foregone conclusion. The straightening of the crooked rests on the
knowledge of the straight, and the exercise of criticism requires a
canon' (1968: 85–6). The problem of establishing a legitimate
canonical authority assumes great importance in Bradley's discussion. While in the balance of the essay his central metaphor is legal
rather than sexual, none the less the stakes remain the same: once
the subjective element in the interpretation of history is accepted,
some rule or law must be invoked to control transgression, to
regulate who among the jarring witnesses may have the authority
to narrate.

Bradley attempts to confront the issue of subjectivity in
historiography head on. His title, he explains, is a statement of his
belief that history without preconceptions – objective history – is a
delusion, and that, in fact, all history is founded upon them. He
proceeds to look at the sublime diversity of the historical field, at
the instability of the historical record, and at the difficulties
inherent in attempts to stabilise or control it:

If we take the simplest historical fact, and reflect on the complex nature of the
transition it attempts to express, it is clear to us that we are concerned with a
number of judgements, the multitude of which wearies our attempts at
analysis.   (1968: 90)

Bradley then moves to an admittedly paradoxical resolution: in
practice the judgements are united, bound up in a single mental
act by which the whole event is apprehended. Historical facts are
themselves conclusions, he decides, posited by the historian
whose judgements and presuppositions inevitably structure any
narrative representation. Such conclusions are never random
inventions, however, but arise from 'the formed world of existing
beliefs'. As a result, Bradley argues, reality appears as a fabric of
inferences, and all facts are inferential. Thus it is possible to get
from episodic chaos to a sense of order through the proper exercise
of judgement – the function of discretion described by Aristotle
and Sidney. This leaves open a fairly wide door. Two questions

regarding Bradley's inferential facts arise: first, what effect does this process of inference have on the 'raw material' of history? And second, how is inferential orientation grounded?

This judgemental process seems to structure perception itself, as Bradley asserts that 'rightly to observe is not to receive a series of chaotic impressions, but to grasp the course of events as a connected whole' (1968: 92). And this is the corrective function demanded of the historian earlier. Our ideas of the past 'become trustworthy solely through a process of constant and habitual corrected recollection; the correction being in every case the determination of an order by fixing its elements in their proper relations' (1968: 93). This mediation or imposition of order is inevitable: in reality, he argues, since facts are theories there are no historical facts whatever which do not depend on inferential reasoning for their existence as well as for their specific narrative organisation (1968: 92). The essential distinction, according to Bradley, is between the historian who is unaware of his presuppositions and the one 'who consciously orders and creates from the known foundation of that which for him is the truth', thus protecting himself '(so far as is possible) from the caprices of fiction' (1968: 96). The end result of this corrective inferential act then is the creation of narrative order, continuity and coherence; it makes sense of history.

But how are the 'proper relations' to be defined? If history is inevitably a matter of inference, the system of judgements from which these inferences arise never begins ex nihilo. The representation of the past 'is never a fragmentary isolated act of our mind, but is essentially connected with, and in entire dependence on, the character of our general consciousness' (1968: 95–6). At this point Bradley seems to accept the stability of consciousness as the necessary corrective to the instability of the historical record. To the charge that consciousness may be no more stable, he replies forcefully, alluding to the power of law in two senses of the word. Following a discussion of scientific laws of nature, he turns (as Hegel does) to human nature, dramatically asserting that if

the actions of man are subject to no law . . . then the possibility of history, I think, must be allowed to disappear, and the past to become a matter of almost entire uncertainty. For, if we are precluded from counting on human nature, our hold on tradition is gone, and with it well nigh our only basis for historical judgement.   (1968: 99)

There is a kind of shift here from an idea of a universal human nature to a particular tradition, from the general to the specific culture whose tradition appears threatened. At the same time the laws of nature, particularly of human nature, begin to merge with the laws of particular social groups and the exercise of power on behalf of 'weightier interests'. The laws of human nature, it seems, are strictly enforced:

where the weightiest interests are at stake, and as long as criminals are executed in many cases by right of what comes to a construction of the laws of human action, so long will there be at least no practical necessity for the discarding of historical evidence in favour of the doubts, or perhaps the dogmas, of any man.

As in Hegel, human nature has shifted almost imperceptibly from being a descriptive term to being a prescriptive one whose norms must be protected. In sum, Bradley argues that the presuppositions structuring history are guaranteed by 'the uniformity of law': a law conflating the laws of nature and of human nature with the legal system of a specific society. And it is a law, it might be added, whose coercive power is clear – weighty interests have a decisive power in delineating the boundaries of the laws of human nature and in prescribing and enforcing the punishment of transgressors. The resulting narrative then demonstrates a sense of unity and order that separates it from the sublime chaos of disjoined and discrepant narrations and renders speechless the jarring witnesses. In this newly unified historical world, he argues, 'critical observation . . . thus in its hands has sentence of life and death' (1968: 103) over historical testimony just as a judge does over the lives of people brought before him. While Bradley no doubt does not intend the rather chilling political overtones of his metaphors, they are none the less appropriate to the stakes involved in legislating the meaning of history.

In arbitrating between witnesses, Bradley's principles of exclusion are twofold: the witness must appear to be reliable and to share, to a degree, our point of view on the events under consideration. The criterion of personal reliability is certainly far from self-evident, yet it is the second criterion that is the focus of much of his attention:

wherever the so-called 'fact' is made by subsumption under a view of the world different from ours, wherever we fail to make out that the judgement rested (consciously or unconsciously) on an ordered system identical with our own, there the 'fact' cannot be affirmed except on analogy; for, since the narrative is based on beliefs different from ours, the facts are affected by the beliefs, or, for anything we know, they may be so; we have no security that they are not affected.   (1968: 107)

As examples of unacceptable narrative agents he includes orthodox Catholics and the uneducated (1968: 109). Although Bradley is addressing himself to an academic problem,[12] nevertheless, in light of England's imperialist power, a legislation of acceptable historical narrative (and, as Bradley acknowledges, implicitly of human nature) that condemns to death (to use his metaphor) the narratives of other cultural groups has an almost explicit political relevance. To judge from the effects of European imperialist expansion for instance, the dependence of other cultures on 'our' ability to understand 'their' situation by analogy has not put them in an enviable position.

Historiography, for Bradley, deals in rational order and unified tradition, not a desire to remain open to the play of cultural difference. Jarring witnesses must be silenced, and the chaos of disjoined and discrepant narrations must be made coherent by coercion or, where possible, by simple elision of the discrepant elements. While we are interested in studying the past, 'where we encounter an alien element which we cannot recognize as akin to ourselves, that interest fails, the hope and purpose which inspired us dies, and the endeavor is thwarted' (1968: 115). He abandons the alien element to the death of hope and purpose, continuing the metaphor of the power of law over life and death that has run throughout his discussion of cultural difference. The oneness of humanity (1968: 114) seems to be connected throughout with the oneness of coherent and continuous orderly narrative which it is the historian's task to create. And the coercive element of legislative power is brought into focus by Bradley's example: historical events, he argues, present gaps which the historian must fill in.

It is a sufficient answer to any difficulties which may be raised as to the construction of a past order to point to the procedure of our police courts, where, in addition to the reconstruction of the witnesses by cross-examination, the sequence of events is reached by an active combination from present data.

(1968: 124)

If the outside limits are prescribed by legal power, within those bounds the unity and coherence of history are guaranteed by the 'personal experience' of the historian who is responsible for narrative reconstruction (1968: 141). If this is so, it follows that narrative perspective depends on whose testimony is privileged, whose personal experience is legitimised as the canon or model by which the police courts of history make their judgements:

Uneducated persons and children transform to their own likeness all they assimilate: and savages are in many cases literally unable to take in what to us seem simple impressions . . . [since] they have no internal world which answers to them, no premises under which to subsume them.   (1968: 141)

Some accounts of history need not be taken seriously because they are not based on 'critical presuppositions'. Orthodox Catholics, the uneducated, and now children and savages join the list of jarring witnesses whose narrations may be excluded. Because such groups lack a rational critical system for the appropriation of facts, he claims, their personal observation and actual experience can be discounted, and thus systematic order is brought to the chaotic field of historical narrative. Yet it remains very much a matter of opinion whose presuppositions are truly systematic and critical, and whose are superstition and dogma. Bradley's argument has led him into a difficult position, yet it is a position that has continued to vex philosophy of history: he recognises that an objective foundation for historiography is unattainable, but he is unwilling to accept the consequences of historiographic relativity. His sense of the vulnerability of his orthodox position is, perhaps, registered in his repeated appeal to the coercive force of law and the need to disallow such illegitimate transgressive history as can be ruled out of order, to silence some jarring witnesses whose narrative testimony can be stricken from the official record and whose agents can be prosecuted to the fullest extent of the law.

COLLINGWOOD AND THE *A PRIORI* IMAGINATION

Like Bradley, R. G. Collingwood in *The Idea of History* (published posthumously 1946 [1956]) works his discussion of the philosophy of history from an engagement with the problem of human nature, yet an important difference separates them.[13] The eighteenth-century historians and philosophers, Collingwood writes, believed that since the creation of the world human nature had remained fundamentally unchanged: 'Human nature was conceived substantialistically as something static and permanent, an unvarying substratum underlying the course of historical changes and all human activities' (1956: 82). The problem of difference could be accounted for only by positing that human nature is 'imperfectly developed in children, idiots, and savages' (1956: 82), a normative use of the term recalling Hegel and Bradley. Instead, a historicised theory of human nature is needed if the Enlightenment idea of universal history is to be replaced,

and this would imply thinking of human nature, the human nature actually existing in eighteenth century Europe, as the product of an historical process, whereas it was regarded as the unchanging presupposition of any such process.
(1956: 84–5)

Collingwood pursues this analysis an interesting step further in his subsequent critique of Herder's conception of history. Herder moved beyond a single monolithic normative human nature; he accepted, writes Collingwood, that there are 'differences between different kinds of men, and that human nature is not uniform but diversified . . . not a datum but a problem' (1956: 90–1). Herder does not offer a theory of a historicised human nature, however, but bases cultural difference on the essentialist idea that each race has specific permanent and inherent traits. Instead of the universal human nature of the Enlightenment, he substitutes the idea of several fixed human natures. Collingwood's rejection of this ahistorical theory, written during the 1930s, becomes scathing as he links it to Eurocentrist apologies for imperialism and racism:

At the present time, we have seen enough of the evil consequences of this theory to be on our guard against it . . . . Today we only know it as a sophistical excuse for national pride and national hatred. The idea that there is a European race whose peculiar virtues render it fit to dominate the rest of the world . . . we know to be scientifically baseless and politically disastrous.   (1956: 91–2)

'Once Herder's view of race is accepted', Collingwood argues, 'there is no escaping the Nazi marriage laws' (1956: 92).

What historians should be interested in, according to Collingwood, is the historical specificity of culture, human nature and social institutions. Historians would then find their subject matter in 'the social customs which [people] create by their thought as a framework within which their appetites find satisfaction in ways sanctioned by convention and morality' (1956: 216). This casts the problem of subjectivity in history in an interesting light and recalls Bradley's distinction between analogous and non-analogous cultural experiences. Historical enquiry, he argues, not only reveals information about past events but also about the historian's own mind: when he finds historical matters unintelligible, 'he has discovered a limitation of his own mind; he has discovered that there are certain ways in which he is not, or no longer, or not yet, able to think' (1956: 218). The problem of what is available to thought, of what is quite literally unthinkable and inconceivable, involves questions of ideology, hegemony and doxa – questions ruled out of order in Bradley's court. Collingwood, however, seems to hover on the brink of this kind of analysis:

Certain historians, sometimes whole generations of historians, find in certain periods of history nothing intelligible, and call them dark ages; but such phrases tell us nothing about those ages themselves, though they tell us a great deal about the persons who use them.   (1956: 218–19)

Having established the problem of what is or is not thinkable as a historiographic problem in itself, Collingwood's next move, a move consonant with his desire to historicise the idea of human nature, might have been to examine the political, social and historical determinations which delineate the horizon of the thinkable. But this is a step he does not take; instead, he works through the individual historian, the strengths and weaknesses (1956: 219) of whose sensibility determine the scope of any historical account.

For Collingwood, individual consciousness constitutes both the subjectivity of the historian and the historical object to be studied. It is the thoughts of historical agents that form the object of historical attention, not the institutions or social structures within which they lived. While Bradley developed his concept of 'presuppositions', Collingwood introduces a theory of a historically variable 'a priori imagination' (1956: 241) structuring individual thoughts and responses at any given time.[14] Just as the imagination of the historian is framed by these a priori structures of thought, so too are the mental habits and cognitive processes of the people the historian studies. Thus social institutions and conventions articulate, perhaps homologically, the a priori imaginations of the people involved in them. As an example, one could cite the idea of hierarchy in mediaeval society: the position of hierarchy as an organisational principle in philosophy, theology and social institutions suggests that some implicit concept of hierarchy might be a basic organisational principle in the mediaeval *a priori* imagination.

Collingwood's insistence on the priority of the individual consciousness separates him from many contemporary thinkers who conversely emphasise the degree to which the thoughts of people are constituted by the institutions within which they live. 'Institutions', he argues, 'are constituted by the way in which they are thought of by the people living under them' (1965: 175). By accepting the existence of incommensurable systems of *a priori* imaginations, the historian could theorise the gap in what appears as thinkable to different cultures at different times. While accepting the existence of this gap, as Louis Mink notes,[15] Collingwood omits an analysis of why it exists or what specifically changes in order to make thinkable what had previously not been so. Indeed, while this is not acknowledged as a problem, it has great relevance to any discussion of jarring witnesses whose judgements might arise from a differently ordered set of *a priori* principles rather than from an incomplete or distorted human nature.

Collingwood goes a step beyond Bradley's idea of a critical history and speaks of a constructive history that is neither arbitrary nor fanciful. This 'construction involves nothing that is not necessitated by the evidence, it is a legitimate historical construction of a kind without which there can be no history at all' (1956: 240–1). He is quite unequivocal about the importance of the imagination which, consciously or otherwise, bridges the gaps between stable facts or authorities in order to give historical narrative its continuity. If the points of stability are frequent enough and connections are constructed carefully, 'the whole picture is constantly verified by appeal to these data, and runs little risk of losing touch with the reality which it represents' (1956: 242). But this model of the historiographic situation is, as Collingwood observes, seriously flawed in its attribution of excessive stability to the authorities and to the empirical data. The fixed points constituted by facts and authorities are not finally static and should never be accepted without an element of scepticism. It is at this point that Collingwood moves to complete

Bradley's 'Copernican revolution in the theory of historical knowledge' (1956: 240).

> I am now driven to confess that there are for historical thought no fixed points thus given: in other words, that in history, just as there are properly speaking no authorities, so there are properly speaking no data . . . . The web of imaginative construction is something far more solid and powerful than we have hitherto realized. So far from relying for its validity upon the support of given facts, it actually serves as the touchstone by which we decide whether alleged facts are genuine.   (1956: 243–4)

And what are the operating principles of this imagination? The historiographic desire to make sense, to make a coherent and continuous picture of the past (1956: 245). Again, as Bradley pointed out, the construction of historical coherence is neither arbitrary nor the fiction of a random invention. 'Whatever goes into it, goes into it not because [the historian's] imagination passively accepts it, but because it actively demands it.' Collingwood argues that while the novelist and the historian both aim at making a coherent unified picture, the latter also has to represent things as they really were and events as they really happened (1956: 246).[16] Certainly, this picture must be constructed through historical evidence, but what is historical evidence? It is, he argues, whatever the historian can recognise as evidence.

> The enlargement of historical knowledge comes about mainly through finding how to use as evidence this or that kind of perceived fact which historians have hitherto thought useless to them . . . . Evidence is evidence only when some one contemplates it historically.   (1956: 246–7)

Unless called into play *as evidence*, such information remains, he concludes, 'historically dumb'. Collingwood's insight is supported by the fact that evidence necessary for the writing of women's history, for example, or histories of the lower classes or colonised races was available long before it was considered historically relevant. The fact that this evidence did not speak, did not appear *as evidence*, suggests the way that the discourse is inevitably subject to extra-disciplinary pressures and constraints. With this we come back, in a sense, to Bradley's sentence of death on those jarring witnesses who with their chaos of disjoined and discrepant narrations remain outside the laws that mark the boundaries of legitimate, coherent and continuous history. Collingwood seems to recognise, rather more sympathetically, the manner in which jarring witnesses can be rendered speechless, aphasic, by the presuppositions or *a priori* imagination of the historian.

WALSH AND COLLIGATION

'One of the things that strikes the outsider most when he looks at history', observes W. H. Walsh in *Philosophy of History* (1951), 'is the plurality of divergent accounts of the same subject . . . differing and apparently inconsistent versions of the same set of events, each of them claiming to give, if not the whole truth about it, at any rate as much of the truth as can now be come by' (1960: 98). In response, Walsh distinguishes between historical scepticism in which subjectivity constitutes an insurmountable obstacle to knowledge (1960: 108), and a perspective theory of historical truth that could accept the fact of historians' sometimes irreconcilable points of view (1960: 109). In terms of the latter position, 'objectivity in history must be taken in a weakened sense: a history could be said to be objective if it depicted the facts accurately from its own point of view'. With this recognition of point of view and consequent abandonment of universality, Walsh admits the jarring witnesses – albeit somewhat reluctantly. This reluctance is registered in his hope that 'objectivity in a strong sense may after all be attainable by historians, since in principle at any rate the possibility of developing a point of view which would win universal acceptance cannot be ruled out' (1960: 109). But this objectivity can only be accomplished if a single historical point of view can be established, and the establishment of such a transcendental point of view inevitably involves a conception of a universal human nature.

While acknowledging that this historical consciousness must be based on a true appreciation of human nature (1960: 118) which is not as yet available, he argues that we must nevertheless continue to hope for the ultimate establishment of a single point of view which all historians might be prepared to accept. To achieve this, a historian needs to know not just how people might behave in a variety of situations, but also 'how they *ought* to behave. He needs to get straight not merely his factual knowledge, but also his moral and metaphysical ideas' (1960: 118). Thus, knowledge of human nature inevitably involves a larger vision of the world, of the universe, in which those humans live: as Bradley pointed out, the correction of the crooked depends on the knowledge of the straight. Walsh admits that many today no longer consider such knowledge possible, but he himself refuses to relinquish hope although the attainment of this perspective does not seem imminent. For the moment there is no escaping the jarring witnesses, and 'objective historical consciousness . . . must remain no more than a pious aspiration.' In the meantime, he concludes, 'we have no alternative but to fall back on the perspective theory' (1960: 118). It is a religious vision to some degree, invoking piety and a sense of a 'fall' from a transcendent vision of history (in which the historian, like Boethius's God, can see and comprehend the totality of human experience) to the secular diverging interpretations and perspectives of finite, heterodox individuals.[17]

In an argument that looks back to the ideas of presuppositions asserted by both Bradley and Collingwood, Walsh observes that every historian has a fundamental set of judgements concerning human nature on which all his thinking depends (1960: 65). The importance of such judgements, encompassing both trivial and essential aspects of human life, must not be underestimated since 'it is in the light of his conception of human nature that the historian must finally decide both what to accept as fact and how to understand what he does accept'. Walsh discusses three possible sources of such judgements. The first source is located in the historian's study of human nature in the social sciences such as psychology and sociology (1960: 66), and the third is the genius, talent or insight of the individual historian whose powers of creative imagination are compared with those of the writers of great literature (1960: 67). The middle term is common sense.

The understanding of human nature shown by historians . . . is not different from that which we all display in our daily lives, and comes from the same source. It is part of that vague amalgam of currently recognized generalities, derived from common experience and more or less confirmed by our own, which we all accept for everyday purposes and know by the name of 'common sense.'   (1960: 66)

The idea of common sense – sensus communis – like that of human nature, is central to the problem under discussion, but finally it does not resolve the difficulties of historical scepticism or perspectivism either. As long as differing accounts of human nature, different versions of common sense, coexist, there will be jarring witnesses and discrepant narrations, and Walsh realises that 'there is in the last resort nothing anyone else can do about it' (1960: 117). It is not even possible to settle the dispute by referring to 'unassailable fact' either, since 'fact on one interpretation is not necessarily fact on another'. Walsh uses as an example the disputes between Marxist and anti-Marxist historians, and while he does not discuss the wider political implications of these disputes, his example suggests an awareness of this dimension that is never fully articulated.

Walsh's best-known contribution to the debate concerning the narrative representation of history is his theory of colligation. He accepts that the historian's aim is 'to make a coherent whole out of the events he studies' (1960: 62), and given the impossibility of doing so (in any final sense) that results from our incomplete understanding of human nature, we are left with the necessity of provisional solutions if we wish to make history coherent. The historian's way of doing this is to locate

dominant concepts or leading ideas by which to illuminate his facts, to trace connections between those ideas themselves, and then to show how the detailed facts become intelligible in the light of them by constructing a 'significant' narrative of the events.   (1960: 62)

This colligation procedure is not perfect and makes no claim to transcendent vision; in fact, he admits, it can achieve at best only partial success. The choice of concepts or ideas to be employed and their proper application is imprecise, and the intelligibility can only be conferred within arbitrarily defined periods. All these caveats notwithstanding, however, Walsh argues that this is essentially what historians do, and he locates the construction of a significant narrative as a central act in the process. A significant narrative as opposed to a 'plain narrative' or chronicle – a distinction that returns us to Aristotle's separation of the episodic from the plotted – has two related characteristics: first, it aims not merely at saying what happened but also at (in some sense) explaining why; second, it is 'a smooth narrative in which every event falls as it were into its natural place and belongs to an intelligible whole' (1960: 31–3).

The historian's task, again, is to make sense of history, to find in or impose on history a coherence and a narrative form that make it seem at the same time *natural*. While Walsh does not interrogate his use of the concept of events in their natural place, the nature referred to here must be related to the conception of human nature held by the historian. Consequently, the intelligibility and coherence are limited once again to those who share to an adequate degree the historian's view of the world – otherwise the sense of a natural place for the events of the narrative, the smoothness of the narrative flow, is disrupted.

Walsh abandons, provisionally at least, the search for a transcendent point of view which might theoretically reconcile or contain all points of view. Instead, he settles for something much more limited, an idea of common sense, a fundamental set of judgements enabling the colligation of historical evidence. A similarity can, to some degree, be recognised between Walsh's terms and Bradley's critical presuppositions or Collingwood's *a priori* imagination. They all attempt to describe the way the historian, however consciously or unconsciously, makes sense of an historical field that does not initially offer itself as a coherent totality, and they all do so through the focus of a point of view on that field based on an already-structured sense of human nature and of reality.

GALLIE AND NARRATIVE FOLLOWING

When W. B. Gallie argues in *Philosophy and the Historical Understanding* (1968) that 'to follow' a narrative 'is to think – to connect, to appreciate continuities, to feel the forward-movement' (1968: 18); the place of jarring witnesses and their disjoined and discrepant narrations is not immediately clear. Nevertheless, 'following', he contends, 'is an essential element in, or basis for, other more complicated forms of historical understanding'. Gallie is adamant that the process of following a story is not ultimately a rational and conscious one, a characterisation that places it, once again, in the category of common sense: 'we are pulled along by it, and pulled at by a far more compelling part of our human make-up than our intellectual presumptions and expectations' (1968: 45).

The act of following a story requires 'the cool application of our general knowledge of human nature' as a means of understanding 'continuous and consistent processes' (1968: 46), but it is not confined to this. There is, as well, the ability to follow events across the apparent discontinuities, contingencies and unpredictabilities that inevitably complicate narration. Without this capacity, the possibility of narrative history could not exist. And just as there is not, for Collingwood, a universal historical imagination, for Gallie there are limits to this capacity: the nature of the discontinuities we are able to accept, without losing the coherence of the narrative, depends in part on 'the set or orientation of our sympathy for some particular character . . . and partly upon the intrinsic nature of the kind of sympathy that has been established' (1968: 46). When the narrative gaps or discontinuities grow too great, the historian has recourse to non-narrative explanation: Gallie uses the example of a commentator at a cricket match who occasionally is forced to interrupt his narrative to explain a rule. But by and large, rational objective knowledge remains subservient to some more fundamental presuppositions through which the sympathies are engaged, otherwise the story would remain incomprehensible, rational knowledge notwithstanding: 'unless we were in some degree emotionally involved in a story, the point, nay the very existence of its climax would escape us' (1968: 47).

Engaging the sympathies depends upon the less-than-universal human interests which a given set of events can be conceived to represent – on their power to appeal to our feelings (1968: 48). To become the object of historical study, human actions and past events must be recognised 'by members of some human group to belong to *its* past, and to be intelligible and worth understanding from the point of view of *its* present interests' (1968: 52). This is close to Collingwood's historiographical aphasia or Bradley's sentence of life and death in historiography, and constitutes an admission that followability is specific to particular social groups at particular times. It is always from a specific location that sense has to be made and that the processes of selection, exclusion and organisation of material must be orchestrated. To be historically comprehensible an event must be seen in relation to other events – both past and present – that are at once its context and its condition (1968: 54). Some principle of selection, conscious or unconscious, must inevitably be invoked if representation is to take place at all. But, as Gallie argues, the selection of the event to be studied as well as the positing of a relation between it and another event is inevitably embedded in the context of present interests.[18]

At one point Gallie, like Collingwood and Walsh, reflects back on the earlier dream of a universal history capable of transcending the specific social and historical situation of the historian, containing and connecting all the main historic themes. Such a history would find its subject matter in the achievements of those nations, religions and cultures that have

served for a period as torch-carriers for the civilization that is now common to 'us all', which to Ranke meant common to all intelligent and educated citizens of any of the great nation-states of Europe and North America. But, alas, every such would-be-Universal history, like every narrower history, must be told with certain pre-selected interests to the fore: e.g. for Ranke those of nineteenth-century national civilizations. Even in his day this selectiveness showed a certain sociological lack of imagination; today it would be simply unthinkable.   (1968: 54)

It might be added that those principles of selection that are accepted as normal or commonsensical here and today may seem equally unthinkable (morally or quite literally) at another point in time or from another point of view. Historiographical blindspots may be inevitable, yet the exigencies of historiography remain: the stories must be told and 'in fairness, some selection of viewpoint must be made if history is to be written at all' (1968: 54). The historical field in its entirety is not a possible starting point and the equation of history with the total past can result only in confusion: 'our ignorance of where the past limit of the proposed slice of space–time should be set, and of the nature and order of importance of the main events that fall within it, is terrifying in its immensity' (1968: 57).

No narrative representation can do justice to the sublime scope of history as a whole. The sense of terror alluded to here is, perhaps, a modern version of the weariness that Bradley speaks of in relation to the magnitude and complexity of the historiographic project. Nevertheless, the ideal of a total history or of one historical world, if unrealisable, remains as 'a demand laid upon the con-science, a challenge set to the passion, of any and every historian' (1968: 61). The paradox persists that the historian's commitment to the perceived interconnectedness and ultimate unity of history must coexist with the obvious and inevitable selectiveness of all historical thinking and writing. And in practice 'it is impossible that he should ever reach, that he could ever have come perceptibly nearer to that ideal goal'. The rhetoric and subject matter here recall Walsh's pious aspiration to achieve objective historical consciousness, but Gallie expresses more fully, perhaps, the problem inherent in any such aspiration: history is not just the totality of the human past.

It is our name for the study of any past human action in so far as it is understood through its interconnectedness with other actions which a particular community or generation regards as of special interest to them.

(1968: 62)[19]

While Gallie does not discuss the political implications of the point, as is the case with Bradley's weightiest interests the political stakes are high, and it is worthwhile underlining the profoundly political nature of the way coherent historical narratives can be shaped by present interest. The point here is not to elaborate a 1984-style conspiracy theory of historiography, but to account for the way coherent historical narrative is built of the testimony of jarring witnesses (or communities of witnesses) and their disjoined and discrepant narrations. Gallie's assertion that ' "our" history is whatever past actions our historians have succeeded in making intelligible to us, whoever "we" happen to be', calls attention to the importance of the first person pronouns in order to make clear the determining influence, whether conscious or unconscious, of social position and community affiliation on the historiographic act.

MINK AND NARRATIVE COGNITION

'[N]othing is more wonderful than common sense', writes Louis O. Mink, and the 'comfortable certainties' (1987: 182) of human nature and of universal human experience present him with his first topic in 'Narrative Form as Cognitive Understanding' (1987). The echoes of Collingwood and of Gallie are clear:

The common sense of an age, we recognize when we compare that age with others, may well be for different times or places beyond the limit of comprehension or even of fantasy. A primary reason for this is that common sense of whatever age has presuppositions which derive not from universal human experience but from a shared conceptual framework, which determines what shall count as experience for its communicants.   (1987: 182)

Mink does not pursue this suggestive aspect of the argument at any length, however, but turns instead to a consideration of a few 'common sense' notions of historical narrative. For Mink, narrative is important not simply as an aspect of history or literature; rather it 'is a primary cognitive instrument – an instrument rivalled, in fact, only by theory and by metaphor as irreducible ways of making the flux of experience comprehensible' (1987: 185). He formulates two essential modes of understanding this flux, synchronic and diachronic, and as the foremost example of the latter, 'narrative as such is not just a technical problem for writers and critics but a primary and irreducible form of human comprehension, an article in the constitution of common sense' (1987: 186).

Narratives contain or express the presuppositions and common sense of their authors, presuppositions and articles of common sense which may be very different. It seems clear, he argues, that we do not necessarily experience life as a narrative but instead give it that form by making it the subject of stories (1987: 186). The fact that we know how to construct coherent narratives, then, suggests that we are in possession of principles of selection and exclusion which may or may not be consciously held. 'Since we do recognize that a given incident is relevant or irrelevant to a certain narrative, it would seem that we must be in possession of implicit *criteria* of relevance.' In principle, says Mink, we should be able systematically to make explicit the criteria structuring our recognition of relevance and irrelevance – this is the critical historian's burden of self-consciousness described by Bradley – yet, he adds, this has still not proved possible (1987: 187).

While systematic explication has remained elusive, Mink nevertheless pinpoints a central presupposition behind much narrative history. This is the idea

that historical actuality itself has narrative form, which the historian does not invent but discovers, or attempts to discover. History-as-it-was-lived, that is, is an untold story. The historian's job is to discover that untold story, or part of it, and to retell it even though in abridged or edited form .... Properly understood, the story of the past needs only to be communicated, not constructed.   (1987: 187–8)

Mink traces this to the powerful concept of universal history, especially as formulated by Schiller and Kant. For Schiller, universal history could potentially explain the contemporary world by identifying and following the chains of events that have led up

to it, events that can be displayed as a coherent unity (1987: 189).
And Kant argued that 'what seems complex and chaotic in the
single individual may be seen from the standpoint of the human
race as a whole to be a steady and progressive though slow
evolution of its original endowment' (1963: 190). As Collingwood
points out, the Enlightenment philosophers felt they had begun to
understand human nature and could therefore articulate a universal history from the point of view of the race as a whole. Mink
delineates four related concepts common to the idea of universal
history: first, the totality of past human events belongs to a single
story; second, a single central subject or theme structures the plot
of that story; third, historical events are unintelligible when seen
only in terms of their arbitrary immediate circumstances and must
be set within the totality to be fully understood; and finally, the
diversity of human events, customs and institutions can be
regarded as variations of a single and unchanging human nature
(1987: 190–1). Each of these propositions has been discredited in
modern philosophy, Mink argues, yet the ideas continue to
permeate historical thinking.

After pointing out a number of contradictions in the idea of
universal history, Mink begins to conceptualise narrative as a form
of cognition rather than of *mimesis* and to discuss some of the
implications:

> The cognitive function of narrative form, then, is not just to relate a succession
> of events but to body forth an ensemble of interrelationships of many different
> kinds as a single whole . . . . The same event, under the same description or
> different descriptions, may belong to different stories, and its particular
> significance will vary with its place in these different – often very different –
> narratives.   (1987: 198)

The problems do not end here, however. Mink asserts that there is
an incompatibility between our concept of *event* and our concept
of *narrative* (1987: 200). The concept of an event is one borrowed
from the physical sciences and becomes awkward when pushed
into history. What are the limits of an event? Is any event not
composed of an infinite number of smaller events? Is it possible to
theorise something like an *eventeme*? Or, on the other hand, as
François Furet concludes in his discussion of the problematic
relationship between narrative and historical events, perhaps
'History is a permanent event' (1984: 60). Strictly speaking, we

cannot refer to events as such at all, 'but only to events *under a description*: so there can be more than one description of the same event, all of them true but referring to different aspects of the event or describing it at different levels of generality' (Mink, 1987: 199–200). At this point the problem posed by jarring witnesses who describe events differently begins to appear more urgent: 'what', he asks, 'can we possibly mean by "same event"?' He then reconceptualises the relation of the two terms in such a way that narratives are no longer seen as built out of events as Bradley argued. Mink, somewhat in the manner of Collingwood's Copernican revolution, goes a step further and reverses the relation: events are *not* the raw materials of narrative, argues Mink, events are abstractions from narrative, and particular narrative constructions, in fact, generate an event's appropriate description (1987: 201).

Mink's analysis threatens seriously to destabilise the mind's perceived ability to grasp discrete, concrete historical events. One is returned presumably to an idea of 'interest' once again in search of a ground for historical knowledge. What then is the criterion of historiographical acceptability? How can we deal with the jarring witnesses and the disjoined and discrepant narrations? Considering his avoidance of the political implications of his argument, Mink's phrasing is remarkable: 'all our experience of narratives suggests that there is no way of settling on standard descriptions other than by arbitrary enforcement' (1987: 201). This insistence on the need for enforcement seems connected to the fact that narrative is inevitably the site of a repression as well as of an expression of the past. Mink does not, however, address the adjacent questions of power which are implied: Who enforces standard or orthodox versions of events? Against whom do they need enforcement? What weighty interests are involved? What, finally, is at stake in the dispute over the terms of historical description?

For Mink, despite the acuity of his analysis, these problems remain suspended, and he concludes that his theory does not undermine our hold on the past completely since individual statements of historical fact are essentially unaffected (1987: 202):

But it does mean that the significance of the past is determinate only by virtue of our own disciplined imagination. Insofar as the significance of past occurrences is understandable only as they are locatable in the ensemble of interrelationships that can be grasped only in the construction of narrative form, it is we who make the past determinate in that respect. If the past is not an untold story but can be made intelligible only as the subject of stories we tell, it is still our responsibility to get on with it.[20]

The sense of peril introduced in the idea of historiographic enforcement is extended here with a reference to 'our responsibility' and the importance of the duty to continue to narrate the past in such a way as to both construct its significance and maintain its truth claims. 'It would be disastrous I believe,' he writes, 'if common sense were to be routed from its last stronghold on this point.' The precise nature of the threatened disaster is nowhere spelled out, but it is clear that in this case there would be no enforceable standard, no orthodoxy, no common sense or sense of community (sensus communis) by means of which the heterodox jarring witnesses could be controlled.

WHITE AND NARRATIVE MEANING-PRODUCTION

In his most recent collection of essays, The Content of the Form (1987), Hayden White asks a familiar historiographic question: 'What is involved, then, in that finding of the "true story," that discovery of the "real story" within or behind the events that come to us in the chaotic form of "historical records"?' (1987: 4). White analyses the narrativisation of historical events through a comparison with annals and chronicles. The central distinction, one that in some ways removes history from the critiques of Aristotle and Sidney, is that in a narrative 'events must be not only registered in their original occurrence but . . . revealed as possessing a structure, an order of meaning, which they do not possess as mere sequence' (1987: 5). Since this coherence is not to be found solely in the events themselves, it must be imposed from a specific narratorial point of view:

It is only from our knowledge of the subsequent history of Western Europe that we can presume to rank events in terms of their world-historical significance, and even that significance is less world-historical than simply Western European, representing a tendency of modern historians to rank events in the record hierarchically from within a perspective that is culture-specific, not universal at all.   (1987: 9–10)

By implication, the same process is at work both in the general selection of events to be narrated and in the selection of details to be included in the representations of those events: no matter how skilful the illusion of comprehensiveness, he observes, every narrative is constructed from a set of events only partially included (1987: 10).

In the annals and chronicle forms, White argues, there is less emphasis on the ranking (and perhaps on the selectivity) that make up the basis of narrative history. But what is ultimately lacking in these forms to lend them narrative fullness and order is, he says, 'a notion of a social center by which to locate them with respect to one another and to charge them with ethical and moral significance' (1987: 11). The key terms in this passage and throughout the article are 'social center' and 'ethical and moral', related terms, for White, with a clear connection to the *sensus communis*, the common sense that provides the epistemological centre of gravity of a society. White goes on to elaborate the relation of these terms to narrative theory, citing Hegel to the effect that the state and its laws provide the social centre without which narrative history is not conceivable: 'it is only the state which first presents subject-matter that is not only *adapted* to the prose of History, but involves the production of such history in the very progress of its own being' (1987: 12). Thus, in order for narrative to go on, there must be a notion of a legal subject whose particular human nature defines the parameters of historical agency and provides the subject of the historical narrative (1987: 13).

Law, historicality and narrativity, he writes in a formulation that recalls Bradley's use of legal metaphors, are intimately related. And this indicates a more general connection as well between narrative and authority (1987: 13–14).[21] The law 'is the form in which the subject encounters most immediately the social system', and it is theoretically a codification of the moral or common sense of that system. The intimate relationship between narrativity and law can thus be extended to include morality or ethics as well, and White concludes that 'every historical narrative has as its latent or manifest purpose the desire to moralize the events of which it treats'. From here it is a small step to the assertion that narrativity may be a function of a basic impulse to moralise reality, and so to identify it with the social system grounding our moral common sense.

This social centre and moral sense implicit in narrative exists in a complex reciprocal relation to authority, both constituting and

LIBRARY
COLBY-SAWYER COLLEGE
NEW LONDON, NH 03257

constituted by social authority. It constitutes the authority of reality by endowing it with the formal coherency – and therefore authority – of a story (1987: 20). Thus it seems possible to endow a particular set of social relations with an atmosphere of reality, a sense of being both natural and desirable which thereby establishes a particular distribution of power as normal, morally as well as narratively coherent. The corollary is that legitimate narrative authority is constituted by social authority, the weighty interests that distinguish reliable from jarring witnesses. White argues that not only the truth claims of any narrative but the right to narrate itself, depends on a relationship to authority. In the end, the authority of the narrative appears interchangeable with the authority of reality (1987: 20). But the sense of reality 'attached to narrativity in the representation of real events arises out of a desire to have real events display the coherence, integrity, fullness, and closure of an image of life that is and can only be imaginary' (1987: 24).

White paraphrases Barthes and Lacan to the effect that narrative is one of the basic social modes of shaping an infantile consciousness into a responsible legal subject (1987: 36). If rule-governed behaviour is a by-product of language-acquisition, then narrativity may be said further to result in the kind of temporal integrity 'which every individual must possess if he is to become a "subject" of (any) system of law, morality, or propriety'. The problem of the function of the imagination in historical narrative then returns, as White asserts that the essential imaginary element of a narrative representation is 'the illusion of a centered consciousness capable of looking out on the world, apprehending its structure and processes, and representing them to itself as having all of the formal coherency of narrativity itself' (1987: 36). White attempts to dispel this illusion by revealing the pivotal role of the imagination in the production of meaning: since any set of events can be variously emplotted (1987: 44), it can only be the imagination that determines the specific shape they will finally assume. This production is not solely a matter of personal preference but an aspect of the way cultures define the limits of the thinkable (Collingwood) or followable (Gallie). 'In the historical narrative the systems of meaning-production peculiar to a culture or society are tested against the capacity of any set of "real" events to yield to such systems.' This interpretation removes narrative

LIBRARY
COLBY-SAWYER COLLEGE
NEW LONDON, NH 03257

history from the dilemma of (true) science versus (false) ideology and recuperates it as part of the cognitive process of defining the boundary between the imaginary and the real of which fiction itself is an integral part (1987: 45). The relation of political power and the imagination then becomes explicit in what amounts, at least in part, to a restatement by White of Gramsci's well-known formulation of hegemony as a variable mixture of consent and coercion. The crucial political problem here

is not whose story is the best or truest but who has the power to make his story stick as the one that others will choose to live by or in . . . . One alternative to 'collective unity' is forced upon us by a combination of master narratives and instruments of control backed by weapons.   (1987: 167)

The difference between White and Mink regarding the ultimately cognitive (Mink) or moral (White) nature of narrative can, perhaps, be resolved by positing a larger term which would contain both, and a number of general theories such as hegemony or ideology might be employed to conceptualise narrativisation as a process that is at once a cognitive apprehension and a moral organisation of reality. In fact, White's own theory of narrative and imagination seems to effect this reconciliation, and we have, in a sense, come full circle. His acknowledgement of the central role of political or social power in the determination of legitimate authority in historical narrative is a return (albeit with a very different emphasis) to Bradley's analysis of the social and historiographic authority – the weighty interests which can be at work in the police courts of history – which is empowered to arbitrate among the jarring witnesses.

Common sense and historical narrative

Each of the theorists discussed thus far has recourse to some category underlying, or providing a foundation for, the coherence of any given historical narrative. Terms such as 'common sense' and 'human nature' recur, along with 'presuppositions', 'a priori imagination' or 'fundamental set of judgements', and indeed it has been strongly suggested that narrative history cannot be written unless it is underwritten by some such foundational notion. These are, however, portmanteau terms carrying within them a good deal of ideological baggage: statements concerning 'human nature' are, as Fredric Jameson has remarked, 'necessarily and irredeemably ideological' (1979: 53). And the idea of common sense (sensus communis), conflating as it does the sense of ordinary and self-evident truth with the sense of the community, begs equally for some kind of ideological analysis.[1] If history, as Jean-Luc Nancy has argued, 'does not belong primarily to time, nor to succession, nor to causality, but to community' (1990: 149), then two options open: either the theoretical discussion can be foregone and attention turned to the narratives themselves, thus potentially allowing the chorus of jarring witnesses to continue vying for narrative authority or arbitrarily suppressing them; or it becomes necessary to explore the relation of community to historical narrative. It should be possible to link theoretically the dynamics of social marginalisation to the structures of narrative marginalisation in such a way as to show how the category of 'jarring witnesses' is produced and how dominant social and narrative structures struggle to contain, even silence them.

Richard Rorty, taking a pragmatist Ockham's razor to the whole matter, might choose the first option, arguing that 'constructing models of such entities as "the self", "language", "nature", "God" or "history" ' is merely a kind of 'tinkering', a matter of 'taste' (1988: 270). Competing versions of the past could then presumably be allowed simply to coexist, since neither the objective represen- tation of historical reality as it is in itself, nor the theories used to buttress those versions, can claim any absolute justification. The result of this neo-pragmatist shortcut, for Rorty, is that 'we-we inheritors of the Enlightenment' (1988: 263) may dispense with such obsolete debates. One's preference for one account or perspective over another should be respected by others – within limits – as we struggle with the real problems of democratic citizenship. Yet even Rorty's tolerant 'we' community, like Bradley's, seems to have a problem with jarring witnesses.

There are times, he admits, when 'we modern inheritors of the traditions of religious tolerance and constitutional government' may refuse the terms of debate. We need not debate with 'fanatics' or the 'mad'. Using the examples of Nietzsche and Loyola, Rorty argues that there are people who, because of their views, cannot be seen 'as fellow citizens of our constitutional democracy, people whose life plans might, given ingenuity and good will, be fitted in with those of other citizens' (1988: 266). Such people, then, are simply not a part of our community, and in such a situation 'we' need not engage the argument on their terms.

Accommodation and tolerance must stop short of a willingness to work within any vocabulary that one's interlocutor wishes to use, to take seriously any topic that he puts forward for discussion' (1988: 268). 'We' take such decisions knowing there is no point in our furthering the conversation with such interlocutors: 'They are crazy because the limits of sanity are set by what we can take seriously' (1988: 267).

While it is not difficult to imagine cases in which Rorty's refusal might be justified, his presumption of ability to decide the sanity of others (the reliability of witnesses, in Bradley's terms) can only work from a position of enormous discursive power, the security of being the judge, not the judged. If we replace Nietzsche and Loyola as examples with North American native people, we can see how the heirs of the Enlightenment traditions of tolerance and democracy have, at times, used the power to decide who is not worth listening to, who need not be taken seriously, and where to set the limits of sanity. While it is, in one sense, an accurate description of the realities of power and conflict, Rorty's model is none the less unacceptable: suppose native people decide that the heirs of the Enlightenment are crazy because of the gap between their rhetoric of democracy and their traditionally exclusionary, even genocidal, practices. Certainly people so blatantly unable to make words and deeds coincide – to observe the legal agreements which they themselves have designed and imposed – are neither worth talking to nor believable; people who seem conveniently able to erase all history not complimentary to themselves must be fanatics. It is worthwhile juxtaposing here Frantz Fanon's depiction of 'this Europe where they are never done talking of Man, yet murder men everywhere they find them, at the corner of every one of their own streets, in all the corners of the globe' (1963: 8). Having quite logically decided this, are they then free, as Rorty is, to suspend discussion?

In a sense they are free to do so, but the outcome is very different since the power to control the present is massively concentrated in the hands of this insane but dominant community. So while 'we' are free to tinker with or reject altogether models of the past, it is worth remembering that not all models are created equal, and that the legacy of the Enlightenment may appear rather different from different perspectives. To the degree that their 'life plans' have not coincided with those of the dominant powers (Bradley's weighty interests), some communities have been simply ignored, excluded from the democratic debate about the 'successful accommodation of individuals'. The ease with which Rorty is able to set up guidelines for judging reliability based on 'our' Enlightenment/democratic/liberal tradition regarding who gets to speak or who deserves a hearing, is disconcerting to say the least. This is not to say that Rorty intends these consequences of pragmatism, but that he provides no adequate framework to safeguard the discursive rights of those groups that liberal democracy has traditionally marginalised. As Richard Bernstein has argued, 'Rorty seems to be insensitive to the dark side of appealing to "we" when it is used as an exclusionary tactic' (Bernstein, 1987: 554).[2]

Although (as Rorty would be quick to point out) the use of theory presents no guarantees, the jettisoning of theory offers no advantage in dealing with historiography – a discourse that has to do both with the past and with the various groups of communal subjects whose identities are bound up with their interpretations of that past. Still, the idea common to some pragmatists and postmodernists that theory, particularly in its tendency to totalisation, poses intellectual and social dangers, ought to be taken seriously. Political theorist Roberto Unger, for example, argues that the great theoretical structures that have traditionally served the left, despite their power, must be rethought as a means to opening up new ways to imagine the world, both as it exists and as it might exist. A new method of critical thought, he suggests, 'must wage perpetual war against the tendency to take the workings of a particular social world as if they defined the limits of the real and the possible in social life' (1986: 108). The echo here of Jean-François Lyotard's call to wage war on totality in The Postmodern Condition is, of course, striking, yet the fact that no single model can circumscribe socio-historical reality need not annul its finite usefulness. 'To live in history', Unger points out, 'means, among other things, to be an active and conscious participant in the conflict over the terms of collective life', a conflict which is played out in all spheres of life including theory (1986: 113). Similarly, Clifford Geertz, in his classic discussion of thick description, warns against placing too much faith in theoretical models abstracted from concrete particulars:

To set forth symmetrical crystals of significance, purified of the material complexity in which they were located, and then attribute their existence to autogenous principles of order, universal properties of the mind, or vast, a priori weltanschauungen, is to pretend to a science that does not exist and imagine a reality that cannot be found. Cultural analysis is (or should be) guessing at meanings, assessing the guesses, and drawing explanatory conclusions from the better guesses, not discovering the Continent of Meaning and mapping out its bodiless language.   (1973: 20)

Narrative theory will not help us arrive at the Continent of Historical Truth, yet theory need not be discarded inasmuch as it can be useful 'in gaining access to the conceptual world in which our subjects live so that we can, in some extended sense of the term, converse with them' (1973: 24). While 'Cultural analysis is intrinsically incomplete', and ethnography (like historiography – and indeed theory itself) is inevitably, as W. B. Gallie put it, 'essentially contestable' (1968: 29), such theory may help us to peer out from our ethnocentric 'we' as well as from our present historical moment. This sense of incompletion (particularly across the lines of race, class and gender that frequently define community borders) impels us to use whatever tools we can find to facilitate improved conversation.

History, whether academic or popular, is a good example of what Norbert Elias calls a means of orientation.[3] Historical knowledge functions as a means of diachronic orientation, a means of plotting the trajectory of a community from one stipulated point in the past to another or to the present or towards an anticipated future. While the possibility of a non-teleological historiography might be considered, there is no doubt that much historical discourse contains a decidedly teleological aspect and functions as a social means of temporal orientation.[4] The power to influence such orientation is, of course, socially contested, and history can be seen as a contributing element in the mixture of coercion and consent that – through provision of a common sense of origins and destinies – characterises hegemony (Gramsci) or the ideological social cement (Althusser) that binds groups together. As we have seen, thinkers from von Ranke to White acknowledge that a specific orientation or point of view (and the common sense that is implicit within it) is a *sine qua non* of coherent narrative historiography. This orientation is generally conceived from a particular (often national or racial) position, and the common sense that is authorised must be related to the common sense of that particular community at a particular historical moment. It is not surprising then that in the interest of social cohesion and the reproduction of specific forms of social relations, the legitimate authority to narrate, to author an historical narrative, must be delegated by social institutions to certain individuals and not to others, must be based on certain privileged versions of the past and not on others – as Bradley so clearly understood.

Furthermore, the presuppositions that must be accepted if the coherence of narrative is to overcome the non-coherence of events *ought* to appear self-evidently true – so true in fact that those presuppositions may be designated common sense in one of the Kantian senses of the term: 'a subjective principle' which operates 'by feeling and not by concepts, but yet with universal validity' (1951: 75). Common sense may thus precede explicit conceptualisation, existing – like Mink's implicit criteria of relevance – in the realm of the taken-for-granted; yet the claim to universal validity, as we have seen in Collingwood's critique of Universal History, is a variation of the enlightenment claim made on behalf of clearly non-universal cultural positions. Kant also distinguishes another variation of the term 'common sense' which 'does not judge by feeling but always by concepts, although ordinarily only as by obscurely represented principles' (1951: 75). In this sense, presuppositions no longer remain in the realm of the taken-for-granted but begin to emerge into the realm of the conceivable, the realm of discourse. In either case, for Kant such principles must transcend particular communities, and be grounded in 'that [element] in the subject which is nature' rather than that which is learned by 'rule and precept' (1951: 189). If there were to be no such shared common sense, he concludes, 'all claim to necessary universal agreement is a groundless and vain fancy' (1951: 191). Ultimately, Kant's community is the universal, the human community, and in historiography this returns us to Mink's struggle with Universal History, a concept that he dismisses with a powerful sense of uneasiness at the thought of the alternatives to it. There is an unavoidable tension inherent in the concept of common sense: if Kant emphasises the universal, others have emphasised the essential historicity and the socially constructed nature of the *sensus communis*. This tension is one that manifests itself in any narrative that attempts to represent human subjectivity beyond the confines of its narrator's community – an attempt that is an integral part of historiography.[5]

BOURDIEU AND ORTHODOXY

The ideas that structure the understanding and writing of narrative history might be represented, then, as a spectrum moving from unconscious and unformulatable preconceptions to conscious and clearly stated principles; a spectrum of belief that may be elucidated with reference to Pierre Bourdieu's theory of *doxa*. In his *Outline of a Theory of Practice*, Bourdieu argues that since various communities have evolved various ways of understanding the world none of those cultural systems is, in an absolute sense, necessary – and each is, to that degree, arbitrary. Yet social groups tend to refuse the arbitrary nature of their interpretations and instead attempt to naturalise their arbitrariness, a naturalisation that results in a '*sense of limits*, commonly called the *sense of reality*' (1977b: 164). At one extreme – doxa – this sense of reality or common sense is absolute and the social world thus appears self-evident. Doxa is distinguished from orthodoxy or heterodoxy, conditions which imply the possible coexistence of different or antagonistic ('jarring') beliefs. Thus, a particular social order may appear not as arbitrary, not simply as one possible order among many others, but as the natural order whose construction of reality tends to remain beyond question (1977b: 165–6). Since a community's temporal orientation is an essential part of its ordering of reality, references to what appears natural in the social world and in historical narrative are, of course, common throughout the discussion of historiography.

Echoing Collingwood's observations on the homology existing between the structure of the *a priori* imagination at a given time in a given society, and the social institutions and knowledge that society creates, Bourdieu argues that the commonsense world is reproduced in discourses (such as history) about the world in which the community's common sense is affirmed. A discourse such as history (as a means of social and temporal orientation) would be a prime example of the power of social discourse to define the world in a particular way, affirming a particular point of view, and thus bringing 'subjective experiences into the reassuring unanimity of a socially approved and collectively attested sense' (1977b: 167). For a wide variety of reasons, other structurations of experience, like the testimonies of jarring witnesses, are not always conceivable or thinkable. As Collingwood observed, there are kinds of evidence, as well as ways of structuring and narrating that evidence which simply remain unavailable, beyond the limits of what can be conceptualised.

The condition of doxa, strictly defined, precludes the possibility of a range of *opinions*, different and equally legitimate positions regarding aspects of the social universe (1977b: 167–8). Not only are some other narrative structurations of the past excluded from discourse then, but questions leading to those other possible structurations cannot, perhaps, even be posed. It is an absolute form of recognition of legitimacy, in short, since 'the very question of legitimacy, which arises from competition for legitimacy', does not arise. The absence of doxic adherence to certain historiographic principles is apparent in Bradley's essay, and his rhetoric, at times, becomes heated when he confronts competing theories. There is a sense of urgency in his drive to contain and arbitrate among witnesses competing for legitimacy. In general, this competition for legitimacy is a necessary condition for the recognition that a doxic state did, in fact, previously obtain:

It is by reference to the universe of opinion that the complementary class is defined, the class of that which is taken for granted, doxa, the sum total of the theses tacitly posited on the hither side of all inquiry, which appear as such only retrospectively, when they come to be suspended practically.

The idea of doxa, then, has much in common with the various theories of fundamental presuppositions or *a priori* imagination which have been posited as the theoretical basis on which practical historical enquiry rests – the 'theses tacitly posited on the hither side of all inquiry'. But these presupposed theses can only be recognised as such when they shift from the realm of the absolute or preconceptual (doxa) to the realm of discourse (orthodox or heterodox), a spectrum which recalls Kant's discussion of the relationship of conceptualisation to common sense. Thus the telling of history was long based on an almost total exclusion of the point of view of women, lower classes and non-Europeans – an exclusion that went largely unquestioned because it rested on the community's tacitly accepted presuppositions about human nature.

Gradually, the *sensus communis* has been changing on this historiographic issue, but a shift such as this does not occur 'naturally'. Instead, questioning of the presuppositions implied a particular way of life occurs, Bourdieu suggests, either as a result of cross-cultural contact or by objective social crisis.[6] This defamiliarisation, which renders into discourse previously tacit presuppositions, occurs when the social world and social facts lose their natural or conventional character (168–9). The idea of an epistemological break in the structure of doxa induced by objective social crisis has great relevance to the philosophy of history because – as theorists as diverse as Bradley and White agree – the authority to narrate and the legitimacy of narration are inevitably tied to social and legal forms of authority and legitimacy. The struggle over the legitimacy of historical narration, over this means of temporal orientation, is only one form of a more general social struggle for legitimacy that extends to the law itself. In his debate with Ronald Dworkin, Stanley Fish has argued that legal interpreters 'are constrained by their tacit awareness of what is possible and not possible to do, what is and is not a reasonable thing to say, what will and will not be heard as evidence' (1989: 98). More relevant still perhaps is the Critical Legal Studies Movement: Roberto Unger argues that modern legal doctrine 'exists in a cultural context in which, to an unprecedented extent, society is understood to be made and imagined rather than merely given'. Unger wishes no longer to avoid, 'as [m]odern jurists and their philosophers have', transforming 'legal doctrine into one more arena for continuing the fight over the right and possible forms of social life' (1986: 18).[7]

A shift out of the condition of doxa does not necessarily entail an absolute loss of meaning or orientation, however. While social crisis can lead to a questioning of doxa, radical critique always has inevitable limits imposed by the situation out of which the critique arises. While the established, dominant interpretations and common sense – Kant's preconceptual or obscurely represented principles – may be brought into focus, articulated, even dislodged in a time of social crisis, there remain horizons of interpretation beyond which it would be impossible to see or nonsense to peer. Nevertheless, Bourdieu maintains, the definition of this horizon is itself at stake:

the drawing of the line between the field of opinion, of that which is explicitly questioned, and the field of *doxa*, of that which is beyond question and which each agent tacitly accords by the mere fact of acting in accord with social convention, is itself a fundamental objective at stake in that form of class struggle which is the struggle for the imposition of the dominant systems of classification.   (1977b: 169)

This struggle over taxonomy and definition, over which opinions define the centre and which occupy the margins, has great relevance to the writing of narrative history and to the presuppositions of the historian regarding the selection and arrangement of whatever is constituted as evidence. Once again, obvious examples might be found in the exclusion of the possibility of an independent legitimate historiographic point of view for colonised peoples, for women or for the working classes. At one time these presuppositions were more or less tacitly accepted; more recently, they have entered into discourse and been disputed as part of the social struggle for legitimacy on the part of various dominated groups who have an interest in contesting the limits of *doxa* and exposing the arbitrariness of its restrictions (1977b: 169). Conversely, dominant groups have an interest in upholding the doxic limits of the world or at least substituting 'the necessarily imperfect substitute, *orthodoxy*'. Historical data may, as Bourdieu argues, be intrinsically amenable to other structurations, but the dominant groups – Bradley's weighty interests – tend to exert pressure toward an orthodoxy that makes it difficult for jarring witnesses with their disjoined and discrepant narrations to be heard. The heat generated recently, not only within the academy but also in newspapers and popular magazines, by debates over the literary canon, over core curriculum materials and over political correctness in the arts, is surprising considering the inattention and unconcern that is characteristic of society's customary attitude toward such topics. This friction cannot be explained in terms of the literature itself; instead, it is symptomatic of the difficulty of altering the social structures of doxa/orthodoxy/heterodoxy to which people are oriented.[8]

Tensions of this sort exist at all times in modern societies, but it is only when dominated groups such as those mentioned above possess the means of rejecting the dominant social classifications and definitions of reality that the arbitrary nature of the principles or presuppositions structuring the social and historical world becomes clear, and it is at this point that it 'becomes necessary to undertake the work of conscious systematization and express rationalization which marks the passage from doxa to orthodoxy' (Bourdieu, 1977b: 169). Orthodoxy may tend toward the preservation of doxa, but that prediscursive state cannot easily be enforced. In a sense, the passage from doxa to orthodoxy seems to be the issue in Bradley's condemnation of jarring witnesses, Collingwood's speechlessness, the horizon of a transcendental point of view in Walsh and Gallie, or Mink's moment of apparent epistemological despair. The difficulty of such a passage is articulated in Bradley's weariness, Gallie's terror or Mink's sense of impending disaster. The move to orthodoxy constitutes the next line of defence in the struggle to contain the heterodox: orthodoxy is an attempt to restore 'the primal state of innocence of doxa, [and it] exists only in the objective relationship which opposes it to heterodoxy, that is, by reference to the choice – *hairesis*, heresy – made possible by the existence of *competing possibles*' (1977b: 169). Bourdieu's use of the term heresy here (and blasphemy later) is strong, but it is appropriate to the strong language used, for instance, by Bradley to condemn heretical accounts of historic reality, or the quasi-religious language used by Walsh and Gallie in their discussions of the possibility of a final authoritative point of view on history.

The writing of history is one form of what Bourdieu calls the production of symbolic goods and, as such, constitutes a contribution 'to the delimitation of the universe of discourse, that is to say, the universe of the thinkable, and hence to the delimitation of the universe of the unthinkable'. When Bourdieu speaks of the ' "aphasia" of those who are denied access to the instruments of the struggle for the definition of reality' (1977b: 170), this loss of the power of coherent speech connects directly to Bradley and Collingwood and their discussion of the silencing of discrepant narrators; the political implications of this aphasia are clear. 'The right to speak, *legitimacy*, is invested in those agents recognized by the field as powerful possessors of [symbolic] capital', Toril Moi notes in her discussion of Bourdieu. 'Such individuals become spokespersons for the *doxa* and struggle to relegate challengers to their position as *heterodox* . . . as individuals whom one cannot *credit* with the right to speak'. (1991: 1022)

There is not, of course, a single voice that expresses society's sense of itself. Instead, a society speaks in many, often contradictory, voices and from many points of view. Indeed, the relations of the various social groups constituting those points of view are frequently at issue, Bourdieu argues, in the various discourses – such as history – in which the limits of the thinkable are defined, established, maintained or enforced.[9] Within those limits, there exists the universe of discourse, of opinion, of jarring witnesses, in which the legitimate authority to narrate the story of the past is contested, in which the struggle for voice and point of view is carried on.

BAKHTIN AND HETEROGLOSSIA

Literature, particularly the novel, is one arena in which the cognitive and ethical limits that bound the *sensus communis* may be affirmed, tested, transgressed or attacked. An overt or covert debate is carried on in the novel, concerning which limits remain invisible and which are to be focused on as sites where social struggles over meaning and power are conducted, concerning the definition of the field of doxa (ortho- and hetero-), and concerning the delegation of the power of legitimate speech and the condemnation to aphasia. A number of these issues have, of course, been explored by Bakhtin, particularly in 'Discourse in the Novel' (Bakhtin, 1981) in a way that interestingly parallels Bourdieu's insights into voice, authority and crisis. While Bakhtin's discussion is not restricted to a particular novelistic genre, his focus on the social situatedness of the novel is especially relevant to the historical novel since it, more explicitly than any other perhaps, necessarily engages the problem of community and representation. A shift in terminology from heterodoxy (Bourdieu) to heteroglossia (Bakhtin) is not difficult if it is kept in mind that Bakhtin defines language in such a way that the connection to Bourdieu is clear: 'We are taking language not as a system of abstract grammatical categories, but rather language conceived as ideologically saturated, language as a world view' (1981: 271). The bond of common sense is introduced into this definition by his insistence that one essential social function of language is that of 'insuring a *maximum* of mutual understanding in all spheres of ideological life'.

Instead of a single doxic view of the world, the novel, as a site for the struggle over legitimacy, over the authority of reality, presents a heteroglot multiplicity of definitions and value judgements (1981: 278). The novelist, in representing the world, 'witnesses as well the unfolding of social heteroglossia *surrounding* the object, the Tower-of-Babel mixing of languages that goes on around any object; the dialects of the object are interwoven with the social dialogue surrounding it'. The representation created by the novelist is, however, neither a simple reproduction of the world nor a collection of episodes including a representative variety of points of view. The novelist, like Walsh's colligating historian, through the creation of a coherent narrative representation from a specific point of view, produces instead an artistically nuanced image of the fundamental voices of this heteroglot reality (1981: 278–9). In the process, it is necessary to confront the heterodox lack of social consensus, the jarring languages constituted by other vocabularies, other semantic and syntactic forms, other points of view (1981: 285). And it is in dealing with this wider lack of a doxic common sense (*sensus communis*) in sorting out the jarring witnesses, that the significance of the novel emerges.

The internal politics of style (how the elements are put together) is determined by its external politics (its relationship to alien discourse). Discourse lives, as it were, on the boundary between its own context and another, alien, context.

(1981: 284)

According to Bakhtin, the kind of monological tendency that Bradley, for instance, demonstrates – his orthodoxy in Bourdieu's terms – is antithetical to the nature of the novel. The demand for a single unified and authoritative point of view and a coherent language with which to represent determinate events is, by this account, finally impossible; jarring witnesses with discrepant narrations and irreducibly alien – heterodox – languages remain, and their traces can always be located. The novel structurally reflects the fact that, at any given historical moment, languages of various periods and social conditions coexist (1981: 291). Indeed, the very possibility of a single stable unitary language is undermined since language itself is always irredeemably heteroglot, embodying the social contradictions of present and past. The various language groups exist in complex relations to each other, relations at times both complementary and contradictory; in Bakhtin's phrase, they are interrelated dialogically (1981: 291–2).

This is not to say, however, that all the languages find equal and adequate representation in narrative. In Bradley's scheme, there is little room for 'jarring witnesses'; the viewpoints must somehow be brought into orthodox line. Bakhtin notes a similar kind of process although his attitude toward it is markedly less draconian. In the colligation of a narrative, the prose writer imposes his or her own intentionality (consciously or unconsciously) on the heteroglossia: 'the intentions of the prose writer are refracted, and refracted *at different angles*, depending on the degree to which the refracted, heteroglot languages he deals with are socio-ideologically alien' (1981: 300). It is the specific organisation of heteroglossia, the orchestration of the languages, not the exclusion of all but a hegemonic language, that is at issue in Bakhtin's theory of the novel. The distinguishing feature of the genre is its organisation of the social diversity of voices into a structured artistic system. In Bourdieu's terms, the novel maps the orthodox and heterodox social relations of a given period or social group; yet as he notes, the existence of heterodoxy does not imply some kind of total epistemological chaos – social and historical limits remain which govern what may be articulated, when and by whom. And for Bakhtin, the dialogic discourse of the novel similarly reflects the social relations of the historical moment and the author's relation to that moment. In the novel, heteroglossia is artistically reworked so that the many voices – orthodox and heterodox – from different social classes and historical periods whose experience echoes in the language are organised according to the position of the author in relation to the surrounding social universe. A tension, then, seems to exist (at least potentially) between the heteroglot nature of the genre and refracting imagination of the author, who may be neither willing nor able to represent the alien languages on their own terms. This tension replicates that identified in the concept of common sense as well: the universal community of humanity contrasts with the specific contradictory socio-historical communities as the source of common sense; while Bakhtin's novelistic heteroglossia of all social voices contrasts with the authorial voice which mediates, and which belongs to a member of a specific socio-historical group.[10]

In one sense it seems possible, following Bakhtin, that history and fiction are, in fact, opposed forms of prose since historical narrative has traditionally tended toward single-voiced statements of factual truth while the novel has tended to complicate this univocity, the former being centripetal and the latter centrifugal in movement. Bradley's attempted banishment of jarring witnesses, for example, allies him with the former. Historians and philosophers of history, of course, are not necessarily interested primarily in realising these dialogic possibilities, but the problem posed does create a kind of generic conflict of interest for novels that attempt to represent history.[11] Prose itself, Bakhtin contends, engages

the historical and social concreteness of living discourse, as well as its relativity, a feeling for its participation in historical becoming and in social struggle; it deals with discourse that is still warm from that struggle and hostility, as yet unresolved and still fraught with hostile intentions and accents; prose art finds discourse in this state and subjects it to the dynamic unity of its own style.   (Bakhtin, 1981: 331)

Nevertheless, despite the author's imposition of stylistic unity, Bakhtin maintains that prose cannot be contained to a single ('sacrosanct') language (1981: 324).[12] No matter how well the writer has managed to purge the jarring witnesses, traces of the heteroglot inevitably remain: even when the novel's unitary language seems to occupy fully the narrative space, it is not incontestable since it is uttered in a demonstrably heteroglot environment (1981: 332). In this sense, the jarring narratives always remain, if only as an absent presence to which the authorial point of view must, however tacitly, respond. For Bakhtin, novelistic discourse is unique in that its orientation does bring it into relation with the larger world of discourse; it exists in a state of necessary contestation in its dialogue with the heteroglossia that surrounds it. Thus, even in what might be termed 'orthoglot' novels, heteroglossia nevertheless continues to determine 'as a dialogizing background, the special resonance of novelistic discourse'.

The novel, then, is an arena in which different, sometimes opposing, language groups assert their ideological identity and represent their particular point of view. This striving for social significance is another version of the struggle to impose the definition of reality that Bourdieu sees as a central aspect of social power relations. In that genre of striving known as the novel, the author, as ideologue, tries out diverse points of view, defending some and attacking others, indifferent to still others (Bakhtin, 1981: 333). Dialogue in the novel tends to underline this striving at times by pushing 'to the limit the mutual nonunderstanding represented by people *who speak in different languages*' (1981: 356). There is, of course, in any narrative representation of this heteroglot situation, an uneven social distribution of fluency and aphasia across this spectrum of discourse. These languages cannot simply speak for themselves in narrative, and Bakhtin acknowledges that they must finally depend to some extent upon the point of view of the author and upon the language privileged by the author.

Authorial language provides the point of refraction for the structure of heteroglossia which constitutes the novel, and in this sense it is normative since one language is generally represented only from the point of view of another, which appears as a social norm (Bakhtin, 1981: 359). Nevertheless, this norm cannot be taken as an absolute. The contestation that is the condition of existence of these languages or ideologies, the striving for social significance, results in the collision between divergent points of view as they 'come together and consciously fight it out on the territory of the utterance' (1981: 360).[13] This collision among jarring points of view over the legitimate power to articulate the sense of reality need have no final outcome: Bakhtin's theory implies no teleology in that sense. It is, in fact, the dynamics of striving that is the point for Bakhtin, not the establishment of a new monoglot authority. At its fullest, novelistic discourse acknowledges the plenitude of social languages, and acknowledges as well that any has the capacity to be a 'language of truth' since the novel is predicated on a presumption of a decentred ideological world (1981: 366–7).[14] Bakhtin's relativism here seems close to Bourdieu's description of culture as arbitrary: neither should be taken in an absolute sense, rather both indicate that the range of available meanings or interpretations must always relate to specific socio-historical worlds.

Heteroglot novelistic discourse emerges when, through cross-cultural contact or objective social crisis, the doxic unity of culture is somehow loosened or decentred, and the possibility of orthodoxy and heterodoxy arises: 'it is necessary that heteroglossia wash over a culture's awareness of itself and its language, penetrate to its core, relativize the primary language system underlying its ideology and literature and deprive it of its naive absence of conflict' (Bakhtin, 1981: 368). The state of doxic innocence or harmony, of monological utterance, can be disrupted if the discourse of 'heteroglossia that rages beyond the boundaries of such a sealed-off cultural universe' (1981: 368) begins to impinge upon the preconceptual (or obscurely conceived) common sense space of doxa. Confirming in his own way Bourdieu's argument, Bakhtin writes that this passage from doxa, this ideological decentring occurs when a culture 'becomes conscious of itself as only one among other cultures and languages' (1981: 370). The relativised sense of culture that results in this situation is fundamentally incompatible with the 'absolute fusion of ideological meaning with language' that is the case in a state of doxa. Internal crisis and cross-cultural contact open up the potential for transgressions of the doxic, monological unity of a culture. When a society or cultural system becomes aware of the arbitrary nature of its own discourse, its monological self-evidence (doxa) becomes insupportable.

One of the novel's primary concerns then, according to Bakhtin, is to explore the dynamics of internally persuasive discourses.

Everyday consciousness 'enters into an intense interaction, a *struggle* with other internally persuasive discourses' and must mediate these jarring 'verbal and ideological points of view, approaches, directions and values' (1981: 346). This heteroglossic interaction, in all its varieties, is a central preoccupation of the novel, especially the historical novel, which is concerned with representing the temporal existence and legitimacy of particular communities and their points of view. We have come, in a sense, to a reversal of the position from which we started, according to which unity was the characteristic of art that separated it from, even elevated it above, an episodic non-unifiable history. The novel appears now as an arena for the heterodox struggle of language groups, a site on which various ideologies are articulated from various points of view and contend for the power of orthodox internal persuasiveness, if not for the status of doxic or authoritative discourse.

One could certainly find earlier examples, particularly in the rich field of German philosophy of history, but for the purposes of my argument, I will locate the unavoidable emergence of pressure on the self-evidence of narrative perspective in historiography with Bradley. This is the kind of passage that Bakhtin is referring to when he describes the way in which other language systems have the capacity to relativise the primary system, thus depriving it of its 'naive absence of conflict'. The struggle with jarring witnesses that he articulates coincides roughly with the beginnings of modernism, and it is a struggle that occurs also in the modernist novels discussed in the next three chapters.[15] This struggle I take to be one definitive characteristic of modernism – not the only one, certainly, but a useful one none the less. I will argue that one modernist strategy regarding this struggle was the attempt to resist or contain particular jarring witnesses – voices that could not always be silenced – rather than to allow them to emerge in a way that would further destabilise the narrative and cultural fabric. This strategy was effected with varying degrees of stress, just as the modernist theorists of history from Bradley to Mink grappled with the problem of point of view with varying degrees of theoretical stress.

In the final section, I will look at less orthodox representations of history: first, from the point of view of African-American women who were typically excluded as human subjects in the orthodox past and who therefore have had to adopt different strategies in order to make their jarring voices heard; and second, a postmodernism which accepts the destabilisation of point of view in order to allow the emergence of jarring witnesses rather than subsuming them within a unifying orthodox perspective. Given the relation between narrative coherence and social power that White points to, it is not coincidental that the erosion of the once self-evident ability of European and American historiographic perspective to render 'the whole story' is roughly contemporaneous with a decline in that culture's confidence in its ability to rule the world.

What remains to be discussed is the specific orchestration of heteroglossia in particular novels. In the name of what authority does the author tend to silence some voices (languages, witnesses) or relegate them to the chorus, while giving solos to others? What is the basis of the legitimacy of such privileging of one voice, or a few voices, from the heteroglot field of historical discourse? How is aphasia socially distributed in the novel? How is the (aphasic) voice of the jarring witness misrecognised and/or represented? What trace of it remains? The following chapters explore ways in which this struggle is articulated in several modern novels which deal with history. My aim is not to correct the historical representations in the novels with a True Version of History, but to juxtapose them with other facts and heterodox – sometimes contradictory – ways of configuring the events in question. Given the inevitable limits of narrative and historiographic point of view – limits at once formal and ideological – this is a necessary part of the interaction between reader and text. As Robert Weimann writes, 'the reader's most basic task in reading a novel is to resolve the irony in the meaning of perspective and to recover that element of wholeness to which point of view is the counterpart' (1984: 266). While I would question the possibility of the reader ever attaining the goal of wholeness in reading any more than the author or narrator can contain it in writing, this kind of readerly engagement is a fundamental aspect of the critical encounter between reader and text.

Modernism and orthodoxy

Nostromo and the 'torrent of rubbish'

Fiction is history, human history, or it is nothing.

Joseph Conrad (1921: 17)

The settler makes history and is conscious of making it. And because he constantly refers to the history of his mother country, he clearly indicates that he himself is the extension of that mother country. Thus the history which he writes is not the history of the country which he plunders but the history of his own nation in regard to all that she skims off, all that she violates and starves.

Frantz Fanon (1963: 41)

Human history? Settlers' history? Conrad's *Nostromo* is, on an immediate level, a representation of violent political conflict in Latin America sometime before the turn of the century. Two opposed communities – one an indigenous guerrilla group, the other made up of settlers with close ties to European and American capital and culture – struggle for legitimacy and control over a region rich in natural resources. It is a struggle for power typical in some ways of the turbulent history of that area, a civil war of a type that continues today and seems familiar even in the American economic pressure and military presence that guarantee the outcome. Given such polarised politics, and given that any power struggle of that nature involves a struggle for discursive legitimacy as well as for military domination, attention to the legitimacy claims of the rival groups and their narratives ought to be a priority; yet critical approaches to the novel's representation of the opposed groups often seem to accept rather than to interrogate its discursive neutrality. Irving Howe reads *Nostromo* as 'a fictional study of imperialism' presenting 'a coherent social world . . . in which all the relevant political tendencies are finely balanced' (1970: 100–1). Avrom Fleishman writes that the novel 'represents the history of society as a living organism', attempting to give an account of historical events 'in their total unity, exhibiting an "organic fullness" ' (1967: 161). More recently, but in a similar vein, Paul Armstrong has argued that 'Costaguana is an attempt to provide an anatomy of the being of society. It serves as a kind of ontological model that allows Conrad to test and explore the social implications of contingency' (1987: 151).

Even those critics who point out a bias seem to consider it of slight importance in light of Conrad's trenchant critique of capitalist imperialism. Abdul R. JanMohamed argues that in *Nostromo* Conrad 'stereotypes the Other, in this case the South American Indian, but uses him as a background in order to examine the imperial process itself'. The novel thus becomes 'a study of the alienating power of exchange-value, emblematized by the silver' (1985: 82). In *The Political Unconscious*, Fredric Jameson remarks that in *Nostromo* Conrad makes it possible

> to overlook the identification of his positive figures among the locals – the so-called Blancos – with the aristocratic party, and that of the evil Monteros with the mestizos . . . . But *Nostromo* is not a political novel in the sense in which it would allow these two political ideals to fight it out on their own terms . . . rather, Conrad's own political attitudes are presupposed.   (1981: 270)

Conrad does make such a critical oversight possible. Indeed, he encourages critical attention to focus instead on the subjectivity of selected central figures and their complex networks of relationships – both interpersonal relationships and relationships to the overall movement of history. But Jameson's meaning here is, in any case, puzzling: what can it mean in a novel to allow political ideals to fight it out on their own terms rather than on the author's or narrator's terms? How can political ideals be said to exist at all in a novel apart from the author, narrator or characters who hold them? Are the political attitudes of some historically and culturally located people not always necessarily presupposed in fiction as in other forms of discourse? Jameson's position here is reminiscent of Lukács's assertion concerning the historical novels of Scott that 'Through the plot . . . a neutral ground is sought and found upon which the extreme, opposing social forces can be brought into a human relationship with one another' (1962: 36).

Yet in the light of Bakhtin's theory of the novel as an author's orchestration of heteroglossia, *Nostromo* must be read as a confrontation of ideologies within a necessarily charged ideological field, whether or not such a reading seems encouraged by the text. *Nostromo* does work the problem out in terms of Conrad's political attitudes, but if the novel is to be studied at all then we are unavoidably drawn into an engagement with Conrad's political attitudes as the narratorial point of refraction for the social heteroglossia that constitutes the novel. The fact that it does not appear as a Lukácsian neutral ground, a level discursive field, is not something to be overlooked but a condition of historical narrative in need of discussion. Whatever degree of irony, ambivalence or outright criticism one may locate in Conrad's attitude to the characters and events in Costaguana, it is still relatively simple to identify the social centre that has – at least as its horizon – the possibility of conferring some ethical and moral significance (White) on events as opposed to the other social group which seems to present itself in the novel as the antithesis of order, coherence and legitimacy. If, as White argues, the efficacy and legitimacy of systems of meaning-production are being tested here against the real events that constitute history, what is the result of the differential treatment given those language groups? It may be that by comparison the natives remain in the background of the novel, yet in this (or any other) narrative *Gestalt*, the relation of foreground to background is not incidental, but is a necessary relation which situates and defines the foreground and without which a foreground cannot be conceived. An analysis of *Nostromo* that overlooks the way that the representation of the marginalised community acts as a constitutive element in the representation of the dominant community, simply reproduces the uneven discursive field of the novel itself.

Nowhere in the novel are the natives given the opportunity – as the Blancos frequently are – to articulate a political position or to narrate a version of historical events. The very existence of their independent historical past is undermined from the outset, and their humanity is metaphorically reduced to a level of bestiality. Denied a voice, such groups remain, in historian Eric Wolf's phrase, people without history. As Michel de Certeau writes: 'Historical discourse makes a *social identity* explicit, not so much in the way it is "given" or held as stable, as in the ways it is *differentiated* from . . . another society' (1985: 45), and it is in this sense that the novel establishes the relative stability and coherence of the Eurocentric foreground. The representation of native people in *Nostromo* constitutes such a negative pole by means of which a modern European-oriented elite – the Blancos – and their supporters may be differentiated and defined. In the juxtaposition of these two groups and the specific characterisations of each in the text, the struggle of the two language groups to be heard takes place on far from neutral ground.

In *Nostromo*, history seems to begin with the introduction of modern capitalism into Costaguana. The opening paragraph presents an Edenic image of Sulaco as 'an inviolable sanctuary . . . in the solemn hush of the deep Golfo Placido as if within an enormous semi-circular and unroofed temple' (1967: 17). This prelapsarian calm is a result of the lack of propitious winds to bring in the sailing ships – and thus modern European commerce. While Conrad acknowledges that Sulaco has a long past, it does not enter into history proper – European history – until the advent of modern steamships able to use the harbour. The pre-Columbian history of Sulaco is not really discussed, and the time from the 'Spanish rule' until the steam age is dismissed since Sulaco 'had never been commercially anything more important than a coasting port with a fairly large local trade in ox-hides and indigo'. The fall into history begins with the arrival of European commerce, of industrial capitalism, when the steamships of the Oceanic Steam Navigation Company arrive 'to violate the sanctuary of peace' (1967: 21). The opening sentences of each of the first two chapters orient the reader specifically in terms of commerce: first, temporally, by defining history in terms of commerce; and second, spatially, by fixing on the 'only sign of commercial activity within the harbour'.

If, as Collingwood argues, the representation of history is inevitably connected to present interest, here that is an interest in modern commerce and its social effects, and any other historical discourse pre-dating or extraneous to these interests – such as the historical situation of the unwillingly colonised – is consigned to the margins of the narrative, the background. As Frantz Fanon notes, the coloniser makes history: 'He is the absolute beginning . . . the unceasing cause' (1963: 41). Since this history is structured around weighty material interests, the native past remains formless, undifferentiated and therefore non-historical from the point of view of the Europeans. The effect (to borrow Walsh's term) of having a communal past that is not colligated into significant narrative – or, more precisely, being a community whose colligation into significant narrative is not recognised by the dominant community – is that the cultural patterns and concerns of the marginalised community, which are embedded in such a past, lose any power to influence the present.

While there may appear to be a note of regret in Conrad's tone, a nostalgia for the peace and simplicity of the era before capitalism, it should be noted that the historical inevitability of this fall parallels the transcendent inevitability of the first Fall and looks forward to the political inevitability of another analogous fall that occurs as American ships arrive near the end of the novel signalling a new shift in power.[1] A further effect of this analogy is the relegation of precolonial cultures to a mythic or religious rather than historical past, a denial of the historical claims of those cultures to relevance and integrity. This is not to suggest that Conrad's novel should or could have represented a different history – from the point of view of colonised people, for instance – but the extremely limited degree to which the existence of that dimension is acknowledged in the opening is notable in a novel celebrated for its comprehensive social vision. The establishment of the existence of that reality as at least a possible point of reference, need not necessitate fully adopting it as a point of view. Yet just as there can be no rational thought of returning to a prelapsarian state, there can, it seems, be no rational thought in Sulaco of opposing the hegemonic power of Western 'material interests'. While the legendary past – like the landscape – may have some exotic appeal or symbolic weight, Conrad uses European commerce as a means of orientation, as an apparent limit to what can 'reasonably' be thought in historical terms. Native South American cultures thus occupy the position of the non-narrated, the heterodox historical presence whose omission from the representation may be seen as a kind of absent centre.[2]

As James Clifford has noted, 'whenever marginal peoples come into a historical or ethnographic space that has been defined by the Western imagination . . . their distinct histories quickly vanish' (1988: 5). Another anthropologist, Johannes Fabian, uses the phrase 'denial of coevalness' to refer to a similar tendency which, he argues, pervades anthropological discourse. This is the practice of placing 'the referent(s) of anthropology in a Time other than the present of the producer of anthropological discourse' (1983: 31). Fabian discusses the practical colonial implications of this tendency quite persuasively as a form of 'Aristotelian political physics':

> it is not difficult to transpose from physics to politics one of the most ancient rules which states that it is impossible for two bodies to occupy the same space at the same time. When in the course of colonial expansion a Western body politic came to occupy, literally, the space of an autochthonous body, several alternatives were conceived to deal with that violation of the rule. (1983: 29)

The first and simplest solution works in terms of space. As Fabian observes, in North America, Australia and South Africa various spatial options have been explored which involve moving the autochthonous community aside whenever necessary, or dividing space up according to rigid but arbitrary principles based ultimately on little but self-interest. The other possible solution, however, 'has been simply to manipulate the other variable – Time. With the help of various devices of sequencing and distancing one assigns to the conquered populations a *different* Time' (1983: 29–30). By thus assigning the native population to an ahistorical or prehistorical time, the dominant interests create a segregated zone – modernity. While modernity is a complex and ambiguous historical condition for those (such as Conrad and his main characters) who inhabit there, it has also been a form of temporal apartheid which arrogates to itself the right to mono-polise discursive and political authority.

Captain Mitchell acts as a kind of guide to Sulaco both for visitors and for the reader, and he also presents the first instance of the novel's ambivalence in its presentation of some of the main characters. Like the narrator of the opening, Captain Mitchell uses European commerce as the touchstone by which historical events may be evaluated, judging 'as most unfavorable to the orderly working of his Company the frequent changes of government brought about by revolutions of the military type' (Conrad, 1967: 22). Early on, in a blend of Captain Mitchell's account and third-person narrative, the novel presents an example of the kind of revolutionary disruption that is bad for commerce. Mitchell characterises the insurgents as 'the rascally mob' (1967: 23), and in the next paragraph the narrator speaks of having to leave 'the town to the mercies of a revolutionary rabble', who 'howled and foamed' outside the company's building. As he escapes, Captain Mitchell is wounded by a razor-blade fastened to a stick – a weapon, as he puts it, very much in favour with the 'worst kind of nigger out here' (1967: 24). For the previous week, 'thieves and murderers from the whole province . . . had been flocking into Sulaco' (1967: 24–5). Fortunately, the Company's property 'and the property of the railway were preserved by the European residents . . . aided by the Italian and Basque workmen who rallied faithfully round their English chiefs' (1967: 25). Some of the 'rabble' can be relied on to behave well (in spite of being an 'outcast lot of very mixed blood, mainly Negroes, everlastingly at feud with the other customers of low grog shops') because they have been so thoroughly intimidated by Nostromo: 'There was not one of them that had not, at some time or other, looked with terror at Nostromo's revolver poked very close at his face' (1967: 25–6). In the end, due to the courage and coercive power of Nostromo and the apparent stupidity of the 'rabble', little actual damage is done. The narrative voice in this passage shifts from Mitchell's to that of the third person narrator, leaving open the possibility that the pejorative terms are Mitchell's rather than the narrator's. Beyond this, however, the question that remains essentially unasked regards the possible motivation, aside from inherent bestiality or irrationality, that these people might have for attacking railway property.

The arrival of the steamship, inaugurating the modern era of history, had by this time been compounded by the development on the part of European capital of an increasingly extensive railway system. The justification of their fear for the safety of the railroad, and for the rebels' presumed desire to damage it are suggested in E. Bradford Burns's discussion of the role played by the railway in Latin America. He argues that the railways were built and controlled by foreigners in order to 'complement the North Atlantic economies' often at the expense of a restructuring of the local economy unfavourable to Latin American people. For example, the extension of the rail network made remote areas accessible, thus conferring great value on land that had previously been left to the peasants since it had not been in demand.

Peasants pushed off this land had little choice but to become part of the commercial agricultural enterprise that had dispossessed them. Thus a subsistence economy based on the labour of many small landholders was converted to an export-oriented economy which increasingly concentrated the land and resources in the hands of a few wealthy holders. 'Indian landholdings in particular suffered incursions in those areas touched by railroads.' Furthermore, he argues, financing the construction of the railroads led to a heavy debtload resulting in 'foreign complications and always to some sacrifice of economic independence' (1986: 150–1). The railway itself is just one sign of modernisation changing the face of Latin America at that time. The chaotic insurrection Mitchell endures may be taken as a suggestion that not everyone was pleased with these changes. Indeed, the march of progress was 'not without discordant chords sounded by the humble classes' for whom progress meant

increased concentration of lands in the hands of ever fewer owners, falling per capita food production with corollary rising food imports, greater impoverishment, less to eat, more vulnerability to the whims of an impersonal international market, uneven growth, increased unemployment and underemployment, social, economic, and political marginalization, and greater power in the hands of the privileged few.   (Burns, 1986: 168)

Here and elsewhere, however, Captain Mitchell's testimony avoids these kinds of issues, and more importantly, neither does the third person narrator augment Mitchell's account to suggest a native perspective. Instead, Mitchell's version demonstrates aspects of epic history in two Bakhtinian senses: first, in the sense of monological official discourse, a fundamentally doxic narrative demonstrating little or no awareness of the limits of its own thought; and second, as Bakhtin writes, it tells of 'the national heroic past: it is a world of "beginnings" and "peak times" in the national history, a world of fathers and of founders of families, a world of "firsts" and "bests" ' (1981: 13). While *Nostromo*'s ironic countermovement is often apparent (for instance, in the lack of children in Gould's life), this is perhaps nowhere more evident than in the way the authority of Mitchell's epic account is undermined.[3] Yet his testimony nevertheless stands, albeit under erasure, and on some details his opinion seems ratified as the novel progresses. If many of the details of Mitchell's historical narrative are shown to be questionable, what of the language in which he represents the rebels? The representation of the native rebels as a mob, the rabble, howling and foaming like animals, or flocking and waiting like vultures, dehumanises them, and this reduction is further accentuated by pejorative references to race, resulting in a denial of their rationality which precludes the necessity of considering their claims to political, discursive or narrative authority. Mitchell's epic account may, in some senses, be shown to be suspect, but the dichotomy he sets up between the 'good' faithful workers and the 'bad' rebellious 'rabble' seems to go fundamentally unchallenged as Conrad simultaneously calls this witness's reliability into question and preserves essential aspects of his perspective.

While Mitchell provides an obvious example of Conrad's ambivalent representation of his major characters, the motives of all the Blancos and their supporters, not Mitchell alone, are subjected to a subtle and complex critique exposing a variety of problems that complicate and compromise their high ideals. Steve Ressler notes in this regard

> Avellano's classical liberalism, Antonia's patriotism, Father Corbelán's religious politics, Viola's heroic republicanism, Emilia's faith in human values, Decoud's love for Antonia, Monygham's chivalrous loyalty to Mrs. Gould, Don Pepe's soldierly fidelity to Charles, Holroyd's purer form of Christianity. Even Mitchell . . . relates his efforts to progress.   (1988: 48)

Gould himself sees the value of the mine, writes Ressler, 'in the law, good faith, order, and security he is certain will result' (1988: 48). Ressler's discussion of these characters is, significantly, entitled 'Versions of Failure', and he shows how each fails in the end to measure up to the ideals he or she professes.[4]

While this analysis of the contradictions and shortcomings of the major characters and the complexity of the narrative representations of them is both useful and insightful, it overlooks one crucial exclusion: the denial of any depth or higher motive to certain 'other' significant characters. The Monteros, for instance, who oppose the Blancos, are characterised in fact as the antithesis of all idealism. If the idealism of the Blancos falls short, appears finally as hollowness or hypocrisy, even this is, on balance, much more than can be said for the Monteros. Consequently, serious opposition to the established hegemonic power structure never for a moment becomes in any way thinkable in the narrative. A reader may sympathise at times, for instance, with Viola and his pride in his Garibaldian past, or Monygham and his torment, while remaining aware of the limitations that Conrad builds into these characters. Such sympathetic identification – however qualified – is never a possibility, with the Monteros (or their followers, such as Sotillo and Gamacho) who, as the jarring representatives of native opposition to the hegemonic powers, exist beyond the horizon of what is thinkable. Were the Monteros merely other characters on the neutral ground of plot, other voices in the heteroglossia of the novel, it would have been possible for Conrad to represent their position simply as another kind of political idealism or illusion, one whose shortcomings and hollowness he could have demonstrated in the same way that he undermines the idealism of the Blancos – showing that opposition, even revolutionary opposition, has no more real positive potential than any of the other ideals represented in the novel. Instead, the Monteros are presented as grotesque, bestial, semi-lunatics, a depiction that indicates, perhaps, a profound anxiety concerning the political possibilities that they represent.[5]

Armstrong argues that in *Nostromo* 'Conrad employs a contradictory narrative strategy whereby he introduces a claim of authority only to call attention to its limits and cast doubts on its pretensions' (1987: 163). For the most part this is valid, yet no matter how much the narrative authority of the Blancos is undermined or their motives and testimonies put into question, there is no equivalent to the portrait, for instance, of General Montero, a man whose claim of authority is never introduced. There is no contradictory narrative strategy whatsoever here, and it is in this comparison that one aspect of the uneven nature of the discursive field may be clearly discerned:

In this gorgeous uniform, with his bull neck, his hooked nose flattened on the tip upon a blue-black, dyed moustache, he looked like a disguised and sinister *vaquero* [cowboy]. The drone of his voice had a strangely rasping, soulless ring.

(1967: 110)

During a formal dinner he fixes a 'lurid, sleepy glance' on Sir John, commits a clear social and political gaffe in his toast, then sits down with 'a half-surprised, half-bullying look'.[6] After dinner he appears equally alien and ludicrous, 'his bald head covered now by a plumed cocked hat'.

The white plume, the coppery tint of his broad face, the blue-black of the moustaches under the curved beak, the mass of gold on sleeves and breast, the high shining boots with enormous spurs, the working nostrils, the imbecile and domineering stare of the glorious victor of Río Seco had in them something ominous and incredible; the exaggeration of a cruel caricature, the fatuity of solemn masquerading, the atrocious grotesqueness of some military idol of Aztec conception and European bedecking, awaiting the homage of worshipers. Don José approached diplomatically this weird and inscrutable portent, and Mrs. Gould turned her fascinated eyes away at last.   (1967: 111)

Again, no matter how much we, as readers, may ultimately harbour reservations about Don Pepe or Emilia, our common sense gaze is encouraged by the narrator to align itself with theirs in a shared distance from this bizarre figure, this jarring witness denied a soul whose very clothing refuses our interpretive codes. Armstrong notes the descriptions of Montero as well as Guzman, Bento and Sotillo but sees them simply as portraits of tyrants who 'seize and abuse power to compensate for wounds to their narcissism' (1987: 160). Of course there have been and continue to be cruel and narcissistic dictators in Latin America and elsewhere. What seems strange about this description is the radically different strategy Conrad uses in representing Montero in comparison with those he employs in representing the Blancos. Here there is no ambivalence, there are no ideals to be demystified, no depth or complexity to be revealed. This analysis – which removes any political content from opposition to the Blancos, ascribing it instead to psychological or ethnic deficiencies – does not take into account two related facts about the representational strategies of the novel: first, that these despicable narcissistic tyrants are all on one side of the struggle, are all against the Blancos; and, second, that no one opposed to the Blancos seems to be the beneficiary of the contradictory and ironic narrative strategy that would suggest a sympathetic human dimension as well.[7] The reader may indeed have serious misgivings concerning the Blancos, but the alternative is unthinkable, literally incomprehensible. While it might be possible to argue that this is simply a technical problem of narrative history to do with the impossibility of establishing a universal point of view containing all sides of a story, it is also the kind of social differentiation de Certeau posits as a central function of historical discourse (1985: 45). Fanon argues that in the representations of the dominant group, the 'colonial world is a Manichean world'.

> Native society is not simply described as a society lacking in values . . . . The native is declared insensible to ethics; he represents not only the absence of values, but also the negation of values. He is, let us dare to admit, the enemy of values, and in this sense he is the absolute evil. He is the corrosive element, destroying all that comes near him; he is the deforming element, disfiguring all that has to do with beauty or morality; he is the depository of maleficent powers, the unconscious and irretrievable instrument of blind forces.
>
> (1963: 33–4)[8]

It would be short-sighted to deny either the acuteness or the subtlety of Conrad's critique of imperialism in *Nostromo* and elsewhere. Conrad undoubtedly succeeds in decentring the mono-logical self-evidence (doxa) of imperialist culture through his portraits of the Blancos. He casts doubt on the meaning of his-torical events and the motives that influenced them. Further, he calls into question the historiographical representations of those events through the many characters, such as Captain Mitchell, Avellano and Decoud, who keep records or narrate events after the fact.[9] Criticism of imperialism was not so widespread at the time, and Conrad's achievement is, perhaps, to move such a critical discourse onto the agenda, into the realm of the thinkable (orthodoxy). But he is clearly not concerned with pushing a step further into a vision of social heterodoxy that would give a voice to disruptive heteroglot elements. The natives remain essentially in a state of aphasia, permitted neither to narrate their own heterodox version of historical events nor to have those social positions represented – or even alluded to – with any seriousness by another narrator. If, as Gallie argues, the coherence or followability of narrative depends to some degree on the orientation of sympathies toward the characters, it must be admitted that Conrad has taken no chances on alienating the reader's sympathies too much. Whatever irony, scepticism or negativity the narrative evokes regarding the Blancos is more than compensated for by a much more serious antipathy towards their opponents: in this way narrative coherence is maintained – in a more complex form certainly, but maintained none the less.[10]

The natives are granted two basic modes of existence in *Nostromo*. First, they are represented as existing anonymously, timelessly, as picturesque essentially premodern scenery, elements of the exotic background setting of the novel. This is the vision that Emilia, for instance, conveys in the description of her first travels in the countryside (1967: 84–5), or in this passage, as they come seeking work in the silver mine:

Whole families had been moving from the first towards the spot in the Higuerota range, whence the rumour of work and safety had spread over the pastoral Campo . . . . Father first, in a pointed straw hat, then the mother with the bigger children, generally also a diminutive donkey, all under burdens, except the leader himself, or perhaps some brown girl, the pride of the family, stepping barefooted and straight as an arrow, with braids of raven hair, a thick haughty profile, and no load to carry but the small guitar of the country and a pair of soft leather sandals tied together on her back.   (1967: 94)

Often in such situations, Conrad distances the picturesque sights through the use of a European observer who sees, as it were, with the reader and offers an interpretive stance. The interposition of the modern European gaze mediates the strangeness by providing a 'familiar' frame for the exotic natives. In the description of Montero cited above, the appearance of this bizarre figure is mediated for the reader through the familiar eyes of Don José and Emilia. A similar mediation takes place here: 'At the sight of such parties . . . travelers on horseback would remark to each other: "More people going to the San Tomé mine. We shall see others tomorrow" ' (1967: 94). In such cases there is no real penetration into the interior space of the natives, indeed little suggestion that such a space exists. The reader is allowed no direct access to the natives and their point of view – representations of them emerge through the perspective of the Europeans, in the language of the dominant group, and tend not to focus on the desperate poverty or the cultural genocide stemming from imperialism that, as Burns's historical study indicates, might lie behind this migration to the mines. The testimony of these witnesses is not part of the novel's historical record.

The other mode of native existence has two aspects, both of which centre on the perceived absurdity or irrationality of their life-styles. Often, this too is presented through the eyes of Europeans in order to foreground the incomprehensibility of the people under scrutiny. Don Pepe is thought remarkable for his ability to remember the identity of so many of the miners; not only does he recognise the men, but he can 'classify each woman, girl, or growing youth of his domain. It was only the young fry that puzzled him sometimes. He and the padre could be seen frequently . . . trying to sort them out, as it were, in low consulting tones' (1967: 95). Their taxonomic difficulty is compounded by the appearance of the children, such as the 'small, staid urchin met wandering, naked and grave, along the road with a cigar in his baby mouth, and perhaps his mother's rosary, purloined for purposes of ornamentation, hanging in a loop of beads low down on his rotund little stomach'. This sense of native absurdity has another, less benign aspect as well however, as evidenced in the description of the bestial and irrational Montero. He not only appears utterly differentiated from the 'civilized' Europeans, but because of the threat he poses to the political stability of the Blancos, his characterisation also adds a powerful element of villainous irrationality to the (sometimes picturesque) absurdity of native existence. If such people seem to possess an interior world at all (which Bradley doubted), it appears as a non-analogous variety of human nature. If they have a cultural system of meaning-production of their own with the potential to make any coherent narrative sense of events, this is nowhere suggested.[11]

The problem, then, is not that the European aristocrats and capitalists are presented as stable and good while the natives are presented as evil. Such a simple opposition entirely misses the complexity of Conrad's understanding of at least one half of the balance. Father Corbelàn, for instance, may be 'fanatical', but he is also fearless, honest and absolutely committed to his ideal. In the 'wilds' the people he preached to are presented in rather more negative terms: 'bloodthirsty savages, devoid of human compassion or worship of any kind'. Because the natives are presented in this light, lacking 'human nature' as we understand it, a number of ironic juxtapositions appear. Father Corbelàn himself is hardly a compassionate man, and, further, he believes 'that the politicians of Sta Marta had harder hearts and more corrupt minds than the heathen' (1967: 168). But if there is a sense that some essential difference between the two cultural groups is being eroded nevertheless, the 'heathens' remain the negative pole on which all such definitions are based. If the Blancos are presented as possessing a range of moral strengths and weaknesses, ideals and the betrayal of those ideals, the natives are granted no such depth or complexity. That strategic historiographic denial constitutes the basis of their political and discursive marginalisation, constitutes Conrad's orthodox means of avoiding the epistemological abyss that Mink faces more thoroughly when forced to consider the possible validity of contradictory and competing historical narratives

There have been, of course, innumerable rebellions against imperialism throughout the history of South America. Such rebellions have been – and continue to be – of many different kinds, having many different motivations, not all wholly admirable by any means. Indian and peasant rebellions were frequent and ubiquitous in the area, challenging both the elitist European- and American-based institutions and the commitment to what those institutions characterised as 'progress' itself. 'More often than not', writes Burns, 'the ideology . . . was vague and contradictory. Somehow, the rebels hoped to save their lands, improve their standards of living, and share in the exercise of power' (1986: 170). In representing one such rebellion – the Monterist – Conrad is refracting the discourse of a socio-ideologically alien group and its struggle for legitimacy or authority. The situation is much like that which Bradley confronts in dealing with the problem of evaluating jarring witnesses, and Conrad's response is similar: to the degree that their historical experience – not to mention their appearance – is alien (non-analogous), their testimony can be refused. Since there is no acknowledgement of any native sense of historical reality on which such a point of view might be based, the heterodox testimony of that community can never impinge on or disrupt that of the modern Blancos.

One incident in Conrad's representation of the native rebellion may serve as a useful example. Late in the novel when the victory of the Monterists seems assured, Pedro Montero (brother of the leader) rides into Sulaco and makes a victory speech. The third-person narrator describes the entry of the rebels in terms that expand on, but do not in essence contradict, Mitchell's representation of them:

And first came straggling in through the land gate the armed mob of all colors, complexions, types, and states of raggedness, calling themselves the Sulaco National Guard . . . . Through the middle of the street streamed, like a torrent of rubbish, a mass of straw hats, ponchos, gun-barrels, with an enormous green and yellow flag flapping in their midst, in a cloud of dust, to the furious beating of drums.   (1967: 318)

This representation functions to discursively disarm these rebels, to inscribe them and their movement as existing beyond the limit of the thinkable. The heterogenous group straggles; they do not march or walk or stroll or move. There seems almost a kind of ludicrous impertinence in their use of an official title: they may call themselves the National Guard, but the clear suggestion is that no right-thinking person would. They are a mob, not an army, and their lack of racial homogeneity seems to count against them as much as the poverty and hardship that results in their ragged clothes. The metaphor employed to describe them is rubbish, garbage, and their humanity is further reduced through the metonymic figure that presents them as 'a mass of hats, ponchos, gun barrels', not as people. Their oversized flag flaps rather than waves, as they straggle through the dust to the furious beating of drums, a cacophony that suggests insanity rather than victory.[12] 'Behind the rabble could be seen . . . the "army" of Pedro Montero.' The word 'army' is contained within ironic quotation marks thus mocking the idea that this military force could possess any real legitimacy, and foregrounding a dubious distinction between this group and a real army.

This is a crucial moment in the novel and in the colonial imagination: the moment when the colonised natives realise their collective power by reclaiming the city, displacing the colonial authorities and reversing the intrusion that began with the steamships and railways in the novel's opening pages. At this point, it is perhaps worth recalling both the earlier description of Montero as well as the look of these people and noting Fanon's argument that the 'natives' challenge to the colonial world is not a rational confrontation of points of view'.

The violence which has ruled over the ordering of the colonial world, which has ceaselessly drummed the rhythm for the destruction of native social forms and broken up without reserve the systems of reference of the economy, the customs of dress and external life, that same violence will be claimed and taken over by the native at the moment when, deciding to embody history in his own person, he surges into the forbidden quarters.   (1963: 33)

This rush into the public square constitutes a very different version of the powerful moment in Pontecorvo's film The Battle of Algiers when the people of Algiers similarly reoccupy their city.[13] As Fanon argues, the dream of insurgent take-over is a constant projection of the desires of the colonised and the fears of the colonial authorities.

To prepare the reader for Pedro's victory speech, Conrad provides some background information and a perspective on the man and his movement. In detailing the means by which Pedro Montero had gained his following, however, Conrad omits entirely the idea that oppressed people throughout history have periodically risen up against those in power in an attempt to change the oppressive conditions of their existence.[14] His influence over the 'rabble' is instead ascribed to

a genius for treachery of so effective a kind that it must have appeared to those violent men but little removed from a state of utter savagery, as the perfection of sagacity and virtue. The popular lore of all nations testified that duplicity and cunning . . . were looked upon, even more than courage, as heroic virtues by primitive mankind.   (Conrad, 1967: 319)

From perverse leadership to pathetic primitive rabble, the revolution is propelled, then, by a combination of racial, cultural and psychological shortcomings on the part of the 'premodern' revolutionaries, rather than by any positive desire to redress the wrongs done to them or alter the power structure that victimises them. No serious political motive seems to influence them at all, living, as they appear to, below the horizon of political consciousness. The 'ignorant and barbarous plainsmen' follow Montero because they 'are always ready to believe promises that flatter their secret hopes' (1967: 319–20), and Montero has been successful in thus manipulating them. Conrad's ironic qualification ('We have changed since') does not, however, ameliorate the effect of the characterisation: while noting a theoretical similarity between 'us' and 'them', it insists on a separate cultural time frame that denies 'them' – to borrow Fabian's phrase – coeval status.

Pedro himself is 'bald, with bunches of crisp hair above [his] ears, arguing the presence of some Negro blood' and is gifted, as members of 'lower races' apparently sometimes are, not with intelligence but with 'an ape-like faculty for imitating all the outward signs of refinement and distinction, and with a parrot-like talent for languages' (1967: 320). The benign and, in the event, misguided 'munificence of a great European traveler' had provided him with some education after which, Pedrito, 'incorrigibly lazy and slovenly, had drifted aimlessly . . . picking up an easy and disreputable living'.[15] Education is obviously wasted on such a person: literacy has done 'nothing for him but fill his head with absurd visions. His actions were usually determined by motives so improbable in themselves as to escape the penetration of a rational person.' Pedro thus stands in bold contrast to those Europeans whose complex motivations and rationalisations are penetrated so subtly in the novel. His mimicry of refinement, however, has been sufficient to delude those who did not know better into temporarily crediting him 'with the possession of sane views'. This denial of rationality and sanity to Montero and his rebellion tends to ensure that any historical testimony he might present need not be seriously considered.

The depiction of Montero as a jarring witness moves between terms of bestiality, insanity and racial inferiority. His insanity, combined with his ability to read, leads him to delusions of grandeur similar to those of the stereotyped madman who believes himself to be Napoleon: Montero, as a result of a misguided reading of French history, thinks he can model himself on the Duc de Morny. In this misguided desire to appropriate European modern culture and history he becomes a parody of the Blancos themselves whose connections to Europe are rather more firmly based. This obviously ludicrous aspiration – not any desire for social justice – 'was one of the immediate causes of the Monterist revolution' (1967: 321), together with 'the fundamental causes' that were 'rooted in the political immaturity of the people, in the indolence of the upper classes and the mental darkness of the lower'. Pedro's delusions of grandeur are not, however, without a practical side as well:

Now his brother was master of the country, whether as president, dictator, or even as Emperor – why not as an Emperor? – he meant to demand a share in every enterprise – in railways, in mines, in sugar estates, in cotton mills, in land companies, in each and every undertaking – as the price of his protection.

The stage has at last been set for Montero's victory speech. With a few theatrical gestures ('from the natural pleasure he had in dissembling' (1967: 322)), he climbs up a few steps to take his place, flanked by Gamacho (who, 'big and hot, wiping his hairy wet face, uncovered a set of yellow fangs in a grin of stupid hilarity') and Fuentes ('small and lean, looked on with compressed lips'), and begins to speak: 'He began it with the shouted word

"Citizens!" ' But that is as far as we are allowed to follow. Conrad jams the speech, somewhat in the way that subversive radio stations are jammed by wary governments. Typically the 'citizens' are not interested anyway, we are told; they are instead, like children, interested only in the histrionics, 'his tip-toeing, the arms flung above his head with the fists clenched, a hand laid flat upon the heart, the silver gleam of rolling eyes,' and so on. And since Montero is clearly a jarring witness, the omniscient narrator chooses not to narrate the speech. Conrad is determined to distance it in every way possible, in the same way that he has made alien the man and his followers. In a sort of cinematic pan, the point of view retreats to a distance from which, apart from the shouts of the crowd, one can make out only

the mouth of the orator . . . opening and shutting, and detached phrases – 'The happiness of the people', 'Sons of the country', 'The entire world, el mundo entiero' – reached even the packed steps of the cathedral with a feeble clear ring, thin as the buzzing of a mosquito.   (1967: 323)

The aphasia of those excluded from power, 'denied access to the instruments of the struggle for the definition of reality' (Bourdieu, 1977b: 170) is what is at stake here. Conrad enforces that aphasia first by making the character thoroughly alien, then by blocking Montero's ability to speak and be heard, metaphorically reducing his utterance to the insignificant and meaningless 'buzzing of a mosquito'.

Chinua Achebe, commenting on a comparable situation of aphasia in *Heart of Darkness*, locates the most significant difference in the novel's representations of the two communities 'in the author's bestowal of human expression to the one [European] and the withholding of it from the other [African]. It is clearly not part of Conrad's purpose to confer language on the "rudimentary souls" of Africa' (1988: 255). This strategy for coping with the jarring native witness is, in essence, what Jean-François Lyotard has defined as a form of terror: 'the efficiency gained by eliminating, or threatening to eliminate, a player from the language game. He is silenced or consents, not because he has been refuted, but because his ability to participate has been threatened' (1984: 63–4). It is one thing to suggest that for whatever reason, uprisings on the part of oppressed peoples are doomed to failure; it is quite another to silence them, to vilify and ridicule them, and to deny the validity of their struggle for power over their own lives. The Monteros are last heard of in a disreputable condition befitting their overall role in the novel: 'General Montero, in less than a month after proclaiming himself Emperor of Costaguana, was shot dead (during a solemn and public distribution of orders and crosses) by a young artillery officer, the brother of his then mistress.' Sexual scandal also surrounds 'Pedrito the Guerillero', who has been seen 'arrayed in purple slippers and a velvet smoking-cap with a gold tassel, keeping a disorderly house in one of the southern ports' (Conrad, 1967: 400).[16]

The power and variety of the rhetorical strategies used to contain the speech of the anti-imperialist revolutionaries suggests, perhaps, a great fear. As Jenkins argues, in *Nostromo*, Conrad's social vision balances uneasily between 'a desire to challenge the existing arrangements of the universe and a fear of summoning up some annihilating specter in the face of which the cruelty of the existing arrangements appears as nothing' (1977: 147). The object of this fear is not so much successful revolution perhaps, but anarchy, chaos, a carnivalesque overturning of authority, a possibility in comparison with which the ruling power structure begins to look more acceptable in the novel. It is as though in order to maintain his delicate political balance Conrad must compensate for his critique of the modern European power structure in Sulaco with a far more extreme and total attack on the native alternatives to it.

One aspect of this orthodox balance might be suggested in the juxtaposition of two passages. The first occurs early in the novel, as Gould explains to his wife the socially beneficial effects of the mine:

What is wanted here is law, good faith, order, security. Anyone can declaim about these things, but I pin my faith to material interests. Only let material interests once get a firm footing, and they are bound to impose the conditions on which alone they can continue to exist. That's how your money-making is justified here in the face of lawlessness and disorder. It is justified because the security which it demands must be shared with an oppressed people. A better justice will come afterwards. That's your ray of hope.   (1967: 81)

By the end of the novel these ideals have not, of course, been realised, and Emilia's despair answers Charles's early idealism:

there was something inherent in the necessities of successful action which carried with it the moral degradation of the idea. She saw the San Tomé

mountain hanging over the Campo, over the whole land, feared, hated, wealthy; more soulless than any tyrant, more pitiless and autocratic than the worst Government; ready to crush innumerable lives in the expansion of its greatness.
(1967: 427–8)

A wide range of the ideological spectrum is covered here: the mine as the ray of hope, the mine as darkest curse. But the political limits of this discourse can perhaps be noted both in the lack of political alternatives presented and in the narrow social spectrum represented. Characters associated with the owners of the mine are given the most profound insights – indeed almost the only insights – into its potential for progress and for destruction. The innumerable crushed lives – unless they are Blancos – remain no more than abstractions whose visions of the mine's significance are never articulated, whose political hopes and social ideals find no expression, and whose historical perspective is not introduced.

The discourse of social critique, of liberation (which has often been a discourse of oppressed groups), is instead displaced onto the privileged groups in three ways. First, the natives themselves are denied the right to voice it: for example, Pedro Montero's 'victory' speech is blocked by the narrator and made incoherent. Second, with this native discourse jammed, the care for native well-being that naturally figures in such a discourse, is then appropriated by the Blancos, who seem to understand the condition of the miners and peasants better than they themselves do – a case in point here is Mrs Gould who, on the dubious basis of having lived for a short time in southern Italy, is credited with an intimate knowledge of peasants and a profound concern for their well-being, and whose vision of the moral failure of the mine seems most profound. Thus, the self-representation of the lower strata is first blocked, then overwritten by the 'truer' representation articulated by the upper. The natives – whether Montero or the peasants – are seen through the eyes of the Blancos, never the reverse. In a passage combining a moral and an aesthetic gaze, whose lyrical poignancy attests perhaps to Mrs Gould's sincerity, Conrad renders another picturesque vision of the natives, one which marks Nostromo's deepest recognition of the interiority of the native subject:

Having acquired in southern Europe a knowledge of true peasantry, she was able to appreciate the great worth of the people. She saw the man under the silent, sad-eyed beast of burden. She saw them on the road carrying loads, lonely figures upon the plain, toiling under great straw hats, with their white clothing flapping about their limbs in the wind; she remembered the villages by some group of Indian women at the fountain impressed upon her memory, by the face of some young Indian girl with a melancholy and sensual profile, raising an earthenware vessel of cool water at the door of a dark hut with a wooden porch cumbered with great brown jars . . . and a party of charcoal carriers, with each man's load resting above his head on the top of the low mud wall, slept stretched in a row within the strip of shade.   (1967: 84–85)

Once again, a European acts as an intermediary for the reader. Her credentials, however, based on a visit to her aunt, seem less than sufficient – not so much because the analogy between Italian peasant ('true peasantry') and South American native is untenable, but because her authority as spokesperson for native experience seems, to say the least, rather unfounded. To understand the sufferings of natives or miners, one would obviously do better to hear the testimonies of the natives or miners in question, rather than to rely on that of the wealthy English wife of the colonialist mineowner.

The third step, completing this displacement of the native discourse of social critique, is to ascribe the real suffering, the most essential ill-effects of imperialist capitalism, to the imperialists themselves who become hollow and enslaved, and who confront a meaningless world as a result of their relation to wealth and power. In the end, the Blancos appear as the real victims of the history of imperialism: the Goulds, Decoud and so on. The social tragedy of the mine that Emilia, for instance, testifies to, moves from the fate of the innumerable crushed lives to the misery of one particular crushed life – her own – in less abstract terms, echoing in a negative context the phrase her husband had uttered as the essence of hope. As she reflects on the shortcomings of her married life, the emotional and reproductive sterility, an

immense desolation, the dread of her own continued life, descended upon the first lady of Sulaco. With a prophetic vision she saw herself surviving alone the degradation of her young ideal . . . all alone in the Treasure House of the World. The profound, blind, suffering expression of a painful dream settled on her face with its closed eyes. In the indistinct voice of an unlucky sleeper, lying passive in the grip of a merciless nightmare, she stammered out aimlessly the words: 'Material interest.'   (1967: 428)

While there is undoubtedly some heuristic value in representing the Goulds, for example, as the real victims, the real slaves, this symbolism obscures a great deal of history as well. It is not just a matter of an apolitical acceptance of the fact that all people – imperialists and peasants alike – are victims. This interpretation of Conrad's tragic, even nihilistic, vision of a universal 'human condition' overlooks the fact that the representation Conrad constructs clearly *does* differentiate between cultural communities, privileging the complex historical sufferings of one group while marginalising that of the other. The transference that occurs here allows the Goulds to be represented metaphorically as the slaves, while the vast numbers of African slaves imported to mine the wealth of South America and the millions of native people who were literally enslaved and worked to death, are left without a legitimate complaint, without even a voice with which to articulate a complaint.[17]

Instead, toward the end of the book, we find that discursive space rather ambiguously occupied by Nostromo himself who, since the events of the rebellion, has developed a radical social conscience. Ironically, the founding of the new regime owes a great deal to his heroic acts. His very name, Nostromo, is a nickname conferred on him by his European superiors, a name meaning not only boatswain (his previous occupation) but, more significantly, 'our man'. We see him in this capacity as he drives the 'unruly brotherhood of all sorts of scum' to work, using his revolver 'to solv[e] the problem of labour without fail'. In this way he patrols the 'slums':

He called out men's names menacingly from the saddle . . . . But if perchance he had to dismount, then, after a while from the door of that hovel or of that *pulperia*, with a ferocious scuffle and stifled imprecations, a *cargador* would fly out head first and hands abroad . . . and the man, picking himself up, would walk away hastily from Nostromo's revolver, reeling a little along the street and snarling low curses.   (1967: 89–90)

This approach to labour relations seems not to be questioned in the novel. ' "The fellow is devoted to me, body and soul!" Captain Mitchell was given to affirm' (1967: 49). While this evaluation of their relationship can hardly be taken at face value, there is no doubt that Nostromo's impressive strengths are harnessed in the service of the 'material interests'. In this capacity he is 'too scornful in his temper even to utter abuse, a tireless taskmaster, and the more to be feared because of his aloofness' (1967: 26). Mitchell's complimentary reference to Nostromo's 'force of character' barely conceals a somewhat less subtle kind of force.[18]

It is strange then to see Nostromo take up the cause of the poor, but even this dramatic conversion is contained within the circle of irony and orthodoxy. The change in his character initially appears as a kind of rebirth: he lies 'as if dead' after his long swim until he arises and says ' "I am not dead yet" ' (1967: 341–2). And it is at this moment of rebirth that he understands his friend Viola's vision of power relations: 'Kings, ministers, aristocrats, the rich in general, kept the people in poverty and subjection; they kept them as they kept dogs, to fight and hunt for their service' (1967: 342). Just as Viola's insight is undermined by his own adulation of the Goulds and his scorn for the peasants, Nostromo's new political vision is similarly questionable.

His new social conscience seems to have its origin not in any real social concern, but in a feeling of having been forgotten, betrayed by his superiors during the revolution. The courageous actions he had performed during that desperate affair in response to their urgent pleas had gone unnoticed, unappreciated, and it is the resulting personal resentment that fuels his alienation from his Blanco superiors more than any serious political ideal or heterodox social insight. Initially, in fact, Nostromo seems almost eager to return to his previous relation to Blanco power. Meeting Monygham soon after, he

> was mollified by what seemed a sign of some faint interest in such things as had befallen him .... At that moment he felt communicative. He expected the continuance of that interest which, whether accepted or rejected, would have restored to him his personality.   (1967: 357–8)

Monygham considers Nostromo's anger a kind of childishness, in accord with the narrator's earlier statement that he 'was simple. He was as ready to become the prey of any belief, superstition, or desire as a child' (1967: 344). Nostromo's new-found political awareness is thus undermined through its non-political basis in his helpless gullibility, childish resentment and naïve pride. As with Montero, oppositional political opinion and action is thoroughly depoliticised through ascription to psychological imbalance.

Nostromo's political critique of the power structure is further compromised by its development in tandem with his decision to keep the treasure for himself rather than return it to its owners. His social conscience appears compromised not only because he is becoming rich on the silver himself – silver which he has stolen, which, as he gradually realises, is the source of much of the injustice he sees around him – but also by the fact that he seems in no hurry to use it to help the poor whose suffering he invokes more frequently the richer he grows. Nostromo, toward the end of the novel, appears as yet another victim of the silver – like the Goulds, a slave to it. The wealthier he becomes, the more he seems a victim of slavery and tyranny: 'to become the slave of a treasure with full self-knowledge is an occurrence rare and mentally disturbing' (1967: 428).[19] His dream of a life for Giselle as splendid as that of Mrs Gould (1967: 443) is ironically undermined in the light of Emilia's despair. As Jenkins concludes, he 'passes from exploitation by the oligarchy to exploitation by the fetishized product of the oligarchy' (1977: 172). Any power Nostromo may have had as a spokesman for the poor and their history of oppression is ultimately eroded in the light of the many ways in which his integrity is compromised.[20]

The alternative discourse of opposition that might accompany the critique of imperialist capitalism is not just undermined, but everywhere discredited in Nostromo. In his portrait of the leader of the new socialist organisation in Sulaco, Conrad employs the same rhetorical skill at making a character appear alien that he used so successfully earlier in characterising the Monteros. He is presented as an indigent, sickly hunchback (1967: 432); a 'hater of capitalists', who, 'small, frail, bloodthirsty . . . perched on a high stool' (1967: 459) near Nostromo's deathbed, 'huddled up . . . shock-headed, wildly hairy, like a hunchbacked monkey' (1967: 460), intent on extracting money from Nostromo, a dying man. This is the last example in the novel of a character who might seem to be involved in a radical attempt to alter the power structure. His obsessive nature suggests a lack of any recognisably rational interior complexity or depth, and his appearance is at once monstrous and – like the natives – bestial. He perches and huddles rather then sits, and to judge by his shock of unkempt hair and his resemblance to a monkey, Conrad seems to be implying that this man too, like the Monteros who also opposed the power structure, may have some dubious racial background.

Not only is oppositional discourse – native or European – thoroughly marginalised, at one point we are given a glimpse of a native who recognises the benefits of the colonial system:

The grave *alcalde* [a civic official] himself, in a white waistcloth and a flowered chintz gown with sleeves, open wide upon his naked stout person with an effect of a gaudy bathing robe, stood by, wearing a rough beaver hat at the back of his head, and grasping a tall staff with a silver knob in his hand.

(1967: 329)

The native is made to seem alien, a figure of ridicule, in much the same way that the Monteros were made to appear bizarre and grotesque. The reader's interpretive gaze is, once again, confounded yet this absurd grave figure is even proud of his costume:

These insignia of his dignity had been conferred upon him by the Administration of the mine, the fountain of honor, of prosperity, and peace . . . which seemed with its treasures to pour down . . . the gifts of well-being, security, and justice upon the toilers.

These opinions are presented as those of the native (and of other natives as well), and the condescending irony of the passage allows the reader a superior vision, a knowledge that the mine is not so benign as these naïve workers believe. Yet if a disbelieving irony distances the reader, there is none the less a degree of sympathy for this native, and for others who peaceably and uncomplainingly ally themselves with the mine and its weighty interests. That sympathy, which extends as well to the quiescent picturesque natives in the countryside, is quite the opposite of the antipathy, revulsion and scorn expressed towards those who, allied with the Monteros, oppose the established structure of 'material interests'. The narrator intercedes to speak even for the pro-Blanco natives, however, addressing the reader over the heads, as it were, of the natives under discussion, offering an historical narrative they might well agree with but would presumably be incapable of colligating themselves:[21]

In a very few years the sense of belonging to a powerful organization had been developed in these harassed, half-wild Indians. They were proud of, and attached to, the mine. It had secured their confidence and belief. They invested it with a protecting and invincible virtue as though it were a fetish made by their own hands, for they were ignorant, and in other respects did not differ appreciably from the rest of mankind which puts infinite trust in its own creations. It never entered the *alcalde*'s head that the mine could fail in its protection and its force.   (1967: 329)

The natives, however, *are* represented as differing appreciably, beginning with the alien appearance that – as in the case of General Montero – distances by simultaneously attracting and repelling the European gaze through anarchic transgression of any recognisable dress codes. These 'half-wild' creatures apparently need some institutional structure imposed from the outside to tame them, and the mine providentially provides it. While the philosophic observation near the close of the passage appears to equate all humanity, at another level this universality is contradicted, and the suggestion subtly remains that on a pragmatic level some sections of humanity can provide order for those benighted 'half-wild' groups who are constitutionally unable to do so for themselves. In the founding of a nation-state controlled by European and North American 'material interests' – however compromised the ideals of those interests may finally be, by wealth and power – there is at least a gesture toward the construction of a more stable social structure: 'For the San Tomé mine', it is asserted, 'was to become an institution, a rallying-point for everything in the province that needed order and stability to live' (1967: 101).

While such endorsements of the mine cannot be taken without a large grain of salt, there is, as well, a kind of blaming of the victims for their difficulties. Historically, the greatest single threat to progress and stability in this society seems to emerge from the natives who irrationally, greedily it seems, rise up periodically to destroy the fragile order that the mine might offer them. History repeats itself in the early nationalist movement, later in the rise of Bento, and finally in the Monterist attempt to seize power. In each case, the anti-imperialist movement is denied political legitimacy, even rationality, appearing simply as (in Emilia's words) 'a puerile and bloodthirsty game of murder and rapine played with terrible earnestness by depraved children' (1967: 53). Before the European invasion, however, the natives of South America had long-established, sophisticated civilisations which were systematically destroyed as part of a genocidal campaign – physical as well as cultural genocide – to plunder natural resources such as silver. The blame for the political chaos which the novel represents is nevertheless directed less towards the Blancos, than towards the greedy subrational natives – both the megalomaniacs who lead and the ignorant but docile ones who passively let themselves be led by these demagogues. *Nostromo*, while critical of the internal logic of imperialism and its ill-effects on the imperialists themselves, never moves beyond the orthodox common sense (*sensus communis*) position that can consider, if not finally wholly endorse, the benign effects of imperialism on the native people. As Terry Eagleton comments, 'alien experience is allowed radically to question civilized structures which in turn gain fresh validation from the encounter' (1970: 31).[22]

Eduardo Galeano points out that silver-mining in Latin America has rarely been benign either in intention or in effect: 'The Indians of the Americas totalled no less than 70 million when the foreign conquerors appeared on the horizon; a century and a half later they had been reduced to 3.5 million.' (1973: 50–1)[23] Natives sent into the silver mines usually died within four years. One mine alone, Potosi's Cerro Rico consumed eight million lives in three centuries of operation. The natives, including women and children, were torn from their agricultural communities and driven forcibly to the mine. 'Of every ten who went up into the freezing wilderness, seven never returned' (Galeano, 1973: 50–1). The anomaly of representing the San Tomé mine as a haven of justice and stability in the eyes of the natives (whether under Spanish or Anglo-American power), the suggestion that the natives themselves are most directly responsible for the political chaos because of their greed and immaturity, and the ascription of *real* suffering and *real* insight into that suffering to the Blancos rather than to the natives is almost grotesque in a way that Conrad's ironic historiographic representation of the situation cannot encompass.

The novel does acknowledge some of this history briefly – although not from the point of view of the natives whose community endured it, but who display little historical consciousness of it. Instead, it is rendered through the thoughts of Mrs. Gould, who is in any case generally seen to be more sensitive to suffering:

Mrs. Gould knew the history of the San Tomé mine. Worked in the early days mostly by means of lashes on the backs of slaves, its yield had been paid for in its own weight of human bones. Whole tribes of Indians had perished in the exploitation; and then the mine was abandoned, since with this primitive method it had ceased to make a profitable return, no matter how many corpses were thrown into its maw. Then it became forgotten.   (Conrad, 1967: 55)

But this era of atrocity is separated from the novel's fictional present by a curious historical rupture. First abandoned, then forgotten, the mine is finally rediscovered in the modern period – not only rediscovered but morally reversed so that the Europeans (significantly now English rather than Spanish) become the apparently blameless victims, and the nationalist governments are the greedy aggressors. Following the War of Independence,

An English company obtained the right to work it, and found a vein so rich that neither the exactions of successive governments, nor the periodic raids of recruiting officers upon the population of paid miners they had created, could discourage their perseverance.

The historical (and rhetorical) division posited here represents the assumption of the changed face of modern imperialism. The era of brutal exploitation by the Spanish imperialists has long ago ended – even disappeared from memory perhaps, like the existence of the mine itself. Now, by contrast, the Anglo-American mineowners are represented as a progressive force in the land, victimised by unfair nationalist governments which do not, apparently, have a 'right' to the mine. These governments then make life difficult for miners who, by virtue of being paid rather than kept in slavery, seem to have given their allegiance to the mining company. It must be pointed out, however, that in Latin America, as in much of the colonised world, allegiance to imperialist modes of production frequently has more to do with military force and the limited options resulting from the deliberate destruction of traditional patterns of life than with a philosophic endorsement of the benign political and economic order imperialism makes possible.

   Yet a representation of the history of colonialist exploitation in Latin America that offers a qualified justification of the imperialist regime is essential to the narrative coherence (tenuous though it sometimes is) of the Blancos. The San Tomé mine under the Goulds must be separated from the history of atrocity that is an integral part of the Latin American colonialist legacy in order to assert, even partially, the legitimacy of the Blancos. The historical division that is suggested in this passage more or less corresponds to the coming of modern capitalism, which is seen to be quite separate from earlier modes of production in that a concern with efficiency leads directly to a concern with the well-being of the miners. The initial reward for this new humane imperialist approach in earlier decades unfortunately was that the native miners, in an interesting twist on the outside agitator theory of popular resistance, 'incited to revolt by the emissaries sent out from the capital, had risen upon their English chiefs and murdered them to a man' (1967: 55). This is, of course, a prefiguring of the crisis that is unleashed on Gould and the Blancos, who apparently have given relatively good government to the natives, have won their trust and loyalty, yet are now faced with the irrational Monterist insurrection.

'The history of Costaguana', asserts Stephen K. Land, 'is a succession of revolutions, oscillating between the rule of a partly-enlightened aristocracy and the tyranny of popular dictatorships' (1984: 111). This response, faithful enough to the historical world Conrad describes, indicates how far from level is the discursive field constituted by the novel. In this formulation, the aristocratic elite are at last partly enlightened and progressive compared with the bestial dictatorial popular tyranny. The point here is not to suggest that the terms be reversed so that the natives are represented as the 'good' in opposition to the imperialist 'bad', but to specify the way that Nostromo's historiographic discourse is structured to legitimate, at least tentatively, some voices – such as the at least 'partly enlightened aristocracy' and to exclude wholly unenlightened others. Just as the wealthy colonialists are represented as the real slaves, so they appear as the real victims of colonial violence and territorial expansionism. No matter how much the legitimacy, authority and moral ground supporting the Blancos is eroded in the novel, never does their situation begin to compare with the moral vacuum or actual evil ascribed to those who oppose them. Mark Conroy, echoing Collingwood's discussion of the limits of historical thought and enquiry, argues that the social dynamic represented in Nostromo is determined by its cultural perspective: since 'this is a European perspective . . . a kind of horizon obtrudes on the narrative, a state of affairs that cannot be seen beyond' (1985: 137). Beyond this horizon, however, this sensus communis, there exists a real community of jarring witnesses whose historical testimony is not registered.

Nostromo operates on the generic border dividing the epic from the novel. It covers the ground traditionally reserved for the epic –

the founding of a nation – but it does not respect one particular central characteristic of that genre: it is neither univocal nor doxic. Too many interpretations of events conflict both in terms of what actually has happened and in terms of the motivations behind the actions. In this way, Conrad's ironic modernist vision virtually parodies the epic possibilities of the Costaguana narrative. Further, in the epic, attention is focused more on the surface of the events themselves, rather than on the complex interiority of the agents; in Nostromo that subjectivity is constantly at issue to the extent that the epic or heroic dimensions of their actions are constantly called into question. Yet a trace of epic remains in that the Republic is founded, the enemy is repulsed by courageous and intrepid – albeit occasionally confused – heroes. In this sense, the centripetal movement of the epic is in evidence, but at the centre there is no epic stability. There is, instead, the instability of the Blanco characters and their narratives, an instability foregrounded by Conrad's demonstration of the difficulty of any closed, completed, true representation of historical events. On the other hand, the centrifugal movement of the work is often over-estimated. While there is finally no solid doxic centre, either in the European characters whose motivations are always open to question or in their interpretations of events which never reveal the 'whole story', the reader is not permitted to move beyond that centre. The potentially centrifugal movement of heteroglossia is checked by Conrad in that the heterodox historical experience or point of view of the native characters remains beyond the orthodox bounds of the speakable or the thinkable, as Collingwood or Bourdieu theorise it.

The novel abounds in irony, as Conrad relentlessly critiques the European characters and their ideals – but that irony at no point impels the reader beyond the space of its object. The irony may call European imperialism into question, it may undermine it, it may be devastating in its critique, but that critique is, in the end, contained within its own discursive space.[24] The European imperialists are the subject of irony, and they are even to varying degrees conscious of it themselves. But Conrad could not then allow the narrative to move the one decisive step further, which would open a discursive space outside, a space that might logically be occupied by an anti-imperialist discourse articulated by or on behalf of imperialism's victims, the natives. Even if that position were then to be subjected to the same sort of critique that Conrad employs to undermine the dominant discourses, it could be articulated rather than made to appear incomprehensible, beyond or beneath rationality. Instead, that critique is internalised within the circle bounded by European characters, and the natives are left without any rationale for their revolution other than apolitical ignorance, greed, psychological or racial dysfunction and barbarity. As a result, they need not be taken seriously – except possibly as a military threat – and their claims for justice or an end to oppression can be largely dismissed. Once again, the point here is not to suggest that the populist or nationalist ideology that the novel portrays so negatively, offers any final solution to the social dilemma represented in *Nostromo*, but to understand the uneven nature of the discursive field and the ideological limits of this ultimately orthodox historical narrative.[25]

This unevenness can be specified in the way that the text (along with many critics) insists on one very important – albeit perhaps negative – stability. While the main Blanco characters are shown to be complex and multilayered both in themselves and in their intricate networks of relationships, the stability that remains arises from the comparative lack of complexity or interiority ascribed to the native resistance. In this asymmetry there remains a limited certainty in the world of the text which reinforces an orthodox image of the historical world since the natives' unapproachable incomprehensibility provides, by negation, a relatively stable centre. It seems as though in *Nostromo*, the relatively familiar interiority and complexity of the characters of the dominant classes is in direct proportion to the denial of any similar familiarity, interiority or complexity in the dominated groups; this dynamic works to safeguard the limited authority of Blanco modernity from the assault of the forces of opposition which are represented as premodern and thereby excluded from authority altogether.

Through Conrad's historical critique of imperialism, the problem is moved into the realm of the thinkable out of the self-evident, into orthodoxy out of the doxic, into the modern novel out of the epic; but the critique is none the less contained. Being contained within the European circle it remains within orthodoxy, that ultimately centripetal discursive space in which issues exist that allow some possibility of differing views, but without allowing them radically to undermine the legitimacy of the hegemonic discursive community. In what may, on one level, seem a contradictory effect, the very critique of the European Blanco community that the novel presents – in crediting only *those* people with sufficient complexity to provide the subject of an ironic critique – simultaneously enacts the exclusion of the heterodox or heteroglossic element that could erode the legitimacy of that group. This is accomplished through the imposition of aphasia onto the natives who, given possession of those same critical insights and that same interiority – granted equal status as full dialogic interlocutors – might potentially be able to contest the legitimacy of their exclusion from possession of three related things: the silver, complex subjectivity and discursive authority. John McClure argues that rather than recognising the legitimacy of popular resistance, Conrad instead balances 'profound criticisms of modern imperialism and vitriolic dismissal of popular movements.' (1981: 166) The second half of the formula, however, results in an interpretation of Latin American political disorder as a reflection of an inherent irrationality.

If commentaries on *Nostromo* . . . have failed to question the validity of its portrait of nineteenth-century Latin America, it is perhaps because Europeans and North Americans have been conditioned to view Latin Americans in the same pessimistic and ultimately dismissive terms . . . . Thus even as *Nostromo* charges Western economic interests with the oppression and exploitation of Latin Americans, it presents an image of Latin America that has long been used to justify external domination and internal tyranny.   (McClure, 1981: 166–7)

The point here is not to suggest that Conrad himself was, or would have become, an active supporter of American or European imperialist policy in Latin America, but rather that the attitude articulated in *Nostromo* has much in common with that policy and contributes, at the very least by default, to its implementation. The narration of history in *Nostromo* is related to the discursive practice Edward Said describes in *Orientalism*, a discourse through which 'European culture was able to manage – and even produce – the Orient politically, sociologically, militarily, ideologically, scientifically, and imaginatively' as part of 'the whole network of interests inevitably brought to bear on (and therefore always involved in) any occasion when that peculiar entity "the Orient" is in question' (1978: 3). Said's comments elsewhere on the imperialist production of space can easily be seen to apply to historical time as well: from the perspective of the metropolitan centre, imperialism

achieves the domination, classification, and universal commodification of all space . . . . To the imagination of anti-imperialism, our space has been usurped and put to use by outsiders for their purpose. It is therefore necessary to seek out, to map, to invent, or to discover . . . [another space] that derives historically and abductively from the deprivations of the present.

(Said, 1990: 78–9)

Such a recreation of space or of time would challenge both the geographical imperialism that allows the Europeans a monopoly of political and economic power, and the temporal imperialism that permits the establishment of a separate historical frame for the 'premodern' other.

Fanon depicts the colonial world as one in which the natives 'form an almost inorganic background for the innovating dynamism of colonial mercantilism' (1963: 41). As historical narrative, Nostromo is not typical of this genre of colonial writing, yet Conrad critiques only half of the colonialist stereotype, leaving the other half – the native half – largely intact. While this is indeed a history concerned, as Fanon puts it, with the cultural perspective of the settler, it must be added that Conrad, a former sailor, was not himself a settler. Even the peculiar intrusion of the first person into the narration (Conrad, 1967: 89) somewhat distances the generally third-person narrator from the colonial events. It is an ironic distance that allows him the space to think the settlers' project in a way they cannot themselves, but it does not give him any more access to the sensus communis of the natives. A sceptical man, Conrad was aware, as few colonial writers were, that, as Fanon puts it, 'In this colonialist context there is no truthful behavior' (1963: 40). His application of this insight is, however, quite uneven, ultimately privileging the colonialists who become thereby sufficiently complex subjects for critique, while the native background – where concepts of truthful behaviour seem not to exist even as a horizon – remains essentially unexplorable, unthinkable and aphasic. As a result, the history that Conrad narrates is neither 'human history' in any comprehensive sense, nor settlers' history as Fanon understands it.

The narratives constructed by the Europeans are all shown to be flawed in significant ways, but the natives are significantly denied the capacity to construct coherent narrative at all; or, what amounts to almost the same thing, they are shown to be irrational and therefore not to be living in terms that any coherent historical narrative might comprehend. As jarring witnesses, their heterodox testimony is disallowed and their actions judged to be narratively incoherent. Furthermore, whenever the discourse concerning the natives shifts its ground from the picturesque to the political, a subsequent transformation immediately occurs whereby political or social categories translate instead into problems of native psycho- or socio-pathology. This kind of cultural difference may itself be read as a form of resistance. Michel de Certeau argues that it can enable the resistance of colonised people 'to avoid being disseminated in the occupiers' power grid, to avoid being captured by the dominating interpretive systems'. Making a virtue of necessity perhaps, this strategy

'maintains' a difference rooted in an affiliation that is opaque and inaccessible to both violent appropriation and learned cooptation. It is the unspoken foundation of affirmations that have *political* meaning to the extent that they are based on a *realization of coming from a 'different' place* (different, not opposite) on the part of those whom the omnipresent conquerors dominate.

(1986: 229)

If it is true to say that final narrative historical authority is never granted to the Sulaco Europeans, it is equally true that not a shred of authority is associated with the rebellious natives, who are not seen to act within a narrative continuum that would allow their actions to have the minimal rationality that is a prerequisite of narrative logic in history, and none of the radical social, political and historical analysis that has been a factor in many anti-imperialist movements in the Third World. If epic unity – doxa – eludes the Blanco characters and their attempts to interpret history, the natives have no authority as historical narrators or even as historical agents; the only position open to them in this modern history is as its heterodox other, whose defeat continues to be an essential constitutive factor in the *relative* stability of orthodox narrative history. Thus there is a sense of acceptance, resignation and inevitability attaching to the narrative and political closure imposed by the 'international naval demonstration which put an end to the Costaguana-Sulaco war . . . [as] the United States cruiser, *Powhattan*, was the first to salute the

Occidental flag' (Conrad, 1967: 400). Whatever disillusion the novel inspires regarding the Blancos, there is no thinkable alternative. This leaves the incomprehensible native other marginalised, discursively disenfranchised and aphasic – essentially excluded from participation in the ongoing description and construction of history and of modernity itself. And it leaves the Blancos, with whom our sympathies have (with whatever reservations) been encouraged to ride, in a complex but very familiar world of irony, fallibility and modernity.

4

Parade's End: 'Has the British this or that come to this!'

I wanted the Novelist in fact to appear in his really proud position as historian of his own time.' Ford Madox Ford (1933: 180)

In his comments about the magnitude of his historiographical ambitions, Ford Madox Ford makes it clear that in *Parade's End* he is attempting something close to a total history of an era. 'The subject was the world', he writes, 'as it culminated in war' (1933: 195). Yet instead of carrying out his initial desire to write a comprehensive novel in which the characters would be represent-ative of the whole social spectrum – heteroglossia – Ford decided to settle for the more feasible task of representing the 'world seen through the eyes of a central observer', a character whose point of view 'must be sufficient to carry the reader through his obser-vations of the crumbling world'. At this point the question of sufficiency must arise: if, as I have argued, there exists a tension in Bakhtin between the social heteroglossia and the authorial refraction of it, how can a fictional central observer be positioned in such a way as to be sufficient to both? If the central observer, as one might expect to be the case, is closely linked to the social position or ideals of the author, will this not tend to produce a containment of heteroglossia, or even impose an aphasic condition on language groups more widely distanced?

The drive to achieve some kind of narrative totality is common to many historical narratives and is never without problems, yet such a comprehensive social vision was even more difficult to attain at a time when the social fabric was under unprecedented strain. Jarring voices were emanating from diverse sectors of society as the tide of imperialist expansion had begun to turn; the dissatisfaction of women was propelling an increasingly militant women's movement; and the working classes were demanding more power both through trade unions and through the rapid growth of the Labour Party. And for Ford, perhaps the most challenging of all was the profound historical impact of World War I – the first modern, even modernist war – on British society, a society in which the historical legacy of traditional hierarchical patterns was resistant to such pressures. The war was widely experienced as a kind of historical rupture from which all these various social tensions emerged into a world that was not the same as it was at the beginning. Indeed, as Paul Fussell has written, this war was 'perhaps the last to be conceived as taking place within a seamless, purposeful "history" involving a coherent stream of time running from past through to present' (1975: 21).[1] If, as Ford's novel seems to concur, the ability to conceive history in this way came to an end in the trenches and on the front lines of First World War Europe, then the attempt to write a comprehensive historical novel in such circumstances was enormously ambitious.

Still, as they have with Nostromo, critics of Parade's End have, in general, endorsed the claim to comprehensiveness with enthusiasm. Joseph Firebaugh writes of Ford's 'comprehension of human life in all its tragicomedy' (1952: 32) for instance, and Robert Green refers to the 'comprehensive totalising realism' (1981: 144) of the work. Similarly, George Core remarks on the 'comprehensiveness' of the work, arguing that since Ford knew 'that it was impossible to present a complete picture of English life from 1908 to 1918', he instead 'shows us the various spheres of action at random but representative moments' through characters who 'are representative of every level of English society' (1987: 97–8).[2] Such claims to narrative totality must be viewed with a degree of suspicion however, and in this case the question that arises is whether the perspective of one observer can be made to contain what seems to be an impossible breadth. To what degree does Ford's orchestration of the social voices of his time in Parade's End in fact comprehend the heterogeneous social reality he is representing? How are the voices of jarring witnesses articulated, if at all? In order to approach these questions, it is necessary to explore the presentation of Tietjens as a character, and to situate him within the social currents of his time.

If all narrative representations of history are to some degree partial – both in the sense of being incomplete and in the related sense of expressing (perhaps through that very incompletion) a bias or partiality – if, as Mink argues, the idea of the whole story is a narrative optical illusion in historiography, a conceptual impossibility – how does Ford's narrative text manage to maintain the illusion of comprehensiveness? The suggestively quasi-allegorical nature of the work encourages an interpretation that conflates to some degree the personal life and problems of Christopher Tietjens and the fate of Tory England or even, perhaps, the fate of England itself.[3] Thus, according to Green, Tietjens must appear to speak for the general condition, 'to be "typical" or capable of universal application. The observer's troubles, Tietjens' disasters, had to be rendered as representative of the common fate' (1981: 132).[4] This identification of the comprehensive consciousness of Tietjens with the social totality, with the state of the nation, is further strengthened by Ford's impressionism which foregrounds the complexity of subjective experience. Much of the real action is not directly narrated by a third person narrator, but is instead represented through the narration of past events by the characters – chiefly Tietjens – who (necessarily) interpret as they narrate their perspective on the events. As Mink might note, it is not events themselves, but the reflections by Tietjens, Valentine and others on the actions and their possible meanings that constitute the bulk of the novel. In this respect, they are themselves like historians who interpret the meanings of, or identify patterns in, historical events – and the partial and selective nature of their interpretations therefore should be examined in order to understand the degree to which the narratorial perspective (whether Tietjens's or Ford's) might better be thought of as normative rather than as truly compre-hensive.

But this partiality is not made clear, in fact it is resisted as Ford seems to present the subjective experience of Tietjens, with all his foibles and eccentricities, as a symbolically potent combination of the true subject of history and an Arnoldian 'best self' of the nation. If his perspective cannot be thought of as comprehensive, as a perspective which rises above and unifies the social diversity, then Tietjens none the less rises above in another sense: as an exemplar of social values and moral imperatives, Tietjens seems to embody an undistorted ideal of human nature, at times to transcend the limits commonly associated with the human condition.[5] Furthermore, the remarkable omniscience that allows Tietjens to correct from memory the errors in the *Encyclopaedia Britannica* (1950: 10) acts as a proof both of his comprehensive mind and of his objectivity. As Paul Armstrong remarks, while 'the *Encyclopaedia* is unreliable as an epistemological origin, Tietjens preserves the authority of "Truth" through his own infallible memory' (1987: 232). Consequently, Tietjens's subjective experience is presented as a kind of qualitative gauge by which objective social and historical conditions can be measured; his ability to make narrative sense of the world around him, measuring the ability of his class to maintain social order, and his point of view constitute the ideological centre of the novel. The historical appearance of the encyclopaedia occurred at a time when the accumulation of knowledge had far outstripped the mind's ability to contain it all. Tietjens's ability to do just that not only suggests his astonishing mental capacity, but in another sense begins to reveal his anachronicity, the sense that he represents a time before consciousness, experience and memory became 'merely subjective', while objective authority – truth – became a property of particular genres of writing. His eventual loss of objectivity and total recall during the war constitutes, accordingly, a fall into a condition of modernity and epistemological uncertainty.[6]

In his study of Conrad, Ford records his observation that 'Life did not narrate, but made impressions on our brains' (1965: 194). As Armstrong argues, Ford's novels, especially *The Good Soldier* and *Parade's End*, 'dramatize the gap between confused, unreflective understanding and reflective interpretation that seeks to compose impressions into a clear, coherent narrative pattern' (1987: 2). Coherent narration is constructed after the fact out of those impressions – or as Bradley writes, 'rightly to observe is not to receive a series of chaotic impressions, but to grasp the course of events as a connected whole' (1968: 92). The ability to connect these impressions into the coherence of narrative form is not solely what is at stake, however.[7] There is also, as Bradley and White agree, the further necessity of having that particular narrative account ratified, legitimated by the general population as well as by the weightiest interests. This process has an explicitly political side, as White remarks, in the struggle to make a convincing coherent narrative that will stick as the one in terms of which people will understand their own lives (1987: 167). This is especially crucial at a time when traditional social categories and trajectories are under pressure, and people are forced collectively and individually to recognise the systems of classification and narratives in terms of which their lives have been and will be organised. Tietjens's narrative authority, the power to supply legitimate descriptions of the world, long presumed to be a birthright of members of his class, is reinforced by his remarkable (comprehensive) intelligence, and is ratified by all the sympathetic characters in the novel, as well as by lower class characters whose acceptance – even adulation – of his authority is pointedly presented on several occasions. However, in *Parade's End*, Ford is dealing with the crumbling of that authority, with the erosion of the claim of Tietjens's class to undisputed authority, and ultimately with the threat of the delegitimisation of the entire edifice of imperial England.

Tietjens's perspective is, none the less, something of an anachronism from the beginning. He is, essentially, a man whose value system belongs to an earlier premodern century – the seventeenth or, at the latest, the eighteenth century – and whose ideals are located in a particular image of the rural social hierarchy of that time. Perhaps the passage most often cited in this regard is his meditation, while under fire in the trenches, on George Herbert's rural life at Bemerton. The extremity of the juxtaposition of these two moments is remarkable, the former as an image of modern reality and the latter not only as an originating point of historical descent but as the Utopian moment from which much of the novel's social critique is directed.[8] A less dramatic example may illustrate this critical strategy as well. Early in their acquaintance, Tietjens and Valentine are on a country path, a pleasantly bucolic setting, and he reflects on the situation:

'This', Tietjens thought, 'is England! A man and a maid walk through Kentish grass fields: the grass ripe for the scythe. The man honourable, clean, upright; the maid virtuous, clean, vigorous: he of good birth; she of birth quite as good .... Each come just from an admirably appointed establishment: a table surrounded by the best people: their promenade sanctioned, as it were, by the Church: two clergy; the State: two government officials; by mothers, friends, old maids.'   (1950: 105)

Tietjens's comments point to a tension between an idealised past
and a present that is simply not up to his high standards. While
they both are undeniably 'of good birth', the man's wife is having
an affair and the 'maid' is a suffragette engaged in civil disobedience. The good establishment is the home of the Duchemins:
Reverend Duchemin is given to periodic fits of violence and sexual
obscenity, and Mrs Duchemin is a hypocritical social climber. The
ironic distance between the image and the reality is vast. Tietjens
muses, 'Walk, then, through the field, gallant youth and fair maid
. . . . God's England! . . . . "Land of Hope and Glory!" ' (1950: 105–
6).

By God, he said, 'Church! State! Army! H.M. Ministry: H.M. Opposition: H.M.
City Man . . . . All the governing class! All rotten! . . . . Then thank God for the
upright young man and the virtuous maiden in the summer fields: he Tory of
the Tories as he should be: she suffragette of the militants . . . . As she should
be! In the early decades of the twentieth century, however else can a woman
keep clean and wholesome! Ranting from platforms, splendid for the lungs.

(1950: 106)

The gap between the ideal and the modern reality widens
though, as he realises that by enjoying this bucolic moment with
Valentine he is compromising her reputation, perhaps causing her
to be struck from the visiting lists of those 'good' hypocritical
establishments. Here and throughout, Tietjens's integrity and
honesty cause him (and ultimately Valentine as well) to be rejected
on moral grounds by a society markedly his moral and intellectual
inferior. This ironic gap between the traditional ideals and the
modern realities encompasses more, however, than the social
difficulties experienced by Tietjens and Valentine, more perhaps
than Tietjens himself might acknowledge. In the early decades of
the twentieth century, ranting from platforms all over Europe were
voices also articulating working class discontent; and ranting from
platforms all over the colonised world were voices articulating
anti-imperialist discontent. These jarring voices occupy the gap
between the traditional ideal and modernity, and the resonance of
Tietjens's invocation of the 'Land of Hope and Glory' must be
measured against the silence of sectors of modernity (and of
heteroglossia) that he does not speak for here as well as those he
does.

One political aspect of his peculiar brand of Toryism emerges
from a conversation with Valentine about women's right to vote.

While he espouses no objection in principal to civil disobedience and even destruction of property as a means, he tends to ridicule the idea of women 'ranting from platforms' and he finds the *goals* of the suffragettes 'idiotic' (1950: 114). 'What good did a vote ever do anyone?' he asks (1950: 115). Valentine cites the example of women seeking equal pay for equal work as a case in point, but he disagrees, arguing that if those women

backed by all the other ill-used, sweated women of the country, had threatened the Under-secretary, burned the pillar-boxes, and cut up all the golf greens round his country-house, they'd have had their wages raised to half a crown next week. That's the only straight method. It's the feudal system at work.

(1950: 115)

It is something of a reversal to support the feudal system on the basis of its offering better access to social justice for the disempowered. Nevertheless, it is this vision of a benign feudal system that Tietjens endorses: social positions well-defined and not yet mystified or reified by modern industrial and bureaucratic institutions, codes of behaviour stable, everyone fulfilling the duties and enjoying the benefits of his or her acknowledged position. This was a position Ford himself seems to have shared with Tietjens: 'We have a vague uneasy feeling', Ford wrote (1915), 'that the old feudalism and the old union of Christendom beneath a spiritual headship may in the end be infinitely better than anything that was ever devised' to replace it (Levenson, 1984: 52). According to this vision, if the system does not at first function properly, there is recourse to direct action. In fact, it would not be difficult to adduce examples from British history in which such a confrontational strategy resulted in the far more violent repression of protest. Tietjens (as well as Ford) omits mention of the fact that while women or the lower classes may have recourse to direct action, the state (and the weighty interests that influence it) has a virtual monopoly on the means of organised violence.

This is, in any case, an odd sort of radicalism. While taking a theoretical stance that seems on the surface more radical than the activists' own position, it none the less has the evident effect of discouraging any further political initiative – without ever explicitly renouncing her feminist militancy, Valentine does not continue her protests much beyond this early point in the novel. Still, Tietjens's question 'What good did a vote ever do anyone?'

does raise a question about democracy and representation. Given the living conditions of much of the population at this time, it was apparent that the gradual extension of the right to vote had not adequately transformed the inequalities of this hierarchic society. Instead of giving them their rights (as Walter Benjamin writes of the growth of fascism (1969: 243–4)), it gave them a chance to express themselves – in this case by means of a vote which had little power to affect significantly the workings of the system in which they were oppressed. If the casting of an ineffectual ballot is the full extent of their democratic voice, then they have indeed moved only very slightly away from the aphasia of earlier forms of political power.

In one of the prefaces to the tetralogy, Ford claims that his attempt to represent modern history through 'the eyes of an extinct frame of mind' (Hynes, 1970: 524) is, however, a strategic one. 'For by the time of my relative youth,' he writes, 'Toryism had gone beyond the region of any practicing political party. It had . . . expired.' Moore argues that since Tietjens's Toryism was already extinct, Ford is able to use it as a perspective from which to view historical developments 'in a relatively unemotional and objective manner, while Tietjens' status as a representative of an outmoded social class endows him with a similarly objective . . . overview of the struggles among various class interests' (1982: 52). There is a strange movement in this argument whereby Tietjens's objectivity is established by his political bias, the centrality of his perspective is guaranteed by his obsolescence, and his relevance to the moment arises from his apparent anachronicity. If Tietjens *is* both objective and critical, as many critics seem prepared to accept, then his witness to modern history is as sufficient as Ford intended it to be; if Tietjens, as a representative figure, articulates a comprehensive critical position then other forms of social critique such as Valentine's modern feminism are rendered superfluous. But such claims to totality can also be used to obfuscate or defuse – even deny the existence of – the testimony of significant witnesses whose perspective jars, whose marginalised positions tend to reveal the arbitrary and selective reality concealed by the illusion of totality. In *Nostromo*, Emilia, whose husband owns the silver mine, is seen to possess the clearest understanding of the world's suffering and as a result it is her vision of the oppression that is privileged rather than that of the oppressed themselves. Similarly, in *Parade's End* a member of the most privileged class is credited with the greatest insight into the ills of the social world. In both cases, their critiques occupy so much discursive space that there is little serious consideration of the heterodox testimony of differently placed witnesses.

Through the character of Tietjens, Ford is able to present a powerful indictment of the ruling classes of his time. This extinct Arnoldian 'best self' not only analyses and criticises the hypocrisies and incompetencies of those in power, but by his opinions and actions (which are almost invariably carefully thought out and above reproach) he alienates almost everyone around him. The novel is replete with examples of his anachronistic moral and intellectual superiority, from his unwillingness to tamper with statistics to his concern with the reputations of others at the expense of his own. On the other hand, from this position the shortcomings of others are glaringly exposed: the outrageously self-centred maliciousness of Sylvia, the gullibility of General Campion who believes her lies, the incompetence of many in positions of bureaucratic and military power, the unprincipled rapaciousness of social climbers such as MacMaster and Edith Ethel. Tietjens's public service class – the class that, as we are told, rules the world (1950: 3) – has historically declined and no longer lives up to its responsibilities. ' "All rotten," ' Tietjens exclaims (1950: 106). While modern Britain is held up for much critical scrutiny in the novel, the position from which the critique is launched is not – Tietjens's version of the stable social hierarchy of earlier centuries seems accepted without question as a positive ideal.

A glimmer of this better world is briefly revealed: Tietjens's personal power, emblematic of the traditional power of his class, is the subject of the opening scenes of the tetralogy:

The two young men – they were of the English public-official class – sat in the perfectly appointed railway carriage. The leather straps . . . were of virgin newness; the mirrors beneath the new luggage racks immaculate as if they had reflected very little; the bulging upholstery in its luxuriant regulated curves was scarlet and yellow . . . the train ran as smoothly . . . as British gilt-edged securities. (1950: 3)

Tietjens and his friend MacMaster are powerful young men at home in this luxury – Tietjens born to it, his friend risen to it.

'Their class', writes Ford, 'administered the world.' If the train had not run smoothly, indeed if any disruptions upset them, the story would not go unreported to the proper authorities – and the narratives of this class carry weight. These are, it might be said, examples of the weighty interests to whom Bradley alludes as the final arbiters of narrative authority.

If they saw policemen misbehave, railway porters lack civility, an insufficiency of street lamps, defects in public services or in foreign countries, they saw to it, either with indignant Balliol voices or with letters to The Times asking . . . 'Has the British This or That come to this!'   (1950: 3)

But the almost doxic sense of harmonious equilibrium based on the unquestioned hegemony of this class is soon shown to be, in reality, already a thing of the past. As Tietjens himself demonstrates, however, in this representation, it is not the class system itself that is the source of the problem, but the fact that the ruling class has not lived up to its responsibilities as governors. If only there were still a ruling class made up of people like this man, the suggestion seems to be, the fine social structures and traditions of earlier centuries might live on. But the rift between Tietjens and his wife Sylvia, indeed Tietjens's growing estrangement from most of his class, is symptomatic of a more general social breakdown characteristic of modernity. The problem is not solely that of the collapse of an older social structure such as that represented by Tietjens and his social vision. Since the transition to modernity is still in process, the old forms, if increasingly fragmentary and moribund, are still extant and coexist uneasily – jarringly – with the new, which are themselves incomplete and in the process of coming into being. Parade's End represents this legitimation crisis – to use Habermas's phrase – primarily as it affects Tietjens whose decreasing ability to construct a coherent narrative is a crucial indication of his class's loss of the narrative power to compel assent.

Still, what kind of world does Tietjens envision? His analogy between religion and social hierarchy offers a clue: God appears here as

a great English Landowner, benevolently awful, a colossal duke who never left his study and was thus invisible, but knowing all about the estate down to the last hind at the home farm and the last oak: Christ an almost too benevolent

Land Steward, son of the Owner, knowing all about the estate down to the last child at the porter's lodge, apt to be got round by the more detrimental tenants.

(1950: 3)

While there is some note of self-parody present, this is essentially the point of comparison by which modernity is condemned. Many early twentieth-century writers turned to these centuries – especially the early seventeenth century – for a myth of a preindustrial 'organic society' or a time previous to the modern 'dissociation of sensibility', in search of a fulcrum from which a critical perspective on the perceived disintegration of modernity could be managed.[9] There is little sense here or elsewhere of the problems afflicting premodern societies; poverty, sexism, class oppression are dissolved in Tietjens's nostalgic idyll. And since the totalising 'objective' vision that the novel articulates belongs to Tietjens – himself the benevolent son of a great landowner – there is no testimony on behalf of those who may have cause to be less starry-eyed about the past than he. Ford's use of Tietjens as his focaliser enables him to dig in his heels against modernity and its problems without having either to confront seriously the problems of premodernity or to posit any alternatives to the existing modern framework.[10]

Tietjens attempts to make narrative sense of his own personal history at several points during the novel. Given his symbolic role in this quasi-allegory, his success or failure bears directly on the political equilibrium of the social system. In fact, his increasing inability to narrate and compel assent represents an integral aspect of the breakdown in the stability of the old social order as the war forces Tietjens into a redefined relation with the 'Other Ranks'. In the opening pages he is able, in conversation with MacMaster, to colligate (Walsh) the events of his recent past into a significant narrative, but as the tetralogy progresses he has increasing difficulty in doing so. In the end he simply cannot do it and, in fact, his consciousness no longer represents the privileged focus of the novel in the final volume. If the strains on Tietjens's narrative capacity are evident almost from the beginning, it is during the war that it reaches a breaking point. In 1911 Ford characterised the modern period as one in which 'any connected thought is almost an impossibility' (Levenson, 1984: 51), and it is clear that the war only exacerbated the situation. As Walter Benjamin has commented, this condition was not restricted to men of Tietjens's class, but had to do with the experience of modern warfare as well: 'Was it not noticable at the end of the war that men returned from the battlefield grown silent – not richer but poorer in communicable experience?' (1969: 84). The consequences of this development for a class whose narratives had traditionally structured much social discourse, however, are far-reaching.

During the fighting Levin brings Tietjens news from home, and the information creates in his mind the impression of 'a singular mosaic of extraordinary, bright-coloured and melodramatic statements . . . without any sequence, and indeed without any apparent aim' (1950: 340–1). This is, of course, unacceptable to Tietjens, who determines to 'go methodically into this! Methodically into the history of his last day on earth' (1950: 345). Accordingly, he decides that the optimal way to be methodical in this case is to make a full narrative account of his recent personal situation, detailing how his current problems came about. He does not at first anticipate just how difficult the construction of 'a deliberate, consecutive recollection' will be (1950: 345), and at this point in *Parade's End*, Tietjens's total grasp on things seems for the first time to be seriously faltering. His mind is too excited for such control and keeps suggesting different attitudes to events, different interpretive possibilities: 'That opened up an immense perspective. Nevertheless, the contemplation of that immense perspective was not the way to set about a calm analysis.' This sublime sense of a bewildering plenitude of interpretive positions – suggestive of the weariness Bradley refers to – is unusual for Tietjens who is a precise man, a statistician whose epistemological authority had at one time surpassed that of *Encyclopaedia Britannica* itself. His attitude to narrative reflects this precision: 'The facts of the story *must* be stated before the moral. He said to himself that he must put, in exact language . . . the history of himself in relation to his wife . . . . "Better put it into writing", he said' (1950: 345). Even this resort to the more stable written narrative form as a means of dealing with the past runs into serious obstacles: recollecting his farewell to Valentine, he knows that they agreed not to become sexually involved, but beyond that, events and interpretations become blurred:

I do not know how we agreed. We never finished a sentence. Yet it was a passionate scene. So I touched the brim of my cap and said: 'So long! . . .' Or she . . . I don't remember. I remember the thoughts I thought and the thoughts I

gave her credit for thinking. But perhaps she did not think them. There is no
knowing. It is no good going into them.   (1950: 347)

Gradually, the pressure of Tietjens's effort to subdue the unman-
ageable past begins to tell, and the emotional and intellectual
strain of the attempt to impose a coherent, disciplined narrative
order on events begins to take its toll: ' "God, what a sweat I am
in!" ' he exclaims. What would once have been a simple mental
exercise now threatens to overwhelm him: 'He became instinct
with a sort of passion to let his thoughts wander into epithets and
go about where they would. But he stuck at it.' Determined to get
the story 'straight', he tries again, but only drifts further into
interpretive uncertainties.[11] Historiography often has to deal with
rather untidy epistemological and interpretive conditions, but
Tietjens's attempt to tidy it up here is doomed to failure. At this
point he gives up in despair of ascertaining the meaning, of finding
a true and final narrative explanation. 'What', he wonders in a
moment of bleak confusion, 'was at the bottom of all the madness
and cruelty?' (1950: 348). No answer follows. Blocked by the
historical world's sublime proliferation of interpretive possibilities which he is no longer in a position to control, Tietjens turns
inward instead and begins self-reflexively to wonder about the
meaning of his impulse to narrate.

What in the world was he doing? Now? With all this introspection? . . . Hang it
all he was not justifying himself . . . . Why, if he, Christopher Tietjens of Groby,
had the need to justify himself, what did it stand for to be Christopher Tietjens
of Groby? That was the unthinkable thought.   (1950: 350)

Literally unthinkable, perhaps, is this questioning of his own
subjectivity and (by extension) the subjectivity and legitimacy of
the ruling class, traditionally the absolute subject of British
history. At this point of personal and social crisis, however, the
unthinkable begins to become thinkable, doxa shifts toward
orthodoxy, as Tietjens's previously total hold on the interpretation
of events is eroded and his narration begins to turn in on itself.

The title 'Tietjens of Groby' itself appeals to a specific narrative
historical discourse, one overtly laden with ideological overtones:
the genealogy of the Tietjens family, the eminence of its members,
its wealth and prominence in British society for centuries, its
massive capital in all of Bourdieu's senses of that word. As a form
of symbolic power accumulated over many generations, compris-

ing educational capital and cultural capital, for instance, as well as financial capital, this constitutes Tietjens's claim to authority. It is Tietjens's inability to narrate coherently and his ultimate failure to recognise narratively the events and impressions that indicate the profound socio-historical change in progress. A 'Tietjens of Groby' should simply be there – importantly, massively there (like Christopher's great physical bulk itself), beyond the need of justification, his narrative perspective automatically authoritative. The erosion of identity and social role signalled in the collapse of his ability to impose a coherent interpretation on the past functions, was a metaphor for the collapse of Tory England that is so often invoked in the novel. The idea that a social inferior such as Levin might claim a right to demand justification from Tietjens violates his sense of the proper order of society, an order that should be guaranteed to the holder of a title such as his. What Levin's question exposes is the fact that ultimately Tietjens's aristocratic authority is not natural, but is a social and ideological construct which over the centuries has come to seem otherwise. Levin's question delegitimises Tietjens, reduces him to the level of those whose authority cannot be assumed but must be established; Tietjens's difficulty in answering it suggests that he is indeed falling to the rank of those who need to contend for authority, a struggle which in itself constitutes, as Bourdieu notes throughout *Distinction*, a conclusive proof of their illegitimacy.

That would be absurd. The end of the earth! The absurd end of the earth . . . .
Yet that insignificant ass Levin had that evening asserted the claim to go into his, Tietjens of Groby's, relations with his wife. That was an end of the earth as absurd! It was the unthinkable thing.   (1950: 355–6)

Once again, the unthinkable is, in spite of his resistance, precisely what Tietjens must think. The social division that separates ranks, compared in the following paragraph with the hierarchic relationship between God and Man, must be maintained, it seems, if the social world is to remain intact. But, in fact, the 'world was foundering' (1950: 359). And the refrain that gives the title to this volume of the tetralogy is invoked here: 'There will be no more parades', says Tietjens, no more of the public display of order and power manifested in the orderly movement of marching presided over by officers of one class demonstrating their authority over soldiers of another. 'A landmark in history,' he sadly reflects later

(1950: 361), one which appeared to signal the end of the rituals of power on display which stretched back to much earlier periods of English history.[12]

Eventually, as his marital situation worsens, Tietjens is faced with the previously unthinkable necessity of justifying himself to Levin – whom he perceives as a military, social and perhaps racial (Turkish–Armenian) inferior.[13] Considering Tietjens's earlier agonised attempts at making narrative sense of his situation, Levin poses the demand in almost impossible terms: 'You will kindly accept an order to relate exactly what happened', says Levin. 'That is what is perfectly damnable' (1950: 460), replies Tietjens, who is aware that the social destabilisation that results in Levin's communicating such an order is part and parcel of the epistemological destabilisation that makes it impossible for him to fully obey. He does, however, endeavour to tell the story, although to do so is to break the gentleman's code of discretion by which he lives and in terms of which he defines himself and his social superiority. Not only is the information he has to relate beyond the bounds of what a gentleman should speak of, but he must relate these private affairs to an inferior. All in all, for a gentleman of Tietjens's station, it is the unthinkable.

The modern destabilisation of the social categories in which the sender and receiver of messages have traditionally been embedded results in the destabilisation of language and communication itself. When Tietjens attempts to discuss his situation with General Campion, his difficulty in achieving clarity and coherence is juxtaposed with McKechnie's ease in doing just that even though his problems concern similar amatory complications. The difference is that while Tietjens strives for an impossible combination of honour and honesty and thus fails to achieve clarity or coherence, the self-interested McKechnie succeeds by sacrificing truth in exchange for coherence. Tietjens is identified here as an eighteenth-century man (1950: 490) and not, as Campion points out, 'modern'. 'That beastly little McKechnie is modern' though, in that his words bear at best a tangential relation to reality. 'What is language for?' wonders an exasperated Campion, 'What the hell is it for? We go round and round' (1950: 492). The tenuous relation of language to modern reality is doubly emphasised: it is in the nature of reality itself to exceed the language of representation; and, in the hands of modern users for whom social status is not so much given but has become instead the stakes of a general social struggle for position, language has become a manipulable tool for gaining advantage rather than a means to the honest communication of reality. 'That's modernism', concludes the General succinctly. (1950: 492).

An almost allegorical enactment of the social world's foundering occurs later when, in *A Man Could Stand Up*, a shell explodes unexpectedly very close to Tietjens and his men. Ford's impressionist technique is well-suited here to the representation of Tietjens's experience as he is tossed through the air:

It was being a dwarf at a conversation, a conflict – of mastodons. There was so much noise it seemed to grow dark. It was a mental darkness. You could not think. A Dark Age! The earth moved.

He was looking at Aranjuaz from a considerable height . . . . The earth turned like a weary hippopotamus. It settled down slowly over the face of Lance-Corporal Duckett who lay on his side, and went on in a slow wave.

It was slow, slow, slow . . . like a slowed down movie. The earth maneuvered for an infinite time. He remained suspended in space.   (1950: 637)

When he returns to earth, thoroughly disoriented, it is to be buried in mud above the waist, a situation that literally gives the physically large Tietjens a new perspective, once again with more than a hint of social allegory implied: 'A man stood over him. He appeared immensely tall because Tietjens' face was on a level with his belt. But he was a small Cockney Tommy really.' He is then rescued by two of his inferiors, and subsequently himself helps pull a subaltern (a term which in this case simultaneously signifies military rank, social class and racial origin – Levantine) to safety. In the light of such a literal and physical – not to mention allegorical – upheaval, social differentiations based on rank or race tend to appear somewhat arbitrary; juxtaposed with such an impersonal and indiscriminate violent force, many forms of social pretension and hierarchy are suddenly pared away.

Even the haughty Sylvia, so critical of Tietjens for lowering himself by taking 'common' soldiers seriously, reacts to the intensity of the barrage by losing momentarily her lofty sense of aristocratic distinction and descending to a language transgressive of her class position: as the volume of the tumult increases,

She screamed blasphemies that she was hardly aware of knowing. She had to scream against the noise: she was no more responsible for the blasphemy than if she had lost her identity under an anaesthetic. She *had* lost her identity . . . . She was one of this crowd.   (1950: 440)

As we see from a number of conversations involving long-time military men, earlier military campaigns had tended to reinforce traditional class divisions by reproducing, even exaggerating, those hierarchies in the military structure, and Tietjens's own nostalgic valorisation of military parades emphasises this same idea. By the First World War, however, the sublime scale of violence had become so vast as to shrink the more arbitrary hierarchic structure of social distinction into insignificance – at least for the moment. Crisis situations in any case, as both Bourdieu and Bakhtin point out, can have the effect of exposing the ultimately arbitrary nature of aspects of the *sensus communis* previously beyond question. As Ford's descriptions demonstrate, modern trench warfare techniques had become so thoroughly dehumanising that all sense of class distinction – a fundamental aspect of personal identity – could be at least temporarily undermined.

Paul Virilio argues convincingly that in modern warfare the terror that dissolves identity is itself an essential aspect of war strategy in that it reduces social and psychological structures to rubble as surely as a bombing raid can reduce buildings to rubble (1989: 5–6). This is precisely the traumatic condition Sylvia diagnoses in her husband, whose normal sense of social hierarchy and personal reserve seems to her to have been destroyed by his experience on the front lines. As she notes despairingly while observing what she considers Tietjens's promiscuous relationships with his social inferiors, 'She had never seen Tietjens put his head together with any soul before . . . . Now! Anyone: any fatuous staff officer, whom at home he would never so much as have spoken to: any trustworthy, beer-sodden sergeant, any street-urchin dressed up as orderly' (1950: 438). This sense of a war-related trauma with broad social and psychological impact is also discussed by Eric J. Leed, who describes this war as a liminal experience with the capacity to dissolve the participant's sense of stable identity. Due to the unfamiliar technology employed, battles were no longer orchestrated in an orderly fashion by generals watching from a distance, but became instead 'an experience of utter chaos' involving 'the fragmentation of spatial and temporal unities. It is the creation of a system with no centre and no periphery in which men, both attackers and defenders, are lost.'

The end result, he suggests, is that this war 'was a modernizing experience ... because it fundamentally altered traditional sources of identity' (1979: 193).

The traditional sources of identity here are at once military and more broadly social, and this aspect of the war experience has been explored by Tim Travers who contrasts the traditional gentlemanly military ideal according to which military rank is a more or less direct reflection of social rank and the modern 'technical, functionally competent, professional ideal' (1987: 5). World War I, he argues, was a period of awkward transition between the two. Traditional attitudes 'reflected the public school experience' and 'stressed such values as ... deference and obedience to the accepted hierarchy', while the technical innovation in weaponry 'forced a new discussion of tactics, ideas and weapons' (1987: 5). The reaction of the British military was essentially conservative, 'perhaps because full accommodation to machine warfare would have required social and hierarchical changes' (1987: 262). Travers recounts the difficulty experienced by officers in coming 'to mental grips with a war that had escaped its pre-ordained boundaries and structures'. This historical change is represented by Travers as a Kuhnian paradigm shift for an officer class which 'wished to retain Victorian moral certainties and social structures ... of morale, character and social hierarchy' (1987: 252–3).

One reason that Tietjens is able to retain his identity as long as he does in the face of the relentless incursion of modernity is that his sense of *noblesse oblige* separates him from the others: he is, for instance, receiving no pay for his military services. In the end, however, even this changes, and Tietjens of Groby not only becomes a wage-earner in the army but is actually reduced to dependence on his salary. Step by step, the distance between Tietjens and the 'Other Ranks' is eroded. For a while it seems as though all the hierarchies that have been set up throughout the novel – based on class, gender, race – may continue tumbling down like a house of cards once the war ends, and the levelling tendency that constitutes one aspect of life in the trenches may assert itself in civilian society afterwards. This social transformation may, of course, be approached in diverse ways. Some commentators at the time argued hopefully that people would no longer be willing to accept the injustices of the traditional class system after the sacrifices of the war.[14] When, however, Tietjens reflects that 'today the world changed. Feudalism was finished; its last vestiges were gone' (1950: 668), he articulates a sense of regret. While the levelling tendency associated with modern trench warfare *can* be seen to have an egalitarian side, this same development in modern warfare can alternately be read – as Tietjens reads it – as a figure for the reification of modern bourgeois life.

Due to the disappearance of the social harmony and the static, hierarchical equilibrium associated with the earlier 'organic' society, all motives appear rationalised into personal grasping for power. In feudal times, according to this schema, relations of power were well enough defined that people could live happily in their stations. Were problems to arise, there existed straightforward face-to-face ways of dealing with them. In modern society, however, those boundaries have lost definition and people (like MacMaster and Edith Ethel) feel encouraged by the system selfishly to get whatever they can for themselves. A kind of social Darwinist struggle for supremacy results from this destabilisation of the traditional social stasis, the biggest losers potentially being the lowest classes, traditionally in the 'care' of the aristocracy but now left on their own. The winners who emerge from this struggle are those whose insensitivity and rapaciousness allow them to overpower, in whatever opportunistic way necessary, anything or anyone that stands in their way. In such a social world, only the strong survive, and a moral code based on idealistic notions of *noblesse oblige* simply does not work under these conditions. Tietjens, with his highly developed sense of principled conduct, becomes, of course, one of the losers. As he loses the struggle for social power – too much of a gentleman even to struggle overtly – he loses as well his power to narrate, and his authoritative account and interpretation of events gradually dissolves.

Much of the thematic tension in the novel is a result of these two strands of interpretive possibility regarding modern history – the ultimately Utopian democratisation of modern society on one side, and the ultimately dystopian reification and rationalisation of modern society on the other. If Tietjens most often represents the latter position, Valentine might be said to represent to some degree the former. Significantly, she shares with Tietjens the position of focaliser on Armistice Day. As *A Man Could Stand Up* opens, Valentine's thoughts and actions reveal a certain apprehension about the future but also a youthful hope:

> She was not going to show respect for any Lady Anything ever again . . . . She was never going to show respect for anyone ever again. She had been through the mill: the whole world had been through the mill! No more respect! . . . No more respect! Was that to be a lasting effect of the cataclysm that had involved the world?   (1950: 506, 509)

Her reiteration of the phrase 'No more respect' echoes, of course, Tietjens's even more frequent reiteration of 'No more parades'. While her morning begins with the duty of maintaining order in a group of six hundred young women – a further ironic reference, perhaps, to the ever-present parallel idea of the male military parade – it ends with her rejection of any such role in school discipline. Her refusal of this form of discipline is juxtaposed with Tietjens's lament for its passing. 'It isn't what I *want* – to be a cross between a sergeant in the army and an upper housemaid' (1950: 540). But if she sees potential for positive social change in the unrest of the war's end, she also observes in the reaction of many the fear of another kind of social upheaval resulting from this historical rupture:

> A quite definite fear. If, at this parting of the ways, at this crack across the table of History, the School – the World, the future mothers of Europe – got out of hand, would they ever come back? The Authorities – Authority all over the world – was afraid of that; more afraid of that than of any other thing. Wasn't it a possibility that there was to be no more Respect? None for constituted Authority and consecrated Experience? . . . You had to keep them – the girls, the populace, everybody! – in hand now, for once you let go there was no knowing where They . . . mightn't carry You.   (1950: 510–11)

The patriarchal structures of the social world seem on the point of disintegration. Echoing Tietjens once again, she realises that 'All the unthinkable sorts of things' might happen, and 'So it was indeed the World Turned Upside Down' (1950: 511). But while Tietjens is not so sanguine about the prospect of social change, for Valentine this historical change represents a potential release from intolerable social restrictions.[15]

These restrictions are indeed temporarily abandoned on Armistice Day in a carnivalesque moment as Valentine joins in a celebration with Tietjens, his fellow-soldiers and the women who accompany them, a celebration that crosses class boundaries and even suggests a transgression of sexual taboos:

An officer, yelling like an enraged Redskin, dealt [Tietjens] an immense blow behind the shoulder-blades. He staggered, smiling, into the centre of the room. An officer gently pushed [Valentine] into the centre of the room. She was against him. Khaki encircled them. They began to yell and to prance, joining hands. Others waved bottles and smashed underfoot the glasses. Gypsies break glasses at their weddings. The bed was against the wall . . . . The whole world round them was yelling and prancing round. They were the centre of unending roaring circles.   (1950: 673)

This moment stands as the antithesis of Tietjens's idealised orderly parade ritual. The references to Gypsies and Redskins refer to 'inferior' races in order to posit a transgression, a shift from the higher to the lower in a Bakhtinian sense.[16] The violence of the moment is the culmination, in a sense, of the disorderly and disordering violence of the war itself which produced similar effects in Tietjens's burial dislocation and Sylvia's transgressive loss of identity. Because of the war, writes Ford elsewhere, 'The sense of values has changed completely . . . . One has grown sentimental incredibly, coarse in a great measure, hungry, thirsty, loud voiced. The pleasures of the drawing room are unknown & not at all valued' (Longenbach, 1984: 164). Indulging in unrestrained revelry with members of lower classes, celebrating in a manner not befitting the upper class, the suggestion of extra-marital sexuality: this is the world upside down for Tietjens and Valentine, and it is precisely at this point that Tietjens finally loses his position as privileged narrator, as the central subject of the tetralogy and of history. The unthinkable has been realised, and for Tietjens the world is forever changed.

In the final volume Tietjens is literally an absent centre. His position and authority had been based on a general acceptance of a certain set of social relations, and in the post-war era they had become untenable outside that set of relations. Of course this result has been developing throughout the tetralogy; the Armistice celebration is merely the dramatic culmination of a long process. Ann Snitow writes that at the outset, Tietjens's 'blood and land and absolute rectitude all entitle him to look down on everybody he encounters. Indeed his snobbery about niggers, Jews, bounders, foreigners, other ranks, decadent gentlemen, aspiring Scots, and society beauties is his birth-right' (1984: 208). By the last volume, however, Tietjens's attitude seems rather altered. In terms of the novel itself, this process has taken only a few years: before the war

Tietjens's upper class authority appears more or less unassailable; at the war's end he is, in a sense, ruined. That Ford is, in fact, telescoping a much larger historical transition into a short period is clear from the allusions to Tietjens as fundamentally an eighteenth- or even seventeenth-century man. While Ford's teleological structure culminates in the social upheaval of the period during and after World War I, the historical decline of upper-class authority to which he alludes actually transpired over a much longer time.

Last Post, the concluding volume of the tetralogy, responds to questions concerning the post-war social power structure in a way that later satisfied neither Ford himself nor some subsequent readers and editors.[17] Rather than continuing the diachronic narration of the earlier volumes, Ford presents a synchronic picture, 'a slice of one of Christopher's later days' as he calls it (Hynes, 1970: 527), although Tietjens is not in fact present through most of the volume. This cross-section of a day may lack the narrative tension provided by the earlier volumes, but it deserves attention none the less for its ambitious attempt to elaborate a model of post-war England, an England whose traditional community structures had been irrevocably damaged by the fact of modern war. Had Ford not continued beyond the carnivalesque, almost apocalyptic, ending of the third volume, all the historical and social contradictions would have been left dissolved in the taxonomic chaos of the Armistice celebration, a real but necessarily transitory moment of apparent abandonment of social division. History, however, cannot stop there. However much the social world is subverted by the moment of the carnivalesque, it is inevitably a moment after which some kind of order must be restored, and it is the burden of *Last Post* to render a representation of the emergent social order. If the final volume of the tetralogy is not wholly successful – neither aesthetically nor sociologically – the magnitude of the task attempted may perhaps mitigate to some extent the reader's sense of disappointment. Still, it does seem as though the process by which Tietjens's narrative has lost the power to compel assent affected his author as well.

While narrative authority is focused largely on Tietjens in the earlier volumes – with some space given to Valentine as well – in the final volume narrative authority is fractured so that no single character or perspective dominates. The multiplicity of narrative points of view could, in fact, be seen as a reversion on Ford's part to his earlier plan to present a comprehensive range of points of view. Nevertheless, it is not (as Valentine's thoughts or the carnivalesque celebration may have suggested) the end of all social order or the World Turned Upside Down. Nor is it the inauguration of the heteroglossic and democratic republic of discourse. After the war a new – or at least a significantly altered – order seemed to be emerging from the ashes of the old, and it was of great importance to Ford to find what continuity he could in his narrative of socio-historical change. As James Longenbach writes, 'Like many of the great modernist writers, Ford felt that the war had severed the modern world from its past' (1984: 150). In *Parade's End* this historical rupture is registered, for instance, in Tietjens's memory loss which 'becomes a synecdoche for the historical memory loss which Ford felt the war had impressed upon the mind of Europe' (Longenbach, 1984: 155). Yet the transition is not without some social continuity.

The first perspective encountered in the final volume is that of the upper classes, the same perspective that was introduced as the point of reference at the beginning of the tetralogy as well. Just as that earlier appearance in the railway car emphasised the solidity of their power ('Their class administered the world'), the later situation draws attention to the apparent waning of that power. Tietjens's dying elder brother Mark has resolved to remain silent and immobile, apparently moribund like the social world – the *sensus communis* – he exemplifies. While Christopher is struggling to adapt to the new situation, Mark's immobility represents his refusal or inability to respond to the altered social world. He has abdicated his social authority, and although his thoughts and impressions continue, they are without effect on those around him due to his refusal of all communication. Having once dominated it, he is now no longer a part of the discursive community, the public sphere. Sylvia, another member of this class, similarly realises that her way of life is almost played out and considers joining General Campion and going to India where, she feels, her style of aristocratic imperialism is still a viable possibility. The condition of modernity which has driven them from their position of authority in England, has, presumably, not yet arrived in the colonies where something like a feudal social structure could be maintained and aristocrats who had become anachronisms in their own land could thrive. Christopher's choice to stay and adapt rather than to leave in search of a premodern world suggests his continuing symbolic importance to the novel in spite of his absence from it at this point.

But if the representation of upper-class life is marked by historical discontinuity, at the other end of the social scale some stability remains. The portrait of the peasantry constitutes a form of exclusion by bestialisation that insists on the continuance of a strong sense of social distinction, a sense of hierarchy undiminished by the levelling experience of the trenches. Gunning is stupid and has 'overlong, hairy arms' that contribute to his 'gorilla-like' appearance (1950: 677). Cramp, the cabinet-maker, is described as 'a remnant of the little dark persistent race that once had peopled Sussex' (1950: 705), and his voice is represented in the heteroglossia as a picturesque rural dialect: "Ard! Thet cider was 'arder than a miser's 'art or 'n ole maid's tongue' (1950: 678). By implication then, the accents of the upper classes become normative, and this bracketing off of the speech of the peasants through written dialect has a marginalising effect, reinforcing the quaintness of what they say by the diction and accent they betray when they say it.

It seems, in a sense, as though Mark Tietjens's refusal of discourse opens the space for peasant speech, creating a sort of discursive vacuum that must be filled. Gunning and Hogben[18] are drawn into that vacuum, and their conversation is, in fact, a parody of the discourse of administrative authority that Mark must once have dominated. In contrast to what we know about Mark's administrative acumen, however, the representation of their territorial dispute makes clear the stupidity that relieves us from having to take the peasants seriously. Furthermore, it makes a mockery of the very real disillusion felt by many of the lower classes and the political left at the inegalitarian social situation that persisted in Britain after the war: 'The war', Gunning and Hogben (a gentlemen's bailiff and a tenant farmer respectively) agree, 'ought to have given tenant-farmers the complete powers of local tyrants; it should have done the same for gentlemen's bailiffs' (1950: 709). The passage ends with a reference to a 'sow grunt[ing] round Gunning's boots'. If there is a sense that, for better or for worse, the traditional rulers can no longer maintain their position in the postwar world, there is certainly no sense that the lower classes are even moderately prepared to step out of their swinish boots in order to fill those shoes by taking on political responsibility.

A broader awareness of the realities of power is briefly demonstrated in a comment that is not ascribed to any one person but seems to issue, as it were, from the general mind of the peasantry. In the midst of an adulatory discussion of what constitutes 'the real Quality' in the upper classes, a peasant says that 'The Quality ought to be told' (1950: 708) about what was going on at Tietjens's house. There are discursive obstacles to this kind of cross-class communication, however:

> But you do not speak to the Quality. Better if they do not notice you. You never know. They sticks together . . . . Queer things the gentry can do to you still if they notice you. It is all very well to say that this is a land fit for whatever the word is that stands for simple folk. They have the police and the keepers in their hands and your cottages and livings. (1950: 708).

This almost furtive insight into the coercive side of hegemony – whether feudal or capitalist – points toward the possibility of a critical position taking into account the perspective of the lower classes, but it is never developed further and the peasants disappear soon after voicing it, leaving behind the trace of a break in their aphasic condition that sounds for a moment then fades. And, in fact, there is something in the phrase 'simple folk', as well as in much of the conversation and behaviour of the peasants presented here, that suggests that these quaint 'simple folks' *are* in need of a certain amount of benign hierarchic protection. Their ignorance of a word other than 'simple folk' in the dominant discourse that designates them as a class indicates their lack of taxonomic and discursive as well as social authority. Do they think of themselves as simple? Or is this the category bestowed on them by the gentry?

In any case, this brief, but complex – anything but 'simple' – moment indicates the breadth of the gulf that separates these language groups, demonstrating how far they are from any substantial dialogic engagement. In this encounter, Ford almost paradoxically enacts a form of symbolic violence (Bourdieu) or discursive terror (Lyotard) by marginalising these characters while simultaneously calling attention momentarily to the fact that this representational violence or terror is routinely inflicted upon them. In lifting the veil of their aphasia for a moment, Ford makes it possible for the reader to sense (as Bakhtin puts it) the way that heteroglossia can wash over the dominant discourse of a novel – even to the extent that Tietjens's earlier argument about the superiority of feudal direct action over the modern ballot box, takes on a new appearance in light of the reference to the coercive force of the gentry. Whatever challenges face the social structure and threaten to destabilise it, there is no sense here that the lower classes have anything to contribute to the debate.

The contest, in the end, is represented as a hegemonic struggle between two groups – the old gentry on the one hand and the 'upwardly-mobile' *nouveau riche* on the other – whose relation to power and capital has undergone an alteration. The lower classes by and large remain dominated and respectful, for the most part without an independent voice.[19] And when they do speak in this pastoral final volume, it is as country bumpkins, rustics generally as devoid of political awareness as of intelligence. The total exclusion of the 'Other Ranks' both from power and from any legitimate claim to a voice is registered in Armstrong's response to Ford's representative occlusion of a large proportion of the social spectrum. In retiring from the sphere of political power,

Mark has given up the struggle. But his proud silence asserts his ascendancy over the political arena he has disdainfully abandoned. With Mark's retirement, *Parade's End* rejects an institutional solution to the social ills of Britain. If the game defeats a player of Mark's stature, or at least forces him to withdraw, social reform on a grand scale does not seem possible.

(Armstrong, 1987: 258–9)

This reading may be justifiable within the text of the tetralogy, but it tacitly affirms the idea that only the rich and well-educated can be players in the game. It implies that the reforms that were on the horizon at this time – an end to child labour, universal access to at least minimal education and health care, universal suffrage and so on – were either unimportant or actually marks of yet further decline from the lofty standards of old Tory England. In a sense, Ford's 'comprehensive' cross-sectional representation of social totality in *Last Post* makes this response possible by eliding the large (and, in part, well-organised and articulate) urban and industrial sections of the working classes and all those who spoke on their behalf. One way of dealing with jarring witnesses is simply to refuse to recognise their existence. Even if the social changes that were introduced around this time are seen as essentially cosmetic, tactical alterations allowing the system itself to remain fundamentally intact, the wholesale exclusion of the participation of the 'Other Ranks' in this representation of the political and cultural process is notable as is the use of only the rural peasantry to represent those 'Other Classes'.

The closeness to members of the 'Other Classes' that Tietjens experiences in the trenches leads to the carnivalesque party on Armistice Day, but the longer-term results of this shoulder-rubbing across class lines should not be overestimated. The picture of life after the war shows Tietjens brought down a notch, but hardly hobnobbing with the peasants. Optimistic readings emphasising the way a new and more egalitarian Tietjens grows in stature ignore to some degree the marked limitations which persist. Thus Armstrong argues that 'Christopher learns that to be in society means to confront across one's horizons manifestations of otherness which defy total management' (1987: 237). Armstrong's acceptance of the implicit positing of a previous or even original state of 'total management' is itself problematic. Furthermore, Tietjens's coping with those manifestations of otherness seem, in the end, to amount to having to work in partnership with Valentine (whom he loves, but who *is* a woman), having to deal with a Jew in the antique business, and indeed being forced to *earn* a living at all. Tietjens's fear about life after the war appears, in a sense, to be fulfilled: 'what was he, Tietjens, going to do! Take orders! It was unthinkable' (1950: 567). In one of the final scenes in the tetralogy, Valentine seems, in fact, to be ordering him around.

The change in Tietjens is neither as radical nor as final as Green argues: 'Although at the beginning of *Parade's End* Tietjens is so closely attached to the loyalties and customs of his own class, by the end of *A Man Could Stand Up* he has transcended them' (1981: 144). While he may, as Ford puts it, have 'outgrown alike the mentality and traditions of his own family and his own race' (1950: 752), this still does not necessarily mean any more than that he has moved, and very painfully at that, from the upper classes to the ranks of the upper-middle classes – and taken the point of view of the novel with him. The degree of Tietjens's actual social transcendence, a transcendence asserted in the text and generally accepted by critics, seems somewhat qualified by such observations as that 'for a little, shivering artistic Jew' such as his new business partner, Tietjens 'was quite capable of feeling a real fondness – as you might for an animal'. In the end, this hardly seems the radical or existential shift it is sometimes made out to be.[20] It is greatly overestimating this transformation to suggest, as Armstrong does, that Tietjens's change of employment from statistician to antique dealer represents evidence of real growth:

> If statistics suggested to Tietjens hermeneutic certainty, timeless truth, and causal logic, then a different, nonreified cluster of implications is associated with his work in antiques: the subjective divination of value, meaning unfolding in history, objects as the embodiment of human creation and social practice. Tietjens's abandonment of numbers for furniture represents an epistemological shift from the positivistic quest for fact to the hermeneutic explication of meaning and value.   (1987: 243)

A less mystified interpretation is that as an antique dealer, Tietjens is simply exchanging his cultural capital for money, both trading on his refined taste and literally selling off some of the heirlooms of his family and of other members of his class, who presumably are also not doing as well in the modern post-war world. By the end of the novel, Tietjens has lost the position of authority that traditionally had guaranteed automatically the legitimacy of his social position, and he is reduced to trading in the market-place, making a living from his enormous cultural (and limited financial) capital.[21]

A doxa, based on the limited and subjective experience of a few powerful people, shifts in the course of Parade's End into orthodoxy, the possibility that there may be other points of view demanding dialogic engagement. A disadvantage of this new dialogic situation, Armstrong writes, is that 'resentment and conflict become possible and even likely as soon as mutual understanding cannot be simply assumed' (1987: 248). But a mutual understanding that has been based on the world-view of the select group of the most powerful people in a society – Bradley's weightiest interests – is surely mutual in only a very qualified sense. It is naïve to suggest that when this hegemonic structure is modified in this way there might be no rules left at all governing delegation of authority within the institutions of social order and hierarchy; yet, Armstrong continues, without 'a stable social hierarchy to establish structures of dominance and subordination, everyone is potentially equal' (1987: 249). This would lead to the conclusion that because Tietjens has at one point to take an order from a military inferior ('unthinkable'), there is no longer any appreciable difference between Tietjens, with his heritage of privilege and wealth going back generations, and the colliers with whom he shares the trenches. It may at times seem that way to Tietjens who now experiences modernity as a bewildering dissolution of the certainties of his social stature, but on the other side, one may doubt whether the colliers or Cockneys, the 'Other Ranks' and other races, felt themselves as privileged as the gentry on the basis of this social upheaval. Indeed, the momentary glimpse the novel affords into the discursive community of the peasants clearly suggests otherwise.

Similarly, because Tietjens's relationship to Valentine demonstrates an increased equality within a context defined by rigid gender roles, one ought not to use this as an indication of the end of the patriarchal social structures that guarantee the marked inequality of the sexes – either potentially or in practice. Like the fleeting insight, articulated by the anonymous peasant, into the coercive apparatus of state power, the feminist critique that appears from time to time in the novel constitutes another oppositional strategy that, although powerful, remains fundamentally underdeveloped. Nevertheless, more than any other element in the tetralogy perhaps, this position – and some of the women who represent it – constitutes the single most significant sociohistorical change represented in the tetralogy. Not only is Valentine accorded the authority to narrate, but so is Marie-Leonie. Nevertheless, while early in the novel suffragettes are beginning to cause trouble in masculine strongholds such as the golf course, the rise of feminism is not finally addressed by Ford as a major issue. Sylvia, at one point during the war, reflects:

These horrors, these infinities of pain, this atrocious condition of the world, had been brought about in order that men should indulge themselves in orgies of promiscuity . . . . That in the end was at the bottom of male honour, of male virtue, observance of treaties, upholding of the flag . . . . An immense warlock's carnival of appetites, lusts, ebrieties . . . . These men talked of these things that occupied them there with the lust of men telling dirty stories in smoking rooms.   (1950: 438–9)

Despite some rhetorical power here, Sylvia is not presented as – in Bradley's terms – a reliable witness.[22] Nevertheless the mere fact of presenting aspects of a feminist perspective in three very different women – Gertie, Valentine and Sylvia – and a strong independent presence in Marie-Leonie, suggests the potential for a critical position that is not fully realised in the tetralogy. Had Ford developed it more fully, in the post-war narrative there might have been a position solid enough to augment or even take the place of Tietjens's earlier critique from the point of view of the obsolete Tory, a position whose critical relevance seems diminished towards the conclusion of the novel. And this erosion of a critical ground that is not reclaimed may, to some degree, account for the inferiority some critics have observed in this final volume.

The feminist and peasant insights remain undeveloped, perhaps, because the novel's 'comprehensive' history *is* inextricably tied to Tietjens's 'comprehensive' consciousness, a consciousness that is not finally so all-embracing. Tietjens is a victim not only of historical change, but also of the limitations of his own ideology. It is because of this that Ford's choice of extinct Toryism as his critical vantage point on modern history, leaves him ultimately with no focused position from which either to sustain a social critique or to suggest an alternative to an historical direction with which he was clearly not pleased. Ford establishes Tietjens's authority and integrity firmly in the opening pages, then demonstrates how it is undermined gradually throughout the rest of the novel. The omniscience that allows him to correct from memory the errors in the *Encyclopaedia Britannica* (1950: 10) ultimately deserts him, leaving him, in fact, dependent on the *Encyclopaedia Britannica* as a source of information. His financial position deteriorates, his view of gender hierarchy alters through his relationship with Valentine, and even the parades, whose passing he laments, are finally (at least implicitly) recognised as belonging to the world of General Campion and a moribund imperialism. Ford represents the transition to twentieth-century modernity as a contradictory combination of social decline mingled with a slight and very tentative sense of hope and openness manifested in the characterisations of Marie-Leonie and Valentine, who (like Gunning and Hogben) come to occupy some of the critical discursive space left vacant in the significant absence of their respective spouses, Mark and Christopher.

There is a strong sense of social equilibrium in the opening of the novel. While troubles are beginning to loom on the horizon, Ford uses Edwardian society, at least superficially, almost as an Eden whose fall has already begun. The causes of that fall Ford locates most particularly within the irresponsible behaviour of the dominant class itself; indeed, the dissolution of 'Tory England' that was occurring at the time of the war seems, in this representation of the history, to be entirely unconnected to any social or historical forces from below such as working class unrest or colonial resistance within the empire. The immense social transformation that Ford represents through Tietjens and his circle of acquaintances does not seem to have any relevance at all to the lower classes. Nor is it seen to stem from the inherent contradictions built into the social structure itself. While there does seem to be some temporary shift in the status quo in the trenches, it is due to the fact that Tietjens is being brought down, not because the lower classes are rising any higher. Tietjens's social 'others' seem to present a stable and stationary background against which his downward social mobility is traced.

The descriptions of the other ranks and other races that Tietjens deals with often condescend to them, present them as lower in nature, a strategy whereby such classes of people are denied a full voice as historical subjects, as historical agents, or as historical narrators. Ford's containment of social heterodoxy even extends so far as to have oppositional positions presented (and thus, in a sense, diffused) by members of Tietjens's own circle. Valentine, for instance, somewhat in the manner of *Nostromo's* Emilia Gould, becomes a voice for the dispossessed early in the novel, at one point even indicating an admiration for Rosa Luxemburg (1950: 120). Another source of such social ideals is introduced towards the end – Mark Jr. even flirts with the 'Marxian communism' fashionable, Ford ironically points out, 'in his set at Cambridge' (1950: 716). Radical political voices, then, are located within the elite group of the upper-class, not beyond, and those positions are not presented with a great deal of seriousness. Both Valentine and Mark Jr. are young and well-intentioned, but their radicalism seems merely a stage they will ultimately grow out of. Indeed, there is not much evidence in the final volume of the radicalism Valentine espoused in the first.[23]

The problem is not so much that this is unrealistic – some young men and women in England coming from the ranks of the most powerful and privileged *have* adopted radical social positions, and in a comprehensive novel about the historical transformation of the nation, it is arguably important to represent them. On the other hand, there is something very limited about restricting the representation of an oppositional point of view to these young and privileged people; it is a rather significant omission to leave out all voices of working-class agitation that led to many of the social changes that the novel is attempting to represent. In pointing to the omission of these jarring voices from Ford's orchestration of social heteroglossia, I do not mean to suggest that the tetralogy is uncritical in its presentation of the social world. Like much modernism, in fact, it is highly critical of that system, but in locating its critical perspective in the mind of Tietjens, who supports pre-capitalist feudal values, Ford in a single move opens up a space for a radical social critique and closes off and contains that space by locating it in an anachronistic and historically dubious sense of benign but absolute social distinction. The critique that seemed initially to offer a radical perspective in the end resolves into an orthodox position. At the same time, any demand to take seriously the more relevant or influential critical positions of his time is pre-empted and defused by Tietjens's 'more radical than the radicals' posture.[24]

Because of Ford's reluctance or inability to grant any independent narrative authority to the 'Other Ranks' – whether by the significant inclusion in the novel of a spokesperson for that perspective, or more simply by alluding to its historical existence – the set of historical possibilities that opens through his analysis of the increasingly democratic or egalitarian nature of modern society, remains curtailed. While we are shown the implosion and collapse of the ideology supporting the old ruling class at a number of points, this social movement does not even seem to be supported by the dominated classes themselves. The workers and tradesmen with whom Tietjens interacts, as well as the soldiers in his command, are all full of respect and admiration for him. When Tietjens knows more about the cabman's horse than the cabman himself, and is then admired for it by the appreciative worker (1950: 11), or when, a few pages later, he jumps on the train under the admiring gaze of the good-natured stationmaster (1950: 22), these examples are meant to demonstrate both the degree to which Tietjens is worthy of the authority that is naturally, it seems, conferred on him, and the harmonious social atmosphere that results from all the members of society contenting themselves with their 'proper' stations. Again, while it is not perhaps historically untrue to say that there were men like Tietjens who were respected and obeyed unquestioningly by their social inferiors, neither is it the 'whole story'. The hegemony exercised by the gentry and aristocracy in the seventeenth and eighteenth centuries was, of course, neither as natural nor as spontaneous as Ford's initial use of Tietjens as a normative figure would seem to indicate. Nor was it as harmonious as this representation might suggest. It was, to use Gramsci's definition of hegemony, a variable combination of consent and coercion; and while it might, in retrospect, be attractive to lessen the coercive element and preserve a nostalgic image of harmonious consent, this remains a very partial representation.[25] Yet at the outset of *Parade's End* the original authority of the dominant class, exemplified in Tietjens (and his brother Mark), is represented as natural, self-evident, apparently well-deserved, historically proven and beyond challenge.

In the end, as Eric Meyer points out, 'Tietjens' real adversary is historical process, and his attempts to reimpose the formal coherency of an earlier world is futile' (1990: 86). In spite of the informing vision of seventeenth-century or even feudal life-style and social structure, in spite of the attempt to retreat to a pastoral life in the final volume, it is impossible finally for Tietjens to escape the set of historical possibilities that results from the increasing reification, rationalisation and bureaucratisation of modern bourgeois life, its crass commercialisation and commodification of spheres of life that once were his sources of real value. But since Tietjens is the centre of the novel, since it is Tietjens and those he represents who are seen as the victims of history, the effects – positive or negative – of the transition to modern capitalism on the rest of the population are left more or less unexamined. Tietjens himself is at least partially left in retreat from modern life, attempting to escape to a pastoral idyll – an anachronism that Ford exposes by having modern life relentlessly intrude on the rural retreat, but one to which he proposes no real alternative. Ford locates his Utopian impulse in a nostalgia for an historical past that arguably never existed (the happy feudal system, organic society, stable hierarchy), and which is certainly unattainable in the twentieth century. Paul B. Rich argues that in spite of the enormous transformation of the economic and social structures related to increasing urbanisation between the wars, the British right tended to cling to traditional class ideals and codes of behaviour based on 'a provincial sense of social hierarchy and place'. This 'nostalgia for a way of life that seemed to be passing' can be seen as part of the invention of the

'myth community' in English social thought [which has] served as a vital buttress to an ideology of rusticity that contained a vision of an English patriotism. It served as a means for neutralising a conception of class warfare and emphasising the homogeneous nature of English society rooted in small town and village life, and spreading up through the shires and counties to that of central government and the organs of national power. (1989: 37)

Neither the desire for a homogeneous society nor the fascination with parades disappeared from the social life of Britain or of the continent after the war, however. In fact, they made something of a comeback in the inter-war years in a way that took advantage of the nostalgia for a purer sense of community. Tietjens's lament over the disappearance of parades seems to be answered by another (though far less benign) man, who attempted to forge a unified sense of social purpose by means of a modern revival of the ideology of (para)military parades in Britain a few years later: Oswald Mosely. Citing a passage from Baudelaire which describes soldiers 'marching like a single animal, a proud image of joy and obedience', Marshall Berman notes that these same soldiers had not long before killed 25,000 Parisians (June 1848), and that Baudelaire himself had fought against them (1982: 137). One ought not underestimate

the tremendous importance of military display – psychological as well as political importance – and its power to captivate even the freest spirits. Armies on parade, from Baudelaire's time to our own, play a central role in the pastoral vision of modernity: glittering hardware, gaudy colors, flowing lines, fast and graceful movements, modernity without tears. (1982: 137)

Berman defines pastoral here as a social vision which neglects the darker potentialities of its economic and political drives (1982: 135), and here we can glimpse something of the way that the nostalgia for hierarchy, communal myth and ritual felt by many modernists, when combined with the historical forces that neither Tietjens nor Ford could hold back, such as modern technology and the political and economic disorder of a later decade, could lead to the fascist aestheticisation of politics described by Walter Benjamin. By means of such rituals of power on display as the military parade, fascism gives the 'masses not their right, but the chance to express themselves' (Benjamin: 1969, 243) while preserving the social hierarchy, promoting patriotism and some version of a homogeneous society.

Ford's disclaimer notwithstanding, some versions of Tory England's *sensus communis* with all its snobberies and privileges still existed as an ideology in his time, indeed still persist today, even if in modified forms. Tietjens, as a symbol of a social class or a social ideology, is wholly neither extinct nor wholly irrelevant, nor is he in a position to offer an objective overview.[26] To accept Tietjens as a historical consciousness in general (Walsh), to lament his passage from the (hegemonic) centre of British life, entails at least the tacit acceptance of the socially constructed and enforced aphasia that long made this monopoly on narrative authority possible. The historical and social changes brought about by the objective social crisis associated with the war clearly altered some boundaries of social discourse, but *Parade's End* struggles to keep orthodox limits in place.

5

Absalom, Absalom!: The 'nigger in the woodpile'

In an interview, Faulkner once asserted that in the South 'there is still a common acceptance of the world, a common view of life, a common morality' (1968b: 72).[1] As Faulkner uses it here, the meaning of the word 'common' is surely a restricted one, the *sensus communis* referred to having certain limits – tacit or otherwise. Around the middle of *Absalom, Absalom!* when the scene first shifts to Harvard and the North, Quentin's identity as a Southerner places him in the position of respondent to questions about the South. *'Tell about the South. What's it like there. What do they do there. Why do they live there. Why do they live at all'* (1971: 143). These are large questions to be sure. Who can legitimately claim the authority to speak for the South, to answer for the community? Who, in fact, has the authority to define what constitutes membership in this community and where its boundaries lie? In an attempt to address these questions historically, the several narrators of *Absalom, Absalom!* (Rosa, Mr Compson, Shreve and, most importantly, Quentin himself) construct various representations of the historical essence of the South. This aspect of the novel has been noted by many critics, and Michael Millgate's response is not atypical: Quentin, 'a young, intelligent Southerner about to leave the homeland . . . seems an appropriate repository for a story which they . . . dimly recognize as embodying some quintessential and symbolic relationship to the whole Southern experience' (1966: 155). Millgate goes on to suggest that the Sutpen story is 'an exceptionally rapid and concentrated version of the history of virtually all Southern families' (1966: 157). As is the case with *Nostromo*, and *Parade's End*, there are

many such statements in the literature on *Absalom, Absalom!*
which suggest the comprehensive social scope of the novel.[2]
The answers offered in the novel to questions posed by Southern historical experience, however, are necessarily constrained by
formal problems of point of view and its attendant restrictions,
restrictions that are further defined by the epistemological and
cultural limits of an orthodox modernism. This orthodoxy registers the loss of doxic certainty associated with traditional cultural
patterns; yet while positing no stable centre, it resists the
potentially further destabilising cultural implications of heteroglossia. In one sense it could hardly be suggested that Quentin
Compson (and his co-narrators) provides the novel with any
degree of epistemological or historiographical stability; yet if no
final guarantee of narratorial authority is presented in the novel,
neither is the gate thrown open to all perspectives that might claim
a voice in a discussion of the history of the South. Since no single
point of view is fully privileged in the novel, it is important to
examine the range of attribution of historiographic authority and
the boundaries beyond which it does not occur. Such narratorial
limits are an important aspect of *Absalom, Absalom!*'s social
taxonomy and *sensus communis*.

Given the deep racial divisions which characterise American
history, and in particular Southern history, the problem of
narrative perspective in historiography is inevitably disturbing.
For centuries, the institution of slavery was made possible
precisely by an absolute denial on the part of the dominant white
community, of the authority and legitimacy of the voices of slaves.
The slave narratives – Frederick Douglass's being the most
influential – are replete with examples of slaves who attempted to
assert authority over their own lives and, through the narratives
themselves, over the language. This denial, which in an extreme
form constitutes a denial of the very humanity of the slave, made
possible the exclusion of African–Americans from any kind of
community with whites which was not ultimately defined and
controlled by the latter. Since the Emancipation Proclamation
legally freed the slaves, the problem has unfortunately continued
in various forms due to the fact that community cannot simply be
legislated but must be accepted at a far deeper level and such
acceptance was not forthcoming. In any case, from the Jim Crow
era to the Rodney King incident, the law can often be seen to

respond to the same pressures and weighty interests as historiography. From the colonial period to the present, African–
American political, cultural and literary history provides abun-
dant evidence that the dominant community, which possesses
better access to the instruments and institutions of discursive
power, can claim normative – even universal – status for its own
particular narrative perspective to the exclusion of the competing,
perhaps incommensurable, narratives of other communities.
Those marginalised narratives, which are by contrast made to
seem merely 'local', then exist in a state of dubious legitimacy,
idiosyncracy and eccentricity.

Who speaks for the South, for Southern history? The question of
voice is central to *Absalom, Absalom!*, and that centrality is
underscored both by its presentation throughout the novel as the
medium of narration, and by the initial description of the
evocative power of Rosa's voice. Her narrative voice is repeatedly
described in the first two pages: 'talking in that grim haggard
amazed voice', '[h]er voice would not cease', 'the voice not
ceasing', 'as if it were the voice which he haunted' (1971: 5–6).
One effect of this voice's narration is to establish in the listener's
(Quentin's or the reader's) mind images corresponding to the
images of the narrative, images having a compelling reality of their
own: 'until at last listening would renege and hearing-sense self-
confound and the long-dead object of her . . . frustration would
appear . . . out of the biding and dreamy and victorious dust'
(1971: 5). In Faulkner's description of the effect of Rosa's
monologue on Quentin's imagination, there is a sense that her
narration virtually makes the historical reality come into existence, a performative speech act that confers the authority of
reality on the events that she describes:

Then in the long unamaze Quentin seemed to watch them overrun suddenly
the hundred square miles of tranquil and astonished earth and drag house and
formal gardens violently out of the soundless Nothing and clap them down like
cards upon a table . . . creating the Sutpen's Hundred, the *Be Sutpen's Hundred*
like the oldentime *Be Light*.   (1971: 6)

There is a double sense of creation in this passage: if Sutpen's
creation of Sutpen's Hundred has something of the *ex nihilo* about
it, so does Rosa's recreation in Quentin's mind of that historical
event. In any case, the historical past depends for its continued

existence and transmission on the power of narration and in *Absalom, Absalom!* that power is considerable.

Rosa has, of course, spent years writing a version of the history of the old South in poetry, attempting to preserve an obsolete image of a previous social structure. It is her desire that Quentin do something similar: 'maybe some day you will remember this and write about it ... and submit it to the magazines' (1971: 7). Whether or not the story gets written (of course it does, in a sense – by Faulkner if not by Quentin), it is clear that this history is seen as a legacy that must be passed on. This epic telling of the story of the South is history in the grand style – describing the founding of a society and its ultimate destruction all under the watchful eye of God (Rosa asks rhetorically, ' "Is it any wonder that Heaven saw fit to let us lose?" ' (1971: 16)). There are complex genealogies, battles, larger-than-life characters, a broad social canvas – all of which convey a whole world-view which is in the process of crumbling with that generation.

Almost by definition, the epic does not reflect too deeply on its own narrative stability. Yet from the outset, as it was in *Nostromo*, the narrative stability of epic history in *Absalom, Absalom!* is undermined and relativised through the use of multiple narrators, most of whom reflect self-consciously on the tenuous nature of their grasp of the material they are narrating. In fact, the narrative situates itself initially by reference to the gap that exists between the narrator (Rosa) and the listener (Quentin), or alternatively in the gap between two Quentins, a gap which reiterates the former but remains none the less ultimately insupportable in epic historical discourse. As he listens to Rosa, there seem to be

two separate Quentins now – the Quentin Compson preparing for Harvard in the South, the deep South dead since 1865 and people with garrulous outraged baffled ghosts, listening, having to listen, to one of the ghosts ... and the Quentin Compson who was still too young to deserve yet to be a ghost, but nevertheless having to be one for all that, since he was born and bred in the deep South the same as she was – the two separate Quentins now. (1971: 6)

This kind of split would be unthinkable within a unified epic consciousness. None the less, in Rosa's position may be seen a kind of residual doxa, a position which permits the epic to continue after the fall of the culture from which it arose. The historical gap that separates Quentin from Rosa (or from the Rosa in himself) is the cultural gap that signals a generic division of epic and modern novel, and further, the shift from doxa to orthodoxy. Quentin's divided modern consciousness here exemplifies Bourdieu's sense of the orthodox condition as one in which tacit faith is no longer available yet remains the point of orientation.

The epic is a good example of the transmission of cultural narratives across generations which, as Lyotard points out in his discussion of narrative pragmatics, is an essential part of the self-reproduction of a community: 'What is transmitted through these narratives is the set of pragmatic rules that constitutes the social bond' (1984: 21). In Quentin's case, the sense of internal division he feels as the narrative is passed on to him reflects the broadly social confusion of a community whose foundational epic can no longer be passed on intact by means of such traditional rituals of initiation. Through the paradigms implicitly or explicitly conveyed by the narratives of a stable culture, the hearer comes into possession of the set of cultural competences that membership in a community demands. If for some reason a blockage obstructs the transmission of traditional cultural competence, then those paradigms will not survive across generations – or, as is the case in *Absalom, Absalom!*, those paradigms will survive only in damaged or imperfect forms. It is the burden of this novel to attempt a reconstruction of a foundational narrative of the events of Southern history, events that could once be encoded in epic form. Now that the monological narrative container which effectively guaranteed the self-evidence of the story has been damaged beyond repair by the crisis of the decisive Civil War defeat, however, those events must be renarrated in order to see what, if anything, survives of that traditional legacy for Quentin to inherit.

Not only are several voices subsequently permitted to narrate, thus complicating the narrative in a definitely non-epic manner, but the complex historical interrelations of these voices are acknowledged. Observing that Quentin sounds like his (Quentin's) father, Shreve reflects, in quasi-historiographical terms, on just how interconnected people (and their narratives) are:

Maybe happen is never once but like ripples maybe on water after the pebble sinks, the ripples moving on, spreading, the pool attached by a narrow umbilical water-cord to the next pool which the first pool feeds, has fed, did feed, let this second pool contain a different temperature of water, a different molecularity of having seen, felt, remembered, reflect in a different tone the infinite unchanging sky, it doesn't matter: that pebble's watery echo whose fall it did not even see moves across its surface . . . . Yes, we are both Father. Or maybe Father and I are both Shreve, maybe it took Father and me both to make Shreve or Shreve and me both to make Father or maybe Thomas Sutpen to make all of us.   (1971: 215)

The orchestration of heteroglossia suggested here and previously ranges from Rosa to Quentin, alternatively including Shreve, Mr Compson and even Sutpen himself – a wide narratorial range. Yet the umbilical water-cord, while permitting a significant degree of imaginative identification, has distinct limits. *Absalom, Absalom!*, by admitting a range of voices into its discursive arena, clearly foregrounds a kind of novelistic heteroglossia; but at the same time, by its significant limitation on which voices are allowed to speak, it resists some of the fuller implications of a social heteroglossia that would allow the dialogic participation of voices outside the *sensus communis* of the Southern community Faulkner invokes in the opening quotation. This resistance is hardly surprising: the racially segregated nature of Southern society at that time is at once recreated in the discursive structure of the novel and mediated by Faulkner's modernist sense of fracture.

If the internal coherence of the community has been damaged, the boundaries which demarcate the community remain relatively intact. When Shreve, for instance, interrupts Quentin to take up the narration himself, saying 'Let me play a while now' (1971: 230), the historiographic *jouissance* this suggests is, nevertheless, inevitably tightly constrained by the ideological limits of the players. As narrators, they are as unable to project a black person as a full historical character as their narrated characters are unable to recognise one, and to this extent at least the communal legacy is maintained. The kind of sympathetic imaginative projection that they can sustain is powerful, but ultimately limited in scope: 'So that now it was not two but four of them riding the two horses through the dark over the frozen December ruts of that Christmas Eve: four of them and then just two – Charles-Shreve and Quentin-Henry' (1971: 275). Complete identification with these characters is available, but virtually none seems possible with any member of the African–American community, who remain thoroughly beyond the limits of the orthodox historical imagination in this case. No black people are admitted into the community of interrelation and identification that constitutes Shreve's pool of understanding. Significantly, no umbilical cord joins marginalised black characters to this network, a network that may no longer legislate a final version of historical truth since none seems finally possible, but which certainly does legislate whose voices will be heard in the discussion, who may legitimately narrate, who may articulate a historical vision. The limits of this umbilical cord of communal vision ultimately define in *Absalom, Absalom!* the limits of an orthodox historical discourse.[3]

It is an orthodoxy that, at a crucial moment late in the novel, has Quentin and Shreve, 'the two of them back to back as though at the last ditch, saying No to Quentin's Mississippi shade [Sutpen]', who remains 'somehow a thousand times more potent and alive' (1971: 231). The magnetic pole that Sutpen constitutes remains the centre, the centripetal organisational point, around which Quentin and Shreve's discourse is ultimately situated no less than is Rosa's. Their last ditch attempt to say 'No' presents the apparently non-transcendable horizon of their discourse, a horizon that guarantees its orthodoxy (despite the degree of discomfort and dissatisfaction they feel with it), and that finally ensures their inability to admit other voices in spite of their earnest and anguished attempts to gain narrative control of the 'whole story'. While *Absalom, Absalom!* may be said to trace a trajectory from a vanishing epic monologic discourse to a strained novelistic and modernist orthodoxy, neither of these genres seems to allow space for the articulation of black historical subjectivity. Nevertheless, the absent narrations by and about black characters have a sort of virtual existence behind the text as it were, constituting the non-narrated or non-narratable that is an enabling condition of every narration. The conscious or unconscious exclusion of certain historical evidence and points of view allows the relative unity of perspective to exist – even in the borderline case of a fractured perspective such as *Absalom, Absalom!* – and permits the attempt to colligate events into a more or less coherent narrative. The enormous difficulties faced by the narrators in their attempt to construct a story that might contain the violent and bewildering past is beyond doubt. Yet their anguished wrestling with the idea of race seems to mark a kind of imaginative limit to their capacity to think about history, as Collingwood put it. This limit is clear in

Rosa's narration, of course, but persists stubbornly with the others as well: while they can face the epistemological aporias of their narrations, the cultural aporias situated at the limiting notion of race seem both more agonising for them and more intractable.

It is conceivable, perhaps, that such an exclusion might constitute an ironic authorial comment on the cultural and historiographical exclusion of that group; but while *Absalom, Absalom!* is certainly more than the sum of its narrators, there is no substantial indication that the novel ought to be read in such a way.[4] One obvious way in which such an ironic stance might be indicated would be the insertion into the narrative of a character, perhaps a black character, who presents at least the elements of the history that the novel occludes. Even a character who does not present such historical evidence would be sufficient if he or she were clearly endowed with the potential to do so. In any case, as Achebe points out with regard to Conrad (cited above), had he wanted to draw a *cordon sanitaire* around the text, Faulkner is certainly a skilful enough novelist to do so. Furthermore, Faulkner's mastery of the modernist narrative as a form could, in principle at least, afford him the technical possibility of introducing such a disruptive voice. The point here is not that Faulkner should, in the 1930s, have written a novel more in touch with the more heterodox sensibilities of the 1990s, but that the horizon of historiographic possibility that structures the novel's perspectival layering needs to be more critically examined than it often is. The belief that the product of literary genius is universal and a timeless insight into a generalised human 'condition' is, perhaps, even less tenable as an approach to historical narrative. The purpose of examining the contours of the narrative perspectives Faulkner employs is not to denigrate his achievement, but to place it more concretely in its cultural context.

The various images of black voices in *Absalom, Absalom!* do not, however, contribute to the creation of such a heterodox representation of historical reality. The first image presented by Rosa's haunted voice is that of a 'man-horse-demon' – Sutpen – imposed on a peaceful scene 'with grouped behind him his band of wild niggers like beasts half tamed to walk upright like men' (1971: 6). The representation of historical reality that is however powerfully or convincingly evoked here, is a specific one and the reference to the bestiality of the 'wild niggers' is unsettling. There are a number of objectionable though hardly surprising aspects of Rosa's racist simile of course, but the particular aspect most relevant here is the consequent denial of the power of speech to these 'wild niggers'. Beasts cannot speak, write or represent themselves through language – a condition not entirely dissimilar to that of blacks throughout *Absalom, Absalom!* The first incidence of actual black speech occurs early in Rosa's narration. The man in question, an anonymous slave whose face is described as 'the wild Negro's perfectly inscrutable one with the teeth glinting a little' (1971: 19), speaks first to a team of horses, suggesting a shared bestiality that is confirmed in the description of that speech: 'something without words, not needing words probably, in that tongue in which [the slaves] slept in the mud of that swamp and brought here out of whatever dark swamp [Sutpen] had found them in' (20).[5] This characterisation suggests a being wholly other, alien, incomprehensible, foul and once again bestial. When, a few lines later, someone, presumably white, attempts to prevent him from beating the horses, he speaks. But his words themselves contain a total abdication of dialogic speech, a removal of the speaker from the arena wherein speech has authority: 'Marster say; I do. You tell Marster.' The slave has authority only to do as he is told and to direct any queries to the master, and as a consequence his speech act constitutes solely an admission of his lack of authority, for whatever reasons, as a participant in discourse. This refusal of speech in any dialogic sense is quite remarkable in juxtaposition with Rosa's strong articulation of her position.

Again, as in *Nostromo* and *Parade's End*, problems of discursive and physical violence underlie the representation of the speech situation here, moving any ideal of undistorted communication far beyond the horizon of possibility. If the anonymous slave's eccentric pronunciation, to which the text calls attention, acts as one signifier of his disqualification from the dominant language group, it is also possible to hear this dialect not simply as a deformation of 'good English' but as an indication of the existence of (in Bakhtin's sense) another language group. The cultural or historical coherence of the 'other' group, which lives in the non-narrated/non-narratable space behind the text, remains unavailable however, as the novel is unable to see or declines to explore too deeply beyond this heteroglossic boundary.

Rosa's investment in this language differentiation and her positing of the not-quite-human category of the 'wild nigger' has interesting parallels to the problem posed by the figure of Caliban in Shakespeare's *The Tempest*. Caliban too seems to exist on the boundary of the human, and his position there is initially defined, at least in part, by his lack of recognisable language. Should he traverse the boundary line into humanity, writes Terence Hawkes, 'it would mean that the category "man" is not the closed, finished and well-defined entity that sustains and is sustained by a European taxonomy' (1985: 26). The taxonomy is no longer, strictly speaking, European but the stakes remain the same: enslavement. For Rosa's social taxonomy and monologic discourse to retain coherence, the humanity of the 'wild niggers' which would pose a challenge to it must remain misrecognised. The line dividing the human from the not-quite-human, Hawkes continues, is vitally important as it defines

the site of the most bitter economic and political competition. Whatever makes a man stands as a major and controlling principle of coherence, both in terms of the present and the past in any society. To make a man is to make sense. And who makes sense, makes history.   (1985: 26)

A radical misrecognition of the language and humanity of the 'wild niggers', then, allows an oppressive power structure to experience itself as coherence – even virtue. And the ability that results to 'make history' must be taken in both related senses: the ability of historical agents to affect events in a meaningful way, and the ability of those agents to construct the narratives in which events are encoded and transmitted.

Rosa's distrust of the alien language spoken by the 'wild Negroes' is later demystified to some degree. The tongue they brought from the mud and swamp turns out to be less foul and mysterious than Rosa and the townspeople assumed: the language in which they and Sutpen communicated is revealed to be 'a sort of French and not some dark and fatal tongue of their own' (1971: 29–30). Their use of (Caribbean) French seems to elevate them, in the opinion of the third-person narrator, in a way that the use of a 'dark and fatal tongue of their own' – which can only mean an African language – would not. The explanation is, however, a sort of backhanded compliment, which in effect takes away as much as it gives. This is Rosa's narration, of course, and given the ideological position she represents, no more sympathetic insight into African–American experience can logically be expected. Much later, however, these problems of language and culture seem to remain unresolved as Quentin, who unlike Rosa is a modern self-conscious narrator, narrates the story of the escape of the architect: maybe

> the niggers saw him go and didn't think it needed mentioning; that being wild men they probably didn't know what Sutpen himself was up to . . . . I reckon the niggers never did know what the architect was there for, supposed to do or had done or could do or was.   (1971: 180)

The ignorance imputed to the slaves – this time by Quentin – implies not only a kind of zero degree of culture, but also, considering their role in building the house, a remarkable lack of ability to observe what was going on around them. Furthermore, this passage seems to lose sight of the fact that the slaves do not speak a 'dark and fatal tongue of their own' but French, the language of the architect. Even a difference of dialect would not account for such a total language failure. One need not postulate lengthy or intimate conversations between designer and workers in order to suppose that in such a situation the 'wild niggers' would know what was going on rather more than they are given credit for. Such an ascription of utter ignorance is consonant with the implication elsewhere that the slaves occupy a position in the hierarchy that leaves them rivalling animals in terms of relative level of civilisation. Whether the representations are those of premodern Rosa or of modern Quentin, the 'wild niggers' are neither demystified nor accepted as possessors of a common human nature within the circle of any recognisable *sensus communis*. They present the stable position of low, dark and inscrutable (incomprehensible) against which all other positions are defined by successive negation. The slaves remain almost subhuman, beneath the acceptable level at which speech is recognised as a legitimate part of social heteroglossia.

The exclusion of slaves from the position of narrators or even interlocutors of history coincides significantly with their exclusion as narrative agents. Sutpen's accomplishment is described here first by a third-person narrator, then by Mr Compson: 'inside of two years he [Sutpen] had dragged house and gardens out of virgin swamp, and plowed and planted his land with seed cotton'

(1971: 33). Sutpen had 'conceived that house and built it in a strange place and with little else than his bare hands' (1971: 42). And twenty African–American slaves, one might add. While black labour is not sufficiently accorded its place in the building of the plantation – and, by implication, in the building of America – Sutpen's success is such that, as Mr Compson puts it, some among his fellow citizens 'believed even yet that there was a nigger in the woodpile somewhere' (1971: 59).[6] If there is, in fact, 'a nigger in the woodpile' of this narrative construction of Southern history, it is the misrecognition or concealment of any significant African–American historical experience or legitimate power of historio-graphical narration.[7]

Bakhtin's suggestion that plot is the backdrop for the struggle of language groups to be heard seems relevant here. And in a novel that attempts to convey a large historical picture, plot formation is necessarily closely bound up with historical interpretation. In one sense, an omission such as this, warns James Snead in his discussion of *Absalom, Absalom!*, is neither 'the vagary of the individual consciousness, or the bad luck of the social outcast, but rather a mechanism of all narrative, one not immune from being abused as social censorship' (1986: 125). The exclusion of African–American historical experience constitutes a refusal to engage (or perhaps an inability to recognise) others which, argues Snead, 'hides under the normal requirement for plot to withhold what does not belong' (1986: 125). It seems that any amount of speculation on and narration of the events, relationships, possible motives of white past is of interest; at the same time, virtually all discussion of black experience is omitted. Faulkner's exploration of the past through the complex subjectivity both of its actors and its narrators is absent in his representation of black characters, who display little developed sense of a subjectivity possessing complex interiority and capable of sustaining a narrative point of view. One obvious conclusion to be drawn is that, as Bradley suggests, blacks are not thought to have an interiority in any degree comparable to whites. Or perhaps if they do, it is assumed to be a subjectivity so alien as to be incomprehensible ('inscrut-able') to whites – a possibility that returns us to Bakhtin's concept of the mutual non-understanding of alien language groups (1981: 356) and the implications that has for plot formation. Rosa, for instance, says that Clytie was so alien to her that *'we might have been not only of different races (which we were), not only of different sexes (which we were not), but of different species, speaking no language which the other understood'* (1971: 126). While Rosa can in no sense be taken as a spokesperson for Faulkner, the cultural abyss she articulates is never really challenged by subsequent narrators.

Bradley's legal model regulating who may reliably act as an historical witness, who therefore may be counted as an equal member of the human community, comes to mind when the younger Bon is taken to court after a brawl which he had apparently started for no obvious reason:

he made no denial, saying nothing, refusing to speak at all, sitting here in court sullen, pale and silent: so that at this point all truth, evidence vanished into a moiling clump of Negro backs and heads and black arms and hands . . . . There had been no cause, no reason for it; none to ever know exactly what happened.

(1971: 166–7).

Bon's actions seem incomprehensible, their rationale lost in an aporia existing on the boundary between black and white communities, in the inability of the White *sensus communis* to comprehend a range of experience outside its own bounds, and because no (white) narrator seems able to imagine what goes on in the narrative gaps in his (Bon's) life: 'none ever to know what incredible tale lay behind that year's absence' (1971: 169). But the 'tale' does seem potentially both narratable and credible, except for the fact that the 'none' clearly means no one white, and therefore no one with the legitimate authority to bestow the coherence of narrative. Again, African–American historical experience is relegated to a non-narrated space which the text cannot comprehend.

When Bon's son returns from his non-narratable absence with a wife, the woman herself is characterised in terms of another absence: an absence of humanity.[8] He returns 'with a coal black and ape-like woman and an authentic wedding license' (1971: 169), the implication being that there might be some doubt about the legality of a man marrying what is clearly depicted as a lower species. She 'existed in that aghast and automaton-like state' in which she had arrived, possibly incapable of narrating ('did not, possibly could not, recount') the story of their union and journey ('how he had found her, dragged her out of whatever two-dimensional backwater ... her mentality had been capable of coercing food and shelter from'). It is a mentality that renders her unable to retain the name of her town or village, leaves her unable even to sign the wedding register with an 'X' so that someone has to guide 'her very hand doubtless while she made the laborious cross', consigns her to such an intellectual abyss that when she married him she apparently knew neither his name nor whether he was black. Nevertheless, he returns, flaunting 'the ape-like body of his charcoal companion' (her mind is significantly absent from this formulation), 'an authentic wife resembling something in a zoo' and 'kenneled her', 'the black gargoyle', in a ruined cabin nearby (1971: 170–3).

If a number of aspects of the representation of African–American culture and humanity can be related to the figure of Caliban, there is as well an associated image that Stephen Greenblatt discusses in connection with Caliban: the Wild Man, 'one of whose common characteristics is the absence of speech' (1990: 21). Other characteristics of the Wild Man noted by Greenblatt coincide as well, such as 'wantonness' and a lack of stable family or social life. The lives of Wild Men are virtually unnarratable because, like Bradley's savages, there are no coherent rules which organise their behaviour, no common sense to give shape to their experience, and so their lives do not take place in any terms that narrative can comprehend. Thus Bon, who is white enough to have culture and narrative, can cross the racial line into a narrative void and reappear with a 'wild' woman from that void who has neither culture, memory nor identity. In the detailed genealogy at the conclusion of this genealogically self-conscious novel, she has no separate entry, but appears anonymously in Valery Bon's as 'a full-blooded Negress' (1971: 316).[9]

Since his skin is very light in colour, Bon's choice of a dark woman signals, apparently, a decision to degrade himself, the relative tone of the skin acting as one indicator in *Absalom, Absalom!* of the relative level of civilisation. Richard Poirier comments:

Though he could pass for a white man, he marries a woman who is an extremely dark Negress, and insists on being recognised as a Negro himself. Considering the social consequences, this is really a conscious form of self-degradation . . . . Valery Bon can define [him]self only horribly. In Sutpen's world, all Valery Bon can do is to assert negatively his potential dignity as a man.   (1984: 30)

Negro equals degradation, extremely dark Negress equals horrible degradation. Poirier's response indicates the way in which the text is unable to transcend its own orthodox horizon; nor, in spite of its radical disruption of dominant discourse, does it encourage readers to challenge fundamentally its agonised and self-defeating racial taxonomy. While it might be maintained that Faulkner's characterisation of this woman, his denial of humanity as well as voice to her, constitutes an ironic comment on the position of oppressed black women in his community, there seems to be no 'objective' or external point of reference from which such a position could be supported. The narrators of *Absalom, Absalom!* apparently see this woman as a subhuman creature; if Faulkner does not, or if he does not intend the reader to, this is nowhere made clear. Judging by the figure of the 'ape-woman', the problem Hawkes discusses – 'what makes a man', or in this case a woman – has remained unresolved in the decades since Sutpen's ascendancy. When, during Shreve's narration of the 'ape-woman's' arrival, Quentin repeatedly protests that he has been told too much to make sense of it all, that he has heard too much to reconcile the disparate strands into coherent narrative (1971: 171), it should be noted that the 'ape-woman' has never spoken, and that until he hears her he has not perhaps heard enough. This typifies, in a sense, what Bourdieu calls 'the "aphasia" of those who are denied access to the instruments of the struggle for the definition of reality' (1977b: 170).

Another black woman, Clytie, is described in terms that similarly emphasise her alterity: while looking at Jim Bond, Quentin fails at first to notice the 'little dried-up woman not much bigger than a monkey and who might have been any age up to ten thousand years . . . her bare coffee-colored feet wrapped around the chair rung like monkeys do . . . [speaking] in a voice almost like a white woman' (1971: 176–7). The sense of difference attaching to this monkey-like woman suggests the problematic nature of the discursive situation. In fact, Shreve at one point posits a separate category for the black equivalents of white (human) feelings: 'Clytie looked at you and you saw it was not rage but terror, and not nigger terror because it was not about herself'

(1971: 289). Furthermore, the idea of timelessness which comes up here and elsewhere in relation to Clytie seems to partake of the image of racial and cultural prehistoricity (or ahistoricity) that anthropologist Johannes Fabian discusses as a common means of denying coeval status and discursive authority to marginalised people. When Rosa confronts Clytie at the stairs, similar terms are used: her face 'antedating time and house and doom . . . [staring with] a brooding awareness and acceptance of the inexplicable unseen, inherited from an older and a purer race than mine' (1971: 112–13). Whether stressing timelessness, racial alterity or bestiality, the end result in either case is to remove the subject from the profoundly historical existence that is the common, intense, even obsessional experience of the white characters in the novel. While it is difficult to 'escape the reductionist use of dichotomies and essences', writes another anthropologist, James Clifford, one 'can at least struggle self-consciously to avoid portraying abstract ahistorical "others". It is . . . crucial for different peoples to form complex concrete images of one another, as well as of the relationships of knowledge and power that connect them' (1988: 23).

At this point, a signal difference between Caliban and the African–American figures in *Absalom, Absalom!* might be stipulated: Caliban ultimately has a say and his disturbing claim to humanity is asserted in however qualified a form. He learns the language well enough to curse, to resist and to afford a glimpse into his world of alterity. As Stephen Greenblatt points out, once Caliban speaks, 'we cannot make it vanish into silence. Caliban's world has what we may call *opacity*' (1990: 31).[10] Instead of meeting with resistance or opacity, the White historical gaze in *Absalom, Absalom!* either bounces off without registering the existence of a world or is absorbed into a kind of narrative 'black hole' of culture from which no light can emerge.

In a novel in which narratives of genealogy have such definitive importance, Jim Bond, son of the 'ape-woman', seems to live outside any narrative framework whatsoever. Had he been asked

if he was Charles Bon's son he not only would not have known either, he wouldn't have cared: and if you had told him he was, it would have touched and vanished from what you (not he) would have had to call his mind long before it could have set up any reaction at all, either of pride or pleasure, anger or grief.   (1971: 177)

He seems to exist in a situation of semi-namedness, between the genealogical certainty of the white Sutpens and the genealogical obscurity and anonymity of the black slaves. When Quentin and Rosa confront Clytie at the end, Jim Bond – a true child of his mother, the 'ape-woman' – appears, 'his arms dangling, no surprise, no nothing in the saddle-colored and slack-mouthed idiot face' (1971: 304). His idiocy is all the more pointed due to the tension of the scene and Quentin's caustic observation that Bond appears an unlikely heir apparent to the house of Sutpen (1971: 304). His lack of positive identity is clear when Quentin shouts, 'You, nigger! What's your name?' Bond's response, 'Calls me Jim Bond', is similar to the earlier black speech strategy, in that there is the same aphasic deflection of assertive statement through passive reflection of the statements of others. Even in his name, there is a slippage from Bon (French) to Bond – a slippage that can be read as a descent from good to bondage but signals as well the loss of essential genealogical continuity.

In all cultures, naming is a means both of conferring identity on an individual and simultaneously incorporating that individual into a collectivity. '[E]ven before he is born', writes Lyotard, 'if only by virtue of the name he is given, the human child is already positioned as a referent in the story recounted by those around him, in relation to which he will chart his course' (1984: 15). Bond, then, is the antithesis of Quentin in terms of intelligence, sensitivity, awareness of the past and even discursive capacity although they both are the novel's heirs: one heir to the house of Sutpen in ruins and the other heir to a culture whose traditional legitimacy is in ruins. In considering the instability of narration and culture we see exhibited in Quentin, it is essential to compare his situation not only to that of more stable narrators of the past, but also to a contemporaneous narrator, Jim Bond, whose relative social and historiographical situation seems infinitely less secure.[11] As Philip Weinstein notes, Jim Bond 'may have a putative soul, but Faulkner has not created it for him, and so we do not imaginatively credit it' (1987: 188).[12]

The seminal subject of all this narrative, Sutpen, does not, as has been suggested, come from a neutral or positive background concerning racial difference. In his study of Faulkner, Irving Howe argues that 'the pioneer innocence of young Sutpen is defined as a freedom from ... racial feeling' (1962: 117). Thadious Davis agrees, arguing that Sutpen's real failure is the betrayal of the original innocence and egalitarianism of his origins.

What Sutpen violates in accepting the principles of the 'monkey nigger' and Tidewater Virginia is precisely a personal code of honor and moral behavior derived from the social and ethical order of his own mountain society. Albeit more primitive, the mountain society has values that are more in keeping with the purer dictates of the human heart to which Faulkner frequently refers.

(1983: 185)

The contention that Sutpen disturbed a pre-existent cultural purity or unity of some kind, an Edenic American moment of harmonious origin, seems dubious – not just as a matter of historical accuracy, but also as a reading of the novel – when it is recalled that these mountain people had a strangely familiar attitude toward the problem of racial difference: 'the only colored people were Indians and you only looked down at them over your rifle sights' (1971: 181).

His first real confrontation with blacks, however, comes in Virginia, and the prevailing attitude among the poor whites is an interesting one. Those blacks, such as the 'broadcloth monkey' (1971: 187), who were at the top of the slave hierarchy were the focus of resentment among lower class whites but the sense remained that they were not the root cause. 'You knew that you could hit them', Sutpen is reported as saying, but 'they (the niggers) were not it, not what you wanted to hit . . . you knew when you hit them you would just be hitting a child's toy balloon with a face painted on it' (1971: 189). The problem is posed here not in terms of the morality of beating blacks, but in terms of whether or not it would be strategically useful. While this may historically have been the attitude of many Southern whites in this peculiar class struggle, the representation is not balanced by a complementary insight into the complex class situation of the blacks on the receiving end. In the description that follows of the beating of one slave the point is brought home. The black victim remains anonymous (1971: 190), and the beating itself, as Quentin describes Sutpen's image of it, is a scene of horror that remained all too familiar in the South for many years:

the torch-disturbed darkness among trees, the fierce hysterical faces of the white men, the balloon face of the nigger. Maybe the nigger's hands would be

tied or held but that was all right because they were not the hands with which
the balloon face would struggle and writhe for freedom, not the balloon face: it
was just poised among them, levitative and slick with paper-thin distension.
Then someone would strike the balloon one single desperate and despairing
blow and then . . . fleeing, running, with all about them, overtaking them and
passing and going on and then returning to overwhelm them again, the roaring
waves of mellow laughter meaningless and terrifying and loud. (1971: 190–1)

The suggestion that there may be a real person inhabiting the
balloon face, of course, is here; but the effect of the perspective
asserted is to elicit understanding, if not sympathy, for the
hysterical and despairing whites whose desperation and powerlessness has driven them to this barbaric act. While it is
undeniably important to understand their point of view, once
again the black perspective – like the face – is almost wholly
occluded. Furthermore, the single blow which is struck gives little
indication of the extent of the racial violence that was routinely
carried out against blacks. The repeated references to the 'balloon
face' of the victim seem to constitute a literal defacing of the other
in Emmanuel Levinas's sense. If, as Levinas argues, 'The epiphany
of the face is ethical' (1979: 199), that ethical imperative is refused
in the occlusion of the victim's face. This dehumanisation not only
enables the violence (physical and symbolic) committed against
him, it allows the perpetrators of that violence to feel little sense of
having violated any code of behaviour which might otherwise curb
such inhumane acts.

Resentment arises among poor whites like Sutpen – and here
Faulkner's historical insight is on the firmer cultural ground of his
own ethnic community – out of their sense of having been

brutely evacuated into a world without hope or purpose for them, who would
in turn spawn with brutish and vicious prolixity, populate, double treble and
compound, fill space and earth with a race whose future would be a succession
of cut-down and patched and made-over garments bought on exorbitant credit
because they were white people, from stores where niggers were given the
garments free.   (1971: 193)

Sutpen is made aware of his condition and inspired to change his
life by the denial of speech inflicted on him by a black doorman.
Knocking on the door of a mansion owned by a wealthy white
planter, he is turned away, and his speech is refused as
illegitimate: 'the nigger told him, even before he had had time to

say what he came for, never to come to the front door again but to go around to the back'. At this moment Sutpen is bested in a speech situation by a 'monkey nigger' (1971: 191), a 'broadcloth monkey' (1971: 187). Such an unthinkable occurrence, a breach of the *sensus communis*, acts as the objective crisis that sparks Sutpen's remarkable career. While others might have reacted violently, Sutpen himself decides not to exact revenge on the 'broadcloth monkey' or on any of the 'monkey niggers' – but his reasoning has nothing to do with any imputation of common humanity. Black faces remain 'balloon-faces'. Instead he realises, quite pragmatically, that in this situation beating or even shooting them would not solve anything, that the only solution is to raise himself to the level to the slaveowner. And it is precisely through violence committed against blacks – initially in Haiti – that he succeeds in his goals.[13]

Faulkner's sense of his own community, the community he refers to in the quotation that opens this chapter, is unparalleled. His representation of that community in *Absalom, Absalom!* and elsewhere reveals its complexities and paradoxes, its opacity, as subtly and profoundly as any novelist could. And he articulates the tensions that might lead a person to embrace this sort of brutality very effectively, providing valuable insight into a genuinely difficult situation. But considering who is ultimately on the losing end of the exchange, considering the history of torture, lynching and rape of blacks that continued long after the Civil War – indeed well into this century and during the time Faulkner was writing – that 'balloon face' deserves a voice with which to narrate the centuries of white brutality.[14] Faulkner notes in passing, as it were, that this man remains anonymous, remains silent, but neither provides the discursive space for him to speak nor suggests that such provision ought to be made. Among the multiple perspectives on history that the novel articulates, there is no point of view in *Absalom, Absalom!* for the 'balloon face', no narrative framework for the 'ape-woman'. Irving Howe writes that

Though he has given us a wider range and taken a deeper sounding of Negro character than any other American writer, Faulkner has not yet presented in his novels an articulate Negro who speaks for his people. No one has the right to demand that he do so, but it is a legitimate problem in literary criticism to ask why he has not . . . Faulkner's honesty, his continuous moral growth, but above all, the inner logic of his own work – all these would seem to require that he

confront the kind of Negro who is in serious, if covert, rebellion against the
structure of the South.   (1962: 131–2)

Although Howe seems here to overlook the entire tradition of
African–American literature in his claim for Faulkner's pre-
emminence, the point is nevertheless well-taken.[15] Little trace of
conscious thought or action is attributed to these people; no sense
of historical struggle and desire for personal and political freedom
is evident.

The low is a condition that any group can be in, white or black.
Sutpen, for instance, begins there. But in the imaginations of all
the various narrators, it seems the unique power of whites to have
the ability to move out of that condition, to be 'riven forever free
from brutehood' (1971: 215). Blacks, on the other hand, seem fated
to remain in a condition close to brutehood, unable to rise not only
as a result of the particular historical set of power relations that
enslaves and brutalises them, but also as a result of some timeless
absence in their make-up that has substituted endurance for
ability.[16] It would be unfair to ascribe to Faulkner responsibility
for any one of the representations of blacks in the novel, or the
opinions about blacks that he puts in the mouths of his characters.
However, the spectrum of such representations and opinions is,
finally, a narrow one – broader certainly than the stereotypes
provided by the racist elements of his community, but orthodox
enough to leave him within the wider bounds of its *sensus
communis*.

In response to an appeal for donations to the National
Association for the Advancement of Colored People (NAACP),
Faulkner refused, because the organisation seemed to him to be
encouraging too radical a position, promoting

actions which will do your people harm, by building up to a situation where
the white people who hate and grieve over the injustice which your people
have to suffer, will be forced to choose either for or against their own people,
and they too, the ones which your people consider the best among my people,
will have to choose the side of the rest of the white people.   (1977: 444)

The possibility that a sense of justice, even among the 'best' of the
white community, could override the racially-based *sensus
communis* is not considered here – white people, it seems, will
stick together no matter what. In the final analysis, a heterodox
alliance, even in the name of justice, outside the bounds of the

white community is not thinkable, no matter how imperfect the orthodox position may be. In a conciliatory letter to W. C. Neill who had publicly taken issue with Faulkner's moderate position on segregation, Faulkner wrote: 'I doubt if we can afford to waste ... that wit which we will sorely need when again, for the second time in a hundred years, we Southerners will have destroyed our native land just because of niggers' (1965: 391). The phrasing is striking not solely because of the final pejorative term, but even more so perhaps because the term 'we Southerners' and the possessive 'our native land' clearly do not include blacks.[17]

This exclusion is essentially consistent with the historiographic orthodoxy of *Absalom, Absalom!* As Lyotard points out, 'The consensus that permits ... knowledge to be circumscribed and makes it possible to distinguish one who knows from one who doesn't (the foreigner, the child) is what constitutes the culture of a people' (1984: 19). Whatever differences may be contained within the cultural spectrum of the Southern community Faulkner describes here – and there are important differences – racial difference was clearly, by consensus, inadmissable at this point in history. The orthodox position does not permit what Bakhtin called 'extopy' (Todorov, 1984: 99), an attitude which recognises and affirms the subjectivity of the other. Faulkner's startling opposition of these two terms – justice and community – constitutes yet another permutation of the problem of jarring witnesses, one to which Bradley himself frequently has recourse. Instead of historical witnesses negotiating questions of truth however, we have legal or moral witnesses negotiating questions of justice – witnesses whose orthodoxy or non-extopic vision ultimately precludes the possibility that the claims of justice have the capacity to transcend or override the claims of a reified *sensus communis*.

The denial of the historical legitimacy and historiographic authority of Black characters which was a central aspect of the earlier community's identity and which seems to continue on beyond the collapse of that community's doxa, does not imply a necessary granting of such authority and legitimacy to the white characters. As a narrative that articulates the damaged or imperfect transmission of cultural identity that results from social trauma, *Absalom, Absalom!* undeniably complicates and qualifies white narrative authority to an extreme degree. Lukács describes the novel genre as 'the epic of an age in which the extensive totality of life is no longer directly given, in which the immanence of meaning in life has become a problem, yet which still thinks in terms of totality' (1971: 56). With its temporal complexity, *Absalom, Absalom!*'s account of the Sutpen story seems to have aspects of both epic and novel. Rosa imparts the epic quality to her narration insofar as it is the epic of the founding of a nation and its subsequent destruction. Her references to God's will and to destiny are resonant with the grand style of the epic. But the whole subsequent movement of the narration, its multiple and unreliable narrators, fundamentally subverts Rosa's attempt to reach epic stature in her retelling of the fall of the old South. The historiographical abyss faced by Quentin in his representation of the past is an index of his distance from her epic certainty: in Rosa's epic treatment of the past, totality still appears graspable, and meaning, if tragic, is relatively unproblematic.

For Quentin, however, the situation is much less straight-forward. Quentin, with the aid of Shreve McCannon, narrates related events, yet Rosa's totality and certainty are no longer available to him as a historical subject. The end of epic history as a real historiographic possibility appears at the moment in Quentin's narration of the last days of the civil war when Bon accepts that there is nothing left of the old South: 'evidently we have done without [God] for four years, only He just didn't think to notify us' (1971: 288). The epic typically asserts for its transcendental legitimacy the favour of God towards the community whose history it celebrates. In the face of God's evident desertion, the consequent military defeat, and the pronouncement that a corner-stone of the community's structure – slavery – was in fact evil, the foundational narratives of community were inevitably shattered. The result is that individuals such as Quentin, whose identities should have been structured by the paradigms transmitted by those narratives, become less unified subjects and confront a less coherent social and historical world. The shadow of that earlier epic vision and its totality though, as Lukács suggests, still haunts his telling. Quentin seems poised between Yoknapatawpha and Harvard, between Rosa and Shreve, and must define himself in relation to both. The position seems untenable for him and he thus occupies that position of homelessness that Lukács characterises as the essence of the novel (1971: 41). In a statement suggesting their distance from the epic model, Mr Compson says that the earlier generation was made up of people in some respects like them, but

victims of a different circumstance, simpler and therefore, integer for integer, larger, more heroic and the figures therefore more heroic too, not dwarfed and involved but distinct, uncomplex who had the gift of loving once or dying once instead of being diffused and scattered creatures drawn blindly limb from limb from a grab bag and assembled.   (Faulkner, 1971: 73)

With this new complexity comes the sense that events seem to occur purely according to chance, with the same lack of logic as when 'a small boy chooses one ant-hill to pour boiling water into in preference to any other, not even himself knowing why' (1971: 84).

Bakhtin writes that the epic past and its apparent certainties are 'walled off by an unapproachable boundary from the continuing and unfinished present' (1981: 30). In the case of *Absalom, Absalom!*, that boundary appears to coincide with the end of the Civil War, and the consequent destruction of the the social fabric of the old South. Nevertheless the attempt to create order among the events and people in history must be made, even though the coherence of the narrative colligation of those events may owe as much to the imagination of the narrator as to the sequence of events themselves. The epic certainty of the narrative and the epic stature of the characters appears to be eroded, as the historical sublime threatens to overwhelm coherence. Mr Compson, situated generationally between Rosa and Quentin, recognises the abyss separating the historiographical 'whole story' from the sublime sum of its parts:

you bring them together in the proportions called for, but nothing happens; you re-read, tedious and intent, poring, making sure that you have forgotten nothing, made no miscalculation; you bring them together again and again nothing happens: just the words, the symbols, the shapes themselves, shadowy inscrutable and serene, against that turgid background of a horrible and bloody mischancing of human affairs.   (1971: 83)[18]

The narrative confusion in *Absalom, Absalom!* regarding what actually happens and when, extends even to its author – Faulkner's appended chronology (presumably designed to clarify the novel) does not, in fact, tally with the narrative itself, but presents yet another contradictory layer of historiographical confusion.[19]

Narrative thus finds its function not simply in the transmission of events but, as Mink argues, in providing a conceptual framework within which events can be cognitively appropriated. This need not be a rigid framework, but it is contained within the spectrum of conceptual possibilities a community encompasses. In relatively stable societies that spectrum can remain more or less intact over generations, but in societies defined by their historicity, it must be transformed as it is passed on if it is to remain adequate to changed circumstances. In a society such as Quentin's, a society that has suffered historical trauma, the narrative can be seen to struggle for adequacy as a community in a continuing state of shock comes to terms with radically changed circumstances and attempts to understand which aspects of its old framework can be salvaged and which are irretrievably destroyed. In his study of intercultural identity, Fredrik Barth notes the difficulty presented by the continuation of differentiated identity in spite of historical change: the continuity of ethnic groups, he argues,

depends on the maintenance of a boundary. The cultural features that signal the boundary may change, and the cultural characteristics of the members may likewise be transformed, indeed, even the organizational form of the group may change – yet the fact of continuing dichotomization between members and outsiders allows us to specify the nature of continuity.   (1969: 14)

Thus, for all the bewildering change taking place within the white Southern community, it is possible for this boundary to remain virtually intact since it is the fact of boundary itself which is at stake in defining a cultural group as much as it is the substantive cultural differences.[20]

As Warwick Wadlington argues, it is 'reductive to regard [Absalom, Absalom!'s] lack of fixity as merely an issue of decidable or undecidable epistemological authority' (1987: 213). In fact, the undeniably polyphonic narrative of Absalom, Absalom! does maintain some quite decidable limits, does not slide from a decentring of authority to a totally relativised rejection of certainty or dispersal of point of view. There is an important margin that must be taken into account: even at its most thoroughly dialogic, the novel maintains a strict control on which voices are permitted to narrate. The epistemological limits of heterodoxy or hetero-glossia are, as Bakhtin and Bourdieu both note, generally deter-mined by the objective realities of the social crisis of the historical moment – in this case a doubled moment of crisis including elements both of Faulkner's moment of writing and the period in which the novel is set. Rosa is reported as saying that 'the stable world we had been taught to know dissolved in fire and smoke', but some world, however unstable and crisis-ridden by compar-ison with the pre-war society, persists. Absalom, Absalom! is concerned with the waning of the authority and legitimacy of a social group whose point of view on history is becoming, if not invalid, then at least no longer absolutely privileged. Its claim to authority, to legitimacy, is displaced to the power of its rhetoric to move, to cast a spell, to summon up the traces of an otherwise lost doxic past, and, as Barth argues, to maintain the continuity of its social boundaries against the discontinuity of historical change.

This compulsive obsessional telling of the past, dwelling on the details, interpreting and reinterpreting, keeps the past from dissolving altogether like the pre-Civil War authority that once legitimised their version of it. And the intensity of that compul-sion seems at times to vary in inverse relation to the availability of historical data, as Quentin and Shreve resort increasingly to fabricating the past they narrate, 'the two of them creating between them, out of the rag-tag and bob-ends of old tales and talking, people who perhaps had never existed at all anywhere' (Faulkner, 1971: 250). Like the lost sense of meaning and totality that Lukács invokes, the sense of lost authority looms over Absalom, Absalom! – whether the authority of Sutpen or the certainty of Rosa, highlighting by contrast the instability of Quentin's position as historical narrator and historical agent. In response to such uncertainty, Peter Brooks argues that 'there seems to be no clear authority, not even a provisional sort, for the telling of the story' (1986: 251). Further, it 'shows us how narration can become fully dialogic, centreless, a transaction across what may be a referential void' (1986: 261–2). Brooks's analysis oversimplifies the situation in one crucial aspect – it loses sight of certain specific residual conditions of the narration. A centre can be recognised – not a doxic, absolute centre, not an epic centre, but nevertheless a centre which seems to regulate, for instance, who is to enter into the dialogue; and the exclusion of African–American voices offering a perspective on the house of Sutpen is a major gap in the novel if it is to be conceived as cultural dialogism. As a point of cultural orientation that Quentin seems unable to refuse for all his efforts, the house of Sutpen refuses equal entrance to blacks and allows little black input on the definition of the communal project. Alice Walker asserts that

Faulkner was not prepared to struggle to change the structure of the society he was born in. One might concede that in his fiction he did seek to examine the reasons for its decay, but . . . [o]ne reads Faulkner knowing that his 'colored' people had to come through 'Mr William's' back door, and one feels uneasy, and finally enraged that Faulkner did not burn the whole house down.

(1983: 19–20)

Despite the eventual burning of the Sutpen house, and the fact that the struggle for the possession of legitimate narrative authority produces no clear winners, there are clear losers who never even get a hearing, whose history seems to exist beneath the horizon of language, well beyond the spectrum of dialogic community that *Absalom, Absalom!* encompasses. If Quentin's ultimate suicide (in *The Sound and the Fury*) undermines still further the ability of this dominant group to continue imposing its definition of the situation, nevertheless the possibility that another group might be able to share power and authority does not exist within the horizon of the novel. The voice that continues to reverberate unintelligibly beyond the end of the novel is that of Jim Bond. Peter Brooks maintains that

The tale he would tell would be full of sound and fury, signifying nothing. He stands as a parodic version of Barthes's contention that the classical narrative offers at its end the implication of a residue of unexhausted meaning . . . . [T]he residual meaning embodied in Jim Bond – seems the very principle of nonsignificance.   (1986: 265)[21]

Such a formulation does not sufficiently recognise the specific location of this remainder – race – which is a problem of doxa and ideology, not a purely formal narratological problem. It seems likely, in fact, that the remainder is never arbitrary but that this position is inevitably reserved for that which, for some reason, does not fit, that which is, potentially at least, radically disruptive to the coherence that the narrative seeks to protect. If, then, we see this as a social as well as a narrative 'residue', the incomprehensibility of Bond or the 'ape-wife' can then be read as an ideological limit of the historical imagination that inevitably coincides with the limit of the narrative colligation. The absence of signification, the ascription of inability to signify, then becomes a function of the inability of the white narrators to read the discourse of the other or of an implicit recognition of the price that would be paid if such signification were to occur. Bakhtin writes that 'the novel must represent all the social and ideological voices of its era, that is, all the era's languages that have any claim to be significant; the novel must be a microcosm of heteroglossia' (1981: 411). Bond howls instead of speaking. But rather than recognising this as the orthodox limit of the narrative imagination, the limit of what is narratively thinkable, the text displaces this lack of coherence onto the black characters themselves. Whereas the narrative of Southern history in *Absalom, Absalom!* gradually grows beyond the grasp of the white narrators, blacks are made to seem beyond (or perhaps beneath) the comprehension of narrative from the outset.

Craig Werner notes that Faulkner's important observation – an observation in tune with much twentieth-century theory of history – that the ' "past isn't dead, it isn't even past," articulates the simple, but all too often ignored, knowledge that the excavation of history is an absolute necessity if we are to make any sense of the present' (1987: 37).[22] He then notes the high cost of excluding sexual or racial 'others' – from *active* participation in the dialogic exploration of history. Faulkner certainly recognises the importance of the dialogic process in coming to terms with the past, but, continues Werner, 'the silences, the gaps in Quentin's excavation – and I suspect in this he shares much with his creator – reflect an unwillingness or inability to apply the implications of . . . his own process and admit the other into active dialog' (1987: 47).[23] While Faulkner is certainly aware that this excavation requires a collective process, there is little actual presence of the 'other' and the narration remains in the control of white male voices. While Rosa's female voice is clearly heard, it is the ghostly voice of the epic past, not a challenge to that doxa. The narrative may have its moment of origin with Sutpen's refusal to accept being silenced by a 'broadcloth monkey', it may subsequently record the rise and fall of Sutpen's authority, but it does not finally transcend its own parallel silencing of black voices and move out from its narrative centre of discursive authority.

The seeming paradox that, as Croce put it, 'every true history is contemporary history' is borne out in *Absalom, Absalom!* As Croce understood to be the case, its construction of history depends on the interests and insights of the narrators as well as on the objective existence of historical evidence. More recently, Foucault has made a similar statement, asserting that his work constitutes a 'history of the present' (1979: 31), and the effect of his work is to demonstrate gaps and discontinuous lines of development which lead to our present discursive formations. Both Foucault and Faulkner call into question the stability of the relationship between historical representation and the past itself, and undermine any 'history whose function is to compose the finally reduced diversity of time into a totality fully closed upon itself' (1977: 152). Despite these similarities, however, an important difference divides them: Foucault's aim in a work such as *Madness and Civilization* is to construct an archaelogy of the silence of the mad in the discourse on madness, thus registering the excluded other of discourse. Faulkner's orthodoxy does not allow him to pursue this alterity: for all his narrators' tendency to bump against the walls of their narrative limits, they remain within a network which – as Shreve's pool analogy demonstrates – is constructed of the language of his own community and renders virtually inaudible or unintelligible the language of difference.

As Philip Weinstein points out, this 'center does not merely "permit" the margin to exist at its side: rather it is constituted by the very notion of marginality' (1987: 170). Weinstein examines the marginal position of blacks in *Absalom, Absalom!* through the characters of Charles Bon, his mother Eulalia and Clytie who seem to have 'symbolic importance for the anguished whites viewing them' but 'no access to their own incandescence; their importance is for *others* alone' (1987: 171).[24] Yet even in placing *these* characters at the margin, Faulkner has created a kind of 'mulatto' buffer zone between white narrators and black experience. Charles Bon is so 'white' – in education, upbringing and pigmentation – that he has no trouble 'passing'. His father is white and his mother has some small fraction of 'negro blood' but certainly passed as white until Sutpen was told that she was invisibly tainted. More important than the arcane measurings of blood percentages that were a part of this peculiar discourse, he seems to have little relation to any African–American community.

Bon occupies the position of a white aristocrat through most of the novel, and he even becomes an officer in the Confederate army. He seems, to say the least, to be an unlikely candidate to represent in any way the African–American historical experience of the South, and the realities of that marginal existence. If the missing narratives of Eulalia, Bon and Clytie define the margin, where are we to locate the absent narratives of the 'ape woman' or her son? As Walter Taylor has argued, Faulkner's fascination with the idea of 'mixed race' outweighs his exploration of the experience of being black in the white-dominated South to the extent that the 'preoccupation with Bon, Clytie, and Valery obscured the problems of their fellow blacks more than it explained them' (1983: 116–17).

The very existence of the mulatto characters, who are situated uneasily on the boundary of racial classifications is, of course, a kind of scandal. The sexual transgression that it implies is, for Southern women such as Rosa, almost as much of a cultural trauma as the war itself. Sexual transgression across racial lines was an inevitable result not only of the proximity of the two groups but also of the power structure of the South when white men controlled to such a degree the destinies of black women. A direct result in *Absalom, Absalom!* is the fall of the house of Sutpen into the hands of the idiot Jim Bond, the illegitimate heir. If ethnic boundaries and the monopoly on cultural coherence that they protect are to remain intact, such sexual contact (and the resulting reproduction) must be rigidly controlled. The problem of miscegenation was nevertheless endemic to the slave South, and the attempts to regulate the boundaries through legalisms concerning the blood percentages of the offspring was less than wholly effective.[25] The cultural force field dividing black and white was breached and contradicted most dramatically perhaps by the frequent sexual transgression of that force field. But the force field itself remained; little sense of common culture arose with the production of common offspring. This is understandable from the point of view of the African–Americans who were the victims of transgression, but as *Absalom, Absalom!* demonstrates, it did put a strain at times on the white culture's sense of coherence. When individuals from different cultures interact regularly, writes Fredrik Barth, it might be expected that cultural differences would be eroded 'since interaction both requires and generates a congruence of codes and values – in other words, a similarity or community of culture' (1969: 16). The fact that boundaries and differences persist despite prolonged, sometimes intimate, contact

implies not only criteria and signals for identification, but also a structuring of interaction which allows the persistence of cultural differences. The organisational feature which . . . must be general for all inter-ethnic relations is a systematic set of rules governing inter-ethnic social encounters.   (1969: 16)

Stable cultural relations, he concludes, 'presuppose such a structuring of inter-action'. In *Absalom, Absalom!*, the rules of sexual contact – the most transgressive because it is the most intimate – across the cultural boundary of race have been broken and the result is a cultural instabilty approaching incoherence. 'So its the miscegenation, not the incest, which you can't bear', says Bon to Henry in Shreve's account of their climactic confrontation (1971: 294). Miscegenation, even more than incest, is the social taboo most to be feared in *Absalom, Absalom!* by those whose reified community boundaries appear threatened.

The odd possibility that there may be no essential difference between black and white, that mere superficial differences obscure the harmonious coexistence of separate but parallel lives, is briefly asserted in one passage that equates black slave and privileged white university student:

only in the surface matter of food and clothing and daily occupation [are the students] any different from the Negro slaves who supported them – the same sweat, the only difference being that on the one hand it went for labor in fields where on the other it went on . . . the hard violent hunting and riding; the same pleasures: the one, gambling for worn knives and brass jewelry and twists of tobacco and buttons and garments . . . the other for the money and horses, the guns and watches . . . the same parties: the identical music from identical instruments, crude fiddles and guitars, now in the big house with candles and silk dresses and champagne, now in dirt-floored cabins with smoking pine knots and calico and water sweetened with molasses. (Faulkner, 1971: 80–1)

Nevertheless, an enormous cultural division based on power is elided in this passage. While there may be a point to such a balancing of the youth of two different cultures, more is concealed than is revealed in such a comparison – not just the liability to violent torture and rape against which the slaves had neither defence nor recourse, but the thousand more subtle minor daily practices of humiliation and forced submission that result from such a state of enslavement, all of which become encoded in the group's *sensus communis* and the narratives that transmit it. Instead, this representation evokes a sense of the 'human condition' or 'family of man' that, as Roland Barthes has observed, occludes the real inequalities which are based on the unequal distribution of power structuring that society.[26] The possibility that Faulkner's meaning at this point is ironic is not easily supported: the inclusion of a voice capable of articulating the point of view of the slaves, a witness for whom the difference would have been obvious, could have created such an ironic juxtaposition – but this is not the case. That this point of view existed historically is attested to by the existence of many black writers, orators and educators whose works went generally unrecognised by the white community of the period – indeed, when their work was, at times, recognised, the penalty some paid was high in a society where black literacy was once a legally-punishable offence and resistance could mean death.

In her essay, 'The Black Writer and the Southern Experience', Alice Walker makes a statement remarkably similar to Faulkner's description of the homogeneity of the Southern community (cited above): 'What the black Southern writer inherits as a natural right is a sense of *community*' (1983: 17). Walker's stipulation of black, however, underscores the fact that Faulkner's community is defined by race as well, but as a member of the dominant community which (as dominant communities often do) sees itself as universal, normative, he is under no obligation to specify the exclusionary taxonomy on which his *sensus communis* depends. Faulkner was once asked whether any of the narrators 'had the right view' or whether it was a matter of 'thirteen ways of looking at a blackbird with none of them right'. Wallace Stevens's modernist classic (the bird's colour notwithstanding) provides an apt epistemological analogy. He replied that 'no one individual can look at truth. It blinds you. You look at it and you see one phase of it. Someone else looks at it and sees a slightly awry phase of it. But taken all together the truth is in what they saw though nobody saw the truth intact.' The suggestion is that the reader, by assembling a composite from the disparate narratives and images provided by the narrators, can arrive at 'his own fourteenth image of that blackbird which I would like to think is the truth' (Faulkner, 1959: 273–4). Still, the question lingers: Who speaks for the South? 'Tell about the South. What's it like there. What do they do there. Why do they live there. Why do they live at all' (1971: 143). One pragmatic answer to the question is that William Faulkner has been considered a spokesperson for the South. In Absalom, Absalom!, his narrative construction brilliantly foregrounds the inevitable inadequacy of attempts to answer these questions in historical terms, but avoids disruptive probing into the constitutive criteria which define who might legitimately respond.

In the act that in a sense sets the whole narrative structure in motion, Quentin is summoned to listen to Rosa's history by means of a 'note which he had received by the hand of a small Negro boy' (1971: 7). The anonymity of the messenger, his diminutive stature, his youth – the racist idiom by which 'boy' signifies all African–American males also comes to mind at this point – his subordinate position as messenger rather than interlocutor, all these factors add to the (in)significance of his position in this major American work of imaginative history. He carries a message between whites, announcing that the time has come to discuss history, to transmit the foundational cultural narratives that structure communities across generations, to pass the torch of historical tradition – in however a complex and incomplete way – from one generation of white Southerner to another. In this almost ritual act of communication and community, the messenger himself remains voiceless, anonymous, a servant of white historiography and historically, a servant. In spite of the threat of narrative disintegration that results from a defeated and traumatised culture, Absalom, Absalom! is unable to move beyond its orthodox boundaries. Instead it lodges itself at the agonised moment of the 'last ditch' attempt on the part of a white community to say 'No' to Sutpen (1971: 231) and to the sensus communis he stands for, neither constructing nor suggesting any representation of what might be involved if that refusal were to be taken as a starting point for a renegotiation of the modern terms of community.

III

Postmodernism and heterodoxy

6

Bearing witness: African–American women's fiction

One . . . jarring chord and a vague and uncomprehended cadenza has been and still is the Negro. And of that muffled chord, the one mute and voiceless note has been the sadly expectant Black Woman.

Anna Julia Cooper (*A Voice From the South*, 1892)

The American museum of unnatural history . . . . It is assumed that all non-Anglo-Saxons are uncomplicated stereotypes. Everybody knows all about them. They are lay figures mounted in the museum where all may take them in at a glance. They are made of bent wires without insides at all. So how could anybody write a book about the non-existent?

Zora Neale Hurston ('What White Publishers Won't Print', 1950 [1979])

In this chapter I would like to examine the strategies by which a group of jarring witnesses who have been marginalised in the orthodox dominant discourse of narrative fiction and history is able to articulate its own perspective, to assert its own discursive space. A number of marginalised groups could be focused on in this respect: categories of class, race, religion, gender, and nationality, for example, have often been used to deny the discursive legitimacy of certain sectors of society. This chapter will explore representations of history in the novels of black American women – a group doubly marginalised, in terms both of race and gender. Zora Neale Hurston's evocative image of the museum display figure without insides echoes almost directly Bradley's assertion that savages have no internal world, and it has been the task of many African–American women writers to correct that image, to assert the authority and legitimacy of the perspectives of black women in a society which has traditionally denied it. Once again, Edward Said's comments on the relation of power to knowledge and discourse are relevant: the dominant culture has been 'able to manage – and even produce – the [dominated] politically, sociologically, militarily, ideologically, scientifically, and imaginatively' as part of 'the whole network of interests inevitably brought to bear on (and therefore always involved in) any occasion when that peculiar entity . . . is in question' (1978: 3). Since historiography has itself been colonised by the dominant power, Said's subsequent prescription coincides precisely with what has been attempted as African–American women have worked to construct another narrative, one 'that derives historically and abductively from the deprivations of the present' (1990: 79).

Men and women do write their own history, but – as Marx might have said – they do not write it under circumstances chosen by themselves. Instead they write it under circumstances directly encountered, given and transmitted by the past, a past that can indeed weigh like a nightmare on the brain of the living. Much African–American literature can be seen as an attempt to awaken from the nightmare of history, or to fan a spark of hope in the past by safeguarding or defending the dead, in the historiographic manner Benjamin describes in 'Theses on the Philosophy of History', from a victorious enemy:

Only that historian will have the gift of fanning the spark of hope in the past who is firmly convinced that *even the dead* will not be safe from the enemy if he wins. And this enemy has not ceased to be victorious.   (1969: 255)

The field of battle, in this case, is that of representation and African–American literary history offers a record of struggle which, for all its diversity, nevertheless demonstrates some remarkably consistent traits involving the establishment of the legitimacy of African–American historical perspectives, the authority of African–American acts of representation – indeed the assertion of African–American humanity itself. This literary and historiographic project dates back to the slave narratives that recorded historical experiences of those oppressed and displaced people whose lives the official discourse refused to legitimate. Following the Civil War, in nineteenth- and early twentieth-century novels such as Brown's *Clotel*, Harper's *Iola Leroy*, Hopkins's *Contending Forces*, or Chesnutt's *The Marrow of Tradition*, historical events and circumstances are evoked either explicitly in prefaces and afterwords, or less directly in the narratives themselves, in an attempt to publically legitimise the historical position of the African–American community.[1] The enormous difficulty of articulating such a perspective against the grain of the dominant configurations of the traditional American narrative of progress and emancipation seems, however, only to have reaffirmed rather than to have discouraged attempts to do so. This historiographic aspect is evident in the work of many contemporary black novelists as well, and confirms bell hooks's argument that memory can be a catalyst for 'collective black self-recovery. We need to keep alive the memory of our struggles against racism so we can concretely chart how far we have come and where we want to go' (1990: 40).[2]

American history, whether literary or political, is itself a site of litigation over the meaning of the past. If African–American historical reality has, until recently, been a somewhat neglected field, this can be seen as an aspect of what Bourdieu has described as the aphasia of those denied access to the instruments for the definition of reality (1977b: 170). As a form of historiography, historical fiction can work against that aphasia by defamiliarising the past, by opening access to previously marginalised perspectives on and definitions of historical experience, by bearing witness. Given the ideological weight of the discourses which bear out Hurston's characterisation of the situation, it is not at all superfluous to point out, Toni Morrison asserts in a recent essay, that 'We [African–Americans] are the subject of our own narrative, witnesses to and participants in our own experience, and . . . in the experience of those with whom we have come in contact. We are not, in fact, "other" ' (1990b: 208).

In a recent essay Thomas C. Holt analyses the historiographical biases that led to the omission of slaves, as human subjects, from the history of slavery (1986: 7). Holt locates the reasons in problems in the definition of evidence and in the relation of knowledge and legitimacy. The situation of black history has much in common, he observes, with that of women's history, working-class history, or the history of oral cultures that have left no written record to be analysed. The reason for this exclusion

is not because they had no history, an impossibility where life and experience exist; nor that that history was unimportant, a notion easily contradicted by reference to almost any political and economic development; nor that there

were no sources from which to write that history – clearly there were and are
. . . . Rather, it was that these sources remained unseen. What we see is a
function of where we stand.   (1986: 7)

This extends Collingwood's insight that there must inevitably be
areas of the past where a given historian's imagination or
conceptual framework simply cannot go.

In the same collection, Nathan A. Huggins argues that it is
perverse to think of American history without African–American
history and women's history. 'A white American and a male
history ought to be, common sense tells us, unthinkable.' Huggins
laments that we have indeed been brought up on 'a lot of perverse
history' (1986: 159). In another sense of the term, of course, a broad
understanding of common sense can reveal a good deal about the
formation of specific historical discourses: from the common sense
point of view of many historians (and others) the displacement of
the White male American central subject of history is precisely
what has been unthinkable. Huggins's use of the term perverse is
also interesting, in a way that relates back to Bradley's insistence
that the straightening of the crooked rests on a knowledge of the
straight (1968: 85–6). The Oxford English Dictionary definitions of
perverse include not only the sense of being turned away from
what is right, true, reasonable and good, but also a legal reference
to a verdict which is against the weight of evidence. The
epistemological limitations described by Collingwood on what can
be conceived as evidence, however, are operative in what appears
perverse to Huggins, yet has remained 'natural' from another
position. As the novels discussed in this chapter repeatedly
demonstrate, the question of admissable evidence is central to the
assertion of narrative legitimacy.

But adding evidence of African–American history to the
discourse as it stands is not enough. What is necessary, Huggins
argues, and what has, in fact, already begun to take place, is an
alteration of the general character of American history, a re-
conceptualising of the field in a more heterogenous context (1986:
158). In the past, American history based itself on a positive myth
of providential destiny – a myth that has never adequately
reflected the historical experience of many marginalised people:
perhaps, he suggests, 'the Afro-American story remains too discordant with progressive assumptions to be comfortably incorporated into the American story' (1986: 167). This discordance has led

the dominant community to a tendency to deal with such groups as anomalies, choruses of jarring witnesses whose historical testimony cannot – indeed need not – be assimilated (1986: 163). Elsewhere, Houston A. Baker has similarly observed the 'Foucaultian "rupture" that exists between traditional American history . . . and an alternative Afro-American discourse' (1984: 57). The exclusion of this perspective from the dominant narratives has important ramifications since the legitimacy of social groups depends on their ability to articulate publically a perspective, to assert with legitimacy their view of the world and of their position in it. Like Mink, whose understanding of the contingency of all narrative representations of history did nothing to negate his sense of its necessity, Huggins calls for 'a new narrative, a new synthesis taking into account the new history' (1986: 160). One response to this call can be located in the many fictional narratives being produced by black American women. In her influential study of Black women's literature, Barbara Christian writes that African–American women need to find their own ways of thinking about history:

for those of us who were not in control of our past or our history and are not now in control of our present, we are clear about the fact that history is a selection of significant events, a means of constructing a coherent pattern out of the past. We know that often what is selected as significant is integrally connected to the point of view, values, and intentions of the historian.

(1985: 166)

This occlusion of the point of view of the female African–American subject is an example of what Jean-François Lyotard has defined as a wrong: not solely a damage to life or liberty, but a damage of this nature that is compounded by the loss of the 'right to testify to the damage' (1988a: 5). Or it could be that the testimony itself is allowed to occur, but is simultaneously negated by being deprived of authority – in this case a witness might speak, but the evidence would not be taken seriously or acted on.[3] The damage done to African–Americans over the centuries of the diaspora has been enormous – literally unspeakable, to use a term taken from the title of Toni Morrison's recent essay on American literary history – yet the testimony of those who suffered this damage has until recently rarely been admitted to the realms of legitimate authoritative discourse. Lyotard writes: 'What is at stake in a literature, in a philosophy, in a politics perhaps, is to bear witness to differends by finding idioms for them' (1988a: 13). Gradually, it seems, such idioms are being found; Morrison agrees that '[s]ilences are being broken, lost things have been found' in recent years as historians and literary historians reinvestigate the colonial and African–American past, moving away 'from silencing the witnesses and removing their meaningful place in and contribution to . . . culture' (1990b: 208).

Frequently, histories which attempt to articulate such differends seek as well to locate a leverage point from which the social world can be moved by redefining the categories and contesting the legitimacy of the principles of division of the social and historical field. The hegemonic *sensus communis*, if not transformed, can at least be thrown into relief through juxtaposition with another, parallel or alternative, perspective that exposes the ultimately arbitrary nature of that social doxa. To this end Amiri Baraka (LeRoi Jones) has called on the black artist to 'provide his version of America from that no-man's-land outside that mainstream' (1966: 114). This call for another 'version of America' – despite the gendered vocabulary – remains exemplary. A definition of a community of sense – as well as a sense of community – is at stake in these novels, and that work of definition is often carried out in historical terms. The symbolic struggle to recast American history in a more heterogeneous narrative can succeed, in fact, only if there is an accompanying modification to the racial taxonomy that divides the nation. It is not sufficient that a liberal historical vision be adopted as a cosmetic surface beneath which the monological epic continues to organise American sensibility virtually unchallenged. A radically heterodox historiography is needed if the traditional exclusionist narratives of progress and emancipation are to be critically challenged.

As Susan Willis points out, a predominant feature in this writing is 'the journey (both real and figural) back to the historical source of the Black American community' (1987: 57).[4] That journey of discovery backward in time is part of the more general project of black women's writing since the nineteenth century, that Hazel V. Carby in *Reconstructing Womanhood* has characterised as an 'attempt to establish an independent and public narrative voice' as a means of developing and legitimising 'their own discourse of black womanhood' (1987b: 38–9). This discursive independence is needed if black women are to counter the reductive and not infrequently offensive images of themselves that have been long produced and reproduced by the dominant discourse.[5] In order to claim legitimacy for their collective historical experience, to establish the authority of their historical narratives, marginalised groups such as black women have first to overcome the accumulated weight of the orthodoxy that has enforced their marginality.

A recurring set of concerns in these novels is the boundary dividing marginal from dominant groups and the social and epistemological dislocation (generated by objective crisis) necessary in order for the experience of the marginal group to become available and comprehensible outside the confines of that group. Further, given an extreme enough degree of marginality and alienation, this experience must be legitimated even for members of the marginalised group itself whose interpretive categories may be overwhelmed by the dominant social and interpretive community that surrounds them. In face of the hegemonic power (weighty interests) contradicting them, these witnesses need, at times, to be reminded of the legitimacy of their own testimony. In a sense, the work that fiction is being asked to do is that of historical or cultural *defamiliarisation*, but in an explicitly political manner not theorised in any detail by the Russian Formalists who, according to Bakhtin and Medvedev, 'radically [distort] the meaning of the device, interpreting it as an abstraction from . . . ideological significance. But, in fact, the whole meaning of the device is in the latter' (1978: 61). It is a defamiliarisation that would make newly visible and comprehensible the past struggles of marginal groups, and legitimise their aspirations for the future. This politicised defamiliarisation acts to counter the naturalisation imposed by ideology on a situation that is in essence historical. To this end the process of defamiliarisation that is attempted must both publicly challenge the existing interpretations that demeaned and marginalised them, and contribute to the public legitimisation of an alternate perspective on the past.

The rewriting of history from the defamiliarised point of view of the historically dominated is an important aspect of the symbolic struggle to produce legitimate representations not only of history but also of the present social world, a world whose meanings depend to some degree on the historical discourses in which they occur. The stakes of this struggle for legitimacy in historical representation, then, include not only the definition of the past, but also of the present and the future. And in order to change the social structures that permit (or enforce) domination, that struggle must contest not only specific dominant historical representations, but also the general view of the social and historical world that produces them. Elizabeth Fox-Genovese argues that for black women writers, history is also 'a map of "where I'm bound." The account of the black women's self cannot be divorced from the history of that self or the history of the people among whom it took shape' (1987: 176–7).

The novels by black American women that I will be discussing do both of these things – they narrate a version of history 'from below' which the dominant historical discourse has not traditionally included, and they engage in various ways the problems of world view and representation that necessarily underlie any specific elaboration of historical narrative. Such novels are a part of the more general struggle in which, as Bourdieu writes, 'the past – with retrospective reconstruction of a past tailored to the needs of the present – and especially the future, with creative forecasting, are endlessly invoked, to determine, delimit and define the always open meaning of the present' (1985: 201). Although this chapter is primarily concerned with more contemporary fiction, essentially the same dynamic can be traced back much further. As Robert Stepto comments, the most impressive element of a slave narrative is the 'strident, moral voice of the former slave recounting, exposing, appealing, apostrophizing, and above all remembering' (1979: 3). The urgency of retaining these memories becomes a recurring theme in later narrative as well, since that communal memory acts as a safeguard against the eradication of African–American historical experience and identity that is a consequence of the dominant discourse. Another recurring feature is the use of a violent juxtaposition or transgression of dominant and marginal social categories in some of the earliest novels by black American women. A representation of characters who cross entrenched social boundaries reveals the arbitrary nature of those boundaries and thus serves the function of breaking down the monological self-evidence of the discourse of the dominant group in order that the historical experience of the dominated group can move toward discursive legitimacy and narrative coherence.

Iola Leroy, or Shadows Uplifted was published in 1892 by Francis Harper, a prominent activist in feminist and anti-racist issues.[6] A first novel, written when Harper was sixty-seven, the book is both sentimental and didactic. Arguing for women's rights, temperance and justice for blacks in a deeply racist and sexist America, *Iola Leroy* is interesting both as a work of fiction and as a work of social advocacy. The novel is set largely in the South, opening in the years preceding the Civil War and continuing into the period of the reconstruction. Spanning two such different eras, it represents two very different ideological positions as well. Iola Leroy, the eponymous main character, is the daughter of a wealthy Southern plantation owner and his wife, the latter a former slave whose fraction of 'negro blood' has never been revealed to the children. Well-educated, genteel, protected from any knowledge of the harsher realities of slavery, she supports that system, becoming an apologist for what she considers a benignly paternalistic social arrangement. As she argues with abolitionist Northern school-mates early in the novel, she occupies one of the accepted white Southern positions of her time. With the sudden death of her father, however, her world is overturned. Due to her fraction of 'negro blood' – until now unknown to her – she is herself remanded into slavery and experiences from the inside the brutality of that system. She falls completely outside her former *sensus communis* in two related ways: she is suddenly and, as it seems, arbitrarily excluded from membership in that community, *and* she realises the degree to which the social representations of that community in fact misrepresent, even misrecognise, the reality of slavery as it is experienced by the slaves.

The transition she is forced to make from one reality, as it were, to another is violent and abrupt. From being a privileged and sheltered upper-class young woman – a more or less autonomous subject – she is thrust into the position of being the property of anyone who purchases her – a dependent object. Remaining within the conventions of the sentimental novel, Iola's sexual violation at the hands of brutal masters is alluded to in order to make clear the profound gulf that separates these social categories. The treatment she receives at this point would have been unthinkable earlier, a juxtaposition that draws attention to the relativity of what is thinkable, what is 'normal', from different cultural points of view. Having previously established a sympathetic identification with the reader, her experience on both sides of this ideological force field makes her a character who can presumably lead the reader to a clearer understanding of the reality faced by slaves.

When Dr Gresham, a white doctor and abolitionist, proposes to Iola, she has the opportunity to resume her comfortable life in the North 'passing' as a white. She declines the offer, preferring instead to dedicate herself to reuniting her dispersed family. This decision has two implications. As Carby points out in her introduction to the novel, this fictional situation is a standard 'metaphor for the African diaspora, a commonly-invoked Afro-American literary convention' (1987a: xviii). The disintegration of family and community that first occurred as a result of the abduction of millions of Africans was later reproduced in America where the destiny of these people was not theirs to decide but rested instead in the hands of white owners whose economic and disciplinary priorities caused them to sell and transport individuals without regard for human relationships. But it should also be noted that the family connection she seeks ultimately to maintain is that of her black ex-slave mother rather than that of her wealthy white father, and that the first result of this decision is her refusal of marriage to a white man. This rejection of Dr Gresham's proposal signals a rejection of white male patriarchy, even in its most benign form, and an affirmation of her African–American heritage. The struggle to which Iola dedicates herself thus concerns both race and gender: she insists on her autonomy as a woman as well as on the legitimacy of black aspirations. The marriage that she does enter into at the end of the novel is a marriage of equals, with both partners working to fulfill the 'grand and noble purposes [that] were lighting up their lives; and they deemed it a blessed privilege to . . . labor for those who had passed from the old oligarchy of slavery into the new commonwealth of freedom' (1987: 271). The versions of historical experience given expression in the novel are sorted through in order that yet another reality might be created in the future: 'From threads of fact and fiction', Harper writes in a concluding note, 'I have woven a story whose mission will not be in vain if it awaken in the hearts of our countrymen a stronger sense of justice and a more Christlike humanity' (1987: 282). History, then, is appropriated in the interest of changing history.

Another novel written not long after *Iola Leroy* employs a similar historical situation. In her preface to *Contending Forces: A Romance Illustrative of Negro Life North and South* (1899), Pauline Hopkins articulates the problem of representation in a way that brings to mind more contemporary discussions of the subject. Narrative is important to any group as a record of development and as a means of preserving cultural values, and, as Hopkins argues, for African–Americans this is especially important:

No one will do this for us; we must ourselves develop the men and women who will faithfully portray the inmost thoughts and feelings of the Negro with all the fire and romance which lie dormant in our history, and, as yet, unrecognized by writers of the Anglo-Saxon race.   (1988: 13–14; Hopkins's italics)

Hopkins's novel is, of course, an attempt to do just that. Like *Iola Leroy*, it begins with a wealthy plantation-owning family whose racial purity is less than secure but whose members never suspect the fate awaiting them. Upon the circulation of a rumour that displeases certain opportunistic white supremacist groups in the area, the father is murdered and his wife and children destined for slavery. While the wife escapes her fate through suicide, the children themselves (who, like Iola Leroy, might have become slaveowners) become slaves. The novel thus is able to explore the historical reality of slavery from both sides: 'I have presented both sides of the dark picture . . . truthfully and without vituperation' (1988: 15). While Hopkins's claim that she has 'tried to tell an impartial story, leaving it to the reader to draw conclusions' may be seen as problematic, there is no doubting the sincerity of her statement of fictional purpose, a purpose that combines, like Harper's, the desire to record the history of a marginalised group with a desire to alter that group's future through legitimising its historical experience. As Hopkins was writing, violence against blacks was reaching unprecedented levels, one result of white determination that, even after legal emancipation, blacks would not be allowed a political voice, and she sees her novel as a way of addressing this situation: 'In these days of mob violence, when lynch-law is raising its head like a venomous monster,' she writes, 'the retrospective mind will dwell upon the history of the past, seeking there a solution of these monstrous outbreaks' (1988: 14).

Hopkins aims her work both at blacks who would find their experience reflected there and at whites who had much to learn about this marginalised group. The faith and optimism suggested in her claim that her novel is a form of 'pleading for that justice of heart and mind for my people which the Anglo-Saxon in America never withholds from suffering humanity' (1988: 15) is more than slightly undermined in the novel itself with its accounts of racist torture, rape and murder.[7] While her hope for social justice in 1899 may have been unfounded, her attempt to find justice through a depiction of the historical sufferings and aspirations of the black population is only one of many based on the perhaps naïve conviction that if only people in power knew what was really happening, they would put a stop to the injustice. What was needed, then, was a portrait of those oppressed people that could penetrate the ideological barriers of the dominant *sensus communis*. Like Frances Harper, Hopkins found that an effective way to accomplish this was to have fictional characters who could speak for the dominant group forced across those barriers. Witnesses whose reliability has already been established – at least in part through their membership in the white community – now speak from the position of the dominated group, have themselves become, in fact, members of that group. The result is that the transgression of the boundary between the two groups exposes the artificiality and brutalising effects of the boundary itself.[8] What had appeared natural – the segregation and stratification of the races – is thus shown to be an arbitrary social and historical creation, subject to further historical alteration. Hopkins's hope that knowledge will lead those in power to a sense of justice not only echoes Harper's similar appeal, it also casts a disturbing light on the long history of such attempts, attempts which continue today as justice remains a distant horizon.

Many novels by black women feature characters whose acceptance of the self-evidence of the status quo is demolished and replaced by an inside knowledge of the heterodox reality of the other – alterity defined here in terms both of race and gender. To accomplish this, a wrenching of the normally experienced reality of social relations is enacted in order to defamiliarise social patterns which have been experienced as natural rather than historical and contingent. The importance of historiography is clear in this context: it constitutes one of the privileged narrative genres that can articulate the realities of people who had remained in a state of aphasia. Bourdieu argues that the capacity to publish, to make public (i.e. render objectified, visible, and even official) that which had not previously attained objective and collective existence ... – people's malaise, anxiety, disquiet, expectations – represents a formidable social power, the power to make groups by making the *common sense*, the explicit consensus, of the whole group.   (1985: 202)

It has been the burden of much black women's writing to develop this kind of discursive power, to overcome a socially-imposed aphasia by articulating an alternative narrative point of view on historical reality, and through this representation to legitimise and valorise the experience of a previously marginalised and oppressed social group. The novels considered here, like many other African–American novels, both represent the situation of the jarring witness in relation to American history and point to the necessary conditions under which that situation might be rectified. There is a pleasing irony in the fact that Toni Morrison, for example, whose novels represent the dilemmas of social aphasia so well, has been awarded the Nobel Prize for Literature. Historically silenced, her characters are no longer historiographically silenced but speak eloquently and to a large audience.

One of the ramifications of such a development might be to enable the articulation of the new, more heterogenous narrative of American history called for by Huggins. This would require the continued elaboration, in Lyotard's sense of the term, of new idioms in which to phrase the historical differend which exists between the black and white communities of America. Such idioms would constitute neither a new version of Universal History nor a vague and token acknowledgement of cultural difference in the midst of 'business as usual', but would – if it is indeed possible – necessitate a fundamental rethinking of some of the organisational principles of historical narrative and the implications of its relation to the *sensus communis*. The central subject of historiography has traditionally been white and male, and his point of view has been authoritative; in the work of contemporary African–American women, the narrative centre organising the events is that of a self-consciously jarring perspective. It remains to be seen what might happen if there were to be no central subject at all, no specific community whose *sensus communis* underwrites the point of view from which the representation is launched.

READ YOUR HISTORY, MAN!'

Paule Marshall's *The Chosen Place, The Timeless People* (1969)
declares its historical concerns in its opening epigraph, a saying
from the Tiv, a West African people whose descendants are
perhaps among the population of the Caribbean island that the
novel depicts.

Once a great wrong has been done, it never dies. People speak the words of
peace, but their hearts do not forgive. Generations perform ceremonies of
reconciliation but there is no end.   (Marshall, 1969: v)

The great wrong that provides a framework for Marshall's novel
has its historical beginning in the forced migration and enslavement of millions of Africans, and the consequences of that great
wrong ramify in complex ways through the lives and relationships
of all the novel's characters. Saul Amron, his wife Harriet and
assistant Allen Fuso arrive in Bourne Island to carry out
anthropological research on this underdeveloped community as
the preliminary phase of a development project sponsored by a
'philanthropic' foundation (Center for Applied Social Research –
CASR). Funding for the 'Center' is provided by several large
corporations, but mainly by 'Unicor', a company which also
controls the sugar-based economy of the island, and a company with which Harriet Amron is connected. Harriet's family
wealth originated with an ancestor who had traded in rum and
slaves, a family business that has changed with the times yet has
maintained economic control over some of the descendants of
those slaves through both the sugar industry (production) and
through the saltfish that provides the basis of the islanders' diet
(consumption).

Marshall's bitter sense of historical irony is evident as she
discusses the motivation behind such a foundation. Frequently
referred to as 'the Center', it suggests as well the hegemonic centre
that it represents, and the relation of margin to centre that it
ultimately enforces. For all its altruistic rhetoric, the Center exists
more fundamentally as a tax shelter. The connection between
philanthropy and hegemony is indeed intimate: since Harriet is
married to the chief academic researcher, it is in a sense her money
that underwrites the whole project – and thus her approval is
necessary to its continuance. As Merle (who acts as a spokes-

person) realises, the power structure has, in some significant ways, not really altered since the English 'were around here selling us for thirty pounds sterling'.

The Kingsley's still hold the purse strings and are allowed to do as they damn please . . . . And the Little Fella is still bleeding his life out in a cane field . . . . Things are no different. The chains are still on.   (1984: 210)

Then, directing her appeal to the island's postcolonial black elite, she concludes by asking: 'Haven't you . . . learned anything from all that's gone on in this island over the past four hundred years? Read your history, man!'

The residents of impoverished Bournehills are, for the most part, victims of this history. The Atlantic ocean, separating them from their ancestral home, crashes in

with a sound like that of the combined voices of the drowned raised in a loud unceasing lament – all those, the nine million and more it is said, who in their enforced exile, their Diaspora, had gone down between this point and the homeland lying out of sight to the east. This sea mourned them. Aggrieved, outraged, unappeased, it hurled itself upon each of the reefs in turn and then upon the shingle beach, sending up the spume in an angry froth which the wind took and drove in like smoke over the land. Great boulders that had roared down . . . centuries ago stood scattered in the surf; these, sculpted into fantastical shapes by the wind and water, might have been gravestones placed there to commemorate those millions of the drowned.   (1984: 106)

The sense here that history is inscribed even on the face of nature suggests the way that Marshall portrays the past as a force determining the very categories of perception available to the people. History, in this novel, is not a separate discourse, however privileged, but the basis on which a culture develops its sense of itself and its relation to the rest of the human community. It is the framework in terms of which all present discourse must be interpreted. The historical sense impinges on all the categories through which the impoverished islanders view the world. As Spillers observes, while slavery has long been legally abolished 'its human and social currencies become the basic archetypal and memorial symbol-pattern that asserts itself in the cultural and daily activities of the community' (1958: 158). If perception and appreciation of the social world, as Bourdieu has argued, are products of 'previous symbolic struggles and express the state of the symbolic power relations' (1985: 200–1), in Bournehills, those previous struggles (symbolic and otherwise) have left people impoverished and defeated, caught in a web of victimisation that is reproduced not simply in their own attitudes, but also in their continued domination by more or less the same forces that enslaved them hundreds of years before. The genealogy Marshall provides, connecting Harriet to the original slave-traders indicates the continuity of this pattern – her non-profit philanthropic foundation notwithstanding.

The power to bestow a name, whether on a place or a person is a frequent motif in many African–American novels. Slaves were given names by their owners and made to live in places whose names were foreign to them – symbolising their enforced lack of control over their own lives, their bodies and their world. The colonial legacy in Bournehills is present in the place names that identify the island – not only Westminster, but outside town as well: Agincourt, Buckingham, Sussex, Lords, Drake (1984: 101). A dispossessed people, their dispossession is registered, for instance, in the fact that they do not name their own land, but depend on the network of names bestowed on the world by those who dominate them. This is typically the case in colonised countries whose official reality is defined in the language of the colonisers and whose prior nominations are either replaced entirely or are absorbed into the dominant language. In this process of linguistic absorption, the original sense can be lost through a semantic shift which results from the rupture in what Saul Kripke refers to as the chain of communication.[9] The problem is even more vexed in the case of African–Americans, who, brought as slaves by the colonisers, can claim no prior possession of the land or its designations.

The great exception in this (synchronic) pattern of naming the island is the great exception historically (diachronically) as well: Pyre Hill. This name registers the island's one great historic moment of resistance:

[O]ne of the biggest estate houses on the island used to be right on top of that hill. People say it stood like a castle there. It belonged to Percy Bryam, the man who owned all of Bournehills and everyone in it in the beginning. People used to have to get down on their knees when he passed.   (1984: 101)

Cuffee Ned, leader of a slave rebellion, killed Bryam and burned his estate to the ground, an event whose success is unparalleled in the island's history. Its value to the islander's sense of the past and of community is expressed by Merle: 'There was never anything like it before or since. It's the only bit of history we have worth mentioning' (1984: 102). And indeed, this moment of insurrection stands in bold relief against the unbroken history of oppression that structures local attitudes to authority and to a future whose bleak prospects are relieved only by the millenarian hope that Cuffee Ned – or some avatar – will return to liberate them once again.[10] With its ritual re-enactment of the slave uprising of Cuffee Ned – complete with the dramatised murder of the imperialists – the carnival later in the novel produces the temporary inversion of the socio-historical reality of the islanders.

This sense of common history seems registered in their very convention of greeting one other: 'they would slowly raise their right arm like someone about to give evidence in court, the elbows at a sharp ninety-degree angle, the hand held stiff, the fingers straight. It was a strange, solemn greeting encompassing both hail and farewell, time past and present' (1984: 103). The legal simile recalls, once again, the metaphor of jarring witnesses, which they indubitably are in the eyes of the dominant community. This image is developed further in the anecdote of the servant charged with the theft of a piece of his employer's property: the servant's (jarring) version of events is not accepted by the court and the employer's complaint is upheld (1984: 76). Their evidence is abundantly clear and powerfully convincing to them, however, and constitutes one of the most fundamental truths that sustain them and order their perception of their place in the structure of power. The greeting is furthermore a kind of ritual of recognition whereby members of a closed community recognise and tacitly affirm each other, and at the same time form a barrier excluding those who do not share in this sense of community.

The gap that distances them from other communities is evident: 'those people are another breed altogether', one of the island's elite women warns Harriet. 'You can't figure them out' (1984: 70). The incomprehension – the mutual incomprehension of alien language groups that Bakhtin observes – is frequently registered, in the 'veiled eyes' (1984: 154), or in the literal distance that separates them from the community of power. When the island's elite meet for drinks at a local bar, a small crowd of people can be glimpsed outside, 'watching from behind the tall split-bamboo fence which secured the hotel from its surroundings ... standing there invisible, their black faces part of the greater blackness of the night' (1984: 75). Even more dramatically, this gap is illustrated by the description of Saul's attempt to communicate the real meaning of his development project to the population of the island who have gathered to hear him. The elite members of the society fill the room, while the rest remain outside. In between, the veranda remains empty 'like some no man's land no one dared cross' (1984: 132) in spite of the fact that those on the outside have been urged to come in. Instead of doing so, they stay on the beach or on the steep steps leading down to it, standing

in great faceless numbers under the far-reaching shadow of the veranda, while behind them, down the stretch of shingle, the breakers pounded and clawed at the land. The torn spume, soaring up into the darkness each time a wave struck, was a brief, brilliant pyrotechnic display in the light from the house.

The play of light and shadow between the house (containing the elite) and the beach (whose surf recalls the millions of dispossessed) conveys much, almost allegorically, about why the gap remains though there is apparently no one present to enforce it. Even Merle cannot convince those 'on the darkened beach below' to 'come up' and challenge the force field that keeps them in a dominated position. 'Each time she called down they would look off, making it appear that she was speaking to someone other than they, gently ignoring her' (1984: 132). As Bourdieu has argued, once a system of objective mechanisms for reproducing the social order is in place, no direct personal intervention is necessary in the maintenance of power relations (1977b: 190) – and, in fact, Saul's well-intentioned intervention in the interests of subverting those objective mechanisms and the social order they guarantee, faces almost insuperable obstacles.

Saul decides to go to them, since they will not come to him. Moving down to the beach, his sense of difference, of distance, in relation to these people becomes even clearer. He tries, with little success, to make contact by looking into their eyes,

deep-set eyes which seemed to be regarding him from the other end of a long dimly lit corridor, whose distance was measurable both in space and time, and down which he was certain he would have to travel if he were ever to know them or they to know him.   (1984: 137)

The basis of the sense of distance is suggested in the loud crash of the wave, which metaporically contextualises all understanding of the present through its memorial to the nameless dead. Just as the memory of the past exerts a force more powerful than this moment can overcome, the roar of the sea with all its sublime associations drowns out Saul's attempt to identify (name) himself as a new and different kind of emissary from the hegemonic centre. Saul is committed to the attempt to cross that cultural barrier, a crossing that requires, as he realises, not only an understanding of the other but also a redefinition of the self. His wife Harriet harbours no such ambitions, and her meeting with them is less of a challenge: her smile is simply a function of her 'unruffled surface', and the 'masked smiles they gave her in return held a profound recognition' (1984: 137). This recognition is a tacit acknowledgement of a whole cultural configuration, a world-view providing well-defined roles both for the Harriets of the world and for the dispossessed, who 'extended their hands in the same slow eloquent manner . . . which seemed to make of them witnesses after some fact', a fact that remains unarticulated but which sounds loudly in the crashing waves.

The eloquence of the salutation is, perhaps, the only eloquence they demonstrate beyond the limits of their own community. The distance that separates them from the community of power expresses itself as well in their particular form of aphasia. Voluble with their peers, their ability to articulate is lost in the presence of others. The most powerful example of this aphasia, though by no means the only example, occurs when Ferguson, a mill worker, resolves to speak to the owner, Sir John Stokes, about the bad condition of the equipment.

'Yes, I'm going to speak to the big man himself,' he said, sobering, 'even if I got to have a few grogs to do it. I'm going to step right up . . . . I'm going to tell him straight, just the way I'm telling you. Mark my words.'   (1984: 156)

When that momentous occasion finally arises, he seems ready: 'more than ever resolved to speak', he stands waiting 'in all his lean tensile grace and authority' (1984: 219) as Sir John comes to look at the equipment. Sir John remains unaware of him for some time, but is alerted eventually by the quality of tension emanating from Ferguson and looks up.

Their eyes met and for a moment they quietly regarded each other down the length of the railing, Sir John vaguely puzzled, questioning, the little commanding lift to his head challenging Ferguson to speak, and Ferguson straining to do so, the veins and tendons that strung together his limbs standing out in a tangle beneath his skin in the effort. But no sound came. He stood silent. Behind his glasses his eyes were eloquent with the speech he was to have given, that he had rehearsed so often.   (1984: 221–2)

The speech situation depicted in this confrontation is an exemplary instance of the discursive blockage which Bourdieu describes as a kind of socially and historically generated aphasia, the symbolic violence of which guarantees the already-existing power structure.[11] The community on the 'other side of the story', represented here by Ferguson, displays both its political and its discursive powerlessness in the face of 'weighty interests' which would, in any case, refuse its testimony. Ferguson's failure to speak suggests his tacit recognition not only that the historical reality experienced by his community is sufficiently non-analogous to that experienced by Sir John as to render understanding impossible, but also that this difference is structured hierarchically so that the linguistic currency he possesses – his names and descriptions of the world – will always already be discounted by those in power. His silence constitutes his implicit awareness of his status as a jarring witness whose testimony will not be accorded the authority it deserves no matter how hard he strains. In the absence of an idiom by means of which he might communicate across the cultural gap, he is left speechless. This aphasia is the result of a long and violent historical process: as Bourdieu argues, in order to establish this imbalance, the dominant classes had to 'work directly, daily, personally, to produce and reproduce conditions of domination, which are even then never entirely trustworthy' (1984: 190). This was the role of the hated Sir Percy and those who followed, but now that position has changed so that the reproduction of 'relations of domination is taken over by objective mechanisms [both institutional and those of social psychology] which serve the interests of the dominant group without any conscious effort on the latter's part'. The ensuing silence can then be interpreted by Sir John (who inherits the situation from Sir Percy) as consent, as evidence of an inability to make judgements or even as an indication of a lack of an internal world (Bradley).

The great exception is, of course, Merle, who speaks endlessly. She acts frequently as a spokesperson for those less articulate than herself, and her logorrhea contrasts sharply with the general aphasia of those around her.[12] As Saul realises, she seems to have no choice:

something in her eyes, a doomed, obsessed glint, did put him in mind of the old mariner in the poem he had read as a boy. She, too, might have been witness to, victim of, some unspeakably inhuman act and been condemned to wander the world telling every stranger she met about it.   (1984: 89)

Her attempt to speak the unspeakable makes little or no impression on those in positions of power. She articulates, in her own way, the history that is the legacy of the islanders, and her suffering – 'wide enough to include an entire history' (1984: 68) – is acknowledged by all. Yet she is not really heard. When the mill is closed, threatening to destroy what little economic independence the people have, her language reaches its highest pitch as she tries to confront the mill boss. He does not respond, does not even come to the door to acknowledge her presence, so that her voice is hurled into an 'unassailable silence':

the abuse she heaped on him sounded hollow, ineffectual, even pathetic. As quickly as the curses rose they fell. Those outside could almost see them falling like downed birds through the air. She, too, must have finally realized the futility of her harangue because her voice suddenly ceased. And as quickly the off-season silence returned. She might not have spoken. (1984: 387)

In a variation on the aphasia suffered by Ferguson, Merle speaks but her voice is not heard since she is speaking in an idiom not recognised by those she is addressing, those who hold power. While Merle and the operators of the mill are, in one sense, members of the same language community, they are here engaged in the struggle over meaning that, according to Voloshinov, occurs at the point of intersection 'of differently oriented social interests within one and the same sign community, i.e., by the class struggle' (1973: 23). Lacking the power to control the official meanings or refractions of the 'multiaccentual' signs in this uneven ideological or discursive conflict, people like Merle and Ferguson are afflicted with a variety of social speech pathologies. While the truth value of their descriptions of events is not, for them, in doubt, no consequent sense of possibility – that, for example, their narrative of events could stick as the one the community will live by – ever materialises.

No simple resolution or synthesis is, however, obvious – either in the world of Marshall's novel or in the political reality it represents. And indeed she makes no real effort to impose an imaginary or aesthetic solution onto this very real dilemma. Reflecting on the writing of this novel a few years later, she comments that in it she brings together her most important themes: 'the importance of truly confronting the past, both in personal and historical terms, and the necessity of reversing the present order' (1973: 110–11). While these themes are amply and complexly dramatised, the social change remains unrealised in the novel. While the urgency of the imperative is not in doubt, no means of achieving it is concretely articulated. Merle's decision to go to Africa seems only a very preliminary step toward defining a new cultural identity from which such social change might then be conceived.[13] 'I am not really talking so much about an actual return', Marshall has commented, instead this journey

is a metaphor for the psychological and spiritual return back over history, which I am convinced Black people in this part of the world must undertake if we are to have a sense of our total experience and to mold for ourselves a more truthful identity. Moreover, I believe this exploration of the past is vital in the work of constructing our future . . . . [A]n oppressed people cannot overcome their oppressors and take control of their lives until they have a clear and truthful picture of all that has gone before, until they begin to use their history creatively.   (1973: 107)

The demand for a 'clear and truthful picture' of history resides uneasily, perhaps, with the injunction to use history creatively – yet this is the tension inherent in all narrative history. An essential difference separates Hopkins's earlier demand for historical truth from Marshall's: while Hopkins's is made in the hope that whites will respond to truth with a sense of justice and common humanity, Marshall's is here directed primarily to blacks who need to redefine their communal identity in order to take power themselves.

Marshall's perspective brings out the tragedy of black history at the expense of most whites who are portrayed in a pointedly unsympathetic manner – who become, in fact, from this point of view, the jarring witnesses to black history and are dealt with in a similarly peremptory fashion. Harriet's suicide seems almost a fitting end for her, a complementary fate to that of her first husband, a scientist whose hand she always imagines on the button that will bring about the nuclear holocaust that completes the long history of the blind destructive white quest for power. Allen Fuso is likeable enough, perhaps, but he is represented as lacking character and sexual identity as a result of his racial and cultural background.[14] Merle's lesbian ex-lover in England seems almost pathologically perverse, Sir John and his minions on the island are thoroughly reprehensible, and so on.

There is, however, a difference between Marshall's reduction of the complex humanity of her white characters and the similar (but contrary) reduction by white writers of black characters, and that difference has to do with history and power. Marshall attributes her original understanding of narrative to hearing her mother and her friends, maids and cleaners for wealthy New Yorkers, telling stories of their experiences in the fine houses of the rich during the Depression. Those conversations, she writes, and the narratives they contained were therapeutic, 'it was their way to exorcise the day's humiliations and restore them to themselves'.

> The people they worked for were usually the first thing to come under the whiplash of their tongues. For hours at a stretch they would subject their employers to an acute and merciless analysis . . . . But this has long been a standard phenomenon in Black-White relations in America. The oppressed has to know the enemy – his survival depends on it. While the oppressor, to defend against his guilt, usually chooses not to know us.   (1973: 98)

The caricatures that the black women created of the whites, they created as a means of self-defence, a way of working through their oppression, a survival strategy. Defusion of guilt through a reduction of black humanity appears conversely as the meaning of white caricatures of blacks. While this novel moves no closer to a universal historiographic point of view transcending the historical exigencies of particular communities, the significance of privileging one point of view over another thus depends on the concrete set of social relations involved – a fact which formalist analysis of narrative might overlook.

'As I see it,' writes Marshall, 'the person we are talking about, the Negro woman, has been until recent times almost nonexistent in the prose literature of the country' (1974: 33). After citing examples from Gertrude Stein and William Faulkner to demonstrate her point that representations of black women have denied them complex subjectivity, Marshall connects this to the strategic denial of testimony it enables. The end result was to deny the Negro woman her humanity. For if she was less than human all sorts of crimes could be committed against her and go unpunished. She could be exploited in the fields and kitchens, her body freely used, her children taken from her, her men castrated before her eyes, and yet in the mind of white America this abuse, this outrage, was somehow not serious, was in fact, justified.   (1974: 34–5)

This kind of oppression, then, is directly related to the power to control the historical records and the interpretations of events. The public assertion and affirmation of shared humanity has been one task of black women writers, attainable through the development and articulation of a complex narrative point of view that could no longer be ignored by that *sensus communis* Marshall designates as 'the mind of white America'.

'LEAVING EVIDENCE'

While *The Chosen Place, The Timeless People* urges a return to black history as a means to the recognition and assertion of black identity, the women whose history forms the central narrative of Gayl Jones's *Corregidora* (1975) need no such urging: they are obsessed with their past, and with the historiographic implications of the ability and propensity of those in power to edit retroactively and selectively the historical record. This is one extreme version of history as textuality which recognises the added fact that the text of history has always been under the control of those in power. By this account, African–Americans, as a group, are allowed no claim to legitimacy that cannot be rescinded at the whim of the whites in power. One character tells how his father had put every cent he could save into the purchase of a small plot of land 'so the generations after him would always have land to live on' (1986: 78). When, after his death, his widow attempts to claim the land at the courthouse, the deed is missing, a historical document torn from the book. The son has no choice but to accept this legal disinheritance since 'they ain't nothing you can do when they tear the pages out of the book and they ain't no record of it. They probably burned the pages.'

Another character comments bitterly that the authorities will put little effort into investigating the murder of a black woman: 'as soon as you leave, they say, "Here put it in the nigger file." That mean they get to it if they can. And most times they can't. Naw, they don't say put it in the nigger file, they say put it in the nigger woman file, which means they ain't gon never get to it' (1986: 134). Hayden White's point, that the coherence of narrative depends on the existence of a social centre which grounds and legitimises it, is here extended by the struggle over discursive power that divides and subdivides the American social world. The African–American social centre exists but the police recognise neither it nor the coherence of the narratives which emanate from it. Like the black hole into which the narratives of Faulkner's Valery Bon or the 'ape-woman' disappear, 'the nigger woman file' is the dead end of this chain of communication, and the evidence given by African–American women produces in the legal authorities no sense of an imperative to act.

Corregidora traces a line of matriarchal descent over four generations of women. The bond that joins these women is forged in response to a legacy of historical and historiographic injustice: 'My grandmama', says Ursa, 'said when they did away with slavery down there they burned all the slavery papers so it would be like they never had it' (1986: 9). In order to keep this historical record alive, an oral counter-tradition is invoked which recalls the urgency Robert Stepto speaks of as an aspect of the slave narrative tradition (1979: 3):

My great-grandmama told my grandmama the part she lived through that my grandmama didn't live through and my grandmama told my mama what they both lived through and my mama told me what they all lived through and we were suppose to pass it down like that from generation to generation so we'd never forget. Even though they'd burned everything to play like it didn't never happen.   (Jones, 1986: 9)

This is their collective strategy to avoid the Lyotardian predicament whereby there is no evidence remaining to document the past and no one to remember what happened. In fact, their main purpose in life seems to be to preserve this memory – even the bearing of children is justified with reference to passing the memory through generations.

This transmission of cultural narrative as a means of structuring individual identity within a shared sense of community is similar in a sense to that which is found in Faulkner's *Absalom, Absalom!*: like Quentin Compson, Ursa is heir to a legacy which is difficult to assimilate. The great-grandmother, with the five-year-old Ursa in her lap, tells the same story over and over. She tells of her life as a slave to Corregidora, a Portuguese plantation owner who

> took her out of the field when she was still a child and put her to work in his whorehouse while she was a child .... 'He would take me hisself first and said he was breaking me in. Then he started bringing other men and they would give me money and I had to give it over to him.'   (1986: 10–11)[15]

If these women do not preserve this history, it is unlikely that anyone else will. And while Ursa is unsure how to respond to it, she is in no doubt of the intensity of the sense of duty bequeathed to her by preceding generations. When she questions the truth of the story, she is slapped and told that her mission in life is to remember so that when their testimony is finally called for, it will be ready. When this time comes aphasia will no longer block their powers of legitimate speech and the oppressors will be judged:

> they didn't want to leave no evidence of what they done – so it couldn't be held against them. And I'm leaving evidence. And you got to leave evidence too. And your children got to leave evidence. And when it come time to hold up the evidence, we got to have evidence to hold up. That's why they burned all the papers, so there wouldn't be no evidence to hold up against them. (1986: 14)

While the horizon of justice suggested here has been substantially deferred in comparison with the appeals made by Harper and Hopkins in their narratives, Jones's implied teleology suggests an end-point at which the rights and wrongs of history will be reckoned, a point analogous to the millenarian moment of post-Diaspora reunification alluded to in Marshall's *The Chosen Place, The Timeless People*, the moment implicit in Walsh and explicit in Benjamin at which the past becomes 'citable in all its moments' (1969: 254). The role inherited by Ursa is that of continuing the generations and the story until this apocalyptic moment of judgement, truth and final justice. As her grandmother reminds her, 'They can burn papers but they can't burn conscious, Ursa. And that's what makes the evidence. And that's what makes the verdict' (1986: 22). When this day of judgement comes, it will provide a verdict that will rectify the Lyotardian wrong by bringing to light and to discourse all the 'Days that were pages of hysteria', the 'suppressed hysteria' on which their survival depended (1986: 59), as Corregidora incestuously fathered children in subsequent generations while living off the prostitution he forces them into. Jones's textual metaphor suggests that these pages, once suppressed, will then become a matter of public record. If, as Bradley suggests, correction of the crooked in the record of history depends on the knowledge of the straight, these women have understood the need for maintaining their sense of the straight, even though the dominant definitions of the weightiest interests contradict all their experience. Their sustaining faith is that ultimately their historical testimony, their truth, will prevail.

The historical text of male possession begins in her mother's story *'about the Portuguese who fingered your genitals. His pussy.* "The Portuguese who bought slaves paid attention only to the genitals." *Slapped you across the cunt till it was bluer than black'* (1986: 54). And again in the blunt warning Corregidora delivers, 'I don't wont nothing black fucking with my pussy' (1986: 127). The most graphic such incident narrated concerns a couple on an adjacent coffee plantation, and it reveals the destructive effect of slavery on human relationships as black women were forced to be sexually available to white men. The violence contained in this brief episode becomes an integral part of the novel's thematic structure.

The master shipped her husband out of bed and got in the bed with her and just as soon as he was getting ready to go in her she cut off his thing with a razor she had hid under the pillow and he bled to death, and then the next day they came and got her and her husband. They cut off her husband's penis and stuffed it in her mouth, and then they hanged her. They let him bleed to death. They made her watch and then they hanged her.   (1986: 67)

These suppressed pages of hysteria constitute a foundational text in which the degraded African–American woman and the castrated African–American man are produced literally and symbolically by white power. The crushing of black resistance in this narrative suggests the power and ruthlessness of the dominant white group who imposed and enforced slavery, sexual and otherwise. Blacks were not often in a position to resist this brutal dehumanisation, and as Jones shows, the disjunction between what they felt and how they could act inevitably affects their relationships, with ramifications reaching down to the present.

This is the history that is passed down in Ursa's family, from mother to daughter, from grand- and great-grandmother to daughter. And there is a related injunction passed down. Not only must historical events be remembered, but even more difficult perhaps, the ideological or psychological after-effects of that history must be dealt with. Ursa's mother tells her

They burned all the documents, Ursa, but they didn't burn what they put in their minds. We got to burn out what they put in our minds, like you burn out a wound. Except we got to keep what we need to bear witness. That scar that's left to bear witness.   (1986: 72)

What has been put in their minds as part of the basic material of subject-formation is the memory of the violence, both physical and symbolic, committed against them as African–Americans, as women. It carries over as a residue from the slave era when male–female relationships and family relationships were subject to the disruptions brought on by the slaveowners who asserted a right to sexual possession of black women (or disposal of their husbands and children).[16] These patterns have scarred their minds and continue to operate even in the absence of the white owner who instigated the destructive behaviour. As Ursa tells Mutt, ' "you taught me what Corregidora taught Great Gram. He taught her to use the kind of words she did," ' words like ' "You fucking me, bastard" ' (1986: 76). Mutt reiterates the language of possession in the same terms as Corregidora: the phrase 'his pussy' implying proprietorship of her body.

The sense of degradation belied by these words exemplifies a significant aspect of the legacy of gender relations inherited by Ursa's generation. This destructive attitude, internalised from the centuries of slavery, structures Ursa's relationships with men and lies behind the brutality of men to women in this novel. As Jones represents this legacy, the disruption of normal sexual relationships enforced by the slaveowner leaves men prone to sexual violence and women unable to reconcile degradation and desire, even generations later. The historical and hysterical text of slavery is thus inscribed in their present behaviour: since the violent sexual possession is repeated to some degree in the relations obtaining between black men and women of Ursa's generation, that suppressed hysteria is repeated as well. Reflecting back on her relationship with Mutt, and its violent end, she wonders 'Is that the way you treat someone you love? Even my clenched fists couldn't stop the fall. That old man [Corregidora] still howls inside me' (1986: 48). She bears a literal scar where her husband's possessive violence has led to an injury resulting in a hysterectomy. This is added to the list of historical injustices awaiting the time when testimony can be given, when the voices of black women will be finally heard and the ghost of Corregidora that continues to possess them can be exorcised.

In an interview, Jones stated that in writing *Corregidora* she was attempting to convey an

intimate history, particularly a personal history, and to contrast it with the broad, impersonal telling of the Corregidora story. Thus, one reason for Ursa's telling her story and her mother's story is to contrast them with the 'epic,' almost impersonal history of Corregidora.   (Tate, 1988: 92)

The epic story that the older women tell carries a great moral weight in the novel, but the weight of the past is a double-edged sword. While there is a discourse of ultimate liberation structuring it, the obsessive attachment to the past nevertheless leads to the inability of the characters to rise above it in the present.[17] The bearing of children that has been an integral part of bearing witness becomes an impossibility for Ursa, and her position is thus greatly complicated. This rupture in the generational passage of the legacy forces Ursa to reconsider her own personal position: deprived even of the legitimacy that inheres in the preservation of the memory of slavery, she must rethink her relation to that memory. As Keith Byerman notes, just as the historical record can be altered, bearing children as a form of bearing witness can be prevented as well, 'destroy[ing] the truth itself by effacing the future' (1985: 178). Forced by this objective physical crisis to redefine her place in the generational responsibility of succession, she realises that not only her great-grandmother and grandmother – slaves to Corregidora – have histories. In order to understand the more recent past that has been overwhelmed by the distant 'epic' slave past, she decides to visit her mother, a woman who was not possessed by Corregidora, but whose life has been lived in his shadow. For this reason the mother is acutely aware of the necessity to understand how they have been affected and to burn out the ill effects without losing sight of the history that produced them. She understands, but does not herself have enough distance on the legacy of the past to overcome its destructive effects.

Although Ursa specifically asks to hear her mother's personal memories, the mother slips back periodically into the further past, the epic past that has obsessed all the Corregidora women:

It was as if she had more than learned it off by heart, though. It was as if their memory, the memory of all the Corregidora women, was her memory too, as strong with her as her own private memory, or almost as strong. (1986: 129)

This possession by the past and by Corregidora whose name she still bears, affects her ability to respond in the present, to see her own life as having historical significance in itself, and prevents her from thinking about her life in ways not provided for in the Corregidora epic narrative. As her mind goes from real or imagined encounters with her ex-husband Mutt, to recitations of the epic, to recalling the story of her mother's failed attempt to reach beyond the limits of that epic past to embrace a contingent present, Ursa realises that by preserving the Corregidora epic of past male brutality and blaming Mutt for her present troubles she is motivated not just by a desire for justice. As Keith Byermann writes, it 'also reveal[s] evasion of one's own responsibility' (1985: 178). Leaving her mother, Ursa wonders if 'now that Mama had gotten it all out, her own memory – at least to me anyway – maybe she and some man . . . . But then, I was thinking, what had I done about my own life?' (1986: 132). The point here is not to deny the past, but to realise the way that the hangover from the past reaches into the present to poison it as well and to find a balance that can integrate that past with the present. Mutt, at one point, insists on a separation from the past: ' "Whichever way you look at it, we ain't them" ' (1986: 151). The simplicity of this separation is lost on Ursa, however, who thinks 'the way I'd been brought up, it was almost as if I was'. And in fact, Mutt's violence toward her suggests that such a simple separation does not adequately represent their dilemma.

Like her mother, Ursa has been unable to respond in the present, and the story of her relationship with Mutt and its failure becomes the subject of her memories in the final section of the novel. When she realises this, she begins to reinterpret the meaning of the breakdown in her relationship in the light of her personal as well as her family or cultural history. This allows her to conceive of her relationship with Mutt in more complex terms than those bequeathed to her by the Corregidora story, and she is able to begin integrating the insights derived from that story into the sense of interpersonal responsibility she has learned from her mother's narrative. Again, defamiliarisation brought about by objective crisis leads to a redefined relationship to present circumstances. The penultimate section of the novel begins with a declaration of a new historical and personal perspective. 'It was June 1969. I was forty-seven' (1986: 168). When Mutt returns, she resumes her relationship with him in a confrontation combining all the elements of love and hate, fear and desire, past and present that structure the novel.

I didn't know how much was me and Mutt and how much was Great Gram and Corregidora – like Mama when she had started talking like Great Gram. But was what Corregidora had done to her, to them, any worse than what Mutt had done to me, than what we had done to each other, than what Mama had done to Daddy, or what he had done to her in return? (1986: 184)

The result of this conflation is that she realises in this moment of mutual vulnerability that she too has power: ' "I could kill you," ' she realises in what might, in another situation, be a moment of sexual submission echoing the earlier account of sexual torture of the black couple that acts as a kind of foundational narrative. It is up to Ursa and Mutt to throw off the cycle of violence and degradation, to rewrite the historical text of sexuality as one of mutual respect rather than to continue its inscription as violence, power and possession. Corregidora is long dead, and their relationship must escape from the brutal definitions he had imposed upon it, must somehow recuperate a sense of love and equality. Gradually the implications of this mutual vulnerability become clear to both of them. 'I don't want a kind of woman that hurt you,' Mutt says in response to the violence of her statement. 'I don't want a kind of man that'll hurt me neither,' she replies (1986: 185). The ensuing embrace seems to signal a truce.

Melvin Dixon has noted that the word 'Corregidora' comes from a Portuguese term meaning 'a former judicial magistrate'. If the slaveowner Corregidora once passed judgement on these women and sentenced them to a brutal captivity, then Ursa Corregidora, who still bears the name and lives out the legacy of the sentence, herself becomes not only a jarring witness, but simultaneously, as Dixon puts it, a female judge 'charged by the women in her family to "correct" the historical invisibility they have suffered, "to give evidence" of their abuse, and "to make generations" as a defense against their further displacement and annihilation' (1986: 110). There is, as well, another aspect of her charge: as Ursa's mother realises, 'We got to burn out what they put in our minds, like you burn out a wound' (1986: 72). The rupture that occurs in Ursa's life prevents her from carrying out all these tasks, but enables her finally to begin using her historical legacy as a tool with which to rethink the present on terms other than those contained in the story of the past she inherits, to possess the past rather than being possessed by it.

One aspect of the historiographical problem of jarring witnesses that is dramatised very clearly here, one that is not recognised by Bradley and perhaps insufficiently acknowledged in more recent discussions, is the tenacity and persistence of unofficial versions of the past. The fact that the dominant group may fail to recognise any other social centre or narrative coherence does not mean that such forms of resistance disappear. Until the millenarian verdict is pronounced in the light of a past citable in all its instances (Benjamin), the testimony must be preserved; but in the meantime, the racist and sexist images that are its legacy must be worked through. While the apocalyptic moment of transcendent historical truth seems no closer, in the end she is able, very tentatively, to balance the history that has had such a deleterious structuring effect on them both – he violent and jealous, she unresponsive and withdrawn – with a sense of personal responsibility. This resolution, partial though it is, emerges in Corregidora only with a new understanding of African–American history, history not as it is conceived by the dominant white community but also not as the epic of black suffering whose unalterable shadow looms over them, determining every present act. By itself, history is not enough to sustain, not even the vital history from the margins that the Corregidora women keep alive. Because they seem to live only for that witness, they ultimately remain captive to it – indeed their continued enslavement is registered in the fact that they keep the name of the slaveowner for generations. It is Ursa's task as a modern woman to live in the absence of faith in a final authoritative tribunal, yet to maintain her jarring testimony and use the past to develop a narrative sufficient to sustain her in the contingent present.

'MAMMY'S NAME'

While *The Chosen Place, The Timeless People* demands a return to history in the name of the voiceless dead, and *Corregidora* registers the importance of preserving the historical testimony of jarring witnesses, both demonstrate the cultural limitations resulting from a foundational narrative of brutal oppression. Sherley Anne Williams's *Dessa Rose* (1986) undertakes the rewriting of the historical record in order to locate in it a site of possibility by means of her own selective appropriation of history. In the 'Author's Note' which introduces the novel, she relates her narrative first to two separate historical incidents, then to a more general reflection on power and historical discourse. In the first incident,

A pregnant black woman helped to lead an uprising on a coffle (a group of slaves chained together and herded, usually to market) in 1829 in Kentucky. Caught and convicted, she was sentenced to death; her hanging, however, was delayed until after the birth of her baby. (1987: ix)

The delay was, perhaps, due to the prospective market value of the baby. In the second, historically unrelated, incident, 'a white woman living on an isolated farm' in North Carolina in 1830 'was reported to have given sanctuary to runaway slaves' (1987: ix). Williams's sense of regret that these women never met is registered in her imaginative rewriting of these incidents so that they do meet.

Her more general deliberation on the writing of history begins with her admission of 'being outraged by a certain, critically acclaimed novel . . . that travestied the as-told-to memoir of slave revolt leader Nat Turner' (1987: ix). The William Styron novel she alludes to was found offensive by a number of black writers – an example of the fact that even on those occasions when black history found its way into mainstream literary discourse, sufficient attention is not always paid to the perspective of that community.[18] 'Afro-Americans,' she writes,

having survived by word of mouth – and made of that process a high art – remain at the mercy of literature and writing; often, these have betrayed us. I loved history as a child, until some clear-eyed young Negro pointed out, quite rightly, that there was no place in the American past I could go and be free. I now know that slavery eliminated neither heroism nor love; it provided occasions for their expressions. (1987: ix–x)

Williams counters this sense of alienation from both historical legitimacy and historical discourse, establishing a space of qualified freedom by testing and transgressing the limits of the *sensus communis* both of slave and of slaveowner. 'Maybe it is only a metaphor, but I now own a summer in the 19th century' (1987: x), writes Williams; taking possession of that historical ground is not a simple process however.

Dessa Rose contains three main sections, and the different narrative point of view employed in each presents a different cultural perspective on the possibilities for dialogic communication and understanding across the racial boundaries that seemed almost absolute at that time. The first section, 'The Darky', recounts the efforts of a white writer, Adam Nehemiah, to understand the actions of Dessa Rose, a pregnant slave captured following an uprising, so that he can include her in his book on slave revolts, a book that he hopes will find a wide audience among slaveowners who fear the outbreak of such actions on their own plantations. As Deborah McDowell notes, this choice of names is particularly apt: the biblical Adam named the world thereby imbuing it with synchronic order and identity, and Nehemiah chronicled its events thereby bestowing diachronic order (1989: 148). In the course of his conversations with her, she narrates in fragments the events leading up to the violence precipitating her imprisonment. In this section the gap separating black and white senses of reality is virtually uncrossable, and the narrative foregrounds this mutual non-comprehension of alien language groups by shifting the focalisation from one to the other. Bakhtin's phrase is particularly appropriate here, as the disjunction between Dessa and Nehemiah is registered in their language as well as in many other ways. 'He hadn't caught every word; often he had to puzzle overlong at some unfamiliar idiom or phrase, now and then losing the tale in the welter of names the darky called' (Williams, 1987: 10). For Dessa the separation and constraint is simultaneously physical and linguistic: 'She clutched the bars of the window and peered at him through them. She had not understood the half of what he had said, catching only the meaning of "camp" and "runaway" ' (Williams, 987: 64).

Towards the beginning of the chapter Nehemiah tries to deal with his difficulty in making sense of her story by listing the certain facts that he can put together – and runs into exactly the narratorial problems that Collingwood describes. Whenever he moves beyond the narrow confines of those facts to fill in the background or interpret their context he is betrayed by his presuppositions about 'darkies' to such an extent that he is unable to assimilate the facts which this jarring witness does provide. Her tale of captivity and desire for freedom, of the cruelty of treating husbands, wives and children as saleable property without respect for their familial links, falls on deaf ears since he does not think of slaves as human subjects. By the end of the chapter though, Williams has elaborated two separate but parallel universes of experience. The two interpretive communities – one white and powerful, one black and subjected to that power – concur on individual facts, such as that Dessa took part in the violence that resulted in a number of deaths, but beyond this the narrative colligations diverge radically according to the *sensus communis* of each. Since he does not regard her as fully human, Nehemiah resorts to supernatural, or non-human categories in order to explain her actions. Dessa's murder of whites, for instance, is a simple fact to her, the inevitable outcome of comprehensible, even obvious, social pressures. From his perspective, however, such an explanation is not thinkable:

He had understood then something of what the slave dealer, Wilson, might have meant when he talked of the darky's 'devil eyes' her 'devil's stare'.
   'I kill white mens,' her voice overrode mine, as though she had not heard me speak. 'I kill white mens cause . . . I can.'   (1987: 13)

Her 'bald statement . . . seemed to echo in the silence. This was the "fiend", the "devil woman" who had attacked white men and roused other niggers to rebellion' (1987: 13). While violence against blacks appears in the white discourse as a normal and acceptable, if sometimes regrettable, fact in the disciplining of an inferior species, Dessa's violence against whites is inexplicable to Nehemiah who, lacking the resources to construct any other followable narrative (Gallie), has to resort to the non-rational in order to account for it. Dessa's escape from literal imprisonment at the end of the chapter registers as well Nehemiah's ultimate inability to confine her within the interpretive categories available to him.

   The second section, 'The Wench', begins to bridge that gap as Dessa joins a group of escaped slaves living on land belonging to

Rufel, a white woman. A good deal of tension, sexual jealousy and resentment, as well as racial misunderstanding continues through this section as the point of view now shifts between Dessa and Rufel. When Dessa regains consciousness in an unfamiliar 'whitewashed' (1987: 82) room and finds a strange white woman leaning over her, her automatic response articulates a serious cultural division: 'she fought to untangle her arms and legs from covers. The white woman would kill her kill her and . . . the baby. Baby. Her ba – She freed an arm and smashed it into the white woman's face' (1987: 83). When she next awakens, she is somewhat more cautious; through half-closed eyes she guardedly surveys the strange room to get her bearings in these 'white' surroundings:

Dessa watched the white woman . . . watching the white woman through half-closed lids. The white woman stood at the door . . . . A white woman moving very quietly around her bed . . . a white woman white stared at her . . . . The white woman moved. Her heart thudded in her chest. The white woman passed beyond her line of vision.   (1987: 83)

In all her experience, nothing good can be expected from being under the watchful eye of a white person, and her tension and suspicion is obvious. Until the sequence of events of her own personal history begins to come back to her, she assumes from the strangeness of it all that she must be dreaming. Seeing her new baby in the arms of the white woman just increases her sense of bewilderment and estrangement, as she can only conclude that her baby has fallen into the hands of the whites – a fate worse, perhaps, than death.[19] The situation that obtains at this plantation, however, is unlike any that Dessa has previously encountered.

The dissolution of the hegemonic white *sensus communis* is revealed as the narrative focus shifts to Rufel's point of view. The absence of her husband – the white male authority figure – from the plantation indicates the loss of the power centre, a vacuum in the patriarchal hierarchy that results in a more egalitarian social organisation. Rufel's harbouring of runaway slaves, far from being based on any conscious ethical position, occurs originally as a path of least resistance. The slaves have more or less gradually taken over in the absence of the master, and they tolerate the mistress in the same way that she tolerates them – out of necessity. They keep the plantation running for her, she provides a legitimate setting for them, and all sides seem to feel it is best not to delve too deeply into the transgression of social order that is going on. On the surface Rufel is still in charge and the slaves are still below her; she clings to the remnants of that belief and they do not upset it too much for fear of upsetting as well the uneasy balance that has been established. 'They couldn't start using the Glen like a regular hideaway, she would think fearfully, and push the speculation aside' (1987: 99). Such speculation about the definition of her position comes closer to the surface in encounters such as her run-in with Annabelle, who is supposed to be her maid:

> Rufel had stood posing in front of the mirror, lifting her hair from her neck, tugging at the waist and bodice of her dress . . . and she prattled to the girl, as she used to do with Mammy, about fashions and hair styles.   (1987: 102)

The ensuing events mark the separation of these two language groups as surely as Nehemiah's earlier interrogation of Dessa had. As Rufel talks, assuming the role of Southern belle for which she was raised, Annabelle quietly walks out of the room. Such a flagrant and insubordinate breach of roles and protocols upsets Rufel, and she tries to summon up the authority that she has lost as well as the racial categories that substantiated it. 'Nigger . . . you come back here,' she calls, 'You know you don't just walk away from a white person without a by-your-leave.' Annabelle's initial silence and subsequent mocking response upsets whatever shreds of authority Rufel might have left, reducing the mistress to the level of spoiled child.

> Hands on hips, Annabelle leaned toward Rufel, grinning in her face . . . . A thousand imps seemed to dance in her eyes as she said on a rising note of incredulity, 'Mistress 'Fel? Miz Rufel?'   (1987: 103)

This use of a pet-name given by a slave to a child openly subverts Rufel's authority. 'Shaking, Rufel screamed, "My name is 'Mistress' to you!" and fled before the silent laughter in the girl's eyes' (1987: 103). This laughter at the brink of articulation performs the function Bakhtin ascribes to laughter in his work on Rabelais: directed toward the upper classes – in this case Rufel's insistence on her title of distinction – it defeats the fear inspired by power and expresses an unofficial truth about social hierarchy.

Although conventional racial roles frequently continue to guide appearances through this chapter, it is clear that the objective crisis arising from Rufel's literal estrangement from her white society is eroding her sense of community. She is gradually edging towards an acceptance of the fact that she is now, in reality, affiliated with an autonomous black community – black not only in terms of population, but, more importantly, in terms of leadership. Her gradual absorption into this previously alien community leads to the inversion of a number of stereotypes. Rufel, a nursing mother herself, at one point breastfeeds Dessa's baby in order to pacify it: 'More of that craziness, she knew; but then it had seemed to her as natural as tuneless crooning or baby talk' (1987: 105). Despite moments of self-consciousness, embarrassment and guilt, she decides that no one ever need know. She continues dozing and feeding the baby, until she is awakened by the entry of Ada and Harker, two of the escaped slaves who share her farm.

> Their consternation had been almost comic. Ada had stuttered and Harker had gaped. In the pause Rufel had recovered her own composure, feeling somehow vindicated in her actions by their very confusion. She had confounded them – rendered Ada speechless. Still, she had felt some mortification at becoming wet nurse for a darky.   (1987: 105–6)

The speechlessness is symptomatic of the fact that this transgression of the boundaries that define language groups is unspeakable. The role reversal depicted here, a white woman precariously close to becoming 'Mammy' to a black child, is as unthinkable for the black adults who come upon her as it would be for a 'normal' white woman of the time.

But Rufel is no longer normal; her normal world is disintegrating and the social taxonomies that once guided her are disintegrating with it. In one sense she is 'crazy', as she notes – at least in terms of the norms of rationality understood by her husband, her family, the society that produced her. Having moved outside the behaviour expected of her by both the black and the white community, she is not the only one to question her sanity. After realising that Rufel is not trying to harm her or her baby, Dessa wonders 'Was the white woman crazy? . . . . Maybe she was crazy, Dessa thought, but not a killer . . . but touched, maybe; strange in the head' (1987: 120–1). As the nickname the blacks have evolved for her ('Miz Ruint' (1987: 120)) indicates, her position in her own community is ruined.

Bourdieu argues that that difference, such as (in this case) a hierarchical racial taxonomy, can only exist for a subject capable not only of perceiving differences but of recognizing them as significant, interesting, i.e. only for a subject endowed with the capacity and inclination to *make* the distinctions that are regarded as significant in the social universe in question.   (1985: 203)

As the traces of Rufel's original community become fewer and fewer, the systems of difference and distinction on which that community based its sense of itself come to exert less and less of a claim on her perception of the social world. The constellations of significance that had previously ordered her social universe become fainter, less distinct. The 'systematic set of rules governing inter-ethnic social encounters', which, as Fredrik Barth contends, are necessary for the maintenance of social boundaries (1969: 16), lose their authority. As a member of the white aristocracy she is ruined; but another perspective on the social world gradually fills the vacuum left in the disintegration of her sense of herself, and in the light of this she reconstitutes her community and redefines her *sensus communis*. While her ability to distinguish the skin colour of the people among whom she lives is obviously unimpaired, the significance for her of such a system of classifications based on race, and her interest in maintaining such a system of differences, gradually evaporates.

If Rufel's name has been the site of some conflict earlier, the disjunction separating Dessa and Rufel – who as mothers and as lovers become doubles to some extent – is, perhaps, clearest when they conflict over the identity of 'Mammy', one of the central figures in the social universe of the old South. Rufel's thoughts turn back nostalgically to the days before her marriage and isolation at Sutton's Glen, to a time when the hierarchies of her earlier world remained firm. Her beauty, her social status, and most importantly her 'mammy', who evidently loved and cared for her – all the luxuries of the Southern aristocracy guaranteed her happiness and privilege.

She used to dress me up so pretty. Even the Reynolds girls – and their daddy owned the bank; everyone said they wore drawers made out of French silk. They used to admire my clothes ... but I always said 'Oh, this is a little something Mammy ran up for me.' So when I walked into the great hall at Winston, I had on a dress that Mammy made.   (1987: 124)

For Dessa though, the end-point of a very different chain of communication (Kripke), the word 'mammy' brings to mind her own mother and a very different set of images in terms of which Rufel's nostalgic reverie is simply offensive. Dessa is more volatile than Annabelle, who had simply walked away, and she attacks this chauvinistic construction of 'mammy' on two levels. First, she rejects the idea that Rufel had a mammy at all – mammy literally means mother, and of the two only she, Dessa, had a black mother. As well, she assaults Rufel's nostalgic image of 'mammy' by showing that Rufel had never really known the person that she called by that name. 'You ain't got no "mammy" ', says Dessa,

' "Mammy" ain't nobody name, not they real one . . . . You don't even not know "mammy's" name. Mammy have a name, have children . . . . Child don't even know its own mammy's name. What was mammy's name?'   (1987: 125)

The authority of Rufel's response ('Mammy . . . . That was her name') is severely undercut by Dessa's angry assertion – ' "Her name was Rose" ' (1987: 125). Dessa is propelled by this encounter to a series of memories of her own about her mother, whose name was Rose, and who had many children – some of whom died, some of whom became slaves like her, and were taken and sold away. 'Remembering the names now the way mammy used to tell them, lest they forget, she would say; lest her poor lost children die to living memory as they had in her world' (1987: 126). While no millenarian sense of ultimate reunification fuels this ritual of pronouncing the names of the lost as it did in Marshall's *The Chosen Place* or in Jones's *Corregidora*, once again, the need to preserve such an otherwise irretrievable past haunts the characters in all these novels.

Dessa's response has the effect of defamiliarising Rufel's comforting idea of 'mammy', forces her to rethink the identity of the woman whose memory seems so important to her but whose real name, 'Dorcas', seems so unfamiliar. 'It was as if the wench had taken her beloved Mammy and put a stranger in her place.' This stranger whose human face begins to appear through the mask of 'mammy' may even, Rufel realises, have had a life of her own. 'Had Mammy had children, Rufel wondered . . . and how had Mammy borne it when they were taken away – That's if she had any . . . . Mammy might have had children and it bothered Rufel that she did not know (1987: 136). Rufel's questioning of the identity of the person known to her as 'Mammy' leads her to find out some information about the woman ('maybe she had a couple of kids. But they was sold away or maybe she just lost touch with them early on . . . it's doubtful Dorcas even know her own children, if she had any' (1987: 146)). This indeterminacy concerning the slave's family relationships signals a rupture in the generational and temporal continuity that is history, a rupture of family and community which is one of the most frequent figures in African–American writing. Rufel's rethinking of all this suggests a new and generalised awareness of the human reality and complex subjectivity that underlies such stereotypical masks as 'Mammy'.

The difference between Rufel and Dessa presents an example of what Lyotard has characterised as the inevitable conflict arising from the 'universalisation of narrative instances': 'Traditions are mutually opaque. Contact between two communities is immediately a conflict, since the names and narratives of one community are exclusive of the names and narratives of the other.' There thus occurs 'a litigation over the names of times, places, and persons, over the senses and referents attached to those names' (1988a: 157), and one way of dealing with that litigation is to rule the senses and referents of the other community out of order. Although she is the product of a white aristocratic community, Rufel can no longer rely on the support of that community's 'weightiest interests' (Bradley) and so cannot relegate the other to the aphasic category of jarring witness. Or again, as Bourdieu points out, the power to bestow identity through naming becomes especially crucial 'in crisis situations, when the meaning of the world slips away' (1985: 203). This is precisely the situation – objective crisis – that obtains at Sutton's Glen, as the previously recognised limits and definitions of the social world are slipping away and the once-assured connotations of 'Mammy' have collapsed. Rufel's breakthrough in understanding the crucial signifier 'mammy' as it is uttered in an 'alien language', and therefore something of that group's experience of reality, reworks the opening situation which focused on Adam Nehemiah's (the namer and chronicler) inability to do so. The traditional chains of communication that once held names and referents together, that controlled not only denotation but also to some extent connotation, have been challenged and reformed.[20]

In the final section, 'The Negress', the narrative perspective shifts to the first person as Dessa Rose completes the story – in her own voice at last – with a rapprochement between white woman and black woman before they go their separate ways. Rufel joins with a group of the runaway slaves in order to perpetrate a fraud on the white slave-buying public. She accompanies them to various towns, posing as their owner and 'selling' them. They then escape immediately, meet at a pre-arranged location and continue on to the next town considerably richer. Rufel's actions here constitute a further development of her alienation from her original community. Whereas her previous transgressions of what should be her common sense might loosely be characterised as passive, since her involvement with Nathan that is no longer the case. She now takes an active role in subverting the authority of the dominant social order. Ironically, in light of their earlier clash, the charade they act out as they travel requires that Rufel become the proper Southern aristocrat and Dessa become the 'mammy'. Initially, these roles cause some friction as pretense and reality are easily confused, but in the end the relationship is strengthened through Dessa's gradual acceptance of Rufel's redefinition of her sense of community and through their realisation that as women they share a common perspective that can potentially transcend racial division. After helping Rufel fend off a would-be rapist, for example, Dessa realises that in some ways their positions are similar. 'The white woman was subject to the same ravishment as me; this was the thought that kept me awake. I hadn't knowed white mens could use a white woman like that, just take her by force same as they could with us' (1987: 220).

At the end of the novel, Dessa is recognised on the street of a small Southern town by Nehemiah who attempts to force her back into slavery. Her fate then rests on Rufel's commitment to saving her, even though doing so means considerable danger for both if they are caught. Nevertheless, having moved away from the doxa that allowed for the justification of slavery, Rufel betrays her own (White) community in order to protect Dessa. While the laughter of slaves was previously at Rufel's expense, the subversive (Bakhtinian) laughter that unites the two women at the end (1987: 256) signals their inward emancipation from the text of slavery. Thus *Dessa Rose* projects a past in which racist divisions could be overcome even at the moment of their greatest orthodox influence. In this novel Williams creates historical characters who, with some difficulty, not only defamiliarise their own *sensus communis*, but seem finally to rid themselves of the inclination to make the distinctions on which the racist system depends. In doing so, she articulates a hope that the narrow and divisive sense of community that victimises those it excludes, may be overcome.

'BEARING WITNESS'

Toni Morrison's concern with narration and history as a means of recognising and articulating the perspective of her marginalised community is evident throughout her work, but her exploration of the problem is, perhaps, most direct in Song of Solomon and Beloved. The question of the relative discursive authority of divergent language groups is raised almost immediately in Song of Solomon, and the specific issue in terms of which difference is posited relates to the historical basis of community identity. According to the official town maps, there exists a street by the name of 'Mains Avenue, but the only colored doctor in the city had lived and died on that street, and when he moved there in 1896 his patients took to calling the street . . . Doctor Street' (1977: 3–4). The unofficial nomination never gains official status however, never achieves legitimacy. When city legislators, in an effort to suppress this subversion, post notices advising the black population that the street is not Doctor Street, they obligingly and ironically defer to authority, renaming it Not Doctor Street (1977: 4). The problem of naming is a recurrent one in these novels, and through this minor anecdote Morrison suggests a great deal about the relative discursive power of the two communities and their power to bestow legitimate identity or orientation. Furthermore, on Not Doctor Street there is a hospital (Mercy Hospital) which has never, until the day on which the novel opens, admitted a black patient and thus has come to be known as No Mercy Hospital. The connection established between authority, historical experience and names (signifiers of identity) is worked out in some complexity throughout the novel. The same set of discursive power relations operates, for example, in the (mis)naming of Macon Dead, Milkman's father. One aspect of Milkman's quest, then, is to recover his family's true name, and thereby their identity. An awareness of the relations of power that are present in the according of a name is more immediate in a community whose power to bestow names – even on themselves – could not always be taken for granted.

The authority of one community over another is further
registered when, during an emergency, a white nurse approaches a
black woman and her children and demands, ' "Are these your
children?" ' The woman turns, 'her eyebrows lifted at the
carelessness of the address'. When she sees it is a white woman
who has spoken, she lowers her brows, veils her eyes and replies
'Ma'am?' (1977: 6). When the nurse peremptorily issues an order to
one of the children, the woman tries to tell the nurse the boy's
name, but the strangeness of the name to the nurse's ears renders
her unable to register it.

'Guitar, ma'am.'
'What?'
'Guitar.'
The nurse gazed at the stout woman as though she had spoken Welsh.

(1977: 7)

In issuing her order to him, the nurse speaks very slowly, as one
would to someone not likely to understand. She tells him to go to
Admissions, spelling it out for him incorrectly: ' "You left out a s,
ma'am," the boy said. The north was new to him and he had just
begun to learn he could speak up to white people. But she'd
already gone' (1977: 7).

The implications are manifold. The white woman has the
authority to control the dialogue to the degree that she has the
privilege of initiating it, of enforcing her authority through it, of
organising the action or results that come from it, of terminating it
at will and without warning, excuse or apology. She can command
respect, comprehension and response without displaying these
qualities in return. While she is free to disregard any claim to
authority others might make based on their own cultural competence, they are not at all in a similar position in regard to her
authority since it is legitimised in ways theirs cannot be. As the
exchange with the boy indicates, her discursive authority is not a
simple function of linguistic competence. It stems from a social
taxonomy that has arranged the ground on which the communities
meet, a taxonomy whose imperatives necessitate the recognition
by blacks of the definitions of reality imposed by whites, but
imposes no such reciprocal demand on whites. As Bourdieu
argues, 'Language is not only an instrument of communication or
even of knowledge, but also an instrument of power' (1977a: 648).

In the background of the discursive violence enacted on the black community, never too far from the surface, there lies the spectre of physical violence as a method of coercive suppression when more subtle methods fail to maintain order. While Milkman is too self-centred to take much interest, the men at the barbershop listen intently to the radio reports concerning a

young Negro boy [who] had been found stomped to death in Sunflower County, Mississippi. There were no questions about who stomped him – his murderers had boasted freely – and there were no questions about the motive. The boy had whistled at some white women, refused to deny he had slept with others, and was a Northerner visiting the South. His name was Till.   (1977: 80)

The reference is to the notorious murder of Emmett Till who in 1955 was abducted, tortured and beaten to death.[21] In spite of world-wide publicity and international protest, in spite of the fact that the identity of the killers was not in serious dispute – in fact, there was eyewitness testimony given by a (black) man who witnessed the abduction – no one was convicted. The Emmet Till case was important in one sense, however, since at that time it was one of the rare instances in Mississippi of an African–American testifying in a murder case against a white. Certainly the testimony of this jarring witness seems to have carried little weight in court, and, understandably fearing for his life, he left Mississippi after his courtroom appearances and never returned (Juan Williams, 1987: 37–57). In Lyotard's phrase, this constitutes a wrong not in that the victims were denied the means to make their witness public, but in that their testimony was deprived of authority.

The response of the men in the barbershop focuses first on whether or not the incident will be reported in the newspaper, an allusion to the process of selection that creates news – and by analogy, history. Given the nature of the social centre from which such official narratives emerge, coverage is by no means guaranteed and informed coverage is virtually unthinkable. Their subsequent discussion of right and wrong in the case underlines the variety of positions held by members of the black community in response to such a brutal attack. One feels that Till should have known better, in a sense blaming the victim for his torture and murder; another fiercely resents such a suggestion as an acceptance of the restriction of the humanity and liberty of African–

Americans. The final disagreement focuses on the subject of the dispensation of justice to the murderers. When one suggests that the murderers will be caught, another replies sardonically,

> 'Catch 'em? Catch 'em? . . . You out of your fuckin mind? They'll catch 'em, all right, and give 'em a big party and a medal.'
> 'Yeah. The whole town planning a parade.'
> '. . . Ain't no law for no colored man except the one that sends him to the chair.'   (1977: 82)

Two very different responses to the situation are represented in the positions taken by the two friends Guitar and Milkman. Guitar, who has listened to the conversation about Emmett Till with a certain visible intensity, tells Milkman that he is no longer able simply to express pity for the black victims of white pathological violence; the time has come, he believes, for a stronger move. Guitar becomes involved with a group called the Seven Days, a group whose rationale reflects the problem of being in the position of jarring witness in the eyes of the nation's 'weighty interests'. The group is made up of a few black men willing to take revenge in a quasi-judicial fashion:

> when a Negro child, Negro woman, or Negro man is killed by whites and nothing is done about it by their law and their courts, this society selects a similar victim at random, and they execute him or her in a similar manner if they can. If the Negro was hanged, they hang; if the Negro was burnt, they burn; raped and murdered, they rape and murder.'   (1977: 155)

This response is understandable, perhaps, in a land where, as Guitar puts it, 'The earth is soggy with black people's blood. And before us Indian blood' (1977: 159). The group has originated, apparently, in response to historical incidents of racial violence: 'when that private from Georgia was killed after his balls were cut off and after that veteran was blinded when he came home from France in World War I' (1977: 156). And Guitar himself remembers seeing 'that picture of those white mothers holding up their babies so they could get a good look at some black men burning on a tree' (1977: 157). At issue is not only a sense of revenge, but of justice, of historical witness finally taken seriously, of jarring witnesses seeking a way to have an effect without the backing of weighty interests. ' "Where's the money, the state, the country to finance our justice?" ' asks Guitar.

Do we have a court? Is there one courthouse in one city in the country where a jury would convict them? There are places right now where a Negro still can't testify against a white man. Where the judge, the jury, the court, are legally bound to ignore anything a Negro has to say. What that means is that a black man is a victim of a crime only when a white man says he is. (1977: 160–1)

This representation of the situation is consonant, once again, with Bradley's legal metaphor for history and with Lyotard's definition of a wrong as testimony denied. It is doubtful, however, whether a retaliatory response of this nature could ever be adequate. While satisfying a basic desire for revenge – justice in the barest 'eye for an eye' sense – the wrong remains. Unless there is some authoritative public testimony, neither the original white crime nor the black response to it can become part of any larger narrative capable of organising events into a meaningful structure. Because of the need for absolute secrecy, no one but the members of the Seven Days and a few close friends – not even the white victims themselves – knows that this violent response to racist violence is linked to any particular political motive. Without some publicly-acknowledged legitimacy, the wrong remains unchallenged and the retaliation appears merely random and pathological. As Hayden White might put it, the systems of meaning-production of this society are unsuccessful when tested against these real but unyielding events.

The major historical focus of the novel is not Guitar however, but Milkman, a young man in some ways like Quentin Compson in that responsibility for the transmission of his community's historical heritage falls on his shoulders. Milkman shows little sign of interest in these issues early in the novel, pursuing personal material success instead. He is dismissive of the Emmett Till incident, choosing to focus instead on his own problems with his family, with money and women. A series of personal crises compel him to rethink this position, however, and his subsequent quest constitutes a long symbolic excursion into the history and community that has shaped his present. As the narrative of his family history begins to take shape, one of the first stories he hears concerns the murder of his own grandfather. Milkman has heard some of the details before, but not enough to put together or colligate a whole story. He had been murdered by wealthy white landowners who wanted his land, and the story that Milkman hears about the murder repeats the discussion of the death of

Emmett Till in such a way as to problematise Milkman's prior separation of personal (private or family) and public affairs.[22] When Milkman asks if his grandfather's murderers were ever caught, Reverend Cooper's answer echoes elements of the barber-shop conversation for Milkman – who wasn't listening the first time.

> 'Catch?' he asked, his face full of wonder . . . . 'Didn't have to catch 'em. They never went nowhere.'
> 'I mean did they have a trial; were they arrested?'
> 'Arrested for what? Killing a nigger? Where did you say you was from?'
> 'You mean nobody did anything? Didn't even try to find out who did it?'
> 'Everybody knew who did it . . . . Wasn't nothing to do. White folks didn't care; colored folks didn't dare . . . . Besides, the people what did it owned half the county.'   (1977: 234)

Those people were the Butlers. Milkman gradually pieces together the narrative as a detective might, finding that the woman who took his father and aunt in when their father was murdered worked for the same Butlers. He finds her still in the Butler house, and in an almost-Faulknerian scene, Morrison does one thing that Faulkner could not – she articulates the point of view of this old woman, Circe, a character reminiscent perhaps of Clytie in *Absalom, Absalom!*, but with a difference. She has remained in the house long after the deaths of the Butlers, and Milkman suspects that she has done this out of a misguided sense of loyalty to people he now considers oppressors. But the truth of the matter lies elsewhere, closer to Alice Walker's wish (see above) that Faulkner had burned the house down: the Butlers had loved the house

> Brought pink veined marble from across the sea for it and hired men in Italy to do the chandelier that I had to climb a ladder and clean with white muslin once every two months. They loved it. Stole for it, lied for it, killed for it. But I'm the one left . . . . And I will never clean it again. Never. Nothing. Not a speck of dust, not a grain of dirt, will I move. Everything in this world they lived for will crumble and rot. The chandelier already fell down and smashed itself to pieces. It's down there in the ballroom now. All in pieces. Something gnawed through the cords. Ha! And I want to see it all go, make sure it does go, and that nobody fixes it up. I brought the dogs in to make sure . . . . You ought to see what they did to her bedroom. Her walls didn't have wallpaper. No. Silk brocade that took some Belgian women six years to make. She loved it – oh, how much she loved it. Took thirty Weimaraners one day to rip it off the walls. If I thought the stink wouldn't strangle you, I'd show it to you.'   (1977: 249–50)

This is, of course, a version of history from below, a servant or slave's eyeview of the accumulation of wealth and material success confirming Benjamin's well-known statement that every document of culture is also a document of barbarism.

By the end of his journey South, Milkman understands his place as an African–American male in a community that has, in the course of the novel, been represented both synchronically (his geographical journey allows him to recognise differences between his own Northern urban situation and that of the traditional rural South) and diachronically (his family genealogy is traced back to a slave origin, and by implication, even earlier to the African homeland to which Solomon has flown). He is then able to understand the relation of history to identity – particularly in the way that history's traces are everywhere left in the names that represent things, places and people. This epiphanic realisation opens a whole new dimension of experience – a defamiliarised historical dimension.[23] Travelling by bus back to the North in autumn, he passes states whose history had previously meant nothing to him. Now he reads roadsigns with interest, speculating on the history and community struggles they commemorated:

The Algonquins had named the territory he lived in Great Water, *michi gami*. How many dead lives and fading memories were buried in and beneath the names of the places in this country. Under the recorded names were the other names . . . . Names that had meaning . . . . Names that bore witness.

(1977: 333)

Names, in *Song of Solomon*, bear a jarring witness to the historical existence of communities whose history has not been otherwise recorded, testify to a buried history shaped by oppression and exploitation from without and community solidarity from within. The possibility of the imminent dissolution of that community's traditions is very real in the novel, and the archeological research into the names of the generations is made in order to maintain a sense of historical continuity, even into the future.

The final moment of the novel shows a kind of uneasy unification of the oppositions the novel has posited. Milkman and Pilate – one male, one female; one young, one old; one representing modern bourgeois individualism, the other a powerful representative of historical continuity – are brought together to bury the remains of an ancestor. As she dies in his arms from a sudden gunshot, he sings for her a song she had taught him containing the names of the dead, finally bearing witness to the generations of struggle. Milkman then launches himself from atop a hill into the arms of her murderer, Guitar, whose desire for violent revenge against whites has gone out of control and obliterated the sense of love for his people that first inspired the violence. It is, in a sense, a dialectical leap: on one hand, these two opposed positions may destroy each other; on the other hand, a synthesis of the two – Guitar's anger and determination and Milkman's newfound insights into history and community – suggest the possibility of a positive redefiniton of the African–American community and its history.

Morrison's more recent novel, Beloved, articulates a similar historiographic imperative. Rather than a quest for the past however, here the past returns, demanding the attention of the present in the memories of slavery recounted by the various characters, in the after-effects that to some degree determine the horizons bounding their lives, and in the presence of a ghost, Beloved herself, whose complex existence both testifies to the horrors of her own short life and revives related but hitherto repressed memories in those around her. The novel is based on an historical event that took place shortly before the Civil War. Margaret Garner, an escaped slave about to be captured and returned to slavery, tried to kill her children rather than see them live as slaves, and succeeded in killing one before being taken (1990a: 60–1).[24] Given the legal circumstances of the period, she was tried not for murder but for theft of property – her children – was convicted and returned to her owner. This represents in the starkest terms another aspect of a Lyotardian wrong: a differend in which the settlement of a conflict is made in the idiom of one of the conflicting parties (the slaveowner) while the injury from which the other (the slave) suffers does not signify in that idiom. As in the Emmett Till case a century later, questions of bearing witness, of testifying to a wrong, of legitimacy and authority, have many ramifications that the novel registers in its narration of the attitudes of the various characters involved, some of whom have similar stories in their slave past that they deal with through a torturous combination of memory and/or refusal of memory.

It is difficult, to say the least, to work through such traumas, yet in Beloved as in Corrigedora, the inability to do so results in an inability to function in the present and inevitably cancels out any sense of future possibility. Though living in the post-slavery era, Sethe is unable to break the destructive patterns of slavery that remain a determining influence in her life: for example, her surviving sons disappear from her life as children of slaves did when sold, never to be heard of again – a continuation of the Diaspora originating in the institution of slavery. Other basic family relationships are similarly difficult to maintain, and her sexual and emotional relationship with Paul D. is disrupted as surely as it might have been under slavery. As in *Corregidora*, there is no escaping the after-effects of slavery, and Sethe is not the only one whose house is haunted by the historical legacy of slavery. When, early on, Sethe suggests simply moving to another house to evade the ghost, her mother-in-law replies 'What'd be the point? Not a house in the county ain't packed to its rafters with some dead Negro's grief' (1988: 6). Such healing as is possible comes about through an intense engagement with the ghost of her murdered child who has returned to defamiliarise the past. In her demand to know why her life was destroyed, Beloved takes on the weight of all those – particularly women – whose lives were truncated, ruined, by slavery and racism. In her presence there are echoes of the middle passage across the Atlantic into slavery, echoes of plantation life, of a variety of atrocities – sexual and otherwise – committed against African–Americans over a period of centuries.

These atrocities are documented, dramatised in the novel and are compounded by the fact that, as Schoolteacher so brutally demonstrates, since the 'definitions belonged to the definers . . . not the defined' (1988: 234), there is no possibility of authoritative testimony against those committing the atrocities. In relegating slaves to an intermediate position between the human and the animal, for example, Schoolteacher's social taxonomy effectively denies their discursive legitimacy, their humanity, their selfhood, and this denial is itself an essential and perhaps strategic part of the overall assault on the subjectivity of the slave. As Sethe puts it,

anybody white could take your whole self for anything that came to mind. Not just work, kill, or maim you, but dirty you. Dirty you so bad you couldn't like yourself anymore. Dirty you so bad you forgot who you were and couldn't think it up.   (1988: 308)

While this image of a breakdown in the very constitution of the subject – strikingly similar to the process described by Marshall – refers in the first instance perhaps to sexual and economic exploitation, this was justified within the discourse of slavery through the denial of legitimacy of the slave's very self, a denial of subjectivity whose devastating impact is charted in Sethe's struggles to articulate her past, to testify to the damage that led her to respond by taking the life of her child.

Beloved's presence and its significance for the black community resonates in Stamp Paid's anguished response to the situation:

1874 and whitefolks were still on the loose. Whole towns wiped clean of Negroes; 87 lynchings in one year alone in Kentucky; four colored schools burned to the ground, grown men whipped like children; children whipped like adults; black women raped by the crew; property taken, necks broken. He smelled skin, skin and hot blood. The skin was one thing, but human blood cooked in a lynch fire was a whole other thing.   (1988: 221)

When he finds a piece of ribbon attached to a piece of hair, itself still attached to a bit of a child's scalp, Stamp Paid understands the meaning of the ghostly presence in Sethe's house, the incomprehensible (aphasic) voices he hears within: It is a chorus of jarring witnesses:

The people of the broken necks, of the fire-cooked blood and black girls who had lost their ribbons.
What a roaring.   (1988: 222)

It is said that ghosts exist because an unresolved past will not let them and their stories settle. Lyotard, in fact, claims that 'The dead are not dead so long as the living have not recorded their death in narrative' (Bennington, 1988: 112). These roaring voices constitute the aphasic testimony of all those whose witness to the damage done to them continues to be denied, whose loss remains unresolved, continues to seek a proper hearing.[25]

It is, finally, Sethe herself who must work through all this if she is to live on and make a future. Her name has echoes that suggest the process she is engaged in: on one hand, the peculiar spelling suggests Lethe, the classical river of forgetfulness in Hades; on the other hand, as Sethe, it means atonement. Thus the tension between repressing the traumatic past and working through the trauma is built into her name. Atonement is the supplying of satisfaction for a wrong that has been committed; yet it is impossible to supply satisfaction for the damage that was done – it cannot be undone. But it is perhaps possible at least to satisfy – albeit much belatedly and insufficiently – the wrong that has resulted from the refusal of testimony itself. An historical testimony is required that *would* test the society's systems of meaning-production (White) and thus make possible an escape from the residual effects of that damage, just as Denver, Beloved's surviving sister manages to escape. While Beloved represents a sort of collective victim, her sister Denver (who survives) has equally broad symbolic reference: 'Everybody's child was in that face' (1988: 302), we are told as Denver desperately attempts to reconstruct a sense of possibility by contacting the community. When, with the aid of Denver and the community, Sethe begins to emerge from her descent into the traumic past, she sees a white man with a whip in his hand approaching her house. Mistaking him for the slavehunter whose previous appearance devastated her life, she does not this time turn the ice-pick in her hand on her daughter, but attempts to wield it instead against the white man in defence of her family – a sign that a turn from self-destruction is becoming possible, a sign tentatively confirmed by the gesture of reconciliation that takes place between Sethe and Paul D. at the end.

Yet since the past cannot be undone, those ghosts wait, ready to disrupt the present with their strange histories again, demanding that their names be called and their testimonies be heard, that the unresolved traumas of the culture be worked through. As bell hooks has observed, *Beloved* constitutes an attempt 'not just to describe slavery but to try and reconstruct a psycho-social history of its impact . . . [which is] a necessary stage in the process of collective black self recovery' (1990: 209–10). Beloved is, finally, not a name but the single word on a gravestone, a memorial to all those – sixty million and more, Morrison writes in the dedication – whose names and testimonies have not been recorded. 'Everybody knew what she was called, but nobody anywhere knew her name', Morrison writes at the end of the novel. 'Disremembered and unaccounted for, she cannot be lost because no one is looking for her, and even if they were, how can they call her if they don't know her name? Although she has claim, she is not claimed' (1988: 336–8).[26] In a recent interview, Morrison stated one aim of

the novel in terms of filling this historical gap and reconstituting a
chain of communication: 'There is no place you or I can go, to
think about . . . to summon the presences of, or recollect the
absences of slaves.'

There is no suitable monument or plaque or wreath or wall or park . . . . There's
no 300-foot tower. There's no small bench by the road . . . in Charleston or
Savannah or New York or Providence or, better still, on the banks of the
Mississippi. And because such a place doesn't exist (that I know of), the book
had to.   (1989: 4)

Beloved constitutes, in a sense, a corrective to this situation: not
only does it stand as a monument to the shameful history of
slavery, but like Song of Solomon and many other novels by
African–American writers, it legitimises and authoritatively testifies to the life experience of Hurston's museum figures 'without
insides'. Morrison's narratives contribute importantly to this long
process of bearing witness and testify to the continuity of the
historical (and historiographical) struggle. She once described her
project as a writer in terms not so far removed from those of
Bradley himself: 'My work bears witness and suggests who the
outlaws were, who survived under what circumstances and why,
what was legal in the community and what was legal outside it'
(1981: 26). Her novels constitute an eloquent response to the
aphasic situation she had encountered in her reading of literature:
'There were no books about me,' she has stated, 'I didn't exist in all
the literature I had read . . . this person, this female, this black'
(McKay, 1988: 45).

7

V.: In the rathouse of history with Thomas Pynchon

'One would have to exorcise the city, the island . . . . The continents, the world. Or the western part,' as an afterthought. 'We are western men.'

(V., Pynchon, 1963: 451)

Hayden White's argument 'that the conviction that one can make sense of history stands on the same level of epistemic plausibility as the conviction that it makes no sense whatsoever' (1987: 73) seems to echo a recurring concern in Thomas Pynchon's works. Stencil in V., Oedipa Maas in *The Crying of Lot 49*, and Slothrop in *Gravity's Rainbow* all seek to discern some order or pattern in the world and its history. An inevitable problem then arises to haunt them throughout the novels – is this pattern, order, meaning (if located) a property of the world and of history, or is it a projection of the ordering perception of the one who is searching for meaning? If the order or meaning perceived is primarily a property of the interpreter's perception, how then is that sublime object of interpretation – historical reality – to be approached? And what are the political implications of this problem?

While many critics have discussed the epistemological lems presented in Pynchon's work, less attention has been paid to the precise setting or context in which Pynchon locates those problems. Yet these are essential components of the work. V. explores the aporias of epistemology at a series of specific and critical junctures in modern Western history, documenting the breakdown of white imperialist hegemony. His concern with science and various abstract bodies of thought is certainly important, but Pynchon's radical questioning of power, politics and historical events (as well as philosophy of history) ought to be taken seriously. There is an almost Pynchonesque irony in the way many critics have, until very recently, maintained a blind spot in their readings of Pynchon's texts, a blind spot that occludes the explicitly social and political dimensions of the work. William Plater, for instance, dismisses the overt political history in Pynchon quite lightly in favour of a more abstract grounding of the work: 'colonialism', he writes, 'is only one of Pynchon's several metaphors for the uncertainty relations of reality and illusion. Others work equally well' (1981: 112). John Stark, perhaps, is most adamant: 'Occasionally he does discuss moral or social issues, but he usually subordinates them to other issues . . . . As a general rule, however, he focuses on literary, epistemological, and metaphysical problems' (1983: 23–4). 'Pynchon does not often refer to social and political history' (1983: 105). Elsewhere he speaks of 'the relatively minor importance of politics' in V. (1983: 169). Quite often, however, even those critics who, like Thomas Schaub, do acknowledge the social and historical dimension of Pynchon's work devote most of their commentary to his more abstract philosophical and scientific concerns. Those recent critical studies which draw on contemporary theories such as deconstruction also have a tendency to emphasise textual and formal aspects of the work at the expense of the political.[1] In this chapter I attempt instead to present Pynchon as a profoundly political and historical novelist whose conception of the political and historical field has much in common with contemporary historiographical theory and whose engagement with the postmodern and historical sublime encourages and enables a different access to the perspectives of jarring witnesses.

According to Hayden White, prior to the formation of the discipline of history in the nineteenth century, the subject was considered a branch of the more general field of rhetoric, 'the source and repository of tradition, moral exemplars, and admonitory lessons' (1987: 64). White writes that

as long as history was subordinated to rhetoric, the historical field itself (that is, the past or the historical process) had to be viewed as a chaos that made no sense at all or one that could be made to bear as many senses as wit and rhetorical talent could impose on it.   (1987: 65)

As history came to constitute a distinct discipline, rules of evidence and a more rigorous sense of factuality came into play, regulating not only the kinds of narratives a historian could produce but also altering the underlying conception of the nature of the historical field itself: 'For this tradition, whatever "confusion" is displayed by the historical record is only a surface phenomenon' (White, 1987: 71) subject to correction by subsequent historians.

White goes on to relate these dichotomous conceptions of history to the concurrent debate on the nature of the sublime and the beautiful. The irreducible confusion and the ultimately unrepresentable nature of the total historical field is associated with the idea of the sublime while the conception of history as possessing order, logic or sense falls into the aesthetic category of the beautiful. As aesthetics superseded rhetoric and the beautiful gradually displaced the sublime as a category of judgement, the narratives both of history and of fiction were expected to display a more thorough sense of coherence, to make sense in a more complete and sustained way. Any single historical narrative should ideally exhibit both an internal coherence and a fidelity to 'the facts' such that it could be seen as one chapter of a narrative that, if extended long enough, could theoretically recount and account for all of history. This view of history is supportable, however, only by the exclusion of the historical sublime: history as an awesome, perhaps incomprehensible, terrifying, multifarious, unrepresentable spectacle.

The attempt to represent history in a narrative form, of course, gives rise to some difficulties – the problem is not that history cannot be interpreted as much as the fact that it can be, endlessly it seems, and in contradictory ways. As Paul Ricoeur argues in *Time and Narrative*, no matter which historiographical methodology is applied, events are never fully interpreted: 'the event is restored at the end of each attempted explanation as a remainder left by each such attempt . . . as a dissonance between explanatory structures, and finally, as the life and death of the structures themselves' (1984: v.1, 224).[2] Similarly, Jean-François Lyotard argues in 'The Sublime and the Avant Garde' that the sublimity of the pure event subverts any attempt at final or full representation. The sublimity of the event is thus precisely what must be repressed in order for representation to occur. The exhaustive narrative is, by definition, impossible, and any history is necessarily a selective one. Selection of the events deemed worthy of narration, selection of narrative point of view and selection of the narrative techniques employed are thus determined, at least in part, by a compulsive need for narrative coherence, a compulsion that prompts White to ask: 'what kind of notion of reality authorizes construction of a narrative account of reality in which continuity rather than discontinuity governs the articulation of the discourse' (1987: 10). With a few exceptions, notably in modern literature,

narrative strains for the effect of having filled in all the gaps, of having put an image of continuity, coherency, and meaning in place of the fantasies of emptiness, need, and frustrated desire that inhabit our nightmares about the destructive power of time.   (1987: 11)

The continuity of the narrative realist form of historical discourse, its tendency to totalisation, has another aspect, one that White describes with reference to Hegel: an 'intimate relationship' seems to exist, he writes, 'between law, historicality, and narrativity' and, he observes, this suggests 'that narrative in general, from the folktale to the novel, from the annals to the fully realised "history", has to do with the topics of law, legality, legitimacy, or, more generally, authority' (1987: 13). It may not be stretching the point too much to infer that problems of narrative continuity have to do with problems of authority in a more general sense as well. History is generally, as the saying goes, written from the vantage point of the victors; to this may be added Frantz Fanon's observation that objectivity has always been on the side of the coloniser (1963: 61). In a similar vein, White argues that

For subordinant, emergent, or resisting social groups ... opposition can be carried forward only on the basis of a conception of the historical record as being not a window through which the past 'as it really was' can be apprehended but rather a wall that must be broken through if the 'terror of history' is to be directly confronted.   (1987: 82)

A number of historians and philosophers of history, including White, have called attention to Chateaubriand's heroic conception of the vocation of the historian as the bearer of a particular kind of liberatory narrative – and, as the previous chapter argued, numerous examples of this can be found in African-American literature:

In the silence of abjection, when the only sounds to be heard are the chains of the slave and the voice of the informer; when everthing trembles before the tyrant and it is as dangerous to incur his favor as to deserve his disfavor, this is when the historian appears, charged with avenging the people.   (1987: 79)

White does not, however, advocate a more rigorous 'scientific' approach to the writing of history, nor does he seek a return to the Covering Law Model: the possibility of a historical discourse of liberation lies elsewhere. Instead, a breakdown in the idea of objective narrative realism and the recovery of the historical sublime may, he argues, be a 'necessary precondition for the production of a historiography of the sort that Chateaubriand conceived to be desirable in times of "abjection" '.[3]

This postmodern version of the historical sublime differs from its predecessors though. Fredric Jameson remarks that the experience of the sublime has changed since the Romantics: it

is no longer *subjective* in the older sense that a personality is standing in front of the Alps and knowing the limits of the individual subject and the human ego. On the contrary, it is a kind of non-humanist experience of limits beyond which you get dissolved.   (1987: 30–1)

This sense of dissolution that marks the sublime can be taken to refer as well to the dissolution of the continuity and coherence of narrative itself and of its claim to represent reality realistically. If narrative coherence is threatened, as White's remarks on the relation of narrativity and legality would seem to imply, then not only is Jameson's individual subject facing dissolution, but the cohesion of the social system producing the narrative is also being threatened. Along with the weakening of the authority of the narratives through which society understands and authorises itself, comes a concomitant crisis in that society. It is surely no coincidence that much postmodern fiction was produced in a period of social upheaval, a period during which many of the basic beliefs (the *sensus communis*) of European and North American society were subjected to radical critique. The potential dissolution of individual subjectivity resulting from the sublime corresponds on the social plane (in terms of White's historical sublime) with a dissolution of certain kinds of traditional social and narrative authority. 'With the sublime', writes Lyotard, 'we go a long way into heterogeneity' (1987: 175). In this sense, postmodern historical relativism can be seen as the dissolution or delegitimisation of any one cultural group's claim to sole authority in the construction of historical narrative, an authority that is ultimately political in nature. This acts then as a challenge to the monopoly on the tools for the legitimate definition of reality that, as Bourdieu argues, results in the discursive marginalisation (aphasia) of all but the dominant culture or cultural group.

This crisis in narrative authority has ranged from a questioning of the various aspects of the art of narration to a wholesale scepticism toward the very possibility of adequate narrative representation given its structural tendency to exclude the heterogeneous. Edward Said writes that, for some contemporaries, narrative itself, 'which poses an enabling *arché* and a vindicating *telos*, is no longer an adequate figure for plotting the human trajectory in society. There is nothing to look forward to: we are stuck within our circle' (1986: 50). Yet it is a central function of artists and intellectuals to try to think a way out of this situation, to work through this crisis of narrative in the Western world. To some degree, as Nathan Huggins' argument (cited above) suggests, the way through seems to lie in a recognition and an acceptance of a more heterogeneous narrative discourse of history and fiction – a heterogeneity that is rendered impossible by the dominance of monolithic 'objectivity' and 'realism' in historical and fictional narrative. Such a heterogeneous discourse would, by definition, work to include the alterity which has been repressed by an imperialist culture and its totalising narratives – recuperating the testimony of some of history's jarring witnesses.

The problem of separate, perhaps incommensurable, heterogeneous worlds of experience and a concurrent separation in the representation of that experience, has long been a central one for Pynchon and he has often been quite specific about the social and political implications. As a student in the late 1950s influenced by the Beat movement, he began 'to get a sense of that other world humming along out there' (1985: xvi–xvii) beyond the privileged world of Cornell. His own early short fiction often turns on themes of class or racial separation, anticipating the social turbulence of the 1960s. About that era, Pynchon writes that

The success of the 'new left' . . . [was] limited by the failure of college kids and blue collar workers to get together politically. One reason was the presence of real, invisible class force fields in the way of communication between the two groups.   (1985: xv–xvi)

As its title suggests, one of Pynchon's few published essays, 'A Journey Into The Mind of Watts', is an attempt to map one such force field and to articulate some aspects of the subjective experience of the residents of Watts as the possibility of riot simmered, once again, at the brink of boiling. At 'the heart of L.A.'s racial sickness is the coexistence of two very different cultures: one white and one black'. These two cultures, each with its own internal logic and historical trajectory, all too frequently confront each other over the barrel of a police revolver: 'your life trembling in the crook of a cop's finger because it is dark, and Watts, and the history of this place and these times makes it impossible for the cop to come on any different, or for you to hate him any less' (1966: 35). The eastern boundary of Watts, he writes, looks 'like the edge of the world' (1966: 80). The idea of mental geography and frontiers continues in another image of the ghetto as a 'country which lies, psychologically, uncounted miles further than most whites seem at present willing to travel' (1966: 78), a country whose customs, dress codes, hairdos and history simply do not mesh with the norms of hegemonic white culture. These points, made in 1966, have lost none of their relevance nearly thirty years later as the events surrounding the arrest of Rodney King demonstrate.

While insisting on the existence of an invisible force field of race and class separating the inhabitants of Watts from the dominant white culture, Pynchon nevertheless attempts to bridge that gap, to interpret and represent the experience of the 'other' with empathy, intelligence and decency. In a very similar vein, Said, in his essay on postcolonial intellectuals, argues that we must accept that while 'there is an irreducible subjective core to human experience, this experience is also historical and secular'. It is, as a result, 'accessible to certain kinds of analysis' although 'not exhausted by totalizing theories marked and limited by doctrinal lines or by analytic constructs'. It is of the utmost importance that we use such tools as we can to gain access to the historical experience of jarring witnesses:

we must be able to think through and interpret together discrepant experiences, each with its particular agendas and pace of development, its own formations, its internal coherence and its system of external relationships. (1986: 55–6)

In Pynchon's work, images such as 'the edge of the world' and 'invisible force fields' posit a human universe made up of 'non-synchronous' (to use Ernst Bloch's term) systems of 'discrepant experiences', and Pynchon's frequent invocation of this difference, whatever its epistemological consequences, is firmly based in social and historical observation.

It is by means of this grounding in concrete social and historical experience that Pynchon manages to avoid the trivialisation that is sometimes a consequence of moral or cultural relativism. For example, early in V. he states the problem in miniature. Profane is riding the subway, 'yo-yoing' back and forth from one end of the line to the other for hours; during the course of the day he sees the atmosphere change radically:

> The shuttle after morning rush hour is near empty, like a littered beach after tourists have all gone home. In the hours between nine and noon the permanent residents come creeping back up their strand, shy and tentative. Since sunup all manner of affluent have filled the limits of that world with a sense of summer and life; now sleeping bums and old ladies on relief, who have been there all along unnoticed, re-establish a kind of property right, and the coming on of a falling season.   (1966: 37–8)

Although the beach image suggests that the bums and old ladies have actually gone somewhere, Pynchon assures us that they have not. Instead, their power to impose the definition of what Sidney Stencil would call 'The Situation' has been eclipsed: the affluent have 'filled the limits of that world', that is, defined it according to their own limited experience, then moved on without having been touched or affected in any way, without even having recognised the existence of an alterity whose definition of 'The Situation' it has occluded. This little epistemological parable describes an important yet frequently overlooked aspect of discursive power relations between the relatively rich and the relatively poor.

This kind of reference to the limits of a particular world recurs in the novel. Early on, Rachel Owlglass, an upper-middle class young woman who feels constrained by the limits of her world, laments that 'Daughters are constrained to pace demure and dark-eyed like so many Rapunzels within the magic frontiers' (1966: 25). Since she realises that she may not be able to escape, she asks Profane to tell her about the world outside: 'How the road is. Your boy's road that I'll never see . . . . What it's like west of Ithaca and south of Princeton. Places I won't know' (1966: 27). Ithaca and

Princeton function here as ideological boundaries as much as geographical locations and the epistemological limits arise through gender as well as class.[4] Those 'magic frontiers' recall 'the limits of the world' mentioned above and look forward to yet another similar instance: Esther meets a college boy who leads a conventional middle-class life but is attracted to the bohemian life-styles of a group known as The Whole Sick Crew:

> He will straddle the line, aware up to the point of knowing he is getting the worst of both worlds, but never stopping to wonder why there should ever have been a line, or even if there is a line at all. He will learn how to be a twinned man and will go on at the game, straddling until he splits up the crotch and in half from the prolonged tension, and then he will be destroyed.   (1966: 58)

This time the split between worlds separates what might be termed a counter-culture from the mainstream.

The 'invisible force fields' separating cultural groups find metaphorical expression in V. as well in the profusion of siege imagery – the siege of Malta and Foppl's siege party are the most detailed, but there are many other passing references. The military siege with its focus on a wall separating opposing groups finds its epistemological correlative in the idea of fundamentally irreconcilable discrepant experience, or perhaps in White's epistemological 'walls that must be broken through'. The most extensive exploration of this problem in V., however, revolves around certain aspects of racial difference, examining a series of critical moments in the history of European imperialism when the West quite deliberately and strategically denied the validity and the reality of non-synchronous Third World experience as part of the brutal enforcement of its own priorities. Not only has imperialist Western culture not often cared to 'think through and interpret . . . discrepant experiences' together with other cultural groups, it has, in fact, attempted to eradicate some of those cultures entirely. Pynchon writes of the 'racist, sexist, and protofascist' spirit of the time preceding the publication of the novel in 1963, a time when 'John Kennedy's role model James Bond was about to make his name by kicking third-world people around, another extension of the boy's adventure tales a lot of us grew up reading' (1985: xxi). V. is, in a sense, a parody of those books – by Kipling, Buchan, Haggard and others – that contributed to the construction of the 'Manichean' racial difference that Abdul JanMohamed locates at the very heart of that colonialist literary genre. Clear though Pynchon's political position seems here, perhaps the most critically neglected aspect of V. is his political use of epistemological and historiographical problems as a means to break down the wall of objective realism to which White alludes, a wall that has served to protect the hegemonic culture of Western society from an awareness of its own historical relativity.

The general epistemological dilemma in V. is given one central formulation by British agent Sidney Stencil, who 'remembered times when whole embassiesful of personnel had run amok and gibbering in the streets when confronted with a Situation which refused to make sense no matter who looked at it, or from what angle' (1966: 189). As a result he problematises the very existence of an objective reality. 'He had decided long ago that no Situation had any objective reality: it only existed in the minds of those who happened to be in on it at any specific moment' (1966: 189). In order to minimise confusion – a costly danger in the espionage business (which is not merely an epistemological metaphor but also, and perhaps more importantly, a straightforwardly political one) – Stencil Sr. has developed an alternative to objective appraisal: a form of epistemological teamwork. But this approach too is not without difficulties:

Since these several minds tended to form a sum total or complex more mongrel than homogenous, The Situation must necessarily appear to a single observer much like a diagram in four dimensions to an eye conditioned to seeing its world in only three. Hence the success or failure of any diplomatic issue must vary directly with the degree of rapport achieved by the team confronting it.
(1966: 189)

'The sublime' writes Lyotard in a similar vein, 'bears witness to the incommensurability between thought and the real world' (1985: 7). If, as Lyotard argues, the terror and the sublimity of the event lies in part in its unrepresentability, then for Stencil there is at least safety in numbers. Truth and knowledge thus ultimately become problems not of verification (or at least not of verification alone) but of consensus, privileging the homogeneous and orthodox over the heterogeneous. In fact, one of the lessons of V. concerns the final impossibility of representing the world coherently and fully from any single perspective, an unrepresentability that brings us back as well to White's historical sublime. Stencil

Jr.'s subsequent quest for V. demonstrates both the futility of the attempt and the inevitable distortions that must result from such an obsessive and totalising vision. In developing his consensus approach to reality and The Situation, Stencil Sr. stresses the need for a 'degree of rapport' – a shared *sensus communis* – among those witnesses attempting to form the composite picture of it, suggesting that otherwise they would 'form a sum total or complex more mongrel than homogeneous' (1966: 189).

The word 'mongrel' carries here, as usual, a pejorative sense and in V., with its acute awareness of race and colonialism, it carries a less abstract meaning as well – a racial mixture. Stencil's insistence on a 'degree of rapport' suggests an ethnocentrism which serves to protect his version of The Situation from epistemological and political dissolution, and it guarantees the exclusion of the kind of discrepant or non-synchronous experience that Said and Bloch speak of. Like many of his generation, Stencil Sr. acknowledges with regret the passing of an imperialist era which protected the homogeneity of representation and power. Arriving in Florence at a time of political instability, he wonders disconsolately 'What sort of Situation could one expect from such a scurvy and heterogeneous crew?' (1966: 190). Later, as an anti-colonialist movement gathers momentum in Malta with its 'motley of races' (1966: 310), he reflects with resignation that 'There were no more princes. Henceforth politics would become progressively more democratized, more thrown into the hands of amateurs. The disease would progress. Stencil was nearly past caring' (1966: 489). Stencil's desire for rapport among his analysts of The Situation suggests as well the narrative structure of *Nostromo*, *Parade's End* and *Absalom, Absalom!*: the multiple narrative perspectives remain within a more or less homogeneous social group.

In the world of Stencil Jr. however, that difference – while still central – is far less divisive. Racial purity, a fetishised principle of exclusion in the historical sections of V., is at times almost parodied. The members of the Whole Sick Crew, and their associates, are by and large, as Rachel puts it, 'Deracinated' (1966: 382) in both senses of the word: rootless and without sharp racial distinctions in the manner of Stencil Sr.'s generation: Profane is Jewish–Irish, Rachel is Jewish, Sphere is black, Fergus Mixolidian is an Irish Armenian Jew. Profane spends part of the novel living and working with a Puerto Rican family, and while Esther does get a nose job, turning her 'Jew nose' into an Irish retroussé, this is questioned by her friends and even by the doctor who performs the operation (1966: 103). Most important of all, perhaps, is the identity of Paola Maijstral, who is Maltese. Malta is located in the middle of the Mediterranean, literally the middle of the middle of the world, a point where imperialist Europe and colonised Africa intersect. It is referred to as 'a cradle of life' (1966: 382) and echoing Stencil Sr.'s strictures against a 'mongrel' reality, the people of Malta are characterised as a 'motley of races' (1966: 310). Furthermore, her last name, Maijstral, suggests the wind, and in V. the wind is associated with exclusion, suffering and dispossession on a number of occasions.[5] Malta is the site of several key episodes in the novel, and in one of the most powerful scenes the children of this 'motley of races', among the ruins of European World War II bombing, disassemble V., who has come to be identified with a particularly evil form of reified racist colonialism.

Ironically, when Stencil Jr. tries long after the fact to represent The Situation of 1898, his narrators constitute precisely the sort of 'mongrel' assortment his father – a participant in the events – would have rejected: P. Aïeul, Arab café waiter; Yusef, another Arab, a kitchen worker; Maxwell Rowley-Bugge, a disgraced expatriate English paedophile; Waldetar, a Portugese Jew working on the railroads in Egypt; Gebrail, an Arab taxi driver; Girgis, an Egyptian acrobat and burglar working with a team of Syrians; and Hanne, barmaid in a German-style beerhall in Egypt. All of these characters try to interpret the behaviour of the same group of diplomat-spies, attempt to construct a version of The Situation. In this way Stencil Jr. attempts to come to terms to some degree with the idea of a non-homogeneous interpretation of reality in which the varying narrations spin off in diverse and inconclusive directions instead of adding up to a complete picture of the events in question.

Nevertheless, Stencil Jr. does, finally, ressemble White's traditional historian attempting to discover both meaning and narrative coherence in historical events themselves. His facts, of course, are incomplete, so in an effort to represent certain historical moments of importance to his overall narrative he must go beyond hard facts, blurring further the line separating fiction and history. History according to Herbert Stencil, as his name might suggest, is

made to fit a pattern; or as Eigenvalue puts it, it has been
'Stencilized' so that places and characters whose names begin with
the letter 'v' become prominent. While Stencil's V motif may seem
implausible and contrived at times, the suggestion remains that
many other more conventional ways of configuring the events of
the past also impose interpretive schemes whose justification lies
at least as much in the interpreter's perspective as in the evidence.
At times the shaky coherence of the V-plot constitutes a parodic
exaggeration of the historiographic attempt to emplot history
coherently. In any case, within the novel it is largely through
Stencil's narratives that we have access to history:

> Around each seed of a dossier, therefore, had developed a nacreous mass of
> inference, poetic license, forcible dislocation of personality into a past he
> didn't remember and had no right in save the right of imaginative anxiety or
> historical care, which is recognized by no one.   (1966: 62)

The first historical dossier that Pynchon, via Stencil, presents
concerns the Fashoda episode, a critical moment in the history of
European imperialism when the 'rush for Africa' brought the
colonising powers perilously close to a head-on collision. In any
narrative, focalisation or point of view determines a great deal;
Chapter 3 presents a series of fictional events related to the
historical crisis, each from a different point of view but always
with the guiding vision of Stencil's combination of 'imaginative
anxiety or historical care' in the background. The eight separate
focalisers in the chapter offer very different perspectives on the
events they observe. In more conventional narratives, writes
Shlomith Rimmon-Kenan, the 'norms' of the text 'in accordance
with which the events and characters' are evaluated 'are presented
through a single dominant perspective, that of the narrator-
focalizer' (1983: 81). Pynchon's use of multiple focalisers undermines any single sense of norms as interpretive guides. In this kind
of situation, Rimmon-Kenan observes,

> the single authoritative external focalizer gives way to a plurality of ideological
> positions . . . . Some of these positions may concur in part or in whole, others
> may be mutually opposed, the interplay among them provoking a non-unitary,
> 'polyphonic' reading of the text.   (1983: 81)

This 'non-unitary, "polyphonic" ' reading may presumably be
extended to encompass the reading (and writing) of history itself, a

reading that could allow space for non-synchronous and disparate experience.

In the other 'Stencilised' chapters as well, this technique is employed. Whether it is a shifting focaliser (Chapter 7), Stencil's adaptation of someone else's story (Chapter 9), or the rendering of someone else's diary (Chapter 11), 'the single authoritative external focalizer' is always undermined. Pynchon's use of this technique allows him to undermine the cultural force fields that seal off communities in monological discourse, to present glimpses of the world from heterogeneous perspectives, and to attempt imaginatively to cross the 'magic frontiers' that separate different phrase universes (Lyotard) or communities of discourse. We are reminded, however, of the difficulty of doing so, of escaping from our towers, by the fact that both the focalisers who provide a centre of consciousness and to some degree the events related have been 'Stencilised'. Yet balancing this narrative instability is the historical detail: the Mahdi, the Fashoda episode, the seige of Malta. These are matters of historical fact and Pynchon does not seem concerned with challenging that status. According to the history books, the Herero uprising of 1904 *did* occur and *was* suppressed by von Trotha in the manner Pynchon relates, and in 1922 the Bondels, led by Abraham Morris *did* unsuccessfully rise against the white South African government. Steven Weisenburger, in a discussion of the historical elements in *Gravity's Rainbow*, notes that the learning evinced in Pynchon's work 'by whatever fortuitous circumstances it was found, was nonetheless won by human labor and a profound sense of care for the importance of engaging oneself, as a witness, before the nightmarish spectacle of recent history' (Pearce, 1981: 141).[6]

It is worth pointing out that whatever the epistemological traps that lie tangled within Stencil's obsession with V., the subtext of every historical narrative he produces has to do with imperialist conquest or violence, with a steady current of racism – and the reality of these events is not ironically subverted. Even in the chapter 'V. in love', the least overtly political of the historical chapters, there occurs a profusion of references to race and imperialism which probes the 'erotic and aesthetic fascination with "the Orient" ' that Andreas Huyssen similarly characterises as a 'deeply problematic' element of European modernism (1984: 51). The echoes in this chapter of the infamous opening night performance in Paris of Stravinsky's ballet *Le Sacre de Printemps*, an exemplary modernist moment, are notable.[7] 'Somehow the performance had taken on a political cast', comments Pynchon/ Stencil, 'Orientalism – at this period showing up all over Paris in fasions, music, theatre – had been connected along with Russia to an international movement seeking to overthrow Western civilisation' (1966: 412).

From the 'Negro girl' dancing at the café L'Ouganda in Paris (1966: 398) to the brutality of the Herero episodes, it is in these images and themes of race and colonial history that the continuity of V. lies, and it is a continuity – tenuous though it sometimes appears – that remains undisturbed by the epistemological aporias presented by the novel. However much the possibility of final knowledge is undermined and narrative shown to be unstable, Pynchon seems at times to address the reader directly and without a trace of epistemological distress:

[D]uring the Great Rebellion of 1904–7 . . . the Hereros and Hottentots, who usually fought one another, staged a simultaneous but uncoordinated rising against an incompetent German administration. General Lothar von Trotha, having demonstrated to Berlin during his Chinese and East African campaigns a certain expertise at suppressing pigmented populations, was brought in to deal with the Hereros. In August 1904, von Trotha issued his 'Vernichtungs Befehl,' whereby the German forces were ordered to exterminate systematically every Herero man, woman and child they could find. He was about 80 per cent successful. Out of the estimated 80,000 Hereros living in the territory in 1904, an official German census taken seven years later set the Herero population at only 15,130, this being a decrease of 64,870. Similarly the Hottentots were reduced in the same period by about 10,000, the Berg-Damaras by 17,000. Allowing for natural causes during those unnatural years, von Trotha, who stayed for only one of them, is reckoned to have done away with about 60,000 people. This is only 1 per cent of six million, but still pretty good.

(1966: 244–5)

All this information is a matter of verifiable historical 'fact'. The only trace of irony in this section occurs in the last sentence, and it does nothing to undermine the certainty of the account – instead it draws attention to the horror of these genocidal events and links them quite directly to the racist holocaust of World War II.

While Pynchon may sometimes seem to accept a relativist position, he has not rejected the possibility of moral judgement – difficult, relative and tentative though it may be. Mondaugen, at one point during the seige party, sets off in search of the power generator so that he can tap some of the electricity for his experiments. The generator he actually finds is of a more symbolic nature than he had intended, however: it is in a planetarium

> a circular room with a great wooden sun, overlaid with gold leaf, burning cold in the very center and round it the nine planets and their moons, suspended from tracks in the ceiling, actuated by a coarse cobweb of chains, pulleys, belts, racks, pinions and worms, all receiving their prime impulse from a treadmill in the corner, usually operated for the amusement of the guests by a Bondelsch-wartz [slave], now unoccupied.   (1966: 239)

Ignoring the reference to slavery, one might argue that the epistemological metaphor here concerns the way we construct our reality, our universe, and suggests that our constructions are, like Stencil's, rather clumsy at times. Mondaugen has, odd though it may seem, danced into the room with a young woman whose declared 'purpose on earth is to tantalize and send raving the race of men' (1966: 239). The rhythm of the music they had been dancing to is transformed into a kind of cosmic rhythm as he

> skipped to the treadmill and began a jog-trot that set the solar system in motion, creaking and whining in a way that raised a prickling in the teeth. Rattling, shuddering, the wooden planets began to rotate and spin, Saturn's rings to whirl, moons their precessions, our own Earth its nutational wobble, all picking up speed; as the girl continued to dance, having chosen Venus for her partner; as Mondaugen dashed along his own geodesic, following in the footsteps of a generation of slaves.   (1966: 239)

Again, it is possible to read this as a demonstration that love (or at least desire) makes the world go round. And Pynchon with his fine sense of cliché perhaps intends this. But the final allusion once again is to slavery, oppression. Without knowing it, Mondaugen has found the generator, although not the one he was looking for. So 'breathing heavily', he 'staggered off the treadmill to carry on his descent and search for the generator' (1966: 240). For the reader at least, there should be less ambiguity surrounding the power *generator* and the *generation* of slaves as Mondaugen reaches bottom in his descent and finds, perhaps, the very slave whose place as generator on the planetary treadmill had been unoccupied.

> As if the entire day had come into being only to prepare him for this, he discovered a Bondel male, face down and naked, the back and buttocks

showing scar tissue from old sjambokings as well as more recent wounds, laid open across the flesh like so many toothless smiles .... Mondaugen approached the man and stooped to listen for breathing or a heartbeat, trying not to see the white vertebra that winked at him from one long opening.

(1966: 240)

The seemingly incongrous images that accompany this scene, of smiles and a wink, underscore with a grim irony the power of metaphorical representation.[8] The wounds that Mondaugen sees from the point of view of the white community as smiles and winks can, of course, also be read as the literal inscription of the desire and power of the oppressor on the body of the slave. Eventually he decides to leave the white enclave whose perspective he has until now passively accepted: 'Mondaugen this time withdrew, preferring at last neither to watch nor to listen' (1966: 278). The absence of a strong moral statement in relation to Mondaugen's departure is notable, and this is one of the moments that has led critics to comment on the novel's postmodern inability to establish sufficiently a position of resistance.

Nevertheless, his dramatic crossing of the ravine separating the seige party from the rest of the world is highly symbolic – the seige is, in V., political and epistemological as well as military. He drops a plank across a narrow part of the abyss and works 'his way gingerly across, trying not to look down at the tiny stream two hundred feet below' (1966: 278–9). The ravine represents a significant epistemological gap with overt moral consequences, and Mondaugen is crossing one of the 'magical frontiers', going beyond 'the limits' of that particular world. He makes his way through the scrubland until he meets a Bondel on a donkey. The man has lost his right arm – presumably in colonial resistance of some kind – and is a (jarring) witness to the violence of imperialism.

'All over', he said. 'Many Bondels dead, baases dead, van Wijk dead. My woman, younkers dead.' He let Mondaugen ride behind him. At that point Mondaugen didn't know where they were going. As the sun climbed he dozed on and off, his cheek against the Bondel's scarred back .... Soon as they trotted along the Bondel began to sing .... The song was in Hottentot dialect, and Mondaugen couldn't understand it.   (1966: 279)

Disoriented and in many ways uncomprehending after the literal bridging of a sublime abyss, a 'magic frontier', an 'invisible

forcefield', he has arrived at the conditions of possibility of
another state of mind, beyond the seige mentality. His non-
comprehension of the alien Bondel language is no longer passively
allied with a genocidal threat to the existence of that language. The
scarred back of this Bondel can itself be considered a kind of text
that is readable in different ways in different cultural and
historical situations (even as 'smiles' and 'winks'), but the
existence of the scars themselves is not in doubt. Although 'history
is not a text' writes Jameson, 'it is inaccessible to us except in
textual form' (1981: 35). Here the text of history is inscribed in the
scars on the backs of its victims. Writing of another colonised
group – Latin American Indians – Michel de Certeau asserts that in
the body language of scars, some cultures

> preserve a painful recognition of four and a half centuries of colonization.
> Dominated but not vanquished, they keep alive the memory of what the
> Europeans have 'forgotten' – a continuous series of uprisings and awakenings
> which have left hardly a trace in the occupiers' historiographical literature.
> This history of resistance marked by cruel repression is *marked on the Indian's
> body* as much as it is recorded in transmitted accounts – or more so.
>
> (1986: 227)

For them, these 'scars on the body proper – or the fallen "heroes"
or "martyrs" who correspond to them in narrative' constitute as
well 'the index of a history yet to be made' (1986: 227) which will
end this condition of subjugation. This is, in a sense, the history
that orthodox narratives such as *Nostromo* leave out, are unable
even to recognise, preferring instead to explain anti-colonial
resistance with categories of irrationality and stupidity, bestiality
and vice.

There is a clear moral and historical imperative governing
Pynchon's representation of 'real' historical events and their
apparently repetitive pattern. It can be detected, for example, in
the way the Bondel's postrevolutionary song (a failed revolution)
echoes in *V.* through decades and across cultures: in Porcepic's
appropriation of African polyrhythms for white European modernist music (1966: 402),[9] and in Sphere's African-American jazz with
its 'rising rhythms of African nationalism' (1966: 60). While a
number of patterns do repeat in the historical and contemporary
chapters, it is an overstatement to claim, as Molly Hite does, that
reality in *V.* is somehow 'static . . . which suggests that past and
present exist simultaneously or even that they are reversible . . . in

V. past and present reflect each other in receding vistas' (1966: 51). There can be no question, for example, of reversing the genocidal atrocities carried out against the Hereros, and to suggest an equivalence to 'Mafia Winsome's intellectual racism' is clearly as disproportionate as is her equivalence of Foppl's seige party (with its racist torture, murder, rape and depravity) and the relatively mild bohemianism of the Whole Sick Crew (1966: 64–5). This response to the novel is quite common, however, and results from approaching it as a formalist epistemological puzzle (albeit a puzzle that may not allow the possibility of a solution), or an abstract philosophical statement, to the exclusion of the overt social and historical detail.

Most critics would no doubt agree with Richard Patteson that for Stencil, 'V. is in a sense a vast hall of mirrors in which . . . an indefinite number of variations' may be discovered, 'but no way out of his dilemma' (1984: 25). The recurrence of mirror imagery in discussions of V. is symptomatic of a prevalent problem in postmodernism: the possibility that an acceptance of relativity entails a trivialising of interpretation – even a kind of solipsism. Ernst Bloch argues that in some versions of historical relativism

The very process of history is broken up . . . historical relativism is here turned into something static; it is being caught in cultural monads, that is, culture souls without windows, with no links among each other, yet full of mirrors facing inside.   (Fabian, 1983: 44–5)

A dangerous tendency of cultural relativism, Johannes Fabian adds, is the fact 'that such mirrors, if placed at propitious angles, also have the miraculous power to make real objects disappear' (1983: 45). Bloch and Fabian undoubtedly have an important point: certainly there are aspects of postmodernism and cultural relativism that effectively derealise history – it has been argued that some of Hayden White's work lends itself to this possibility, for example. Yet this need not be the case. There is a corollary to this mirror imagery: if placed at certain other propitious angles, mirrors have an equally miraculous power to make present objects and perspectives previously unavailable to perception. Pynchon's postmodern mirrors may indeed conceal many things and present many illusions and deceptions, but they also re-present historical situations and events that had hitherto remained obscured from sight. By means of a postmodern historical relativism, rather than making events disappear, he is making present what seems to be a remarkable history of Western racism, from the atrocities of colonialism to the somewhat more covert and subtle racism of America at the time of writing. This history is, in fact, one that somehow managed to elude generations of historians and novelists – including realists, modernists and others.

It is also not entirely accurate to claim, as Hite does, that 'in V. ... nobody seems to learn anything' (1983: 51). Sphere, Rachel, Maijstral all seem to experience a change for the better in their understanding of the world. And while it is true that 'Benny Profane's last words in the book are "Offhand I'd say I haven't learned a goddam thing" ' (Pynchon, 1966: 51), Profane is not set up as an ideal or universal specimen. Nor is Stencil, whose policy towards knowledge is either obsessive or 'Approach and avoid' (1966: 55), to be considered a universal epistemological model:

it hadn't really ever stopped being the same simple-minded, literal pursuit; V. ambiguously a beast of venery, chased like the hart, hind or hare . . . . And clownish Stencil capering along behind her, bells ajingle, waving a wooden, toy oxgoad. For no one's amusement but his own.   (1966: 61–2)

Surely there is a middle ground between Profane (who claims to understand nothing, to learn nothing) and his opposite, Stencil (who seeks to comprehend the totality of experience). Much of the book is written in a slapstick tone which encourages at best a limited identification with the characters. As readers we need not choose only between the two: instead, it ought to be possible to learn something ourselves. However subjective our interpretation of Pynchon's interpretation of history might be, there are, in the end, facts that are presented in V. as history, narratives that are presented to convey meaning, and these are often related to themes of real political oppression. Regardless of whether the characters seem to grasp the meanings and morals as firmly as one might wish, Pynchon's condemnation of the atrocities of racism and imperialism ought not be in doubt.

The point here is neither to hypostatise facts nor to relativise them out of existence. As Said contends, 'Facts do not speak for themselves but require a socially acceptable narrative to absorb, sustain and circulate them' (1984: 14). And, 'where are the facts', he continues, in a tone almost reminiscent of Chateaubriand, 'if not embedded in history, and then reconstituted and recovered by human agents stirred by some perceived or desired or hoped-for historical narrative whose aim is to restore justice to the dispossessed?' (1984: 16). Pynchon's postmodern history is an attempt to remind us about certain aspects of our heritage that we might prefer to overlook as we select the materials from which to construct our narrative of the past. And no matter how much it is argued that the past is our own creation, we create it out of a limited supply of building materials:

> People read what news they wanted to and each accordingly built his own rathouse of history's rags and straws. In the city of New York alone there were at a rough estimate five million different rathouses . . . . Doubtless their private versions of history showed up in action. (Pynchon, 1966: 225)

Doubtless everyone's version of history does show up in action, which is why it is so important to examine the construction of history in order to come to an understanding of the complex relationship between ideology and praxis. In theory there may be an infinite number of designs for the rathouse, but in practice there is a finite (and remarkably consistent) number of headlines to build with, and many rathouses display a certain similarity. The building of an historical rathouse is not simply a matter of *jouissance*, of the free play of the imagination: such a 'Postmodern Style of History' would, as Hal Foster fears, 'signal the disintegration of style and the collapse of history' (1984: 73).

In Pynchon's work, however, history is in no danger of collapsing under the weight of jarring witnesses and their heterogeneous discourses. The Herero–Bondel episode in V. is not at all an isolated one. The Mahdi, alluded to in Chapter 3, was a nationalist, millenarian movement which had attempted to repell the colonising British. Historical accounts of the Battle of Omdurman (1898), yet another of V.'s sieges, are chilling. Against a large army of Sudanese, most of whom fought with spears, the British forces used heavy artillery with the result that on the battlefield, more than 10,000 Sudanese died immediately and uncounted more men, women and children died of wounds or in the shelling of the city. As a fitting conclusion to this military destruction, the tomb of the Mahdi, the only building of size in the city and 'an object of veneration . . . the focal point of the religious and political life of the capital' was destroyed after the fighting was over (Daly, 1986: 4–5). Thus, the decimation of the population was accompanied by the destruction of the symbolic centre or orientation point of their *sensus communis*, an act intended to eliminate further military threats by eliminating at its cultural source the system of meaning-production (White) that might project a narrative of resistance.

Elsewhere, one of Stencil's impersonations considers the strange history of Egypt's Lake Mareotis:

> Beneath the lake were 150 villages, submerged by a manmade Flood in 1801, when the English cut through an isthmus of desert during the siege of Alexandria, to let the Mediterranean in. Waldetar liked to think that the waterfowl soaring thick in the air were ghosts of fellahin. What submarine wonders at the floor of Mareotis! Lost country: houses, hovels, farms, water wheels, all intact.
>
> Did the narwhal pull their plows? Devilfish drive their water wheels?
>
> (1966: 79)[10]

Here again we are given historical fact without epistemological complication but accompanied by a quiet, powerful, even lyrical, sense of historical pathos. The incident is a kind of historical curiosity as well, since it occurred as part of the British campaign against the French led by Napoleon, and neither nationality remained in Egypt long after the battle. It was, in a sense, a precursor to the Fashoda crisis which also pitted the British against the French, but without the overt colonialist motive for the British. E. M. Forster discusses the incident in his book on the city of Alexandria and, as an example of historical relativism and the derealisation of history, it is worth juxtaposing his account with the account Pynchon gives to Waldetar. What is now 'Lake Mariout [sic] was almost dry', Forster writes. 'It contained a little fresh water, but most of its enormous bed was under cultivation.' In a strategic move to isolate the French troops in Alexandria the British opened a channel. 'The salt water rushed in, to the delight of the British soldiers, and in a month thousands of acres had been drowned.' The move was a military success. The French surrendered and both imperialist armies retired: 'we had accomplished our aim, and had no reason to remain in the country any longer; we left it to our allies the Turks' (Forster, 1961: 93). Forster's elision of the inhabitants from this narrative is made all the more strange by use of the metaphor 'drowned' to describe the acres instead of the people whose fate does not, in this account, merit notice. Indeed, Forster suggests, they should be grateful for receiving the attention of Europeans; brief though it was, it rescued the area from a kind of native stupor:

But the sleep of so many centuries had been broken. The eyes of Europe were again directed to the deserted shore. Though Napoleon had failed and the British had retired, a new age had begun for Alexandria. Life flowed back into her, just as the waters, when Hutchinson cut the dyke, flowed back into Lake Mariout. (1961: 93)

The problem of point of view in history is central here. Deserted by whom? The imperialist forces who returned immediately to Europe? The inhabitants whose lives were submerged beneath the salt water? White argues that although we claim 'to rank events in terms of their world historical significance . . . that significance is less world historical than simply Western European,' representing 'a perspective that is culture-specific, not universal at all' (1987: 9–10).[11] Forster reiterates the kind of culture-specific historical narrative that White criticises and Pynchon is self-consciously undermining. As one of V.'s characters points out,

We can always so easily give the wrong reasons . . . can say: the Chinese campaigns, they were for the Queen, and India for some gorgeous notion of Empire. I know. I have said these things to my men, the public, to myself. There are Englishmen dying in South Africa today and about to die tomorrow who believe these words as – I dare say you believe in God. (1966: 169)

It is at a point such as this that his technical manipulation of narrative together with his overt subject matter combine to subvert the standard historical accounts. This reference to South Africa is as timely today as it was in 1963 when it was written, or perhaps more so, as South Africa gradually undergoes a momentous political alteration – yet another illustration of historical or historiographical relativity. White, whose linkage of narrative and authority was quoted earlier, argues that the 'more historically self-conscious the writer of any form of historiography, the more the question of the social system and the law which sustains it, the authority of this law and its justification, and threats to this law occupy his attention' (1987: 13). Pynchon's self-consciousness as a historian and otherwise have often been observed, but the problem of social or political authority has not generally been considered central to V. Yet the novel is replete with examples of this kind of reference to authority both in the events of history and in the narrative representations of those events. Whether the examples are drawn from Egyptian, Sudanese, Namibian or Maltese history, the rooms in Pynchon's rathouse exhibit a consistently radical rereading of European imperialism.

Yet Pynchon is no dogmatist: any final interpretation – of history or of his story – remains thwarted. As Schaub argues, 'he is adamantly opposed ... to the creation of any stable, fixed "history" ' (1981: 110). Pynchon's project is not primarily a reconstruction of history from the point of view of its victims, although elements of this are present in the novel. Instead he works to decentre the established authoritative 'objective' Western account of historical events. Mink argues that, as a form of cognition, narrative does not simply relate a sequence of events, but

bod[ies] forth an ensemble of interrelationships of many different kinds as a single whole. In fictional narrative the coherence of such complex forms affords aesthetic or emotional satisfaction: in historical narrative it additionally claims truth. But this is where the problem arises.   (1987: 144–5)

Pynchon, of course, seems well aware of the problem and at the possible expense of 'aesthetic or emotional satisfaction' has sacrificed, to a large degree, the totality implied in the idea of 'single whole' story. Instead, he is faithful to the fact that, as Mink observes, one event may appear in different stories, told by different narrative communities, and its significance may vary enormously with its place in these different narratives (1987: 144–5). Hegemony, in a Gramscian sense, lies in the power to control, by means of a variable combination of coercion and consent, the terms in which the event enters into legitimate discourse – the society's system of meaning-production. Pynchon's postmodernism is an example of a discourse that works to erode the hegemonic cultural system of meaning-production that has served to oppress and marginalise those aphasic, jarring witnesses traditionally excluded from legitimate discourse.

While speculation is perhaps idle, it is at least possible that Pynchon might even agree with Jameson that postmodernism's resort to the sublime and to relativity need not necessarily remain an end in itself; the point is rather 'To undo postmodernism homeopathically by the methods of postmodernism ... to reconquer some genuine historical sense by using the instruments of what I have called substitutes for history' (1987: 42). Defining a 'genuine historical sense' here might prove difficult of course, yet in any case, Pynchon's historiographical practice in V. amounts to the implosion of the culture-specific historical narrative that White has outlined. As Stencil Sr. observes, The Situation is an n-dimensional mish-mash (1966: 460) and Pynchon demonstrates this technically by undermining to such a degree the stable representation of historical fact, stuffing the novel full of references to every theory of history imaginable, and yet continuing to render historical facts. Despite Stencil's impersonations, V. does not, by itself, articulate a discourse of the 'other' to any great extent. But, by fragmenting the monolithic Western narrative of 'objective' historical realism, it works towards opening the heterodox discursive space within that dominant discourse in which narratives of alterity, of non-synchronous and discrepant experience may be articulated and, possibly, even understood by readers not native to those other cultures.

'There's no organized effort about it,' explains the narrator of V. in relation to the inhabitants of exotic lands, 'but there remains a grand joke on all visitors to Baedeker's world: the permanent residents are actually humans in disguise' (1966: 78). The similarity to Zora Neale Hurston's comments on the American Museum of Unnatural History, another cultural tourist attraction, is noteworthy, and Pynchon's fiction constitutes an attempt to reveal the human behind what the West has traditionally seen as the native disguise, to create the conditions of possibility under which jarring historical witnesses might testify and be heard. In Gravity's Rainbow, Pynchon introduces a radio image to describe this: temporal bandwidth – 'the width of your present, your now' (1973: 509). The narrower the bandwidth, the more tenuous is the connection of present experience to past and future; the broader the bandwidth, the better the reception of the various perspectives and discourses on events that (however uneasily) coexist. Weisenburger writes of the importance that a broad bandwidth and a wide open radio dial has for Pynchon, a writer 'who often seems capable of listening to an impossible cacaphony . . . . [yet] never insists on keeping the different channels discrete'. In novels such as V. and Gravity's Rainbow, 'Each channel is history, in the most open sense of that word' (Pearce, 1981: 149). Ideally, such a postmodern discourse would be a realisation of the Bakhtinian polyphonic ideal. 'Polyglossia', or the 'interanimation of languages', is what makes the novel possible, writes Bakhtin, and it developed 'in a complex and centuries-long struggle of cultures and languages' (1981: 82–3). The unitary, monological language of epic history would be dissolved: as Bakhtin puts it, with the move to novelistic heteroglossia,

Every event, every phenomenon, every thing, every object of artistic representation loses its completedness, its hopelessly finished quality and its immutability that had been so essential to it in the world of the epic 'absolute past,' walled off by an unapproachable boundary from the continuing and unfinished present. Through contact with the present, an object is attracted to the incomplete process of a world-in-the-making, and is stamped with the seal of inconclusiveness.   (1981: 30)

If unitary language and completeness are the marks of a sealed-off homogeneous culture, this sense of the radical inconclusiveness of any representation has much in common with Lyotard's discussion of the sublimity of the event, and with the sense of the cultural differend that follows from it. In its Utopian aspect this polyphony would be resolved into a non-hegemonic harmony; in its dystopian aspect it would dissolve into discursive warfare with no one holding a balance of power. In the meantime there is, as Pynchon observes, the value – aesthetic and political – of a wide bandwidth.

In his retrospective introduction to *Slow Learner*, published twenty years after *V.*, Pynchon considers the possibility that 'racial differences are not as basic as questions of money and power, but have served a useful purpose . . . in keeping us divided and so relatively poor and powerless' (1985: xxi). Yet in *V.*, written while the American civil rights movement gathered momentum, it is racial difference that is explored most fully. Early in the novel, Paola teaches her friends a song that she had learned from a French paratrooper on 'leave from the fighting in Algeria'. Algeria, as well as being just beyond Europe, on the other side of the Mediterranean (middle of the world), was no doubt in the news while *V.* was being written, as the site of the most well-publicised anti-colonial war immediately prior to the American involvement in Viet Nam.

Demain le noir matin
Je fermerai la porte
Au nez des années mortes;
J'irai par les chemins.
Je mendierai ma vie
Sur la terre et sur l'onde,
Du vieux au nouveau monde. (1966: 18–19)

This song is echoed in a different key later, perhaps, by the 'girl [who] sang about her love, killed defending his homeland in a faraway war' (1966: 191). Closing the door on the dead years for this soldier can only mean closing the door on the historical era of colonialism and its legacy of war and death in faraway places. No activist or rebel, he was probably 'a man-of-no-politics as brave as anyone ever is in combat: but tired, was all, tired of relocating native villages and devising barbarities' (1966: 19). To refuse the various politics of barbarism is to choose to wander, a state of Deleuzian deterritorialisation much like the 'deracinated' characters who are discussing him. As he had done, most of the many military characters in V. live below the horizon of historical consciousness, participating in it without much awareness of the political and historical pressures behind military action. When the Suez crisis occurs, the sailors in V. talk of many things, but not of the historical or political background. The lack of awareness on the part of the characters in V. has been commented on by a number of critics as has the novel's lack of tangible hope. But there may be, as V.'s Eigenvalue says, folds and crests in the fabric of history

such that if we are situated . . . at the bottom of a fold, it's impossible to determine warp, woof or pattern anywhere else . . . [and] it is assumed there are others, compartmented off into sinuous cycles each of which come to assume greater importance than the weave itself and destroy any continuity. Thus it is that we are charmed by the funny-looking automobiles of the '30's, the curious fashions of the '20's, the peculiar moral habits of our grandparents. We produce and attend musical comedies about them and are conned into a false memory, a phony nostalgia about what they were. We are accordingly lost to any sense of a continuous tradition. Perhaps if we lived on a crest, things would be different. We could at least see. (1966: 156)

V. may then be read as an attempt to foster, if not clear vision, then at least the necessary conditions in which a broader vision (or bandwidth) might be possible, one that is able to focus on the lives of the dispossessed and the victims, in relation to the discourses of power that oppress them. To this end, Pynchon examines some of the implications of cultural and historical relativism and of the historical sublime – the latter present in both aspects discussed by Lyotard. The first – the ultimately unrepresentable nature of the event and the plurality of historical interpretation – has been discussed earlier. 'The art object', writes Lyotard, 'no longer bends itself to models [of the beautiful] but tries to present the fact that there is an unpresentable' (1985: 12). The other aspect of the sublime is perhaps more peculiarly contemporary: 'the sublime', he writes, 'is kindled by the threat of nothing further happening . . . . What is terrifying is that the It happens that does not happen, that it stops happening' (1985: 10). Lyotard's idea of nothing further happening entails the end of the narrative, and the end of the social possibility of creating narrative can only coincide with the destruction of that society – as the plight of the Mahdi in 1898 or the Namibian Hereros in 1904 demonstrates,[12] or as Said has argued in reference to the Palestinian question (1984).

The end of the unfolding narratives of history on a global scale is apocalypse, the sublime spectacle of unrepresentable terror. 'The sublime has not lost its link to terror', writes Huyssen. 'For what could be more sublime and unrepresentable than the nuclear holocaust, the bomb being the signifier of an ultimate sublime' (1984: 46). As long as events continue to unfold, however, it is possible to represent them in one way or another as something happening, continuing the narratives as it were. But the possibility echoes throughout V. that the end of the story, the end of history, may be imminent, as 'the balloon' appears set to 'go up' on a number of occasions and Western society seems about to tear itself apart in war yet again. The novel ends as the troops prepare for another neo-colonial showdown – Suez. 'The Middle East', says Stencil Jr., 'cradle of civilisation, may yet be its grave' (1966: 387). This ending signals an attempt to connect the historical record and the novel itself to present conditions in the world, to historicise contemporary politics in a radical context. Pynchon is contributing another dimension to the design of the historical rathouse that is to be built out of the headlines about the Suez crisis.

Writing of the story that became Chapter 3 of V., Pynchon observes that although World War I takes on the power of an 'apocalyptic showdown',

Our common nightmare The Bomb is in there too. It was bad enough in '59 and is much worse now, as the level of danger has continued to grow . . . . Except for that succession of the criminally insane who have enjoyed power since 1945, including the power to do something about it, most of the rest of us poor sheep have always been stuck with simple, standard fear. I think we have all tried to deal with this slow escalation of our helplessness and terror in the few ways open to us, from not thinking about it to going crazy about it. Somewhere on this spectrum of impotence is writing fiction about it.   (1985: xxix)

Pynchon's approriation of epistemological relativism and the historical sublime constitutes, in many ways, an early example of a more general social shift: away from segregation for example, the American version of apartheid, and toward an ideal of trans-cultural non-coercive understanding that was to become a central tenet of the Civil Rights Movement and of radical politics in the 1960s. In a study of the liberational possibilities of cultural relativity, Arif Dirlik writes:

Hegemony requires a center, not only in space but also in time. The decentering of the hegemonic group, be it class or nation, deprives history of a center and the hegemonic group of its claims upon history. Culturalism that achieves this end points to a liberating possibility, if only as a possibility.   (1987: 27)

Yet the fragility of this sense of possibility must be noted. Indeed, as Dirlik (and many others) points out, some kinds of postmodern thought have the effect of derealising concrete historical experience quite thoroughly, compounding rather than helping to ease the postcolonial situation. What is ultimately needed is not only 'an epistemology the goal of which is to discover abstract truths, but an epistemology with an intention, one that seeks to overcome the alienation that is implicit in the notion of truth conceived abstractly' (1987: 45). There is no reason to assume that postmodernism per se, as an 'ism', can provide the appropriate concrete historical, philosophical or political frame-work. If it can, writes Huyssen, it 'will have to be a postmodernism of resistance, including resistance to that easy postmodernism of the "anything goes" variety' (1984: 52). As a postmodern historio-graphical novel – a novel about historical representation as well as about historical events – Pynchon's V. does point in that direction.

Conclusion

In *The Historical Novel*, one of the first modern studies of the genre, historian Herbert Butterfield maintained that

> Whatever connection the historical novel may have with the history men write and build up out of their conscious studies, or with History, the past as it really happened, the thing that is the object of study and research, it certainly has something to do with . . . that mental picture which each of us makes of the past; it helps our imagination to build up its idea of the past.   (1924: 2)

Since it concerns our ideas – however *we* is defined – history, fictional or not, is a story that concerns the present, even the future, as well as the past. The present situation exerts a determining influence on how the past is perceived and thus on how it can be represented; the future, as a projected continuation or culmination of the past and present, draws both to it in ways that alter their shape. Moreover, history is a story that is not solely concerned with time and events: in its representations of those times and events, it functions as a powerful form of self-representation and self-definition. Indeed it is through such shared narratives that the social identity of communities is constituted, both positively (by inclusion) and negatively (through exclusion or demonisation, for example). Such narrative exclusion can occur either by means of a representation of an alien, somehow dangerous or suspicious 'other', or simply through an absence of representation that occludes the other altogether. Following de Certeau's reasoning, it could be argued, in fact, that the discourse of history has acted precisely to create and preserve difference as a means of consolidating a sense of community. The jarring witness, then, is not an accidental or coincidental product or problem of historical narrative but one fundamental *raison d'être* of a discourse and discipline that arose along with the ideologies of nationalism, imperialism and modern class structure. The jarring witness is a category which has functioned to legitimise, for example, the bourgeoisie of specific nations (for whom history and genealogy were not already synonymous as they were for the aristocracy), to justify (implicitly or explicitly) the colonial conquest of cultures deemed premodern or even prehistoric, or to perpetuate the exclusion of women from historical agency in a patriarchal society.

As a general characterisation of historical discourse, this is, of course, at once too negative and too reductive. Historical narrative has done other things as well: Chateaubriand's depiction of the historian as hero 'charged with avenging the people' ought not be dismissed. The questions, however, remain: Which people? For whom or against whom does the historian strike the blow for truth and liberty? In the name of what community is justice sought? Can there be a universal community? While questions of community or of common sense are, as Jean-Luc Nancy has remarked, basic to the discussion of historiography (1990: 149), the nature of the *sensus communis* itself is also deeply problematic.[1] Throughout this study, I have attempted to show the degree to which community affiliation inevitably structures narrative representations of the past. One danger in such an approach appears in the tendency, which I have tried to avoid, to reify community in such a way as to see its structures as immutable or monolithic. The nature or constellation of community affiliation is a product of history, as well as a producer of historiographic representations, and is therefore subject to change. The shifts in the nature of community which have been occurring in this century are reflected in narratives which both dramatise that social crisis and intervene in the general social struggle to define what constitutes community affiliation.

The recent controversy over the canon, for example, is an issue of literary history involving the question of community as deeply as other forms of history. To raise the questions of race, class and gender in relation to the canon is to call into question the definition of the community whose sense of itself has been reflected and moulded there. The struggle over the canon, then, is a somewhat disguised argument concerning the shifting nature of community, and the current revisions to the canon – like all previous constructions of it – are based on a re-imagining of the literary past which is inevitably structured by present interests. The point of challenging an orthodox traditional canon is not only to locate texts perhaps suppressed by the weightiest interests, or to reread texts in light of these considerations, it is also – and more controversially – to be part of a more general redefinition of the community whose identity is displayed and consolidated in its choice of 'sacred texts'.

Eric Hobsbawm, in a recent lecture entitled 'The New Threat to History', dismisses 'the rise of "postmodernist" intellectual fashions . . . which imply that all "facts" claiming objective existence are simply intellectual constructs' (1993: 63). 'Facts' can thus, as he points out, easily be manufactured and mobilised in the service of one community or another in order to advance its claim to dominance. Surely this practice does not originate with postmodernism, however; nor need the adoption of a postmodernist position entail an inability to distinguish fact from fiction. Another postmodern avenue opens, in fact, in Hobsbawm's remark that there is no 'unambiguous way to choose between different ways of interpreting [a historical fact] or fitting it into the wider context of history'. The postmodern attempt to approach history in terms of narrative and community is not necessarily then, as some fear, to abandon the past to a relativist abyss of empty textuality, however. As Linda Hutcheon has commented, 'History is not made obsolete; it is, however, being rethought as a human construct' (1987: 21). Like any human construct, it is carried on within the discursive practices of some community whose cultural horizons, as Gadamer has argued, both enable and limit the construction of knowledge. Accepting that knowledge is situated in this way, of course, entails difficulties, not the least of which is the often-repeated complaint that such a position can lead only to political paralysis. Jean E. Howard, in a discussion of feminism, postmodernism and history, poses the question this way:

Once one acknowledges the multiple positions from which knowledge is made and the loss of a ground of absolute truth, how does one avoid mere relativism and the loss of politics which always involves exclusions, choices and privileging of one perspective over another?   (1991: 115)

Howard's answer is that a postmodern yet politically commit-ted historical practice is indeed possible. First, like Louis Mink for example, she argues that standards of coherence and accuracy can and must be maintained even in the absence of 'belief in true, complete and unmediated accounts' of reality (Howard, 1991: 117). Second, like Arif Dirlik she insists on the importance of assessing knowledge not only in terms of its objectivity but also in terms of its effects. The importance of feminist historiography, for example, lies in 'its effects or consequences in disrupting and displacing historical narratives which at the crudest level erase women subjects and so further, in the present, an androcentric, oppressive understanding of the world'. The potential for resis-tance afforded by postmodernism exists, then, but is not a necessary condition of that position. Only the postmodern subject who desires to resist will find the outlines of a postmodernism of resistance; a more passive postmodern liberalism is equally possible, even a postmodern conservativism. But this has always been the case anyway with other *isms*; the only difference perhaps is that postmodernism acknowledges this fact more openly.

The perils and possibilities of a postmodernism of resistance have been discussed by a number of commentators of course. Teresa Ebert, for instance, has distinguished two postmodernisms. Ludic postmodernism, in its ironic deconstruction of signifying systems, may 'denaturalize and destabilize the dominant regime of knowledge and the naturalisation of the status quo in the common sense', but it 'cannot provide the basis for a transformative political practice' (Ebert, 1991: 293). Echoing Voloshinov, she argues that a resistance postmodernism, however, rather than accepting difference as a condition of all signification on the level of textuality or language alone, 'contends that textuality and difference – the relation of the signifier and signified – are themselves the sites of social conflict and struggle' (Ebert, 1991: 293). A resistance postmodernism must address the way social power in all its forms functions to structure the specific operations of difference in the production of various ways of making sense of human experience, various versions of common sense. In doing so, it ought to be possible to recover the narrative coherence of at least some voices rendered aphasic by the power politics of difference. A plural sense of history thus replaces the impossible dream of a Universal History: as Gianni Vattimo succinctly puts it, 'modernity ends when . . . it no longer seems possible to regard history as unilinear' (1992: 2). Ideally a notion of community might be evolved in which the law of political physics Johannes Fabian discusses, might be repealed and it could become thinkable for a number of social groups to occupy non-coercively the same social space and time (1983: 31).[2]

These problems are tied up with the more conventional literary issue of point of view. Following Lukács, who saw such dilemmas as symptomatic of a kind of modern homelessness (another form of a crisis of community), Robert Weimann has traced the evolution of point of view from the epic through to the modern novel. The modern concentration on the problem of literary point of view is, he asserts, a reflection of 'a changing and increasingly complex world in which the artist, in order to create, can no longer take wholeness for granted' (1984: 234).[3] For Weimann, point of view is not simply a matter of literary technique, since literary values and social values are finally inseparable:

> the teller of the tale is faced, not simply with a series of technical problems and not only with the rhetorical task of communication, but with a world full of struggle and change where the writer, in order to transmute his experience into art, has constantly to reassess his relations to society as both a social and an aesthetic act. (1984: 237)

Narration, argues Weimann, is neither total nor objective but is rather an act of representation, of 'selective communication' that is only made possible by the adoption of a specific perspective and the engagement in a process of evaluation. Otherwise

> no narration is possible: how else could the narrator . . . hope to comprehend and arrange the multitude of details that he – in summary or silence – thinks fit to condense or pass over? But to achieve the necessary selection and evaluation is impossible without a point from which to select and evaluate, and this view point (whether consciously or unconsciously taken) is indeed the absolute prerequisite of all narrative activity. (1984: 246)

The limits imposed by point of view, then, both constrain and enable narrative. Unlike the epic, 'The modern novel is born in the consciousness of its narrative perspective', writes Weimann, and one is tempted to add that in the twentieth century, particularly in the last decades, that consciousness becomes more precisely a narrative self-consciousness.[4]

The novels I have discussed concern themselves with history in both diverging senses of the term – events in the past (res gestae) and the narrative discourse about those events (historia rerum gestarum) – and in fact this divergence is itself a major theme. What the novels articulate beyond the narrated events themselves is the struggle among social groups over the power and authority to narrate, the struggle for possession of the power to impose the legitimate categories in terms of which the narration is to be carried on. It is, in a sense, a struggle over point of view, over the power to select from among the jarring witnesses the accounts that may be accepted as legitimate testimony. Von Ranke's insight that the writing of history is, finally, impossible without the selection of a point of view (cited above) is borne out here – his other great insight concerning history as the more or less transparent account of 'what actually happened' notwithstanding. The practical difficulties involved in arbitrating between the groups of jarring witnesses, in taking a position with respect to the selection of (and versions of) events to be privileged in narrative, is a longstanding problem to which philosophers of history have often returned. In some ways the distance between F. H. Bradley and Hayden White is less than one might expect: both emphasise the importance of the present social forces that are inevitably influential in the orchestration of the narrative past; both understand clearly that the weightiest interests are at stake in the representations of the past that are produced; and both explore the determining role of tacit presuppositions on the construction of historical knowledge and narrative.

One could certainly find earlier examples, particularly in the rich field of German philosophy of history, but Bradley provides a starting point for the Anglo-American discussion of the emergence of a specifically modern pressure on the certainty of narrative perspective in historiography. The struggle with jarring witnesses, he articulates, coincided with the beginnings of modernism, and it is a struggle that occurs as well in the modernists whose novels I have discussed. This struggle – and I take it to be one of the definitive characteristics of modernist fiction – has been waged in order to resist, contain or otherwise cope with such other voices as could not be silenced or ignored, rather than to let them speak their version of the past. Such a (sub)version, if permitted, could further destabilise a cultural and social fabric reliant on narrative doxa or orthodoxy for its coherence. This strategy was effected in modernism with varying degrees of narrative stress, just as theorists from Bradley to Mink have grappled with problems of authority and coherence in narrative with varying degrees of theoretical stress.

In discussing the limits of the historiographic perspective in modernist novels, my intention is not to attack the novels but to understand the limits that inevitably bound them. Conrad, Ford and Faulkner were men of their time and of their communities; no purpose is served in regarding them as transcendent geniuses expressing timeless and comprehensive wisdom. They did not write from the point of view of the Universal: their novels articulate the tensions present at that time within those social groups – indeed, it would be strange if the ideological structures, tensions and boundaries of their social worlds were not present in their works. Insightful as they are, some of their perceptions of the social world are not wholly adequate to the more heterodox reality of the present. This has been a busy century, and we are separated from them by much history. Their value to us exists not in our wholesale acceptance of their social visions, but in understanding the ideological (and aesthetic) structures and pressures that enabled those specific orchestrations of heteroglossia, distinguishing what will no longer suffice (to borrow Wallace Stevens's phrase) from what will, and attempting to work out new approaches to the dilemmas of modernity that they have helped us to define.

Edward Said has recently argued that a fundamental historical problem of modernism is that the dominant Western social groups were being put in the position of having to take some jarring witnesses seriously: 'The subaltern and the constitutively different suddenly achieved disruptive articulation exactly where in European culture silence and compliance could previously be depended on to quiet them down.' As a result of the social crisis caused by this refusal of culturally-imposed aphasia, the sense of a single sacrosanct language (Bakhtin) can be seen to be breaking down; in response to increasing cross-cultural contact and conflict, the image of a doxic unity of culture becomes even less tenable; in face of the jarring narratives of many different cultural groups, the great metanarratives of European culture gradually lose their legitimising power. To this (multi)cultural challenge, writes Said, 'modernism responded with the formal irony of a culture unable to say yes, we should give up control, or no, we shall hold on regardless' (1989: 222–3). Consequently, modernism frequently 'foundered on or was frozen in contemplative irony' and paralysing self-consciousness. This summary description, while reductive as a comprehensive characterisation of the modernist achievement as a whole, does point toward a significant pattern in the three novels discussed in Part II. In all three cases, the certainty of the epic monological position is shown to be irrevocably undermined, yet the language groups constituting the 'other' of those dominant groups are not granted any significant power of speech. A sense of impasse thus results.

In *Nostromo*, the residual trace of epic unity is at once displayed and discredited; yet Conrad does not then reach beyond the orthodox limits of his own culture in search of other voices, supplemental or alternative definitions of the historical or cultural situation. Instead, the novel remains within the ironic bounds of a conservative nihilism that offers a critique but no challenge to the existing power structure. Taking Tietjens initially as a representative figure for the best of British upper class tradition, Ford records the demise of the authority and centrality of that class in relation to what is perceived as a far more general social decline. Yet, since it is made in the name of these specific, if increasingly obsolete, class interests, and since no other groups are given serious consideration, the critique mounted against modernity suffers a consequent loss of critical focus in the final volume of *Parade's End*. Faulkner's inability to move beyond an essentially negative position – expressed, for example, as the struggle to say 'No' to the legacy of Sutpen or Quentin's final repeated 'I don't hate it' – leaves him straining against the narrative limits of his historical *sensus communis* to a degree almost unparalleled among white American writers of his time, but rarely penetrating through to whatever might lie beyond.

Still, in all these novels the authority or legitimacy of the central characters, narrators or focalisers is questioned in terms of their narrative privilege. Kenneth Burke notes that the question of stable authority has been a recurrent one. At 'different periods in history, there have been quarrels as to the precise vessel of authority that is to be considered "representative" of the society as a whole'. This sense of a stable, generally accepted point of view –

a problematic concept in much historiographical theory – is predicated, at least in part, on the existence of a stable social organisation. In the absence of that social stability, when the struggle for legitimacy is more intense, the stability of narrative point of view is also thrown into question. 'Periods of social crisis', writes Burke, in a formulation that seems close to Bourdieu,

occur when an authoritative class, whose purpose and ideals had been generally considered as *representative* of the total society's purposes and ideals, becomes considered as *antagonistic*. Their class character, once felt to be the *culminating* part of the whole, is now felt to be a *divisive* part of the whole.   (1957: 23)

In the novels discussed here, the dominant group in question is not considered divisive perhaps, but they are seen to have slipped from their position of representative centrality and that slippage is reflected in the ironic and self-conscious narration that abjures its claim to narrative totality as a result of – almost as a casualty of – the intense modern struggle for the possession of the legitimate point of view.

The consequent instability of modern (and modernist) historical existence is, in effect, stabilised at least relatively by this refusal of the historicity and of the historiographic voices of the 'premodern' marginalised groups. In *Nostromo*, for example, the rebellion of the Monterists is not only a political or military rebellion: it constitutes as well an attempt to force an entry into a history and into a modernity defined and controlled by another community, and this attempt is decisively refused. Their attempt to voice their historicity is refused as thoroughly as is their attempt to exert control over their present and future conditions. The natives who do not rebel, however, who remain picturesquely premodern and more or less silent, pose no threat and are spared Conrad's rhetorical violence. Similar tensions along lines of race, class and gender occur in Ford and Faulkner, and the urgent need to contain that tension results from an apparent sense that if such marginalised groups were allowed to succeed in asserting their historicity and authority, then even the relative stability of the orthodox modernist position – undercut as it is by irony and self-consciousness – would be in danger of dissolving.

The ironic self-consciousness which occupies such an important place in modern narrative fiction is, according to Hayden

White, an important factor in historiographic narrative as well. White has observed, for example, the relationship between the rise of irony and 'an atmosphere of social breakdown or cultural demise' (1973: 232). Echoing Bakhtin's (or even Lukács's) similar model of the passage from epic to novel, White notes that irony signals 'the passage of the age of heroes and of the capacity to believe in heroes', and this trajectory is charted in *Nostromo*, *Parade's End* and *Absalom, Absalom!* Furthermore, argues White, with irony 'the problematical nature of language itself has become recognized . . . and brings its own potentialities for distorting perception under question' (1973: 37). But if the distortion of vision is recognised, is a non-distorted vision also possible? Robert Weimann argues that 'the reader's most basic task in reading a novel is to resolve the irony in the meaning of perspective and to recover that element of wholeness to which point of view is the counterpart' (1984: 266). Whether or not the whole story can be recovered and told, whether or not the whole story is even a conceptual possibility, narrative is, as Mink concludes, a fundamental form of cognition and it remains our responsibility (at times our pleasure and comfort as well) to get on with the narrativisation of our world.

The final chapters examine two alternative approaches which attempt to provide access, if not to a wholeness, at least to a perspectival difference that the orthodox representations of the earlier novels do not allow: first, the non-ironic retrieval of suppressed African–American historical experience; and second, the adoption of a more thoroughly ironic postmodern mode of historical narrative capable of relativising the claims of specific hegemonic cultural groups and locating historical knowledge accordingly. If the novels of Part II internalise self-consciousness, the novels discussed in Part III, since they stand in a very different relation to the dominant discourses, respond very differently. The repeated problems that these texts encounter are posed by the difficulty, for marginalised groups, of recovering suppressed history, of keeping it alive, of legitimising that testimony and those witnesses, and of living in the present and constituting a future with the legacy of that past. The narrative self-consciousness of these novels by African–American women is expressed not so much through formal self-reflexivity or irony regarding point of view or focalisation; instead, it is expressed as the self-consciousness of the witness who knows that she is perceived as a jarring witness yet whose testimony *must* nevertheless be rendered. The self-consciousness is related then not towards the formal possibility of narrative authority *per se*, not towards an ironic critique of historiographic Truth, but towards the difficulty of overcoming the aphasia imposed by a powerful and alien dominant language group that has always accepted her testimony under erasure at best. The burden in these novels is to move beyond the irony to a position recognising the experience of those whose discourse has not been heard in the dominant institutions and is therefore not in any need of ironic demystification. Some forms of irony had become, in any case, almost a way of life or even a means of survival among people whose situation it was as human subjects, to be trapped in the false definitions of them imposed by the dominant discourses of racism and slavery.[5] The literature of African–American women has had as one of its most pressing imperatives the assertion of the very historicity and historiographic authority that orthodox (and of course doxic) dominant discourses have felt compelled to deny in order to shore up a precarious racial and gendered monopoly on legitimacy.

Pynchon's *V.*, like much postmodernism, takes modern narrative self-consciousness to an extreme through the formal self-reflexivity of both narrator and characters, through parody directed at the great metanarratives, and through an exploration of the ethnocentricity that is evident in both the events of colonial history and in the historiographic accounts of those events. *V.* embraces the irony that is a condition of modern narrative more fully, and in doing so points out the less-than-dialogic basis of the communication that has been carried on in this century between different language groups. Postmodern discourse – some of it at least – attempts to grasp the implications of a fuller historiographic instability, one not guaranteed finally by the exclusion of the others with whom the heterodox historical moment is, after all, shared. A destabilisation of the hegemonic hold on historical discourse would allow those marginalised people to emerge as equal historical subjects and narrators, and might thus make it more difficult not just to marginalise them discursively but to continue ignoring their claims to historical agency in the present as well. The 'weighty interests' have not wished to hear the voices of jarring witnesses precisely because, obedient to Fabian's orthodox laws of political physics, they have not wished to share modernity with them.

It is increasingly difficult to imagine, with E. M. Forster, 'the English novelists . . . seated together in a room, a circular room, a sort of British Museum reading-room – all writing their novels simultaneously' (1949: 12). While Forster himself confronts certain aspects of the problem of cultural pluralism in *A Passage to India*, and while he makes it clear that he is using the term 'English' here to refer to the language and not to the nation, it is doubtful whether he could have foreseen just how many diverse social groups, each with its own perspectives, would have to be represented in that circular room before the century was out. The relative tranquility of the room that had for so long depended upon the tacit ascendancy of a particular set of perspectives or presuppositions, has been endangered by the heterogenous discourses of so many jarring witnesses. But the ensuing creative dialogue concerning the significance of the past and the diverse narratives of temporality and social identity emerging more and more from such a dialogic situation constitutes an important mode of working through the long objective social crisis that this century has experienced. We are, indeed, fortunate as readers to have access to such a variety of narratives, historical perspectives and versions of common sense. And that plenitude of historiographic testimony is, perhaps, the closest we can ever approach to grasping 'the whole story' of the past.

Notes

FOREWORD

1. 'The whole intricate question of method, in the craft of fiction,' writes Percy Lubbock, 'I take to be governed by the question of the point of view' (1957: 251). See Robert Weimann's *Structure and Society in Literary History* for a discussion of point of view both as a technical problem and as a problem of specifying the writer's relation to his or her own social world.
2. The common language referred to here is English, a language shared – in Bakhtin's sense of the phrase – by many diverse cultural language groups. See especially his exploration of language groups, the novel and heteroglossia in *The Dialogic Imagination* (discussed below). See also Voloshinov's *Marxism and the Philosophy of Language* (a work often attributed to Bakhtin) for a detailed discussion of the social basis of language.
3. Bourdieu defines his use of the terms 'doxa', 'orthodoxy' and 'heterodoxy' most clearly in *Outline of a Theory of Practice* (discussed below).
4. Definitions of race are notoriously difficult, and in this study the term refers to culturally-defined social groups rather than to biological or other essentialist differentiations. For discussions of this term, see Appiah (1990), Gates (1986) or Higginbotham (1992) among many others.

HISTORICAL NARRATIVE AND THE POLITICS OF POINT OF VIEW

1. See White's 'The politics of historical interpretation: discipline and desublimation' (in *The Content of the Form*, 1987) for a discussion of some of the implications of this development.
2. While much has been written for and against this model, the central statement of the position is in Hempel's 'The Function of General Laws in History'. A number of problems with this model, and with the modified versions of it that have been advanced, are discussed in Mink's *Historical Understanding*. See also Ankersmit (1986) for a brief survey of recent developments in the field, or Stone's 'Revival of Narrative' for a discussion of various attempts to establish a scientific history.

3. Ricoeur characterises the overall plot of Braudel's *The Mediterranean and the Mediterranean World in the Age of Philip II* as 'the decline of the Mediterranean as a collective hero on the stage of world history' (1984: v.1, 215). Hans Kellner also argues for the narrative dimension of Braudel's work in 'Disorderly Conduct: Braudel's Mediterranean Satire' (*Language and Historical Representation*, 1989), characterising it as a Menippean satire.

4. Lawrence Stone, for example, compares *Montaillou* with modern fiction as part of his discussion of narrative and the 'new historians' in 'The revival of narrative: reflections on a new old history'.

5. These terms are Windelband's. For a discussion of the applicability of these terms, see Collingwood (1956: 166–8).

6. Gramsci writes: 'It is essential to destroy the widespread prejudice that philosophy is a strange and difficult thing just because it is the specific intellectual activity of a particular category of specialists or of professional and systematic philosophers. It must first be shown that all men are "philosophers", by defining the limits and characteristics of the "spontaneous philosophy" which is proper to everybody' (1971: 323).

7. Ricoeur's discussion of Aristotelian mimesis (imitation) and muthos (emplotment) is valuable here:

> The whole problem of narrative *Verstehen* is contained here in principle. To make up a plot is already to make the intelligible spring from the accidental, the universal from the singular, the necessary or the probable from the episodic. (1984: v.1, 41)

But through the act of emplotment which accomplishes this, the events undergo a transformation. Mimesis in narrative is thus not simply 'a copy of some preexisting reality', but 'a creative imitation' (1984: v.1, 45).

8. I use Stern's translation here because the phrase 'what actually happened' has been a much-quoted one. All further references to von Ranke are to the more recent edition by Iggers and von Moltke who in this instance favour 'how, essentially, things happened' (1973: 137).

9. In his influential anthropological study of time and history, Mircea Eliade remarks that Hegel

> was obliged to see in every event the will of the Universal Spirit . . . . How could Hegel know what was *necessary* in history, what, consequently, must occur exactly as it had occurred? Hegel believed that he knew what the Universal Spirit wanted.

'We shall not insist on the audacity of this thesis', Eliade concludes dryly (1971: 148).

10. 'I do not believe', Kellner declares, 'that there are "stories" out there . . . waiting to be resurrected and told.'

> Getting the story crooked . . . means looking at the historical text in such a way as to make more apparent the problems and decisions that shape its strategies, however hidden or disguised they may be. It is a way of looking honestly at the *other* sources of history, found not in archives or computer databases, but in discourse and rhetoric. (1989: vii)

11. See Collingwood (1956: 134–43) for a discussion of Bradley's position and the context of this debate.

12. As indicated above, Bradley's essay was written partly in response to the debate between Christian supporters of the historical truth of the Bible, and those – most notably the Tübingen school of Biblical criticism including F. C. Bauer and David Strauss – whose rational positivism tended to make them sceptical of much in the Bible. Dispute centred most intensively on the accounts of miracles since they violated laws of nature which for positivists appeared inviolable. See Lionel Rubinoff's introduction to the book, as well as Collingwood's discussion of Bradley in *The Idea of History*.

13. Collingwood refers to Bradley as 'the greatest English philosopher of our time' and, while admitting its shortcomings, declares that *The Presuppositions of Critical History* 'bears the stamp of his genius' (1956: 238–9).

14. W. H. Dray discusses this concept in 'R. G. Collingwood and the A Priori of History'. See Alan Donagan for a full discussion of Collingwood's work.

15. See Mink, *Mind, History, and Dialectic: The Philosophy of R. G. Collingwood*. Mink's study of Collingwood evidently influenced his own work in the philosophy of history in the same way that Collingwood himself was influenced by Bradley.

16. In *The English Historical Novel*, Avrom Fleishman disputes even this limited distinction between the novelist and the historian, arguing that it 'breaks down even in his own terms'. Since the historian's picture is an imaginative reconstruction, the fact that its coherence is based on documents and artefacts does not necessarily distinguish it markedly from the novelist's coherent picture (1971: 5).

17. Walter Benjamin's similar formulation is more explicit: 'nothing that has ever happened should be regarded as lost for history. To be sure, only a redeemed mankind receives the fullness of its past – which is to say, only for a redeemed mankind has its past become citable in all its moments' (1969: 254).

18. Not surprisingly, the term 'interest' comes up frequently throughout the discussion of historical representation from Hegel onwards. The idea of innocent interest or curiosity is not always easy to distinguish from a sense closer than that of 'vested interests' – for example, the way the phrase 'defending American interests' has been used. The difficulty is most pronounced, perhaps, when the idea of Universal History blocks awareness of the variable, but inevitable, operations of more specific interests. Similarly, Clifford Geertz argues that the anthropologist's tendency 'to imagine himself something more than an interested (in both senses of that word) sojourner . . . has been our most powerful source of bad faith' (1973: 20).

19. Walter Benjamin writes: 'As flowers turn toward the sun, by dint of secret heliotropism the past strives to turn toward that sun which is rising in the sky of history . . . . For every image of the past that is not recognized by the present as one of its own concerns threatens to disappear irretrievably' (1969: 255).

20. In his introduction to Mink's essays, Vann reads this paragraph as a more

or less unsuccessful attempt by Mink to shore up the ground of historiographic certainty that he had eroded in his own critique of the event, as though he were not entirely comfortable with some of the radical consequences of his own analysis (1987: 25).

21. Edward Said persuasively cites this point in his discussion of the need for a Palestinian national narrative in 'Permission To Narrate'.

COMMON SENSE AND THE HISTORICAL NARRATIVE

1. Common sense, according to Foucault, is a way of handling difference: he writes of a 'common sense which, turning away from the mad flux and anarchical difference, invariably recognizes the identity of things'. Rather than confront difference as such, 'Common sense extracts the generality of an object while it simultaneously establishes the universality of the knowing subject' (1977: 181–2).

2. See also Bernstein's 'Rorty's Liberal Utopia' reprinted along with this essay in The New Constellation. Elsewhere, Rebecca Comay, in 'Interrupting the Conversation', argues that Rorty's we 'becomes as stern as an Un-American Activities Committee. You don't cooperate, we see no point in continuing this conversation' (1987: 96).

3. '[W]hat we call knowledge', writes Elias, 'is the social meaning of human-made symbols . . . in its capacity as a means of orientation' (1984: 252).

4. One classic study of various cultural conceptions of time is Mircea Eliade's The Myth of the Eternal Return or, Cosmos and History. Eliade draws attention to the philosophical and social problems of modern linear and teleological time frames by comparison with 'archaic societies' which have demonstrated a 'rejection of profane, continuous time' (1971, ix). The possibility that a postmodern culture might move away from the linearity and diachronicity of the modern era is a site of interesting speculation.

5. For a recent historical overview of the concept of common sense that traces the term back to its Greek origins, see Fritz van Holthoon and David R. Olson (eds), Common Sense: The Foundations for Social Science. See Lyotard's 'Sensus Communis' (1988b) for a postmodern discussion of Kant and the concept of common sense.

6. Bourdieu distinguishes this from the purely intellectual or conceptual break such as the 'intellectual operation which phenomenology designates by the term epoche, the deliberate, methodological suspension of naive adherence to the world' (1977b: 168).

7. Unger's understanding of power and society can be related to Bourdieu's on a number of points, but curiously their greatest difference is in their attitudes towards the possibility of positive social transformation. While Bourdieu often seems to emphasise the degree to which we are confined in our imagined places, Unger constantly envisions escape through our power 'to transcend the limited imaginative and social worlds' that we construct (1986: 26).

8. The major attacks on 'political correctness' include William J. Bennett (1984), Allan Bloom (1987), Dinesh D'Souza (1991) and Roger Kimball (1990).

9. Raymond Williams' discussion of the dominant, residual, and emergent elements in culture (*Marxism and Literature*) is relevant here. See also Ernst Bloch's 'Nonsynchronism and the obligation to its Dialectics.'

10. In contrast to Bakhtinians, who accept the multivoicedness of novelistic discourse uncritically as a kind of Utopian discursive space, a free republic of heteroglossia, Ken Hirschkop argues that Bakhtin at times overlooks the 'uneven structuring of language'. The world of discourse consists not simply of

> speaking individuals, but of a series of interacting structures or forms of discourse, which vary according to the durability of the utterance, the size and nature of speaker and audience, the degree of literacy required for participation, as well as the social factors highlighted in Bakhtin's own work. (1992: 111)

See also Bourdieu's 'The Economics of Linguistic Exchanges' for an examination of the relation of language to power.

11. A similar generic distinction made by Bakhtin is that between the epic and the novel. Whereas the epic tends towards the centripetal and monoglot (doxic), the novel tends towards the centrifugal and heteroglot (heterodox). 'For Bakhtin,' writes David Carroll, 'the epic is nationalistic, religious, hierarchical, and univocal; it is an "official literature," that of the ruling classes, a product of their institutions' (1983: 77). See also Lukács's very different view in *The Theory of the Novel* of a fall from epic presence and totality to the necessarily partial representations of the novel. Robert Weimann discusses this generic distinction as well in relation to the problem of point of view (1984: 234–66) and in relation to fictional representation and totality (1988).

12. Again, Bakhtin's allusion to the sacred here is not surprising if we recall Gallie's and Walsh's use of similar language in defence of an ideal of a single universal truth. Barthes similarly characterises realist historiography as a form of 'secularized reliquary', whose immense importance is evident in the fact that 'the profanation of these relics is tantamount to the destruction of reality' (1970: 155). Durkheim's discussion of the relationship between religion and the social totality in *The Elementary Forms of the Religious Life* has, of course, great relevance to this problem.

13. See also Voloshinov's discussion of ideology and language in which he argues that the 'sign becomes an arena of the class struggle' (1973: 23). As well, this striving, contestatory description recalls Lyotard's characterisation of the field of discourse as essentially agonistic (1984: 10).

14. A distinction must be maintained between such disparate terms as ideological worlds, fictional worlds and possible worlds. While the former refers to the world as it is imagined, perceived or constructed by specific social groups, a fictional world is the world of the story and is made up of the totality of ideological worlds represented (and refracted) in the story. Possible worlds, however, differ from both. Gregory Currie, who dislikes the vagueness of the term 'fictional worlds', argues that if there are any, they 'cannot be assimilated to possible worlds' (1990: 54) since possible worlds are logically consistent and determinate with respect to truth,

whereas fictional worlds need be neither. For extended discussions of possible and fictional worlds, see also Wolterstorff (1980), Pavel (1986) and Walton (1990).

15. See Michael Levenson's discussion both of Bradley's relationship to T. S. Eliot's modernism, and of the epistemological problem of objectivity/subjectivity in modernism.

NOSTROMO AND THE 'TORRENT OF RUBBISH'

1. As early as 1821, John Quincy Adams's references to America's manifest destiny register this sense of inevitability: it is 'unavoidable', he argued in a debate with Henry Clay over the future of Latin America, 'that the remainder of the continent should be ours' (Fuentes, 1985: 44). Since that time, writes E. Bradford Burns, 'The United States, which considers itself a paragon of democratic government, has actively and generously supported in this hemisphere every type of repressive dictatorship, governments that have tended to preserve, indeed to strengthen, those iniquitous institutions from the past that hobble Latin America's progress' (1986: viii–ix).

2. My use of the term 'native' is, I realise, an awkward oversimplification, as is my use of the terms 'Blanco' and 'European'. Jameson uses the term 'mestizo', and others have used 'Indian' to designate the historical 'other' that is presented in *Nostromo*. With all of these terms there are problems related to the difficulty of achieving taxonomic clarity in a social reality whose complexity resists rigid classification, but the differentiation referred to here, as in the novel, is nevertheless, I hope, sufficiently clear.

3. Benita Parry observes that since many of the events are narrated by Mitchell, 'the text is able openly to mock the idea of history as the linear record of prominent persons participating in or precipitating great and noteworthy public occurrences that coalesce to issue in the glorious climax of progress' (1983: 118).

4. Noting that almost all the main characters are identified with a powerful ideal, Armstrong proposes a similar list, then shows how the novel alternately endorses and demystifies the positions it portrays (1987: 174–5).

5. In theory the possibility remains that all the narrators – even the third person narrator whose voice ultimately controls the novel – are unreliable and that Conrad's attitude to the perspectives on the natives presented is ironic. Chinua Achebe's response to such an approach to *Heart of Darkness* seems relevant to *Nostromo* as well:

   if Conrad's intention is to draw a *cordon sanitaire* between himself and . . . his narrator his care seems to me totally wasted because he neglects to hint however subtly or tentatively at an alternative frame of reference by which we may judge the actions and opinions of his characters. It would not have been beyond Conrad's power to make that provision if he had thought it necessary. (1988: 256).

6. The eyes function frequently as a window on the soul in *Nostromo*, distinguishing moral character as well as support for the Blanco regime.

The government official Gould has to deal with, has a 'dark olive complexion and shifty eyes' (1967: 85), while Montero here moves from 'a lurid, sleepy glance' to an 'imbecile and domineering stare' (1967: 110–11). Don Pepe, on the other hand, has 'a kindly twinkle of drollery in his deep-set eyes' (1967: 92), and Barrios has 'a black silk patch over one eye. His other eye, small and deep-set, twinkled erratically in all directions, aimlessly affable' (1967: 141).

7. Ressler writes that 'Because of cultural conditioning and insufficient modes of perception fashioned on assumptions of rationality, measure, and progress, the Westerners are unable to comprehend the alien and primitive forces of Costaguana.' But there is more at stake than simple neutral incomprehension. Gould, for instance, realises at times 'that he, too, shares in the country's moral contagion' (1988: 50–1), an extremely negative characterisation. Ressler is, perhaps, accurate enough in his assessment of the text, but seems to accept uncritically this representation of the situation as an adequate one rather than questioning the very dubious ascription of 'moral contagion' to this country and its people.

8. For recent discussions of Fanon and literary theory, see Bhabha (1986), Gates (1991), JanMohammed (1985), Parry (1987) and Said (1989).

9. See Edward Said's *Beginnings* for a discussion of these historiographic representations.

10. If Conrad relentlessly exposes the illusions of the Blancos, nevertheless, as Jenkins observes, in *Nostromo*

> All illusions are equal but some are more so, and just as the society of post-revolutionary Sulaco may be *in fact* better while, *theoretically,* no different from any other, so the same can be said of the beliefs and actions of the characters siding with the Blanco party. (1977: 158)

11. See Wlad Godzich's 'Correcting Kant: Bakhtin and Intercultural Interactions' for a relevant discussion of the problem of confronting a cultural other.

12. At times, however, *even* Europeans can be affected by this noise: 'The barbarous and imposing noise of the big drum, that can madden a crowd, and that even Europeans cannot hear without a strange emotion' (Conrad, 1967: 115).

13. See Marx's *Eighteenth Brumaire* for a similarly described surge, one that threatens to destabilise Marx's own historical narrative about another insurrection.

14. As a Pole, Conrad was certainly aware of such political movements. The distinction seems to lie, perhaps, in the fact that since the natives are an 'inferior' group, the situation is simply not (in Bradley's terms) analogous.

15. The narrator's use of the diminutive form 'Pedrito' ('Little Pedro') itself has the effect of reducing whatever claim to authority he might have asserted. By contrast, the formal titles of the Blancos are frequently used (Don Carlos, Don Pepe), thus tacitly affirming the greater legitimacy of their social positions and aspirations.

16. The use of explicitly sexual terms here to represent degradation recalls Bakhtin's analysis of images of the lower bodily stratum, or Mary Douglas's

discussion in *Purity and Danger* of the transferral of images of pollution from the body politic to the physical or sexual body. See also Stallybrass and White, *The Politics and Poetics of Transgression*.

17. Ressler's response is not unusual: 'In the depth of her suffering and in her grasp of the darkest realities, Mrs. Gould endures the fullest burden of tragedy in the novel' (1988: 56). The grim realities faced by the native people seem to be wholly elided from such a formulation, which focuses instead on the suffering of a person whose relative comfort stems directly from their oppression.

18. See also a passage cited earlier, 'There was not one of them that had not, at some time or other, looked with terror at Nostromo's revolver poked very close at his face' (1967: 25–6). While many *Nostromo* critics express admiration for Nostromo's power, it ought to be pointed out that Latin American history is unfortunately replete with examples of just such ruthless attitudes towards the working classes as 'material interests' enforce their position.

19. The point is repeatedly emphasised: 'And the feeling of fearful and ardent subjection, the feeling of his slavery ... weighed heavily on the independent Captain Fidanza' (1967: 431). 'He yearned to clasp, embrace, absorb, subjugate ... this treasure, whose tyranny had weighed upon his mind, his actions, his very sleep' (1967: 433).

20. There is a striking historical and literary irony in the fact that the edition I am using – Penguin – has on its cover a reproduction of a portrait of Zapata, the Mexican revolutionary peasant leader. The portrait is presumably meant to refer in some way to Nostromo, but Zapata, curiously, was leader of a revolution against everything that Nostromo and the Blancos stand for. Indeed, as a native leading a popular insurrection, Zapata seems closer to Montero than to Nostromo.

21. As Said's *Orientalism* makes clear, this way of speaking for the native is common to other forms of cultural representation as well. See also Clifford, Fabian and Asad for discussions of the way anthropological or political discourse about native peoples has rarely included them as real interlocuters.

22. While there are many passages that illustrate the negative effects of the mine on the owners and those associated with them, there is very little description of any suffering undergone by the native miners or their families. Kenneth Graham, citing descriptions of miners and their families seeking work and the 'uncritical ... description of the mine itself', argues that 'the current in the book that would judge the mine adversely ... is more than counterbalanced by the way it is also shown to teem with individual and collective vitality' (1988: 119).

23. On this, the 500th anniversary of Columbus's arrival, a historiographic debate is being conducted over these statistics with people of various political persuasions finding figures that are amenable to their opinions. The addition or subtraction of a few million victims, however, does not alter the monumental scale of this tragedy.

24. This is analogous to the problem Malcolm Lowry located in *Heart of Darkness*: 'that story – great though it is – is at least half based on a

complete miscomprehension'. Critical of European imperialism, Conrad was none the less unable to look outside it to see what coherence or legitimacy another culture might have. 'Comrade Joseph did not allow himself to be corrupted by any savages,' writes Lowry ironically, 'he stayed in Polish aloofness on board in company with some *a priori* ideas' (1967: 236). Conrad's (or Marlow's) determination to stay on board his ship here is analogous to the refusal in *Nostromo* to move beyond the confines of historiographic orthodoxy.

25. Benita Parry argues that a political reading of *Nostromo* must 'confront the working out of discrepant discourses on the construction of historical meaning.' She identifies three strands of discrepant discourse in the novel:

> The teleological view of capitalism as the high point in human development and bourgeois democracy as its appointed end is negated by two mutually incompatible counter-arguments, the one belittling history as an arbitrary series of contingent occurrences producing nothing and going nowhere, the other reordering these same events as manifestations of processes initiated by human agency and developing in directions determined by permutations in the strength of competing class forces. (1983: 118)

Insightful as this reading is into the way the text articulates discursive tensions, yet another level of discursive discrepancy exists in the text: the discrepancy between the representation of native discourse and that of the dominant group.

PARADE'S END: 'HAS THE BRITISH THIS OR THAT COME TO *THIS*!'

1. See also Samuel Hynes's *A War Imagined: The First World War and English Culture.* For a discussion of the First World War as a modernist war, see Modris Eksteins's *Rites of Spring.*

2. As well, Gene M. Moore argues that the tetralogy constitutes a 'comprehensive and broadly social attempt to restore a lost sense of continuity', a comprehensiveness Ford presents through the 'consciousness of "the last English Tory" ' as a means of representing 'a vast social vision of historic continuity-in-change' (1982: 49–50); and Samuel Hynes describes it as 'the history of his own time on an immense and public scale' (1970: 516).

3. See, especially, Firebaugh's insightful early (1952) reading in which he asserts that '*Parade's End* is an allegory of social decay' (23). Similarly, Marlene Griffith notes that 'once we begin hunting for allegory we find ourselves amply rewarded' (1972: 141). Richard Cassell also agrees that the tetralogy can 'be easily read as allegory' (1961: 267).

4. In his discussion of the historical novel, Avrom Fleishman, responding to Lukács's concepts of representative and world-historical figures in such novels, argues that 'the relation of the representative hero to the society of his time is . . . [one of] symbolic universality. The heroes of historical fiction represent . . . man in general, conceived as a historical being' (1971: 11).

5. As Moore puts it, he represents 'what society ought to be, by embodying its most honored values' (1982: 52). Leer makes a similar point, arguing that 'Tietjens is finally seen as a Fordian ideal . . . grow[ing] to embody Ford's most complete affirmation' (1966: 105).

6. Michael Levenson's *A Genealogy of Modernism* is particularly illuminating concerning 'the disintegration of stable balanced relations between subject and object' in modernism, 'and the consequent enshrining of consciousness as the repository of meaning and value' (1984: 22) if no longer of truth.

7. Again, see Levenson's discussion of Conrad, consciousness and authority in the first chapters of *A Genealogy of Modernism*.

8. The turn to the past for a social vision is a familiar strategy, one that can potentially be used to support almost any political position. For a discussion of this use of history – although of another period – see Christopher Hill on 'The Norman Yoke'. See also Raymond Williams's discussion of the uses of the past in *The Country and the City*, especially 'A Problem of Perspective'.

9. 'The breaking up of the grand Narratives,' argues Lyotard in *The Postmodern Condition*, 'leads to what some authors analyze in terms of the dissolution of the social bond and the disintegration of social aggregates into a mass of individual atoms.' Lyotard himself disagrees, however: 'Nothing of the kind is happening: this point of view, it seems to me, is haunted by the paradisaic representation of a lost "organic" society' (1984: 15).

10. For discussions of focalisation, see Gérard Genette's *Narrative Discourse: An Essay in Method* or Shlomith Rimmon-Kenan's *Narrative Fiction: Contemporary Poetics*.

11. Within one page, these hesitancies occur as well: 'I took it to mean . . . .'; 'It might just as well mean . . . .'; 'She was of the opinion that it meant . . . .'; 'It was difficult to follow . . . .'; 'The interview ended rather untidily' (1950: 348).

12. I take the phrase from Leonard Tennenhouse's *Power on Display*, which examines the enactment of analogous rituals in the Elizabethan theatre.

13. Levin's inferior military rank is only one strike against him. Even a military superior such as Lord Beichan garners Tietjens's contempt – for reasons partly personal, partly ethnic. 'Tietjens, his breath rushing through his nostrils, swore he would not go up the line at the bidding of a hog like Beichan, whose real name was Stavropolides, formerly Nathan' (1950: 372).

14. Historian Brian Simon, for example, writes that a resolve was formed by many – less enamoured of England's rigid class system – 'that after the war things would be different, social evils and injustices abolished, and a brave new world emerge from the years of frustration, horror and mass slaughter' (1965: 345). A disillusioned R. H. Tawney wrote that 'Reconstruction and a better world have been have been promised to the nation as a reward for the losses and tireless labours of the Great War' (1964: 32). Yet still,

There are classes that are ends and classes that are means – upon that grand original distinction the community is invited . . . to defend, and to perpetuate the division of mankind into masters and servants. How delicate an insight into the relative value of human beings and of material riches! How generous a heritage into which to welcome the children of men who fell [in the war] in the illusion that in their humble way, they were servants of freedom. (1964: 51)

15. For a reading of the novel which places the progressive attitudes of Valentine in a dialectical relation to those of the traditional Teitjens, see Marianne DeKoven's 'Valentine Wannop and the thematic structure in Ford Madox Ford's *Parade's End*'.

16. The concept is developed in Bakhtin's *Rabelais and His World*. Also see Peter Stallybrass and Allon White for an elaboration of this idea of transgression. Valentine's remark about the 'World Turned Upside Down' is of course also relevant here.

17. Some editors have gone so far as to omit the volume, thus creating a trilogy. See Hynes (1970: 521–3) for a discussion of this editorial problem.

18. Hogben's name is interesting both in its closeness to pigpen, and because hogs and pigs are mentioned so frequently in this short section. For a discussion of the social semiotics of the pig that explores the way pigs have come to represent all that which is socially base, see Stallybrass and White.

19. The confrontation between Gunning and Sylvia (1950: 803–7) is, obviously, anything but respectful. The reason for this is, however, that Sylvia has transgressed the accepted hierarchic code of behaviour and thereby forfeited her right to be treated as a lady of 'Quality', not because Gunning presumes any democratic sense of equality.

20. While Tietjens seems to be relaxing his standards somewhat, historian David Cesarini writes that during this period Jews in Britain saw their social position further eroded, a result that

flowed inevitably from an unwillingness, an inability, to comprehend and accept the differences of minorities within society. In this sense, the problematic exists not at the level of specific instances of conflict . . . but in the realm of ideology . . . . [In World War I British Jews] fought and died for an England and an idea of Englishness that remained stubbornly impermeable to the particular needs and aspirations of the varied peoples which comprised the country's true population.' (1990: 76)

21. See Bourdieu's *Distinction* for an examination of the exchange rates that obtain between different forms of symbolic capital.

22. Ford's more sympathetic portrait of Valentine notwithstanding, he was highly critical of the anti-war stand he attributes to her and to Sylvia – a position he saw, according to Leer, as 'childish and dishonest' (1966: 109).

23. Or, for that matter, of the radicalism that occasionally is expressed by Tietjens, such as his opinion that there should be a minimum wage 'of four hundred a year and every beastly manufacturer who wanted to pay less [should] be hung. That it appeared was the High Toryism of Tietjens as it was the extreme radicalism of the extreme Left of the Left' (1950: 79).

24. See, for instance, his discussion (cited above) with Valentine in which he argues – albeit with a degree of irony perhaps – the futility of granting women the right to vote (1950: 115).

25. In response to Matthew Arnold's similar sentimental invocation in *Culture and Anarchy* (Arnold, 1960–77) of a golden age of the enlightened aristocracy, Henry Sidgwick astutely replied: 'Our historical reminiscences seemed to indicate that [their] passion for making reason and the will of God prevail ... was of a very limited description; hardly, indeed, perceptible to the scrutiny of the impartial historian' (1898: 216–17).

26. There are, of course, many kinds of Tory, and it would be a mistake to confuse Tietjens's social vision with a contemporary Tory position such as Thatcherism. In 1924, in fact, while maintaining his stance as a traditional Tory, Ford distanced himself from the Conservative Party because he felt that it represented 'nothing that was conservative except the so-called conservative banking interests' (Leer, 1966: 113).

ABSALOM, ABSALOM!: THE 'NIGGER IN THE WOODPILE'

1. In a similar spirit, as Richard Gray observes (1983: 165), in *Intruder in the Dust* Faulkner has Gavin Stevens declare: 'We are defending ... our homogeneity ... only from homogeneity comes anything of a people or for a people of durable and lasting value' (1972: 154). See also T. S. Eliot's well-known comments in *After Strange Gods* (noted by Richard Poirier in this context) on the South as a positive example of community. He suggested that tradition and community were still possible in the South because there was less 'difference of language or race' (1934: 16).

2. Melvin Backman, for example, argues that *Absalom, Absalom!* constitutes a 'search for the truth about a whole society' (1966: 88). Peter Brooks has recently made a similar point: we have, he writes, 'at least the postulation of a story that may equal history itself' (1986: 251).

3. This is not to say that Faulkner's fictional representations of Blacks remain static throughout his novels. But while he abandons the rather simple Black stereotypes employed in an early work such as *Sartoris*, nevertheless his representations of the racial 'other' rarely significantly challenge the boundaries of Southern orthodoxy.

4. Indeed, a reading of Faulkner's letters, essays and speeches does not encourage such a position. His many public statements on the matter maintain an orthodox position. In an address given at the University of Virginia, for instance, he suggests that 'Perhaps the Negro is not yet capable of more than second class citizenship. His tragedy may be that so far he is competent for equality only in the ratio of his white blood.' Faulkner accepts that this need not always be the case, however. If 'the Negro' is to be made 'capable of ... the responsibilities of equality', then

> we, the white man, must take him in hand and teach him that responsibility .... Let us teach him that, in order to be free and equal, he must first be worthy of it .... He must learn to cease forever more

thinking like a Negro and acting like a Negro. This will not be easy for him. (1965: 155–7)

5. Africa is later characterised as 'the dark inscrutable continent from which the black blood, the black bones and flesh and thinking and remembering' originate (1971: 206). In the attribution of inscrutability both to the continent and to the people, similar to the sense of moral contagion ascribed to both the continent and the population of South America in *Nostromo*, there appears to be little self-conscious sense that the inscrutability may have more to do with the inability or unwillingness of Faulkner's community to confront the dynamics of cultural difference, than with an inherent, almost ontological, darkness or obscurity. Allon White argues that such modernist textual obscurity is 'obscurity not simply of style, but of narrative, of symbolic and metaphorical structure, and of scene. What fears were allayed, or what desires fulfilled, by the evasion, equivocations, enigmas, and obliquities of these novelists?' (1981: 3).

6. *Brewer's Dictionary of Phrase and Fable* defines the phrase 'nigger in the woodpile' as '[o]riginally a way of accounting for the disappearance of fuel; it now denotes something deceitful or underhanded; a concealed troublemaker or suspicious character' (Evans, 1981: 784).

7. In a discussion of 'what America has done for them', Faulkner, in a speech given to the Southern Historical Society in 1955, characterised Afro-American history in these terms:

> the people who only three hundred years ago were eating rotten elephant and hippo meat in African rain-forests, who lived beside one of the biggest bodies of inland water on earth and never thought of a sail, who yearly had to move by whole villages and tribes from famine and pestilence and human enemies without once thinking of a wheel . . . in only three hundred years in America produced Ralph Bunch and George Washington Carver and Booker T. Washington. (1965: 149)

Beyond the slight to African cultural history, it is perhaps worth noting as well Faulkner's choice of black heroes. No radicals here: all espoused a conciliatory position that offered little challenge to white hegemony. See also Walter Taylor's discussion of the complexities and contradictions in the positions Faulkner advocated.

8. The specific narrator who characterises her in these terms is Mr Compson, but again there is no sense elsewhere that this characterisation is meant to be contested. In fact, some of the pejorative terms are repeated later in the conversation between Quentin and Shreve, once again without apparent qualification.

9. For another, very different, representation of an African–American wild woman, see Toni Morrison's *Jazz*.

10. Greenblatt concludes, 'Europeans in the sixteenth century, like ourselves, find it difficult to credit another language with opacity.' Recognition of this quality of opacity can only be attained through a recognition of the specificity of language and culture in question.

> But as we are now beginning fully to understand, reality for each society is constructed to a significant degree out of the *specific* qualities of its

language and symbols. Discard the particular words and you have discarded the particular men. And so most of the people of the New World will never speak to us. That communication, with all that we might have learned, is lost to us forever. (1990: 32)

11. Due to the destabilisation often imposed on African–American families and communities by slavery – the sale of family members who would be unable to remain in contact with those they had left behind, the sexual possession of black women by male owners – genealogical continuity was indeed tenuous in many cases. But this condition need not imply the cessation of narrative; indeed, as the next chapter will argue such conditions can create the ground for narratives of some urgency.

12. Coincidentally, another Faulknerian idiot, Benjy in The Sound and the Fury, in a sense Bond's white double, is granted both a voice and a soul, as well as an urgent if not always coherent narrative competence.

13. Sutpen is no stranger to interracial tension, having quelled a slave rebellion at a sugar plantation in Haiti, an island with a 'rank sweet rich smell as if the hatred and the implacability, the thousand secret dark years which had created the hatred and the implacability, had intensified the smell of the sugar', an island whose 'soil [was] manured with black blood from two hundred years of oppression and exploitation' (1971: 204–6). Once again the racial discord is registered but remains an abstraction in the absence of any black narrative perspective. For another fictional perspective on the historical role of sugar in the problems of the third world, see Paule Marshall's The Chosen Place, The Timeless People, discussed in the next chapter.

14. Phyllis R. Klotman cites a figure of approximately 4,000 lynchings of Blacks between 1882–1937. No figures are available for rape and assault or other common forms of violence inflicted by whites on blacks. See also Trudier Harris's discussion of this horrific subject.

15. Howe's own comments, in a sense, reflect the kind of aphasia to which he refers. One can, obviously, find better insight into 'Negro character' in the works of any number of black writers. While lacking Faulkner's novelistic complexity, such writers as far back as Harriet Wilson (Our Nig, 1859) or Frances Harper (Iola Leroy, 1892) demonstrate more awareness of black experience and character. Howe's remark is all the more surprising coming as it does in the revised edition (1962) of the book, long after the publication of works by Langston Hughes, Gwendolyn Brooks, Ralph Ellison, James Baldwin, Ann Petry, Richard Wright and numerous others. It is interesting to note that in the 1975 edition, Howe altered the phrase 'any other American' to read 'most other American'.

16. By the 1950s, Faulkner accepted, at least in principle, the idea that blacks can rise up from their low condition. But overlooking the long struggles of the black intelligentsia and community leaders, he saw it as a southern white man's burden. 'So we alone' he argued, speaking of the southern white community, 'can teach the Negro the responsibility of personal morality and rectitude – either by taking him into our white schools, or giving him white teachers in his own schools until we have taught the

teachers of his own race to teach and train him in these hard and unpleasant habits' (1965: 157–8).

17. Elsewhere, in an interview conducted apparently while Faulkner was under the influence of alcohol and the strain of the threat of federal government intervention in the civil rights crisis, he put the matter more strongly. 'If I have to choose between the United States government and Mississippi, then I'll choose Mississippi . . . . But if it came to fighting I'd fight for Mississippi against the United States even if it meant going out into the street and shooting Negroes' (1968b: 260–1). While the degree to which Faulkner may be held responsible for a statement that he subsequently clearly regretted making is debatable – at another time he said that given such a situation he would be forced to leave the South – the depth of his commitment to an orthodox *sensus communis* is not. For a different assessment, see Louis Daniel Brodsky's discussion in 'Faulkner and the racial crisis, 1956' (1988: 791–807).

18. This vision of history looks back to the historical sublime of Schiller and Burke, and forwards to White (discussed further in Chapter 6).

19. While Cleanth Brooks dismisses the discrepancies as errors on the part of either the author or his characters (1963: 424–6), Robert Dale Parker argues that they are a deliberate part of Faulkner's strategy for 'refus[ing] authority and suspend[ing] his readers in fictionality' (1986: 196). Snead suggests that this confusion demonstrates that the novel's main concern is not with specific events themselves but with the way events are constructed as narrative (1986: 104).

20. The situation described by historian George H. Fredrickson in *The Black Image in the White Mind* has to some degree continued into the twentieth century as well: 'the tragic limitation of the white racial imagination of the nineteenth century . . . [was] its characteristic inability to visualize an egalitarian biracial society' (1971: xiii). In the early twentieth century, he concludes,

> an ideal approximating a benevolent internal colonization came to dominate national thinking about the race question. This was a point of view permitting liberals and moderates to manifest some concern about Southern blacks, but it also sanctioned their acquiescence in the basic Southern policies of segregation and disenfranchisement. (1971: 325)

Thus the respective imperatives of ethnic boundaries and of conscience could be reconciled.

21. The residue of meaning has been a concern not just of Barthes. See also the discussion of this problem in relation to Ricoeur, Adorno and Lyotard in Chapter 6.

22. See also Werner's 'Tell Old Pharaoh: The African–American Response to Faulkner' for a discussion of the way African–American writers have incorporated aspects of Faulkner's techniques.

23. On the question of the connection between Faulkner and Quentin, Poirier writes that in *Absalom, Absalom!* 'one is almost obliged to associate the problems of the author with the problems of Quentin Compson' (1984: 25).

24. As James Baldwin observes, 'Faulkner could see Negroes only as they related to him, not as they related to each other' (1985: 472–4). See also 'Faulkner and Desegregation' in the same collection (1985: 147–52)).

25. As late as 1983, the state of Mississippi, still struggling with this taxonomic problem, upheld a law defining those with 1/32 African ancestry as 'Negro' (Yinger, 1986: 21–2).

26. See Barthes's discussion of 'The Great Family of Man', a well-known photographic exhibit showing 'the universality of human actions in the daily life of all countries of the world'.

> Everything here, the content and appeal of the pictures, the discourse which justifies them, aims to suppress the determining weight of History; we are held back at the surface of an identity, prevented ... from penetrating into this ulterior zone of human behavior where historical alienation introduces some 'differences' which we shall here quite simply call 'injustices'. (1973: 101)

BEARING WITNESS: AFRICAN–AMERICAN WOMEN'S FICTION

1. See Dickson D. Bruce Jr.'s *Black American Writing from the Nadir: The Evolution of a Literary Tradition 1877–1915* for an extensive discussion of the African-American literature of this period.

2. A vital concern with history animates the work of many contemporary African–American writers such as Toni Cade Bambara, David Bradley, Octavia Butler, Alice Childress, Charles Johnson, Gloria Naylor, Ishmael Reed, Alice Walker, Margaret Walker and John Edgar Wideman, as well as those writers studied in this chapter.

3. Not long ago, Los Angeles experienced what may have been its worst riot ever. The original legal acquittal of the police officers who beat Rodney King, in spite of what appeared to be the overwhelming evidence of the videotape of the beating, stands as yet another example of Lyotard's point.

4. Marjorie Pryse writes of a challenge to the 'authenticity and accuracy of an American history that failed to record their voices and a literary history – written by black men as well as white – that has compounded the error of that neglect' (1985: 4). Jane Campbell notes that in recent years, 'Afro-American historians and artists have launched a full-fledged exploration – and celebration – of the past' (1988: xv). This sentiment is not, of course, common only to black women. Ralph Ellison, for instance, has written: 'I have to *affirm* my forefathers and I *must* affirm my parents or be reduced in my own mind to a white man's inadequate conception of human complexity.' James Baldwin, more succinctly, states: 'I mean to use the past to create the present' (Bruck and Karrer, 1982: 289).

5. In the introduction to one of the formative collections of essays in the field of black women's studies. *All the Blacks Are Men, All the Women Are White*, Gloria Hull and Barbara Smith cite Faulkner's incidental characterisation of a black nursemaid, in *Light in August*, in terms of the 'vacuous idiocy of her idle and illiterate kind' (Faulkner, 1968a: 53). They argue that

Faulkner's 'assessment of black female intellect and character, stated as a mere aside, has fundamental and painful implications' (1982: xviii). The fact that the works in which such oppressive images as the vacuous idiot (and the ape-woman) 'appear are nonetheless considered "masterpieces" indicates the cultural-political value system in which Afro-American women have been forced to operate' (Hull and Smith, 1982: xviii).

6. An even earlier novel by a black American woman has recently been rediscovered. Our Nig by Harriet Wilson (1859), a quasi-autobiographical work, narrates the physical and emotional sufferings of a young black girl in the North at the hands of the family who keeps her in servitude. While exhibiting many similarities to the novels I discuss, particularly in its representational insistence on an African–American subjectivity as complex as that of her white 'superiors', it does not have an explicitly historiographical dimension.

7. Hopkins directs readers who doubt the veracity or realism of her narrative to the 'archives of the courthouse at Newberne, NC, and at the national seat of government, Washington, D.C.' (1988: 14).

8. The conventions of the sentimental novel, and the extremity of the social positions to be narrated contribute to the use of quite melodramatic representations of the conflict. In Contending Forces, for example, after her noble husband is murdered by 'white trash', the beautiful and cultured Grace Montfort is tied to a post and whipped, and the 'rough hand of Hank Davis . . . tear[s] her garments from her shrinking shoulders' (1988: 68). The whipping is recounted quite sensationally, and even accompanied by a full-page frontispiece illustration of the scene, accentuating the outrage the reader may feel in the knowledge that the law – an agency which finally legitimises social narrative – is on the side of the villains.

9. As an example of a reference shift, Kripke cites the history of the African term Madagascar which changed in geographical meaning when it was incorporated into the language of colonial geographers (1980: 163). Here in Canada, a mixture of native and European words are used to name the nation: while the etymology of British Columbia (where I live) is simple enough, it is a rare Canadian who knows that Canada is an Iroquois word (kanata) meaning village or community. A linguistic problem in every culture touched by colonialism, this is explored in an Irish context in Brian Friel's Translations.

10. This millenarian hope is expressed explicitly by the sugar cane workers, as well as implicitly in Leesy's redemptive care for the memory of her ancestors and in the hope that her family will be reunited someday on her little plot of land. The theme of family reunification once again expresses a larger communal aspiration (1984: 28, 34).

11. For an extensive discussion of speech and social power, see Bourdieu's 'Economics of Linguistic Exchanges', a revised edition of which is included in his Language and Symbolic Power.

12. Peter Nazareth writes that 'Merle, indeed, is the voice of a voiceless people' (1973: 120).

13. Marshall at one time conceived this novel as part of a loose 'trilogy describing, in reverse, the slave trade's triangular route back to the motherland, the source' (1973: 107).

14. The suggestions of homophobia in the novel appear, perhaps, as signs of Marshall's own cultural frame at the time. In the lesbian relationship from Merle's past, in the scene in Sugar's bar and in Allen Fuso's sexual confusion, homosexuality is used as a metaphor for cultural decadence. See also Spillers's discussion of this aspect of the novel (1985: 172–4, n.6), or Missy Dehn Kubitschek's 'Paule Marshall's women on quest'.

15. Eugene Genovese, in fact, mentions Portuguese slaveowners in Brazil as an extreme example of the sexual exploitation that was common to slavery (1974: 423–5).

16. The other main form of disruption of the family and social fabric was the result of the practice of selling black children at an early age without regard for family relationships. This practice, one aspect of the Diaspora, is described over and over in these novels. In *Corregidora*, when Ursa questions the all-female make-up of her family over four generations, her mother replies: ' "I think there was some boys. I think they told me there was some boys, but Corregidora sold the boys off." ' (1986: 61)

17. Richard Barksdale writes that the historical roots of sexual conflict can be traced back to slavery – 'a time when the system granted every master and every white male overseer the unchallenged right to use and abuse every female slave on the plantation according to his fancy' (1986: 404). He concludes that there gradually 'occurred a mirror-imaging exchange of power, and in his sexual relations with his women the black man replaced his former master' (1986: 407). Genovese points out that these 'incidents of force or seduction under implicit threat of force must have taken a fearful toll. These women paid a high price . . . for it was they who suffered the violence and the attendant degradation of being held responsible for their own victimization' (1974: 428).

18. Styron's novel resulted in the publication of a collection of critical essays dealing with this problem: *William Styron's Nat Nat Turner: Ten Black Writers Respond* (John Henrik Clarke (ed.), Boston: Beacon Press, 1968). See Fleishman's discussion of this debate in *The English Historical Novel* (1971: ix–xii). Williams's Nathan seems to be a reference to Nat Turner, and a number of other intertextual references can be located in this novel as well which suggest the cultural gap separating it from white literary versions of this history. A story is told about a slave named Thomas who betrayed a black conspiracy to the plantation owners, and whose nickname, 'Uncle Tom' has become anathema to the black community (1987: 20–1). Also, there is some correspondence, coincidental or otherwise, between Bertie Sutton (Rufel's husband) and Thomas Sutpen of *Absalom, Absalom!* and their respective plantations – Sutton's Glen and Sutpen's Hundred. The book's many references to the attempt to go West in search of freedom begs comparison with *Huckleberry Finn*. That they have such difficulty doing so, because of the racist climate of opinion that extends far beyond the slave states, seems a bitterly ironic comment on that particular manifestation of the 'American Dream'.

19. Because of the future apparently in store for her child, Dessa regrets her pregnancy during her imprisonment and at one point considers killing the child when it is born. A similar desperation frames events in Toni Morrison's Beloved, as a mother kills her daughter when it appears they will be sent back into slavery, and in David Bradley's The Chaneysville Incident a group of escaping slaves chooses death over slavery.

20. 'Mammy' has been, of course, a common character in much Southern fiction – Faulkner's Dilsey being a case in point. Another perspective on that institution is provided in Alice Walker's The Color Purple. Historian Leslie H. Owens argues that 'references by southern leaders . . . to their motherly mammies should be treated as more than simple affection for a tragic figure' (1986: 33). Owens also notes that when Southern congressmen in the 1920s attempted unsuccessfully to have a federal statue erected to the black mammy in the District of Columbia, their 'efforts met with considerable resistance within the black community' (1986: 32).

21. According to Aldon D. Morris, 'By 1955 the South had become an extremely dangerous place for blacks. In 1955 a number of hideous murders took place. One was the killing and removal of the testicals of a fourteen-year-old black boy named Emmett Till, who was visiting Mississippi from the North. Till was killed for allegedly whistling at a white woman' (1984: 29–30). The Emmett Till incident has been the subject of literary treatment previously as well: Gwendolyn Brooks's poem 'A Bronzeville Mother Loiters in Mississippi. Meanwhile, A Mississippi Mother Burns Bacon' explores the perspective of the woman at whom Till whistled, and 'The Last Quatrain of the Ballad of Emmett Till' is a brief study of Till's mother. Morrison herself returned to it in a play Dreaming Emmett (1986).

22. Echoes of the reference in the earlier conversation to the violence against blacks that took place after the war are heard as well, as Reverend Cooper shows Milkman a lump on the side of his head:

> Some of us went to Philly to try and march in an Armistice Day parade . . . . We were invited and had a permit, but the people, the white people, didn't like us being there. They started a fracas. You know, throwing rocks and calling us names. They didn't care nothing 'bout the uniform. Anyway, some police on horseback came – to quiet them down, we thought. They ran us down. Right under their horses. (1977: 235).

The bitter irony is that such events could occur immediately after a war which should have unified the population. Once again, public history is made personal by such testimony.

23. As Susan Willis comments, 'For Morrison, everything is historical. Even objects are embedded in history and are the bearers of the past' (1984: 268). As he passes through his crisis 'the possibility of a past opens out to him like a great adventure . . . . Milkman comes to realize that only by knowing the past can he hope to have a future.' (1977: 270)

24. See Marilyn Sanders Mobley's 'Memory, History and Meaning in Toni Morrison's Beloved' for a discussion of the relation of the novel both to this historical incident and to the slave narrative tradition as well.

25. A similar ghost appears several times in *Song of Solomon* as well: the ghost of the first Macon Dead who is seeking a proper burial and, more importantly perhaps, seeking to restore the continuity of his family narrative by passing on his wife's true name.
26. Problems of naming and identity have figured prominently in African-American literature, Baldwin's *Nobody Knows My Name*, John A. Williams's *The Man Who Cried I Am*, and Ellison's *Invisible Man* being only a few examples.

V.: IN THE RATHOUSE OF HISTORY WITH THOMAS PYNCHON

1. One exception is Steven Weisenburger who, in 1979, maintained that 'To Pynchon, the novel is a means of bridging the epistemological gap between the past we reconstruct with language and the actual events we narrate, rearrange, transform, even forget. Its purposes are ultimately political' (Pearce, 1981: 146).
2. Adorno asserts in *Negative Dialectics* that 'objects do not go into their concepts without remainder . . . the concept does not exhaust the thing conceived' (1973: 85).
3. Bourdieu argues that the 'heretical power' and 'liberating potency' of such heterodox discourses derive not from their claim to Historical Truth, but 'from their capacity to *objectify* unformulated experiences, to make them public – a step on the road to officialization and legitimacy' (1977b: 170–1).
4. The image is evidently an important one for Pynchon: his second novel, *The Crying of Lot 49*, employs a similar image of a woman trapped in a socio-epistemological tower, and documents her attempts to escape. Oedipa had 'gently conned herself into the curious, Rapunzel-like role of a pensive girl somehow, magically prisoner' (1990: 10). See Catherine Stimpson's discussion of women in Pynchon's work. See also Paul Coates, 'Unfinished business: Thomas Pynchon and the quest for revolution' for a discussion of the politics of this novel.
5. A mistral is a cold northerly wind experienced in the Mediterranean (OED). Charlie Parker's soul 'had dissolved into a hostile March wind nearly a year before', writes Pynchon, but 'Outside the wind had its own permanent gig. And was still blowing' (1966: 60). Like the metaphor of the streets that 'fused into a single abstracted Street' (1966: 10), the wind image recurs throughout.
6. While some critics have questioned the veracity of Pynchon's historical detail in the light of the evident fertility of his imagination, Arnold Cassola argues that 'Pynchon has taken the trouble to investigate everything to the last detail. His "historical" narrative is based on documentary evidence' (1985: 311).
7. Some Stencilish V-detective pleasure is added by the fact that Stravinsky's original title for the piece was *The Victim*. Furthermore, Stravinsky's work, like Porcepic's *Rape of the Chinese Virgins*, culminates in the death of a virgin – although in the latter the death actually occurs. Modris Eksteins sees *The Rite of Spring*, 'the dance of death, with its orgiastic-nihilistic

irony' as 'One of the supreme symbols of our centrifugal and paradoxical century, when in striving for freedom we have acquired the power of ultimate destruction' (1989: xiv).

8. The idea that wounds and mouths have a certain similarity is not original to Pynchon: 'Mouths are often likened to wounds in Shakespeare. The image may derive from their appearance, and from the idea that they could speak as witnesses to what caused them' (Abrams et al., 1987: 515, n.9). Pynchon's use of one wound as an eye and another as a mouth thus combines both witnessing and testifying possibilities.

9. Stravinsky's Rite of Spring, evidently a partial model (along with Petrushka) for Porcépic's ballet, was described by a reviewer of the time as Hottentot music (Eksteins, 1989: 50).

10. There is an affinity here with the sense of a vast and perhaps irretrievable native history that Toni Morrison's Milkman experiences in Song of Solomon as he reads the Algonquin place names and has his realization about the relation of history, community and power.

11. While my own efforts to find out what happened to the people who lived there were by no means exhaustive, I did consult a couple of sizeable research libraries as well as a specialist in Middle Eastern history. Among other records, I found an eyewitness account by a British soldier who was involved, but the impact of the strategy on the inhabitants is left unclear. It was suggested finally that I should continue the search with the University of Cairo – a course of action Stencil would no doubt have pursued but I did not. Even the limited search that I did carry out was sufficient to demonstrate once again the influence of cultural perspective on the reconstruction of the past.

12. The difficulties of the Namibian Hereros, of course, continue – until very recently as longstanding victims of an illegal South African occupation. See Karla Poewe's The Namibian Herero for a discussion of the cultural effects of their traumatic history.

CONCLUSION

1. For recent discussions of these topics, see both Nancy's The Inoperable Community (1991) and the collection of essays which followed, Community at Loose Ends (ed. Miami Theory Collective, 1991). See also Giorgio Agamben's The Coming Community (1993).

2. See Iris Young's discussion of community and difference in which she concludes with a call to develop a 'concept of social relations that embody openness to unassimilated otherness with justice and appreciation' (1986: 23).

3. Weimann accepts a Lukácsian interpretation of epic wholeness rather than the Bakhtinian view of epic as monologic official culture. Regardless of one's position on this issue, his remarks on point of view in the novel are germane.

4. Adorno argues, in fact, that although the novel as a genre requires narrative, 'it is no longer possible to tell a story'. This is because 'The identity of

experience in the form of a life that is articulated and possesses internal continuity – and that life was the only thing that made the narrator's stance possible – has disintegrated' (1991: 30–1).

5. See Blassingame's *The Slave Community* for the classic historical study of African–American double consciousness. More recently, see Henry Louis Gates's discussion of signification in *The Signifying Monkey*. He argues that in the doubling and redoubling of meaning in black language, 'What we are privileged to witness here is the (political, semantic) confrontation between two parallel discursive universes .... We bear witness to a protracted argument over the nature of the sign itself' (1988: 44–5).

References

Abrams, M. H. et al., (eds) (1987) *The Norton Anthology of English Literature* (Fifth (edn). *The Major Authors.* New York: W. W. Norton.

Achebe, Chinua (1988) 'An image of Africa: racism in Conrad's *Heart of Darkness'. Heart of Darkness* by Joseph Conrad. Ed. Robert Kimbrough. New York: W. W. Norton, pp. 251–62.

Adorno, T. W. (1973) *Negative Dialectics.* Trans. E. B. Ashton. New York: Seabury Press.

Adorno, T. W. (1991) *Notes to Literature,* v.1. Ed. Rolf Tiedeman. Trans. Shierry Weber Nicholsen. New York: Columbia UP.

Agamben, Giorgio (1993) *The Coming Community.* Trans. Michael Hardt. Minneapolis: U Minnesota P.

Althusser, Louis (1971) *Lenin and Philosophy.* Trans. Ben Brewster. New York: Monthly Review.

Ankersmit, F. R. (1983) *Narrative Logic: A Semantic Analysis of the Historian's Language.* The Hague: Martinus Nijhoff.

Ankersmit, F. R. (1986) 'The dilemma of contemporary Anglo-Saxon philosophy of history'. *History and Theory* Beiheft 25: 1–27.

Appiah, Kwame Anthony (1990) 'Race'. *Critical Terms for Literary Study.* Eds Frank Lentricchia and Thomas McLaughlin. Chicago: U Chicago P.

Aristotle (1968) *Poetics.* Trans. Leon Golden. Englewood Cliffs, NJ: Prentice-Hall.

Armstrong, Paul B. (1987) *The Challenge of Bewilderment: Understanding and Representation in James, Conrad, and Ford.* Ithaca: Cornell UP.

Armstrong, Paul B. (1986) Review of *Modernism and Authority: Strategies of Legitimation in Flaubert and Conrad* by Mark Conroy. *Conradiana,* **18**.1: 64–9.

Arnold, Matthew (1960–77) *The Complete Prose Works of Matthew Arnold,* ed. R. H. Super. Ann Arbor: University of Michigan Press.

Asad, Talal (ed.) (1973) *Anthropology and the Colonial Encounter.* New York: Humanities Press.

Backman, Melvin (1966) *Faulkner: The Major Years*. Bloomington: Indiana UP.

Baker, Houston A. Jr. (1984) *Blues, Ideology, and Afro-American Literature: A Vernacular Theory*. Chicago: U Chicago P.

Bakhtin, M. M. (1981) *The Dialogic Imagination*. Trans. Caryl Emerson and Michael Holquist. Austin: U of Texas P.

Bakhtin, M. M. (1968) *Rabelais and His World*. Trans. Helene Iswolsky. Cambridge, MA: MIT Press.

Bakhtin, M. M. and P. N. Medvedev (1978) *The Formal Method in Literary Scholarship: A Critical Introduction to Sociological Poetics*. Trans. Albert J. Wehrle. Baltimore: Johns Hopkins UP.

Baldwin, James (1961) *Nobody Knows My Name: More Notes of a Native Son*. New York: Dial Press.

Baldwin, James (1985) *The Price of the Ticket: Collected Non-Fiction 1948–85*. New York: St. Martin's.

Baraka, Amiri (LeRoi Jones) (1966) *Home: Social Essays*. New York: Apollo Books.

Barksdale, Richard (1986) 'Castration symbolism in recent Black American fiction'. *CLA Journal*, **29**.4: 400–13.

Barth, Fredrik (1969) *Ethnic Groups and Boundaries: The Social Organization of Culture and Difference*. Boston: Little, Brown and Co.

Barthes, Roland (1970) 'Historical discourse'. *Structuralism: A Reader*. Ed. Michael Lane. London: Jonathan Cape, pp. 145–55.

Barthes, Roland (1973) *Mythologies*. Trans. Annette Lavers. St Albans: Paladin.

Benjamin, Walter (1969) *Illuminations*. Trans. Harry Zohn. New York: Schocken.

Bennett, William J. (1984) *To Reclaim a Legacy: A Report on the Humanities in Higher Education*. Washington, DC: National Endowment for the Humanities.

Bennington, Geoff (1988) *Lyotard: Writing the Event*. Manchester: Manchester UP.

Berman, Marshall (1982) *All That Is Solid Melts Into Air: The Experience of Modernity*. New York: Simon and Schuster.

Bernstein, Richard (1987) 'One step forward, two steps backward: Richard Rorty on Liberal democracy and philosophy'. *Political Theory*, **15**.4: 538–63.

Bernstein, Richard (1991) *The New Constellation: The Ethical-Political Horizons of Modernity/Postmodernity*. Cambridge: Polity Press.

Bhabha, Homi (1986) 'Remembering Fanon: Self, Psyche and the Colonial Tradition'. Foreword *Black Skin, White Masks* by Frantz Fanon. Trans. Charles Lam Markmann. London: Pluto.

Blassingame, John W. (1979) *The Slave Community: Plantation Life in the Antebellum South*. New York: Oxford University Press.

Bloch, Ernst (1977) 'Nonsynchronism and the obligation to its dialectics'. Trans. Mark Ritter. *New German Critique*, **11**: 22–38.

Bloom, Allan (1987) *The Closing of the American Mind*. New York: Simon and Schuster.

Booth, Wayne (1961) *The Rhetoric of Fiction*. Chicago: U of Chicago P.

Bourdieu, Pierre (1977a) 'The economics of linguistic exchanges'. *Social Science Information*, **16**.6: 645–68.

Bourdieu, Pierre (1977b) *Outline of a Theory of Practice*. Trans. Richard Nice. Cambridge: Cambridge UP.

Bourdieu, Pierre (1984) *Distinction: A Social Critique of the Judgement of Taste*. Trans. Richard Nice. Cambridge, MA: Harvard UP.

Bourdieu, Pierre (1985) 'Social space and the genesis of groups'. *Social Science Information*, **24**.2: 195–220.

Bourdieu, Pierre (1991) *Language and Symbolic Power*. Trans. Gino Raymond and Matthew Adamson. Cambridge: Polity Press.

Bradley, David (1981) *The Chaneysville Incident*. New York: Avon.

Bradley, F. H. (1968) *The Presuppositions of Critical History* (1874). Chicago: Quadrangle.

Braudel, Fernand (1972) *The Mediterranean and the Mediterranean World in the Age of Philip II*. 2 Vols. Trans. Siân Reynolds. New York: Harper and Row.

Braudel, Fernand (1980) *On History*. Trans. Sarah Matthews. Chicago: U Chicago P.

Brodsky, Louis Daniel (1988) 'Faulkner and the racial crisis, 1956'. *Southern Review*, **24**.4: 791–807.

Brooks, Cleanth (1963) *William Faulkner: The Yoknapatawpha Country*. New Haven: Yale UP.

Brooks, Gwendolyn (1963) *Selected Poems*. New York: Harper and Row.

Brooks, Peter (1986) 'Incredulous narration: *Absalom, Absalom!*' *William Faulkner: Modern Critical Views*. Ed. Harold Bloom. New York: Chelsea House, pp. 247–86.

Brown, William Wells (1969) *Clotel; or, the President's Daughter: A Narrative of Slave Life in the United States*. New York: Citadel Press.

Bruce, Dickson D. Jr. (1989) *Black American Writing from the Nadir: The Evolution of a Literary Tradition 1877–1915*. Baton Rouge: Louisiana State UP.

Bruck, Peter and Wolfgang Karrer (eds) (1982) *The Afro-American Novel Since 1960*. Amsterdam: B. R. Grüner.

Burke, Kenneth (1957) *The Philosophy of Literary Form: Studies in Symbolic Action*. New York: Vintage.

Burns, E. Bradford (1986) *Latin America: A Concise Interpretive History* (Fourth edn) Englewood Cliffs, NJ: Prentice-Hall.

Butterfield, Herbert (1924) *The Historical Novel: An Essay*. Cambridge, Cambridge UP.

Byerman, Keith E. (1985) *Fingering the Jagged Grain: Tradition and Form in Recent Black Fiction*. Athens, GA: U of Georgia P.

Campbell, Jane (1988) *Mythic Black Fiction: The Transformation of History*. Knoxville: U of Tennessee P.

Carby, Hazel V. (1987a) 'Introduction'. *Iola Leroy, or Shadows Uplifted* by Francis Harper. Boston: Beacon Press, pp. ix–xxvi.

Carby, Hazel V. (1987b) *Reconstructing Womanhood: The Emergence of the Afro-American Woman Novelist*. New York: Oxford UP.

Carroll, David (1983) 'The alterity of discourse: form, history, and the question of the political in M. M. Bakhtin'. *Diacritics*, **13**.2: 65–83.

Cassell, Richard A. (1961) *Ford Madox Ford: A Study of His Novels*. Baltimore: Johns Hopkins UP.

Cassola, Arnold (1985) 'Pynchon, V., and the Malta connection'. *Journal of Modern Literature*, **12**.2: 311–31.

Cesarini, David (1990) 'An embattled minority: the Jews in Britain during the First World War'. *The Politics of Marginality: Race, the Radical Right and Minorities in Twentieth Century Britain*. Eds Tony Kushner and Kenneth Lunn. London: Frank Cass.

Chesnutt, Charles (1901) *The Marrow of Tradition*. Boston: Houghton Mifflin.

Christian, Barbara (1980) *Black Women Novelists: The Development of a Tradition 1892–1976*. Westport, CT: Greenwood Press.

Christian, Barbara (1985) *Black Feminist Criticism: Perspectives on Black Women Writers*. New York: Pergamon Press.

Clarke, John Henrik (ed.) (1968) *William Styron's Nat Turner: Ten Black Writers Respond*. Boston: Beacon Press.

Clifford, James (1988) *The Predicament of Culture: Twentieth Century Ethnography, Literature, and Art*. Cambridge: Harvard UP.

Coates, Paul (1986) 'Unfinished business: Thomas Pynchon and the quest for revolution'. *New Left Review*, **160**: 121–8.

Collingwood, R. G. (1956) *The Idea of History*. London: Oxford UP.

Collingwood, R. G. (1965) *Essays in the Philosophy of History*. Austin: U of Texas P.

Comay, Rebecca (1987) 'Interrupting the Conversation: Notes on Rorty'. *Antifoundationalism and Practical Reasoning: Conversations Between Hermeneutics and Analysis*. Ed. Evan Simpson. Edmonton: Academic.

Conrad, Joseph (1921) 'Henry James: an appreciation'. *Notes on Life and Letters*. Garden City, NJ: Doubleday, Page, pp. 11–19.

Conrad, Joseph (1967) *Nostromo* (1904). Harmondsworth: Penguin.

Conroy, Mark (1985) *Modernism and Authority: Strategies of Legitimation in Flaubert and Conrad*. Baltimore: Johns Hopkins UP.

Cooper, Anna Julia (1988) *A Voice from the South*. (1988) New York: Oxford UP.

Core, George (1987) 'Ordered life and the abysses of chaos: *Parade's End*'. *Critical Essays on Ford Madox Ford*. Ed. Richard A. Cassell. Boston: G. K. Hall, pp. 92–101.

Currie, Gregory (1990) *The Nature of Fiction*. Cambridge: Cambridge UP.

D'Sousa, Dinesh (1991) *Illiberal Education: The Politics of Race and Sex on Campus*. New York: Free Press.

Daly, M. W. (1986) *Empire on the Nile: The Anglo-Egyptian Sudan 1898–1934*. Cambridge: Cambridge UP.

Davis, Cynthia A. (1982) 'Self, Society, and Myth in Toni Morrison's fiction'. *Contemporary Literature*, **23**.3: 323–42.

Davis, Thadious M. (1983) *Faulkner's 'Negro': Art and the Southern Context*. Baton Rouge: Louisiana State UP.

de Certeau, Michel (1985) *The Writing of History*. Trans. Tom Conley. New York: Columbia UP.

de Certeau, Michel (1986) *Heterologies: Discourse on the Other*. Trans. Brian Massumi. Minneapolis: U of Minnesota P.

DeKoven, Marianne (1977) 'Valentine Wannop and the thematic structure in Ford Madox Ford's *Parade's End*'. *English Literature in Transition*, **20**.2: 56–68.

Dirlik, Arif (1987) 'Culturalism as hegemonic ideology and liberating practice'. *Cultural Critique*, **6**: 12–50.

Dixon, Melvin (1984) 'Singing a deep song: language as evidence in the novels of Gayle Jones'. *Black Women Writers (1950–80): A Critical Evaluation*. Ed. Mari Evans. New York: Anchor Doubleday, pp. 236–48.

Donagan, Alan (1962) *The Later Philosophy of R. G. Collingwood*. Oxford: Clarendon.

Douglas, Mary (1966) *Purity and Danger: An Analysis of Concepts of Pollution and Taboo*. New York: Praeger.

Douglass, Frederick (1982) *Narrative of the Life of Frederick Douglass, An American Slave*. Harmondsworth: Penguin.

Dray, W. H. (1983) 'R. G. Collingwood on the *a priori* of history'. *Clio*, **12**.2: 169–81.

During, Simon (1987) 'Postmodernism or post-colonialism today'. *Textual Practice* **1**.1: 32–47.

Durkheim, Emile (1965) *The Elementary Forms of the Religious Life*. Trans. Joseph Ward Swain. New York: Free Press.

Eagleton, Terry (1970) *Exiles and Emigrés: Studies in Modern Literature*. London: Chatto and Windus.

Ebert, Teresa (1991) 'Writing in the political: resistance post(modernism)', *Legal Studies Forum*, **15**.4: 291–303.

Eksteins, Modris (1989) *Rites of Spring: The Great War and the Birth of the Modern Age*. Toronto: Lester and Orpen Dennys.

Eliade, Mircea (1971) *The Myth of the Eternal Return or, Cosmos and History*. Princeton: Princeton UP.

Elias, Norbert (1984) 'Knowledge and power'. Interview with Peter Ludes. *Society and Knowledge: Contemporary Perspectives in the Sociology of Knowledge*. Eds Nico Stehr and Volker Meja. New Brunswick, NJ: Transaction Books, pp. 251–91.

Eliot, T. S. (1934) *After Strange Gods: A Primer of Modern Heresy*. New York: Harcourt, Brace and Co.

Ellison, Ralph (1952) *Invisible Man*. New York: Modern Library.

Evans, Ivor H. (ed.) (1981) *Brewer's Dictionary of Phrase and Fable* (Revised Edition). New York: Harper and Row.

Evans, Mari (ed.) (1984) *Black Women Writers 1950–80: A Critical Evaluation*. New York: Anchor Doubleday.

Fabian, Johannes (1983) *Time and the Other: How Anthropology Makes Its Object*. New York: Columbia UP.

Fanon, Frantz (1963) *The Wretched of the Earth*. Trans. Constance Farrington. New York: Grove.

Faulkner, William (1959) *Faulkner in the University: Class Conferences at the University of Virginia 1957–1958*. Eds Frederick L. Gwynn and Joseph L. Blotner. Charlottesville: U Virginia P.

Faulkner, William (1965) *Essays, Speeches and Public Letters*. Ed. James B. Meriwether. New York: Random House.

Faulkner, William (1968a) *Light in August*. New York: Random House.

Faulkner, William (1968b) *Lion in the Garden: Interviews with William Faulkner 1926–62*. Eds James B. Meriwether and Michael Millgate. New York: Random House.

Faulkner, William (1971) *Absalom, Absalom!* (1936). Harmondsworth: Penguin.

Faulkner, William (1972) *Intruder in the Dust*. New York: Vintage.

Faulkner, William (1977) *Selected Letters of William Faulkner*. Ed. Joseph Blotner. New York: Random House.

Firebaugh, Joseph (1952) 'Tietjens and the tradition'. *Pacific Spectator*, **6**: 23–32.

Fish, Stanley (1989) *Doing What Comes Naturally: Change, Rhetoric, and the Practice of Theory in Literary and Legal Studies*. Durham, Duke UP.

Fleishman, Avrom (1967) *Conrad's Politics: Community and Anarchy in the Fiction of Joseph Conrad*. Baltimore: Johns Hopkins UP.

Fleishman, Avrom (1971) *The English Historical Novel: Walter Scott to Virginia Woolf*. Baltimore: Johns Hopkins UP.

Foley, Barbara (1986) *Telling the Truth: The Theory and Practice of Documentary Fiction*. Ithaca: Cornell UP.

Ford, Ford Madox (1933) *It Was the Nightingale*. Philadelphia: Lippincott.

Ford, Ford Madox (1964) *Parade's End* (1924–28). New York: Signet.

Ford, Ford Madox (1965) *Joseph Conrad: A Personal Remembrance.* New York: Octagon Books.

Forster, E. M. (1949) *Aspects of the Novel.* London: Edward Arnold.

Forster, E. M. (1961) *Alexandria: A History and a Guide.* New York: Doubleday.

Foster, Hal (1984) '(Post)Modern polemics'. *New German Critique,* **33**: 67–78.

Foucault, Michel (1965) *Madness and Civilization: A History of Insanity in the Age of Reason.* Trans. Richard Howard. New York: Random House.

Foucault, Michel (1973) *The Order of Things.* New York: Vintage.

Foucault, Michel (1977) *Language, Counter-Memory, Practice: Selected Essays and Interviews.* Ithaca: Cornell UP.

Foucault, Michel (1979) *Discipline and Punish: The Birth of the Prison.* Trans. Alan Sheridan. New York: Vintage.

Fowler, Doreen and Ann J. Abadie (eds) (1987) *Faulkner and Race: Faulkner and Yoknapatawpha, 1986.* Jackson: U of Mississippi P.

Fox-Genovese, Elizabeth (1987) 'To write myself: the autobiographies of Afro-American women'. *Feminist Issues in Literary Scholarship.* Ed. Shari Benstock. Bloomington: Indiana UP, pp. 161–80.

Fredrickson, George H. (1971) *The Black Image in the White Mind: The Debate of Afro-American Character and Destiny, 1817–1917.* New York: Harper and Row.

Freud, Sigmund (1965) *New Introductory Lectures on Psychoanalysis.* Trans. James Strachey. New York: Norton.

Friel, Brian (1981) *Translations.* London: Faber and Faber.

Fuentes, Carlos (1985) *Latin America at War with the Past.* Montreal: CBC Enterprises.

Furet, François (1984) *In the Workshop of History.* Trans. Jonathan Mandelbaum. Chicago: U Chicago P.

Fussell, Paul (1975) *The Great War and Modern Memory.* New York: Oxford UP.

Galeano, Eduardo (1973) *The Open Veins of Latin America: Five Centuries of the Pillage of a Continent.* Trans. Cedric Belfrage. New York: Monthly Review.

Gallie, W. B. (1968[1964]) *Philosophy and the Historical Understanding.* New York: Schocken.

Gates, Henry Louis Jr. (ed.) (1984) *Black Literature and Literary Theory.* New York: Methuen.

Gates, Henry Louis Jr. (ed.) (1986) *'Race,' Writing and Difference.* Chicago: U Chicago P.

Gates, Henry Louis Jr. (1988) *The Signifying Monkey: A Theory of African–American Literary Criticism.* New York: Oxford UP.

Gates, Henry Louis Jr. (1991) 'Critical Fanonism'. *Critical Inquiry*, **17** (Winter): 457–70.

Geertz, Clifford (1973) *The Interpretation of Cultures*. New York: Basic Books.

Genette, Gérard (1980) *Narrative Discourse: An Essay in Method*. Oxford: Blackwell.

Genovese, Eugene (1974) *Roll, Jordan, Roll: The World the Slaves Made*. New York: Pantheon.

Godzich, Wlad (1991) 'Correcting Kant: Bakhtin and intercultural interactions'. *Boundary 2*, **18**.1: 5–17.

Goldman, Arnold (ed.) (1971) *Twentieth Century Interpretations of Absalom, Absalom!* Englewood Cliffs, NJ: Prentice-Hall.

Govan, Sandra Y. (1988) 'Homage to tradition: Octavia Butler renovates the historical novel'. *MELUS*, **13**.1–2: 79–96.

Graham, Kenneth (1988) *Indirections in the Novel: James, Conrad, and Forster*. Cambridge, Cambridge UP.

Gramsci, Antonio (1971) *Selections from the Prison Notebooks*. Trans. Quentin Hoare and Geoffrey Nowell Smith. New York: International.

Gray, Richard (1983) 'From Oxford: the novels of William Faulkner'. *American Fiction: New Readings*. Ed. Richard Gray. Totowa, NJ: Barnes and Noble, pp. 165–83.

Green, Robert (1981) *Ford Madox Ford: Prose and Politics*. Cambridge: Cambridge UP.

Greenblatt, Stephen (1990) *Learning to Curse: Essays in Early Modern Culture*. New York: Routledge.

Griffith, Marlene (1972) 'A double reading of *Parade's End*'. *Ford Madox Ford: Modern Judgements*. Ed. Richard Cassell. London: Macmillan, pp. 137–51.

Hacking, Ian (1986) 'The archaeology of Foucault'. *Foucault: A Critical Reader*. Ed. David Couzens Hoy. Oxford: Basil Blackwell.

Harper, Francis (1987) *Iola Leroy, or Shadows Uplifted* (1892). Boston: Beacon Press.

Harris, Trudier (1984) *Exorcising Blackness: Historical and Literary Lynching and Burning Rituals*. Bloomington: Indiana UP.

Hawkes, Terence (1985) 'Swisser-Swatter: making a man of English letters'. *Alternative Shakespeares*. Ed. John Drakakis. London: Routledge.

Hegel, G. W. F. (1953) *Reason in History: A General Introduction to the Philosophy of History*. Trans. Robert S. Hartman. New York: Bobbs-Merrill.

Hegel, G. W. F. (1956) *The Philosophy of History*. Trans. J. Sibree. New York: Dover.

Hempel, C. G. (1942) 'The function of general laws in history'. *Journal of Philosophy*, **39**: 35–48.

Henderson, Harry B. III (1974) *Versions of the Past*. New York: Oxford UP.

Higginbotham, Evelyn Brooks (1992) 'African–American women's history and the metalanguage of race'. *Signs: Journal of Women in Culture and Society*, **17**.2: 251–74.

Hill, Christopher (1958) 'The Norman yoke'. *Puritanism and Revolution*. London: Mercury, pp. 50–122.

Hirschkop, Ken (1992) 'Is dialogism for real?' *Social Text*, **10**.1: 102–13.

Hite, Molly (1983) *Ideas of Order in the Novels of Thomas Pynchon*. Columbus: Ohio State UP.

Hobsbawm, Eric (1993) 'The new threat to history'. *The New York Review of Books*, **40**.21 (December 16): 62–4.

Holt, Thomas C. (1986) 'Introduction: Whither now and why?' *The State of Afro-American History: Past, Present, and Future*. Ed. Darlene Clarke Hine. Baton Rouge: Louisiana State UP, pp. 1–10.

hooks, bell (1990) *Yearning: Race, Gender, and Cultural Politics*. Toronto: Between the Lines.

Hopkins, Pauline (1988) *Contending Forces: A Romance Illustrative of Negro Life North and South* (1899). New York: Oxford UP.

Howard, Jean (1991) 'Toward a postmodern, politically committed, historical practice', in Frances Barker, Peter Hulme and Margaret Iverson (eds), *Uses of History: Marxism, Postmodernism and the Renaissance*. Manchester: Manchester University Press, pp. 101–22.

Howe, Irving (1970) *Politics and the Novel*. Freeport, NY: Books For Libraries.

Howe, Irving (1975) *William Faulkner: A Critical Study*. Chicago: U of Chicago P, 1962.

Huggins, Nathan A. (1986) 'Integrating Afro-American history into American history'. *The State of Afro-American History: Past, Present, and Future*. Ed. Darlene Clarke Hine. Baton Rouge: Louisiana State UP, pp. 157–68.

Hull, Gloria and Barbara Smith (eds) (1982) *All the Blacks Are Men, All the Women Are White, But Some of Us Are Brave: Black Women's Studies*. Old Westbury, NY: Feminist Press.

Hurston, Zora Neale (1979) *I Love Myself When I Am Laughing . . . And Then Again When I Am Looking Mean and Impressive: A Zora Neale Hurston Reader*. Ed. Alice Walker, Old Westbury, NY: Feminist Press.

Hutcheon, Linda (1987) 'Beginning to theorize postmodernism'. *Textual Practice*, **1**.1: 10–30.

Huyssen, Andreas (1984) 'Mapping the postmodern'. *New German Critique*, **33**: 5–52.

Hynes, Samuel (1970) 'Ford Madox Ford: three dedicatory letters to *Parade's End* with commentary and notes'. *Modern Fiction Studies*, **16**.4: 515–28.

Hynes, Samuel (1990) *A War Imagined: The First World War and English Culture*. London: Bodley Head.

Iggers, Georg (1975) *New Directions in European Historiography*. Middletown, CT: Wesleyan UP.

Jameson, Fredric (1979) 'Marxism and historicism'. *New Literary History*, **11**: 41–73.

Jameson, Fredric (1981) *The Political Unconscious: Narrative as a Socially Symbolic Act*. Ithaca: Cornell UP.

Jameson, Fredric (1987) 'Regarding postmodernism – a conversation with Fredric Jameson'. Anders-Stephanson. *Social Text*, **17**: 29–54.

Jameson, Fredric (1988) 'Cognitive mapping'. *Marxism and the Interpretation of Culture*. Eds Cary Nelson and Lawrence Grossberg. Urbana, IL: U of Illinois P, pp. 347–57.

JanMohamed, Abdul R. (1985) 'The economy of Manichean allegory: the function of racial difference in colonialist literature'. *Critical Inquiry*, **12**: 59–87.

JanMohamed, Abdul R. (1983) *Manichean Aesthetics: The Politics of Literature in Colonial Africa*. Amherst: U Massachusetts P.

Jenkins, Gareth (1977) 'Conrad's *Nostromo* and History'. *Literature and History*, **6**: 138–78.

Jones, Gayl (1986) *Corregidora* (1975). Boston: Beacon Press.

Kant, Immanuel (1951) *Critique of Judgement*. Trans. J. H. Bernard. New York: Hafner.

Kant, Immanuel (1963) *On History*. Ed. Lewis White Beck. Trans. Lewis White Beck, Robert E. Anchor and Emil L. Fackenheim. Indianapolis: Bobbs-Merrill.

Kellner, Hans D. (1975) 'Time out: the discontinuity of historical consciousness'. *History and Theory*, **14**: 275–96.

Kellner, Hans D. (1989) *Language and Historical Representation: Getting the Story Crooked*. Madison: U Wisconsin P.

Kimball, Roger (1990) *Tenured Radicals: How Politics Has Corrupted Our Higher Education*. New York: Harper and Row.

Klotman, Phyllis R. (1985) ' "Tearing a hole in history": lynching as theme and motif'. *Black American Literary Forum*, **19**.2: 55–63.

Kripke, Saul A. (1980) *Naming and Necessity*. Cambridge, MA: Harvard UP.

Kubitschek, Missy Dehn (1987) 'Paule Marshall's women on quest'. *Black American Literary Forum*, **21**.1–2: 43–60.

Kuhn, Thomas (1970) *The Structure of Scientific Revolutions* (Second edn). Chicago: U Chicago P.

Ladurie, Emmanuel Le Roy (1978) *Montaillou: The Promised Land of Error*. Trans. Barbara Bray. New York: G. Braziller.

Ladurie, Emmanuel Le Roy (1979a) *Carnival in Romans*. Trans. Mary Feeney. New York: G. Braziller.

Ladurie, Emmanuel Le Roy (1979b) *The Territory of the Historian*. Trans. Ben and Siân Reynolds. Hassocks, Sussex: Harvester.

Land, Stephen K. (1984) *Conrad and the Paradox of Plot*. London: Macmillan.

Leed, Eric J. (1979) *No Man's Land: Combat and Identity in World War One.*
Cambridge: Cambridge UP.

Leer, Norman (1966) *The Limited Hero in the Novels of Ford Madox Ford.*
Michigan State UP.

Levenson, Michael (1984) *A Genealogy of Modernism: A Study of English Literary Doctrine, 1908–1922.* New York: Cambridge UP.

Levinas, Emmanuel (1979) *Totality and Infinity.* Trans. Alphonso Lingis. The Hague: Martinus Nijhoff.

Levine, George and David Leverenz (1976) *Mindful Pleasures: Essays on Thomas Pynchon.* Boston: Little, Brown and Co.

Longenbach, James (1984) 'Ford Madox Ford: the novelist as historian'.
Princeton University Library Chronicle, **45**.2: 150–66.

Lowry, Malcolm (1967) *Selected Letters.* Ed. Harvey Breit and Margerie Bonner.
London: Cape.

Lubbock, Percy (1957) *The Craft of Fiction.* New York: Viking.

Lukács, Georg (1962) *The Historical Novel.* Trans. Hannah and Stanley Mitchell. London: Merlin.

Lukács, Georg (1971) *The Theory of the Novel.* Trans. Anna Bostock.
Cambridge, MA: MIT Press.

Lyotard, Jean-François (1984) *The Postmodern Condition.* Trans. Geoff Bennington and Brian Massumi. Manchester: Manchester UP.

Lyotard, Jean-François (1985) 'The sublime and the avant-garde'. *Paragraph* 6: 1–18.

Lyotard, Jean-François (1987) 'The sign of history'. *Post-structuralism and the Question of History.* Eds Derrick Attridge, Geoff Bennington and Robert Young. Cambridge: Cambridge UP.

Lyotard, Jean-François (1988a) *The Differend: Phrases in Dispute.* Trans.
Georges Van Den Abbeele. Minneapolis: U Minnesota P.

Lyotard, Jean-François (1988b) 'Sensus Communis'. Trans. Marian Hobson and Geoff Bennington. *Paragraph* 11.1: 1–23.

Marshall, Paule (1973) 'Shaping the world of my art'. *New Letters,* **40**.1: 97–112.

Marshall, Paule (1974) 'A panel discussion'. *Keeping the Faith: Writings by Contemporary Black American Women.* Ed. Pat Crutchfield Exum. Greenwich, CT: Fawcett, pp. 33–40.

Marshall, Paule (1984) *The Chosen Place, The Timeless People* (1969). New York: Vintage.

Marx, Karl (1964) *The Eighteenth Brumaire of Louis Bonapart.* New York: International.

McClure, John A. (1981) *Kipling and Conrad: The Colonial Fiction.* Cambridge, MA: Harvard UP.

McDowell, Deborah E. (1989) 'Negotiating between tenses: witnessing slavery after freedom – *Dessa Rose*'. *Slavery and the Literary Imagination.* Eds Deborah E. McDowell and Arnold Rampersad. Baltimore: Johns Hopkins UP.

McKay, Nellie Y. (ed.) (1988) *Critical Essays on Toni Morrison*. Boston: Hall.

Medvedev, P. N. and M. M. Bakhtin (1978) *The Formal Method in Literary Scholarship: A Critical Introduction to Sociological Poetics*. Trans. Albert J. Wehrle. Baltimore: Johns Hopkins UP.

Meyer, Eric (1990) 'Ford's War and (post)modern memory: *Parade's End and National Allegory*'. *Criticism*, **32**.1: 81–99.

Miami Theory Collective (ed.) (1991) *Community at Loose Ends*. Minneapolis: University of Minnesota Press.

Millgate, Michael (1966) *The Achievement of William Faulkner*. London: Constable.

Mink, Louis O. (1969) *Mind, History, and Dialectic: The Philosophy of R. G. Collingwood*. Bloomington: Indiana UP.

Mink, Louis O. (1987[1978]) *Historical Understanding*. Eds Brian Fay, Eugene O. Golob and Richard T. Vann. Ithaca: Cornell UP.

Mobley, Marilyn Sanders (1990) 'A different remembering: memory, history and meaning in Toni Morrison's *Beloved*'. *Toni Morrison*. Ed. Harold Bloom. New York: Chelsea House.

Moi, Toril (1991) 'Appropriating Bourdieu: feminist theory and Pierre Bourdieu's sociology of culture'. *New Literary History*, **22**: 1017–49.

Moore, Gene M. (1982) 'Tory in a time of change: social aspects of Ford Madox Ford's *Parade's End*'. *Twentieth Century Literature*, **28**.1: 49–68.

Morris, Aldon D. (1984) *The Origins of the Civil Rights Movement*. New York: Free Press.

Morrison, Toni (1977) *Song of Solomon*. New York: Knopf.

Morrison, Toni (1981) 'The language must not sweat: a conversation with Toni Morrison'. Thomas Leclair. *New Republic*, 21 March: 25–9.

Morrison, Toni (1984) 'Memory, creation, and writing'. *Thought*, **59**.253: 385–90.

Morrison, Toni. (1988) *Beloved*. New York: Plume.

Morrison, Toni (1989) 'A bench by the road'. *The World*, **3**.1: 4–5, 37–41.

Morrison, Toni (1990a) 'Toni Morrison: Novelist'. Interview with Bill Moyers. *A World of Ideas II: Public Opinions from Private Citizens*. Bill Moyers. New York: Doubleday.

Morrison, Toni (1990b) 'Unspeakable things unspoken: the Afro-American presence in American literature'. *Toni Morrison*. Ed. Harold Bloom. New York: Chelsea House.

Morrison, Toni (1992) *Jazz*. New York: Knopf.

Nancy, Jean-Luc (1990) 'Finite History'. *The States of 'Theory': History, Art, and Critical Discourse*. Ed. David Carroll. New York: Columbia UP.

Nancy, Jean-Luc (1991) *The Inoperative Community*, ed. Peter Connor, trans. Peter Connor, Lisa Garbus, Michael Holland and Simona Sawhney. Minneapolis: University of Minnesota Press.

Nazareth, Peter (1973) 'Paule Marshall's timeless people'. *New Letters*, **40**.1: 113–31.

Owens, Leslie H. (1986) 'The African in the garden: reflections about New World slavery'. *The State of Afro-American History: Past, Present, and Future*. Ed. Darlene Clarke Hine. Baton Rouge: Louisiana State UP, pp. 25–36.

Parker, Robert Dale (1986) 'The chronology and genealogy of *Absalom, Absalom!*: the authority of fiction and the fiction of authority'. *Studies in American Fiction*, **14**.2: 191–8.

Parry, Benita (1983) *Conrad and Imperialism: Ideological Boundaries and Visionary Frontiers*. London: Macmillan.

Parry, Benita (1987) 'Problems in current theories of colonial discourse', *Oxford Literary Review*, **9**.1–2: 27–58.

Patteson, Richard F. (1984) 'How true a text? Chapter Three of *V.* and "Under the Rose" '. *Southern Humanities Review*, **18**.4: 299–308.

Pavel, Thomas G. (1986) *Fictional Worlds*. Cambridge, MA: Harvard UP.

Pearce, Richard (1981) *Critical Essays on Thomas Pynchon*. Boston: G. K. Hall.

Pechey, Graham (1987) 'On the borders of Bakhtin: dialogization, decolonization'. *Oxford Literary Review*, **9**.1–2: 59–84.

Plater William M. (1981) *The Grim Phoenix: Reconstructing Thomas Pynchon*. Bloomington: Indiana UP.

Poewe, Karla (1985) *The Namibian Herero: A History of Their Psychosocial Disintegration and Survival*. Lewiston, NY: Edwin Mellen.

Poirier, Richard (1984) ' "Strange Gods" in Jefferson, Mississippi: analysis of *Absalom, Absalom!*'. *William Faulkner's Absalom, Absalom!: A Critical Casebook*. Ed. Elizabeth Muhlenfeld. New York: Garland, pp. 1–23.

Polk, Noel. (1987) 'Man in the middle: Faulkner and the Southern White moderate'. *Faulkner and Race: Faulkner and Yoknapatawpha, 1986*. Eds Doreen Fowler and Ann J. Abadie. Jackson: U of Mississippi, pp. 130–51.

Pryse, Marjorie (1985) 'Introduction: Zora Neale Hurston, Alice Walker, and the "ancient power" of Black women'. *Conjuring: Black Women, Fiction, and the Literary Tradition*. Eds Marjorie Pryse and Hortense J. Spillers. Bloomington: Indiana UP, pp. 1–24.

Pynchon, Thomas (1966a) 'A journey into the mind of Watts'. *New York Times Magazine* (June 12): 34–5, 78, 80–2, 84.

Pynchon, Thomas (1966b) *V.* (1963) New York: Modern Library.

Pynchon, Thomas (1973) *Gravity's Rainbow*. New York: Viking.

Pynchon, Thomas (1985) *Slow Learner*. New York: Bantam.

Pynchon, Thomas (1990) *The Crying of Lot 49*. New York: Perennial Library.

Reilly, John M. (1986) 'History-making literature'. *Studies in Black American Literature*, Vol. 3. *Belief vs. Theory in Black American Literary Criticism*. Eds Joel Weixlman and Chester J. Fontenot. Greenwood, FL: Penkeville, pp. 85–120.

Ressler, Steve (1988) *Joseph Conrad: Consciousness and Integrity.* New York: New York UP.

Rich, Paul B. (1989) 'Imperial decline and the resurgence of English national identity 1918–79'. *Traditions of Intolerance: Historical Perspectives on Fascism and Race Discourse in Britain.* Eds Tony Kushner and Kenneth Lunn. Manchester: Manchester UP, pp. 33–52.

Ricoeur, Paul (1984–88) *Time and Narrative.* 3 Vols. Trans. Kathleen McLaughlin and David Pellauer. Chicago: U of Chicago P.

Rimmon-Kenan, Shlomith (1983) *Narrative Fiction: Contemporary Poetics.* London: Methuen.

Rollyson, Carl E. Jr. (1977) '*Absalom, Absalom!*: the novel as historiography'. *Literature and History,* **5**: 42–55.

Rorty, Richard (1988) 'The priority of democracy to philosophy'. *The Virginia Struggle for Religious Freedom: Its Evolution and Consequences in American History.* Eds Merril D. Peterson and Robert C. Vaughn. Cambridge: Cambridge UP.

Rubinoff, Lionel (1968) 'Introduction'. *The Presuppositions of Critical History* by F. H. Bradley. Chicago: Quadrangle Books.

Said, Edward W. (1975) *Beginnings: Intention and Method.* New York: Basic Books.

Said, Edward W. (1978) *Orientalism.* New York: Pantheon.

Said, Edward W. (1984) 'Permission to narrate'. *London Review of Books,* **6**:3 (February 16): 13–17.

Said, Edward W. (1985) 'Orientalism Reconsidered'. *Cultural Critique,* **1**.1: 89–107.

Said, Edward W. (1986) 'Intellectuals in the post-colonial world'. *Salmagundi* **70–71**: 44–64.

Said, Edward W. (1989) 'Representing the colonized: anthropology's interlocutors'. *Critical Inquiry,* **15**: 205–25.

Said, Edward W. (1990) 'Yeats and decolonization'. *Nationalism, Colonialism and Literature.* Minneapolis: U Minnesota P.

Schaub Thomas H. (1981) *Pynchon: The Voice of Ambiguity.* Urbana: U of Illinois P.

Sidgwick, Henry (1898) *Practical Ethics.* London: Swan Sonnenschein.

Sidney, Sir Philip (1966) *An Apology for Poetry.* Ed. J. A. Van Dorsten. Oxford: Oxford UP.

Simon, Brian (1965) *Education and the Labour Movement 1870–1920.* London: Lawrence and Wishart.

Smith, Barbara (1982) 'Toward a Black feminist criticism'. *All the Blacks Are Men, All the Women Are White, But Some of Us Are Brave: Black Women's Studies.* Eds Hull, Gloria et al. Old Westbury, CT: Feminist Press, pp. 157–75.

Snead, James A. (1986) *Figures of Division: William Faulkner's Major Novels.* New York: Methuen.

Snitow, Ann Barr (1984) *Ford Madox Ford and the Voice of Uncertainty*. Baton Rouge: Louisiana State UP.

Spillers, Hortense J. (1985) 'Chosen Place, Timeless People: figurations on the New World'. *Conjuring: Black Women, Fiction, and the Literary Tradition*. Eds Marjorie Pryse and Hortense J. Spillers. Bloomington: Indiana UP, pp. 151–75.

Stallybrass, Peter and Allon White (1986) *The Politics and Poetics of Transgression*. London: Methuen.

Stark, John O. (1983) *Pynchon's Fictions: Thomas Pynchon and the Literature of Information*. Athens, Ohio: Ohio UP.

Stepto, Robert B. (1979) *From Behind the Veil: A Study of Afro-American Narrative*. Urbana, IL: U of Illinois P.

Stern, Fritz (1956) *The Varieties of History: From Voltaire to the Present*. New York: Meridian.

Stimpson, Catherine (1976) 'Pre-apocalyptic atavism: Thomas Pynchon's early fiction'. *Mindful Pleasures: Essays on Thomas Pynchon*. Eds George Levine and David Leverenz. Boston: Little, Brown and Co., pp. 31–47.

Stone, Lawrence (1979) 'The revival of narrative: reflections on a new old history'. *Past and Present*, **85**: 3–24.

Styron, William (1967) *The Confessions of Nat Turner*. New York: Random House.

Tate, Claudia (ed.) (1988) *Black Women Writers at Work*. New York: Continuum.

Tawney, R. H. (1964) *The Radical Tradition*. New York: Pantheon.

Taylor, Walter (1983) *Faulkner's Search For a South*. Urbana: U Illinois P.

Tennenhouse, Leonard (1986) *Power on Display: The Politics of Shakespeare's Genres*. New York: Methuen.

Todorov, Tzvetan (1984) *Mikhail Bakhtin: The Dialogical Principle*. Trans. Wlad Godzich. Manchester: Manchester UP.

Travers, Tim (1987) *The Killing Ground: The British Army, The Western Front and the Emergence of Modern Warfare 1900–1918*. London: Allen and Unwin.

Tyler, Stephen A. (1987) *The Unspeakable: Discourse, Dialogue, and Rhetoric in the Postmodern World*. Madison: U Wisconsin P.

Unger, Roberto (1986) *The Critical Legel Studies Movement*. Cambridge: Harvard UP.

van Holthoon, Fritz and David R. Olson (eds) (1987) *Common Sense: The Foundations for Social Science*. Lanham: UP of America.

Vann, Richard (1987) 'Editor's Introduction'. *Historical Understanding* by Louis O. Mink. Eds Brian Fay, Eugene O. Golob and Richard T. Vann. Ithaca: Cornell UP, pp. 1–34.

Vattimo, Gianni (1992) *The Transparent Society*. Trans. David Webb. Baltimore: Johns Hopkins UP.

Virilio, Paul (1989) *War and Cinema: The Logistics of Perception.* Trans. Patrick Camiller. London: Verso.

Voloshinov, V. N. (1973) *Marxism and the Philosophy of Language.* Trans. Ladislav Matejka and I. R. Titunik. New York: Seminar Press.

von Ranke, Leopold (1973) *The Theory and Practice of History.* Eds Georg G. Iggers and Konrad von Moltke. Trans. Wilma A. Iggers and Konrad von Moltke. Indianapolis: Bobbs Merrill.

Wadlington, Warwick (1987) *Reading Faulknerian Tragedy.* Ithaca: Cornell UP.

Walker, Alice (1982) *The Color Purple.* New York: Harcourt Brace Jovanovitch.

Walker, Alice (1983) *In Search of Our Mother's Gardens.* San Diego: Harcourt Brace Jovanovich.

Walsh, W. H. (1960) *Philosophy of History: An Introduction* (1951). New York: Harper Torchbooks.

Walton, Kendall (1990) *Mimesis as Make-Believe: On the Foundations of the Representational Arts.* Cambridge: Harvard UP.

Ward, Catherine C. (1987) 'Gloria Naylor's *Linden Hills*: a modern inferno'. *Contemporary Literature,* **28**.1: 67–81.

Weimann, Robert (1984) *Structure and Society in Literary History: Studies in the History and Theory of Historical Criticism* (Second edn). Baltimore: Johns Hopkins UP.

Weimann, Robert (1988) 'Text, author function, and appropriation in modern narrative: toward a sociology of representation'. *Critical Inquiry,* **14**: 431–47.

Weinstein, Philip M. (1987) 'Marginalia: Faulkner's Black lives'. *Faulkner and Race: Faulkner and Yoknapatawpha, 1986.* Eds Doreen Fowler and Ann J. Abadie. Jackson: U of Mississippi, pp. 170–91.

Werner, Craig (1983) 'Tell Old Pharoah: the Afro-American response to Faulkner'. *Southern Review,* **19**: 711–35.

Werner, Craig (1987) 'Minstrel nightmares: Black dreams of Faulkner's dreams of Blacks'. *Faulkner and Race: Faulkner and Yoknapatawpha, 1986.* Eds Doreen Fowler and Ann J. Abadie. Jackson: U of Mississippi, pp. 35–57.

White, Allon (1981) *The Uses of Obscurity: The Fiction of Early Modernism.* London: Routledge and Kegan Paul.

White, Hayden (1973) *Metahistory: The Historical Imagination in Nineteenth Century Europe.* Baltimore: Johns Hopkins UP.

White, Hayden (1987) *The Content of the Form: Narrative Discourse and Historical Representation.* Baltimore: Johns Hopkins UP.

Williams, John A. (1967) *The Man Who Cried I Am.* Boston: Little Brown.

Williams, Juan (1987) *Eyes on the Prize: America's Civil Rights Years 1954–65.* New York: Viking.

Williams, Raymond (1973) *The Country and the City.* Oxford: Oxford UP.

Williams, Raymond (1977) *Marxism and Literature.* Oxford: Oxford UP.

Williams, Sherley Anne (1987) *Dessa Rose* (1986). New York: Berkley.

Willis, Susan (1984) 'Eruptions of funk: historicizing Toni Morrison'. *Black Literature and Literary Theory*. Ed. Henry Louis Gates, Jr. New York: Methuen, pp. 263–83.

Willis, Susan (1987) *Specifying: Black Women Writing the American Experience*. Madison, WI: U of Wisconsin P.

Wilson, Harriet (1984) *Our Nig: or, Sketches from the Life of a Free Black* (1859). London: Alison and Busby.

Wolf, Eric (1982) *Europe and the People Without History*. Berkeley: U California P.

Wolterstorff, Nicholas (1980) *Works and Worlds of Art*. Oxford: Clarendon Press.

Yinger, J. Milton (1986) 'Intersecting strands in the theorization of race and ethnic relations'. *Theories of Race and Ethnic Relations*. Eds John Rex and David Mason. Cambridge: Cambridge UP.

Young Iris (1986) 'The ideal of community and the politics of difference'. *Social Theory and Practice*, **12**.1: 1–26.

Young, Robert (1990) *White Mythologies*. London: Routledge.

Index

Abrams, M.H., 278n8
Achebe, Chinua, 75, 135, 263n5
Adams, John Quincy, 263n1
Adorno, T.W., 272n21, 277n2, 278–9n4
Agamben, Giorgio, 278n1
Althusser, Louis, 40
Ankersmit, F.R., 4, 258n2
Annales, 4–5
Appiah, Kwame Anthony, 258n4
Aristotle, 7, 8, 11, 13, 24, 32, 259n7
Armstrong, Paul, 58, 66, 96, 118–20,
    263n4
Arnold, Matthew, 269n25
Asad, Talal, 265n21

Backman, Melvin, 269n2
Baker, Houston A., 167
Bakhtin, Mikhail, vii, 46–52, 59, 64, 93,
    109, 113, 118, 136, 139, 149, 151,
    153, 155, 169, 179, 196, 199, 204,
    242, 252, 255, 258n2, 262n10,
    262n11, 262n12, 264n11, 264n16,
    268n16, 278n3
Baldwin, James, 271n15, 273n24, 273n4,
    277n26
Bambara, Toni Cade, 273n2
Baraka, Amiri (Leroi Jones), 168
Barksdale, Richard, 275n17
Barth, Fredrik, 152, 153, 157, 201
Barthes, Roland, 34, 159, 262n12, 272n21,
    273n26
Baudelaire, Charles, 126
Bauer, F.C., 260n12
Benjamin, Walter, 100, 103–4, 126–7,
    164, 188, 194, 211, 260n17,
    260n19
Bennett, William J., 261n29

Bennington, Geoff, 214
Berman, Marshall, 126
Bernstein, Richard, 38, 261n2
Bhabha, Homi, 264n8
Blassingame, John W., 279n5
Bloch, Ernst, 224, 227, 235, 262n9
Bloch, Marc, 4
Bloom, Allan, 261n8
Bond, James, 225
Booth, Wayne, vii
Bourdieu, Pierre, vii, 41–6, 47, 48, 50, 51,
    75, 87, 105, 106, 109, 117, 132,
    142, 153, 165, 170, 174–5, 177,
    180, 182, 200–1, 203, 206, 222,
    254, 258n3, 261n6, 261n7, 262n10,
    268n21, 274n11, 277n3
Bradley, David, 273n2, 276n19
Bradley, F.H., vii, 11–17, 18, 19, 20, 21,
    23, 25, 27, 28, 29, 31, 33, 35, 37,
    38, 40, 42–3, 45, 47, 48, 49, 52, 70,
    71, 96, 102, 104, 139–40, 141, 149,
    163, 166, 182, 189, 194, 203, 209,
    216, 251, 252, 260n11, 260n12,
    260n13, 260n15, 263n15, 264n14
Braudel, Fernand, 4–5, 259n3
Brodkey, Louis Daniel, 272n17
Brooks, Cleanth, 272n19
Brooks, Gwendolyn, 271n15, 276n21
Brooks, Peter, 153, 154, 269n2
Brown, William Wells, 164
Bruce, Dickson D. Jr, 273n1
Buchan, James, 225
Bunch, Ralph, 270n7
Burke, Edmund, 272n18
Burke, Kenneth, 253–4
Burns, E. Bradford, 63–4, 69, 71, 263n1
Butler, Octavia, 273n2

Butterfield, Herbert, 246
Byerman, Keith, 191, 192

Caliban, 137, 141, 143
Campbell, Jane, 273n4
Carby, Hazel V., 168, 172
Carroll, David, 262n11
Carver, George Washington, 270n7
Cassell, Richard, 266n3
Cassola, Arnold, 277n6
Cesarini, David, 268n20
Chateaubriand, François-Réné, 220–1, 236, 247
Chesnutt, Charles, 164
Childress, Alice, 273n2
Christian, Barbara, 167
Clifford, James, 61, 143, 265n21
Coates, Paul, 277n4
Collingwood, R.G., 17–22, 23, 25, 26, 27, 28, 30, 31, 34, 40, 42, 45, 61, 86, 87, 134, 166, 197, 259n5, 260n11, 260n12, 260n13, 260n14, 260n15
Comay, Rebecca, 261n2
Conrad, Joseph, 57, 135, 252
Heart of Darkness, 75, 263n5, 265–6n24
Nostromo, vii, viii, 57–92, 100, 123, 131, 136, 227, 234, 253, 254, 255, 270n5
Conroy, Mark, 86
Cooper, Anna Julia, 163
Core, George, 94
Critical Legal Studies, 44
Croce, Benedetto, 156
Currie, Gregory, 262n14

Daly, M.W., 237–8
Davis, Thadious, 144–5
de Certeau, Michel, 59–60, 67, 91, 234, 246
DeKoven, Marianne, 268n15
Deleuze, Gilles, 243
Dirlik, Arif, 245, 249
Dixon, Melvin, 193–4
Donagan, Alan, 260n14
Douglas, Mary, 264–5n16
Douglass, Frederick, 129
Dray, W.H., 260n14
D'Souza, Dinesh, 261n8
Durkheim, Emile, 262n12
Dworkin, Ronald, 43

Eagleton, Terry, 84
Ebert, Teresa, 249

Eksteins, Modris, 266n1, 277–8n7, 278n9
Eliade, Mircea, 259n9, 261n4
Elias, Norbert, 40, 261n3
Eliot, T.S., 263n15, 269n1
Ellison, Ralph, 271n15, 273n4, 277n26

Fabian, Johannes, 61–2, 73, 143, 235, 250, 256–7, 265n21
Fanon, Frantz, 38, 57, 60, 67–8, 72, 90, 220, 264n8
Faulkner, William, 185, 210, 252, 254
Absalom, Absalom!, vii, viii, 128–60, 187, 209, 210, 227, 253, 255, 275n18
Intruder in the Dust, 269n1
Light in August, 273n5
Sartoris, 269n3
The Sound and the Fury, 154, 271n12, 276n20
Febvre, Lucien, 4
Firebaugh, Joseph, 94, 266n3
Fish, Stanley, 43–4
Fleishman, Avrom, 58, 260n16, 266n4, 275n18
Ford, Ford Madox, 93, 252
The Good Soldier, 96
Joseph Conrad: A Personal Remembrance, 96
Parade's End, vii, viii, 93–127, 136, 227, 253, 254, 255
Forster, E.M., 238–9, 257
Foster, Hal, 237
Foucault, Michel, 5–6, 10–11, 156, 261n1
Fox-Genovese, Elizabeth, 170
Fredrickson, George H., 272n20
Friel, Brian, 274n9
Furet, François, 30
Fussell, Paul, 94

Gadamer, Hans, 248
Galeano, Eduardo, 84
Gallie, W.B., 25–8, 34, 39, 45–6, 68, 197, 262n12
Garner, Margaret, 212
Gates, Henry Louis Jr, 258n4, 264n8, 279n5
Geertz, Clifford, 39, 260n18
Genette, Gérard, 267n10
Genovese, Eugene, 275n15, 275n17
Godzich, Wlad, 264n11
Graham, Kenneth, 265n22
Gramsci, Antonio, 6–7, 34, 40, 125, 240, 259n6

Gray, Richard, 269n1
Green, Robert, 94, 95
Greenblatt, Stephen, 141, 143, 270–1n10
Griffith, Marlene, 266n3

Habermas, Jurgen, 102
Hacking, Ian, 5
Haggard, H. Rider, 225
Harper, Francis, *Iola Leroy*, 164, 171–2,
    173, 174, 188, 271n15
Harris, Trudier, 271n15
Hawkes, Terence, 137, 142
Hegel, G.W.F., 8–9, 11, 18, 33, 220,
    259n9, 260n18
Hempel, C.G., 3, 258n2
Herbert, George, 97
Herder, J.G. von, 18
Higgenbotham, Evelyn Brooks, 258n4
Hill, Christopher, 267n8
Hirschkop, Ken, 262n10
Hite, Molly, 234–5, 236
Hobsbawm, Eric, 248
Holt, Thomas C., 165–6
hooks, bell, 165, 215
Hopkins, Pauline, *Contending Forces*,
    164, 173–4, 184, 188, 274n7, 274n8
Howard, Jean E., 248–9
Howe, Irving, 57–8, 147–8, 271n15
Hughes, Langston, 271n15
Hutcheon, Linda, 248
Huggins, Nathan A., 166–7, 175, 222
Hull, Gloria, 273n5
Hurston, Zora Neale, 163, 165, 216, 241
Huyssen, Andreas, 230, 244, 245
Hynes, Samuel, 266n1, 266n2, 268n17

Iggers, Georg, 4, 5

James, Henry, vii
Jameson, Fredric, 36, 58, 221, 234, 263n2
JanMohammad, Abdul, 58, 225–6, 264n8
Jenkins, Gareth, 76, 81, 264n10
Johnson, Charles, 273n2
Jones, Gayle, *Corregidora*, 186–94, 195,
    202, 212, 213

Kant, Immanuel, 29–30, 40–1, 43, 44,
    261n5, 264n11
Kellner, Hans, 10, 259n3, 259n10
Kennedy, John, 225
Kimball, Roger, 261n8
King, Rodney, 129, 223, 273n3
Kipling, Rudyard, 225

Klotman, Phyllis R., 271n14
Kripke, Saul, 178, 201, 274n9
Kubitschek, Missy Dehn, 275n14
Kuhn, Thomas, 10

Lacan, Jacques, 34
Ladurie, Emmanuel Le Roy, 4–5
Land, Stephen K., 86
Leed, Eric J., 109–10
Leer, Norman, 267n5, 268n22
Levenson, Michael, 263n15, 267n6, 267n7
Levinas, Emmanuel, 146
Longenbach, James, 115
Lowry, Malcolm, 265–6n24
Loyola, Saint Ignatius, 37
Lubbock, Percy, vii, 258n1
Lukács, Georg, 58–9, 149–50, 153, 250,
    255, 262n11, 266n4, 278n3
Luxemburg, Rosa, 123
Lyotard, Jean-François, 39, 75, 117, 132,
    144, 149, 167–8, 175, 187, 188,
    203, 207, 209, 212, 214, 219, 221,
    226, 230, 242, 244, 261n5, 262n13,
    267n9, 272n21, 273n3

Marshall, Paule, *The Chosen Place, The
    Timeless People*, 176–86, 188, 195,
    202, 214, 271n13
Marx, Karl, 164, 264n13
McClure, John, 89
McDowell, Deborah, 196
Medvedev, P.N., 169
Meyer, Eric, 125
Miami Theory Collective, 278n1
Millgate, Michael, 128
Mink, Louis O., 20, 28–32, 35, 40, 41, 45,
    52, 71, 95, 152, 167, 240, 249, 252,
    255, 258n2, 260n15, 261n20
Mobley, Marilyn Sanders, 276n24
Moi, Toril, 46
Moore, Gene M., 100, 266n2, 267n5
Morris, Aldon D., 276n21
Morrison, Toni, 165, 167–8, 175, 205–16
    Beloved, 205, 212–16, 276n19
    Jazz, 270n9
    Song of Solomon, 205–12, 216, 278n10
Mosely, Oswald, 126

Nancy, Jean-Luc, 36, 247, 278n1
Napoleon, 238
National Association for the
    Advancement of Colored People
    (NAACP), 148

Naylor, Gloria, 273n3
Nazareth, Peter, 274n12
Neill, W.C., 149
Nietzsche, Friedrich, 37

Olson, David R., 261n5
Owens, Leslie H., 276n20

Parker, Charlie, 277n5
Parker, Robert Dale, 272n19
Parry, Benita, 263n3, 264n8, 266n25
Patteson, Richard, 235
Pavel, Thomas, 263n14
Petry, Ann, 271n15
Plater, William, 218
Poewe, Karla, 278n12
Pontecorvo, Gillo, 72
Poirier, Richard, 141–2, 269n1, 272n23
Pryse, Marjorie, 273n4
Pynchon, Thomas, 217–45
    The Crying of Lot 49, 217, 277n4
    Gravity's Rainbow, 217, 241
    'A Journey into the Mind of Watts', 223
    Slow Learner, 222, 242, 244
    V., viii, 217–45, 256

Rabelais, François, 199
Reed, Ishmael, 273n2
Ressler, Steve, 65, 264n7, 265n17
Rich, Paul B., 125–6
Ricoeur, Paul, 5, 219, 259n3, 259n7, 272n21
Rimmon-Kenan, Shlomith, 229, 267n10
Rorty, Richard, 36–8, 261n2
Rubinoff, Lionel, 260n12
Russian Formalists, 169

Said, Edward, 89–90, 163–4, 222, 223, 227, 236, 244, 252–3, 261n21, 264n8, 264n9, 265n21
Schaub, Thomas, 218, 240
Schiller, Friedrich von, 29–30, 272n18
Scott, Sir Walter, 58
Shakespeare, William, The Tempest, 137
Simon, Brian, 267n14
Sidney, Sir Philip, 7, 8, 11, 13, 32
Sidgwick, Henry, 269n25
Smith, Barbara, 273n5
Snead, James, 139, 272n19
Snitow, Ann, 113
Spillers, Hortense, 177, 275n14
Stallybrass, Peter, 265n16, 268n16, 268n18

Stark, John, 218
Stein, Gertrude, 185
Stepto, Robert, 170, 187
Stevens, Wallace, 159, 252
Stimpson, Catherine, 277n4
Stone, Lawrence, 3, 5, 258n2, 259n4
Strauss, David, 260n12
Stravinsky, Igor, 231, 277–8n7, 278n9
Styron, William, 195, 275n18

Tawney, R.H., 267–8n14
Taylor, Walter, 157, 270n7
Tennenhouse, Leonard, 267n12
Thatcherism, 269n26
Till, Emmett, 207–8, 209, 210, 212, 276n21
Tiv, 176
Travers, Tim, 110
Turner, Nat, 195, 275n18
Twain, Mark, Huckleberry Finn, 275n18

Unger, Roberto, 39, 44, 261n7

van Holthoon, Fritz, 261n5
Vann, Richard, 261n20
Vattimo, Gianni, 249
Virilio, Paul, 109
Voloshinov, V.N., 183, 249, 258n2, 262n13
von Ranke, Leopold, 8, 11, 27, 40, 251, 259n8

Wadlington, Warwick, 152
Walker, Alice, 154, 156, 210, 273n2, 276n20
Walker, Margaret, 273n2
Walsh, W.H., 22–5, 27, 28, 45–6, 47, 60, 103, 127, 188, 262n12
Walton, Kendall, 263n14
Washington, Booker T., 270n7
Weimann, Robert, 53, 250, 255, 258n1, 262n11, 278n3
Weinstein, Philip, 144, 156
Weisenburger, Steven, 230, 241–2, 277n1
Werner, Craig, 155, 272n22
White, Allon, 265n16, 268n16, 268n18, 270n5
White, Hayden, vii, 3, 32–5, 40, 43, 53, 59, 96–7, 187, 209, 215, 217, 218–19, 220–1, 226, 228, 235, 238, 239, 241, 251, 254–5, 258n1, 272n18
Wideman, John Edgar, 273n2

Williams, John A., 277n26
Williams, Juan, 207
Williams, Raymond, 262n9, 267n8
Williams, Shirley Anne, *Dessa Rose*,
    195–205
Willis, Susan, 168
Wilson, Harriet, 271n15, 274n6
Willis, Susan, 168, 276n23
Windelband, Wilhelm, 259n5

Wolf, Eric, 59
Wolterstorff, Nicholas, 263n14
Wright, Richard, 271n15

Yinger, J. Milton, 273n25
Young, Iris, 278n2
Young, Robert, 10

Zapata, Emiliano, 265n20